ADVANCES IN STRENGTH AND CONDITIONING RESEARCH

SPORTS AND ATHLETICS PREPARATION, PERFORMANCE, AND PSYCHOLOGY SERIES

Sports Injuries and Their Effects on Health
Robert R. Salerno (Editor)
2009. ISBN 978-1-60741-507-7

Advances in Strength and Conditioning Research
Michael Duncan and Mark Lyons (Editors)
2009. ISBN 978-1-60692-909-4

ADVANCES IN STRENGTH AND CONDITIONING RESEARCH

MICHAEL DUNCAN
AND
MARK LYONS
EDITORS

Nova Science Publishers, Inc.
New York

For permission to use material from this book please contact us:
Telephone 631-231-7269; Fax 631-231-8175
Web Site: http://www.novapublishers.com

NOTICE TO THE READER

The Publisher has taken reasonable care in the preparation of this book, but makes no expressed or implied warranty of any kind and assumes no responsibility for any errors or omissions. No liability is assumed for incidental or consequential damages in connection with or arising out of information contained in this book. The Publisher shall not be liable for any special, consequential, or exemplary damages resulting, in whole or in part, from the readers' use of, or reliance upon, this material. Any parts of this book based on government reports are so indicated and copyright is claimed for those parts to the extent applicable to compilations of such works.

Independent verification should be sought for any data, advice or recommendations contained in this book. In addition, no responsibility is assumed by the publisher for any injury and/or damage to persons or property arising from any methods, products, instructions, ideas or otherwise contained in this publication.

This publication is designed to provide accurate and authoritative information with regard to the subject matter covered herein. It is sold with the clear understanding that the Publisher is not engaged in rendering legal or any other professional services. If legal or any other expert assistance is required, the services of a competent person should be sought. FROM A DECLARATION OF PARTICIPANTS JOINTLY ADOPTED BY A COMMITTEE OF THE AMERICAN BAR ASSOCIATION AND A COMMITTEE OF PUBLISHERS.

LIBRARY OF CONGRESS CATALOGING-IN-PUBLICATION DATA

Advances in strength and conditioning research / [edited by] Michael Duncan and Mark Lyons.
   p. cm.
 Includes bibliographical references and index.
 ISBN 978-1-60692-909-4 (hardcover)
 1. Physical education and training--Research. 2. Muscle strength--Research. 3. Physical fitness--Research. I. Duncan, Michael, 1955 Dec. 7- II. Lyons, Mark, 1956-
 GV711.5.A38 2009
 613.7'1072--dc22
                    2009000690

Published by Nova Science Publishers, Inc. ✛ *New York*

CONTENTS

PREFACE

Achievements related to human sports performance have recently surpassed what was once thought possible. In part, these developments are due to greater understanding of strength and conditioning science and practice. The strength and conditioning arena has grown dramatically in recent years and draws on a range of academic disciplines including exercise physiology, biomechanics, sport psychology and physical therapy. This book presents recent research in the field that provides a bridge between scientific knowledge and the strength and conditioning practitioner.

Short communication A presents data on the physiological and kinanthropometric profiles of elite British ice-hockey players, short communication B provides the readers with a brief overview of the mechanical basis for the stretch-shortening cycle (SSC) which is clearly applicable to strength and conditioning practitioners due to the extensive use of SSC in sports performance, and short communication C identifies the current awareness of elite powerlifters in terms of their knowledge, use and perceptions of sport psychology. This also provides directions for growth in the provision of psychological support to this particular group of athletes.

A number of research articles are also presented which provide interesting practical applications and directions for future research. Chapter I identifies differences in the anaerobic and aerobic capacity of paddlers across age and gender groups and Chapter II investigates the effect of agility training on agility and dribbling skills in soccer players. This chapter provides a particular point for thought with respect to possible psychological changes that accompany the other responses associated with conditioning programs in sports people. Chapter III provides the reader with background on predicting performance in women's ice-hockey and, through regression analysis, identifies equations to predict key variables related to ice-hockey performance such as speed, agility and acceleration. Chapter IV provides an in-depth overview of the impact of a multi-component training schedule on physiological parameters in an elite Gaelic football player.

Several review articles are also presented which provide the reader with relevant, up-to-date information pertinent to a range of areas within strength and conditioning. Chapter V supplies the reader with key information relating to the efficacy of caffeine in enhancing performance for athletes whilst chapter VI identifies the ergogenic aspects of music, walking poles and compression garments that could be employed in various training capacities. Chapter VII provides an overview of power in resistance exercise, an area key to the strength and conditioning practitioner. Methods used for the assessment of power are also highlighted.

The focus of chapter VIII is the use of ratings of perceived exertion during resistance exercise. This chapter provides applied information that can be used by those working with both high level athletic groups as well as with the general population. Plyometric training is one key area of interest for strength and conditioning professionals which is addressed in Chapter VIIII. This chapter provides an overview of the impact of plyometric training on muscle function and performance of rapid movements. In Chapter X the authors address the practical issue surrounding strength and conditioning program design in several combat sports including judo and tae kwon do. The focus of Chapter XI is on the development of mental toughness, a concept that although somewhat overlooked in the strength and conditioning literature, could be key to enhancing performance. The focus on chapter XII is on the enhancement of performance in ice-hockey with the authors examining both training studies and the ecological validity of training in transfer to skating performance.

It is hoped that this text provides a broad and balanced overview of topics relevant to the strength and conditioning practitioner drawn from a range of disciplines including exercise physiology, biomechanics and psychology. We hope that the information presented here will prompt discussion, further research and stimulate improvements in strength and conditioning practice.

SHORT COMMUNICATIONS

In: Advances in Strength and Conditioning Research
Editor: Michael Duncan and Mark Lyons

ISBN: 978-1-60692-909-4
© 2009 Nova Science Publishers, Inc.

Short Communication A

POSITIONAL DIFFERENCES IN THE KINANTHROPOMETRIC AND PHYSIOLOGICAL CHARACTERISTICS OF ELITE BRITISH ICE-HOCKEY PLAYERS

Michael J. Duncan[1]* *and Mark Lyons*[2]
[1]University of Derby, UK
[2]Newman University College, UK

ABSTRACT

The objectives of the present study were to investigate the kinathropometric characteristics of elite ice-hockey players. Eighteen ice-hockey players from the British 'Elite Hockey League' 2004-05 season's, title winning squad (mean age ± S.D. = 25.1 ± 4.2 years) were assessed on a number of physiological and anthropometric variables. Somatotype was assessed using the Heath-Carter method, body composition (% body fat) was assessed using surface anthropometry, Leg strength was assessed using a leg and back dynamometer and low back and hamstring flexibility was assessed using the modified sit and reach test. Results indicated that defencemen were more endomorphic (p<0.01), more mesomorphic, had greater body mass and higher percent body fat than forwards (all p<0.05). Mean ± S.D. of somatotype (endo, meso, ecto) for defencemen and forwards was 2.9 ± 0.6, 6.2 ± 0.8 and 1.6 ± 0.7 and 2.2 ± 0.5, 5.3 ± 0.8 and 2.2 ± 0.7 respectively. Mean ± S.D. for body mass and percent fatness was 90.5 ± 8.5kg and 16.8 ± 2.7% for defencemen and 79.6 ± 9.5kg and 13.9 ± 2.8% for forwards. There were no other significant differences in physiological and anthropometric variables across playing positions (all p>0.05). Overall, defencemen tend to be endomorphic mesomorphs, whereas forwards tend to be balanced mesomorphs. These results indicate the need for sports scientists and conditioning professionals to take the kinathropometric characteristics of ice-hockey players into account when designing individualised position specific training programmes.

---

* Please address correspondence and requests for reprints to Michael J. Duncan, Faculty of Education, Health and Sciences, University of Derby, Kedleston Road, Derby, England, DE22 1GB or e mail m.duncan@derby.ac.uk.

Keywords: Somatotype, Physiological Profile, Ice-Hockey

An athlete's anthropometric and physical characteristics may represent important pre requisites for successful participation in any given sport [8]. It can be assumed that an athlete's anthropometric characteristics can in some way influence his level of performance, at the same time helping to determine a suitable physique for a certain sport [5, 11]. However, although studies have examined the anthropometric and physiological profiles of athletes from a variety of sports [4, 8, 11], it appears that few studies have examined the anthropometric or physiological profile of ice-hockey players, particularly in relation to their positional role within the sport [12].

Somatotype analysis may be useful in terms of talent identification or development of training programmes as somatotypes, as well as other physical characteristics differ between sports and as a result of positional role and differences in requirements of play within particular positions [5]. It has also been suggested that somatotyping is superior to linear anthropometric measures in differentiating between different competitive sport populations as it combines adiposity, musculo-skeletal robustness and linearity into one rating [5]. Likewise, an awareness of the physiological characteristics of elite level athletes within a given sport may be beneficial in terms of optimising training programmes specific to the requirements of particular sports [4].

This may be particularly important within ice-hockey as it is a physically demanding sport comprising repeated high intensity work bouts over a 60 minute period. Time-motion analysis of men's hockey reveals that the average on ice per work bout is 91.2-146.3 seconds in duration and can be repeated up to 17 times in a game [10]. At the elite level players cover an average of 5160m (range, 4860-5620m) whilst data from university standard teams indicates a distance covered of 5553m with an average skating velocity of 227m/min [9]. It is therefore important for coaches, strength and conditioning experts and sports scientists to understand the off-ice and on-ice fitness components that are associated with elite ice-hockey performance. This type of data are important to establish baseline performance, develop scientifically based training protocols and improve performance [1]. Furthermore, given the complex motor skills involved in skating performance it is important to understand how off-ice fitness variables that are important for success in elite ice-hockey relate to on-ice performance [3]. Recently, studies have predicted ice skating performance from off-ice fitness testing in women's ice hockey and compared on-ice performance of elite and non-elite female hockey players [1, 3, 7]. Bracko and Fellingham [2] also examined differences in physical performance characteristics of male and female junior ice-hockey players and research by Vescovi et al. [12] reported physiological data based on off-ice fitness tests in elite male players. However, it appears that few studies have examined the kinanthropometric profiles or somatotype of elite British, male ice-hockey players and fewer still have presented data in relation to on-ice performance. Therefore, the aim of this study was to examine positional differences in the anthropometric and physiological profiles of elite, male ice-hockey players.

METHOD

Participants

Eighteen elite, male, professional ice-hockey players (mean age ± S.D = 25.1 ± 4.2 years) participated in this study following approval by the College ethics committee and after providing written informed consent. The players comprised 10 forwards and 8 defencemen from the 2004-05 British Elite Hockey League Championship winning team and the study was carried out at the start of the 2004-05 season.

PROCEDURES

Off-Ice Testing

All measures were conducted on the same day and were completed in the standardized order described below. Height and body mass were assessed using a Seca Stadiometer and weighing scales (Seca Instruments Ltd, Germany). Percent body fat was assessed using skinfold measures of four sites using Harpenden skinfold callipers (Harpenden Instruments Ltd, England) and employing the Durnin and Womersley [6] skinfold equation. Somatotypes were calculated using the Heath-Carter method [5]. Leg strength (kg) was assessed using a leg dynamometer (Takei Instruments Ltd, Japan), low back and hamstring flexibility was assessed using the modified sit and reach test. Three tests were completed by all participants with the best effort of each test being used for analysis. All anthropometric measures were completed by ISAK accredited anthropometrists whose TEMs for the sites involved were 2% or better.

On- Ice Testing

Participants wore full kit and carried their stick during on-ice testing. Prior to testing, the players had undergone a 15 min skating based warm-up. On-ice speed was determined using a 44.8m ice-hockey specific speed test [2, 3] assessed by photoelectric speed gates (Brower Systems, USA). Timing gates were adjusted for the height of each participant to ensure that they were placed at approximately shoulder height when the participant was skating at full speed. Three trials of each test were completed by all participants with the best effort of each test being used for analysis. On completion of each trial, participants continued to actively skate in the opposite end of the rink and received approximately 5 minutes recovery time between trials as has been the case in previous studies using this methodology [2]. Following completion of the speed skating test, anaerobic power was determined using the ice-hockey specific equation of Watson and Sargeant [13].

Statistical Analysis

Following completion of the tests, independent t-tests were used to examine any differences in kinathropometric variables according to playing position. Descriptive statistics were also calculated. SPSS version 14.0 was used for all analysis.

RESULTS

Results from statistical tests and mean ± S.D. of all values according to playing position are found in Table 1. Results indicated that the only measures influenced by playing position were on-ice anaerobic power, body mass, body fatness and the endormorphy and mesomorphy components of somatotype. Defencemen had significantly lower anaerobic power (t_{16} = -2.386, $p<0.05$), significantly greater body mass (t_{16} = -2.447, $p<0.05$) and significantly higher percent body fat (t_{16} = -2.122, $p<0.05$) than forwards. Similarly, defencemen were significantly more endomorphic (t_{16} = -2.897, $p<0.01$) and mesomorphic (t_{16} = -2.342, $p<0.05$) than forwards. Classification of somatotypes according to the Heath – Carter method [5] revealed that defencemen were classed as endomorphic mesomorphs and forwards were classified as balanced mesomorphs.

Table 1. Summary of results (Mean ± S.D.)

Measure	Position			
	Defencemen		Forwards	
	Mean	S.D.	Mean	S.D.
Height (m)	1.83	.07	1.8	.04
Mass (kg)	90.5	8.5	79.6	9.5
Leg Strength (kg)	217.1	45.6	197.2	23.5
Sit and Reach (cm)	43.3	4.9	40.1	7.7
Body Fatness (%)	16.8	2.7	13.9	2.8
Endomorphy	2.97	0.6	2.2	0.5
Mesomorphy	6.2	0.8	5.3	0.8
Ectomorphy	1.6	0.7	2.2	0.7
Anaerobic Power (W/kg)	8.2	0.3	8.6	0.2

DISCUSSION

Current findings support previous research with other athletic groups [4, 8, 11] that also reported positional differences in somatotypes. As no prior literature appears to have reported the somatotypes of elite, male, ice-hockey players, no comparisons can be made with prior studies. The differences in anthropometric variables between forwards and defencemen in the current study may however, be due to the different technical and tactical demands of their respective positions. Defencemen are primarily used to breakdown the opposing attack by blocking or 'checking' opposing players. As a result higher body mass, greater body fatness and greater endomorphy may increase inertia for blocking and provide a bigger body surface area for forwards to navigate around. This may be particularly important given that defencemen will generally have to skate backwards whilst forward players should generally be able to outskate defencemen (as they will be skating forwards). The greater mesomorphy scores in defencemen may also be important allowing for more forceful 'checking' of opposition players and sustaining repeated attacks by opposing players. Lower endomorphy scores and higher on-ice anaerobic power in forwards compared to defencemen may also be important where speed and agility of attack are of primary concern. For example, forwards are more likely to cover greater distances during ice-hockey due to the need to forecheck and backcheck (ie check opposing payers in all areas of the rink) whereas defencemen will tend to only backcheck (check opposing payers in their half of the rink).

No significant differences in leg strength, grip strength, modified sit and reach scores, height and the ectomorphy component of somatotype were found in the kinanthropometric profile of these players according to playing position. This may indicate that similar levels of leg strength, grip strength, low back and hamstring flexibility are required for elite level ice-hockey performance irrespective of playing position. Overall, such information may be useful for talent identification, sport selection and planning specific training programmes that correctly consider the physical traits and abilities of the athlete. However, in the current study no on-ice measures of fitness were evaluated. Further researching examining the relationships between on-ice and off-ice fitness testing and analysis of the role that anthropometric and physiological factors play in predicting ice-hockey specific performance would be desirable.

These findings imply that somatotypes differ as a function of positional role within ice-hockey and that Sports Scientists, coaches and strength and conditioning professionals need to be aware of the specific positional requirements within ice-hockey. Consideration of kinanthropometric and physiological factors when allocating resources, selecting playing position and within conditioning programmes may be beneficial in increasing the effectiveness of players within a team.

REFERENCES

[1]   Bracko, M. R. (2001) On-ice performance characteristics of elite and non-elite women's ice hockey players. *J Strength Cond Res*, 15, 42-47.

[2]   Bracko, M. R. and Fellingham, G.W. (2001) Comparison of physical performance characteristics of female and male ice hockey players. *Ped Exer Sci*, 13, 26-34.

[3]   Bracko, M. R. and George, J. D. (2001) Prediction of ice skating performance with off-ice testing in women's ice hockey players. *J Strength Cond Res*, 15, 116-122.

[4]   Callan, S. D., Brunner, D. M., Devolve, K. L., Mulligan, S. E., Hesson, J., Wilber, R. L. and Kearney, J. T. (2000) Physiological profiles of elite freestyle wrestlers. *J Strength Cond Res*, 14, 162-169.

[5]   Carter, J. E. L. and Heath, H. (1990) *Somatotyping – Development and Applications.* Cambridge: Cambridge University Press.

[6]   Durnin, J. V. G. A. and Womersley, J. (1974) Body fat assessed from total body density and its estimation from skinfold thickness: Measurements on 481 men and women aged from 16 to 72 years. *B J Nut*, 32, 77-97.

[7]   Geithner, C., Lee, A. and Bracko, M. (2006) Physical and performance differences among forwards, defensemen and goalies in elite women's ice-hockey. *J Strength Cond Res*, 20, 500-505.

[8]   Gualdi-Russo, E. and Zaccagni, L. (2001) Somatotype, role and performance in elite volleyball players. *J Sports Med Phys Fit*, 41, 256-62.

[9]   Montgomery, D. L. (2000) Physiology of ice-hockey. In: Garrett, W. E., Kirkendall, D. (Eds.), *Exercise and Sports Science.* (pp. 815-828). Philadelphia: Lippincott, Williams and Wilkins.

[10]   Montgomery, D. L., and Vartzbedian, B. (1979) Duration and intensity of play in adult recreational hockey games. In: Terauds, J., Gross, H. J. (Eds.), *Science in skiing, skating and hockey. Proceedings of the International Symposium of Biomechanics in Sports.* (pp. 107-115). Del Mar, California: Academic Publishers.

[11]   Rienzi, E., Reilly, T. and Malkin, C. (1999) Investigation of anthropometric and work-rate profiles of Rugby Sevens players. *J Sports Med Phys Fit*, 39, 160-64.

[12]   Vescovi J. D., Murray, T. and VanHeest, L. (2006) Positional performance profiling of elite ice-hockey players. *Int J Sports Phys Perf*, 1, 84-94.

[13]   Watson, R. C. and Sargeant, T. L. C. (1986) Laboratory and on-ice comparisons of anaerobic power of ice-hockey players. *Can J App Sports Sci*, 11, 218-224.

In: Advances in Strength and Conditioning Research
Editor: Michael Duncan and Mark Lyons
ISBN: 978-1-60692-909-4
© 2009 Nova Science Publishers, Inc.

Short Communication B

THE STRETCH SHORTENING CYCLE: A BRIEF OVERVIEW

Philip Watkins[1]
University of Derby, UK

ABSTRACT

The purpose of this paper is to examine the mechanics of the stretch-shortening cycle (SSC) and its influence on activities with high force and power requirements. The elasticity of muscle and tendons has been shown to enhance performance in SSC movements. Its importance in sprinting and jumping is well-documented and is typically characterised by an eccentric muscular contraction or stretch, followed immediately by a concentric muscular contraction. Specifically, the paper covers the mechanisms involved in the SSC, namely: tension time and the pre-tension effect, neural mechanisms and restitution of elastic strain energy and briefly introduces assessment of the SSC and concludes with practical applications. Coaches should encourage rapid, powerful movements that reduce the eccentric to concentric reversibility times of their athletes as well as emphasise the importance of minimising ground contact times. Measuring the SSC of athletes will enable coaches to monitor training adaptations and examination of ground contact times allow coaches to assess the nature of the SSC (fast or slow) being utilised to prescribe specific and appropriate training programs.

Keywords: Stretch-Shortening Cycle, Muscle Spindle, Golgi Tendon Organ, Muscle tendon Unit, Series Elastic Element.

The elasticity of muscles and tendons has been demonstrated to affect performance in stretch shortening cycle (SSC) movements [32, 33]. The importance of the SSC in sprinting and jumping has been documented [18], and is typically characterised by an eccentric

---

[1] Please address correspondence and requests for reprints to Philip Watkins, Faculty of Education, Health and Sciences, University of Derby, Kedleston Road, Derby, England, DE22 1GB or e mail p.h.watkins@derby.ac.uk.

muscular contraction or stretch, followed immediately by a concentric muscular contraction. Using a stretch immediately prior to a concentric contraction has been shown to increase the concentric phase resulting in augmented force production, power output [29, 17] and a shift in the force-velocity curve to the right [16]. The increased power output evident after a countermovement jump (CMJ) can be explained by the time to build up force, storage and re-use of elastic energy, potentiation of the contractile elements and reflex contributions [37]. Athletes can perform various forms of strength training to improve their ability to exert power using the SSC [23], understanding the mechanisms and assessment methods of the SSC may influence program design and enhance performance.

MECHANISMS OF THE SSC

Tension Time and the Pre Tension Effect

During SSC movements, force rises in the eccentric phase, and the time available for force development is greater [36] than concentric only movements where the movement is performed immediately upon muscle activation. There is very little lengthening of the muscles in this eccentric phase, and the muscle action in the later dip is concentric. At the moment of transition (reversibility) from lengthening to shortening, the force is developed in isometric conditions and so the influence of high velocity is avoided [32, 36]. A continuation of tendon lengthening enables a body to continue to drop downward [36]. The importance of developing pre-tension before muscle shortening has been reported in the literature [13, 14]. Concentric movements that are immediately preceded by either isometric or eccentric actions lead to greater concentric torque when compared with purely concentric actions [30, 14].

For example, when performing a static jump (SJ), the movement begins as soon as force is applied, by the time substantial muscle forces have been generated, velocity has also increased. According to the force-velocity relationship, force must be developed when velocity is slow in order to achieve very high forces. Higher levels of muscle activation earlier in the movement allow muscles to produce greater forces over a range of joint angles thereby optimising performance [2, 5].

During the countermovement jump (CMJ) however, the body descends rapidly before the concentric phase and the total change in momentum (from high negative to high positive) is much greater than in a static jump (from zero to positive). Bobbert and Casius [1] report a 3 to 11cm increase in the maximum height attainable in the CMJ relative to the SJ. The total impulsive force required to achieve large changes in momentum is therefore high. The greater impulse translates to an increased change in momentum in order to maximize velocity at take-off [24]. In most high speed movements, the muscle force is developed in isometric conditions [36] through much of the movement, with the magnitude of lengthening and shortening of muscles depending upon the amplitude of the eccentric and concentric phases and the muscle involved. This near isometric contraction of the muscles allows large forces to be generated in accordance with the force-velocity relationship, as well as operate near their optimal length. Dropping too deeply during a CMJ may compromise jumping ability as a consequence of the muscles being taken beyond their optimal length for force production (8).

Neural Mechanisms

When muscles are forcibly stretched their tension rises sharply. SSC movements cause increases in the excitability of proprioceptors for an optimal reaction by the neuromuscular system. These changes are controlled and partially counterbalanced by two proprioceptors that are most relevant in SSC actions, the muscle spindle and the golgi tendon organ (GTO). Muscle spindles are located in the intrafusal fibres and are innervated by gamma-motor neurons. They are facilitatory mechanoreceptors that react to changes in muscle length to protect the muscle-tendon complex (10). The inevitable unloading of the muscle spindle during shortening of the muscle is counteracted by a concomitant shortening of the intrafusal muscle fibres. This stretch reflex occurs during the yielding phase (when the hip, knee and ankle joints are flexing), and compensates for muscle exposed to forcible stretches.

The Golgi-Tendon Organ (GTO) is located in the extrafusal fibres and innervated by alpha motor neurons [25]. GTOs act as a protective mechanism by responding to changes in tension rather than length and inhibit the agonist muscles and facilitate the antagonist muscles [4]. When muscle contractile forces reach a point where damage to the muscle-tendon complex may occur, GTOs increase afferent activity by inhibiting the motor neurons that innervate the stretched muscles, whilst simultaneously exciting the motor neurons of the antagonist muscles [4, 25]. Plyometric and strength training not only upregulate the stretch reflex, but also reduce the inhibitory reflexes (type III and IV receptors) [14].

Restitution of Elastic Strain Energy

Elastic energy stored in the series elastic elements (SEEs) (tendons, aponeuroses, cross-bridges, actin/myosin filaments, and possibly the giant protein Titin) in the eccentric phase is re-used during the concentric phase. At the onset of shortening, elastic recoil of these elements add to the work output of the muscle-tendon complexes involved in these actions [30]. Tendon recoil speeds are much greater than muscle shortening speeds, exercises with increasing stretching loads result in a reduction in muscle activation and surface EMG [7, 27] indicating an increased reliance on the elastic properties of the musculotendinous unit (MTU) during ballistic actions.

The control of the MTU stiffness has been shown to play an important role in making full use of the benefits of SSC movements [19]. It is defined as 'the property of a system to resist an applied stretch' [20, p653]. When no external forces are present these systems maintain a constant shape, however when acted upon by external forces they generate elastic force to oppose the external force and store and return elastic energy [20]. A stiffer spring-like action in the legs allows humans to run with higher stride frequencies than otherwise possible [9]. Tendon stiffness is constant, however, the stiffness of muscle is variable and depends upon the forces exerted. Fukunaga et al. [11] found that during the stance phase, subjects' medial gastrocnemius muscle contracted isometrically, whereas the tendon lengthened by 7mm indicating greater tendon compliancy. Such tendons work as springs, and allow for storing and recoiling large amounts of mechanical energy at each step [36]. Harrison et al. [12] demonstrated that sprinters used a stiffer leg spring at any given speed when compared with high calibre endurance athletes but suggested that endurance athletes may benefit from the inclusion of SSC related activities in their training. Superior athletes can develop high forces, and the stiffness of their muscles when active exceeds the stiffness of their tendons [36].

When a muscle becomes active, high forces must be applied to stretch it, the greater the muscle tension, the greater the muscle stiffness. Increased stiffness has also been shown to enhance joint functional stability, and therefore plays a positive role in soft-tissue injury prevention [5]. It appears that MTU stiffness is an important variable for superior performance in SSC movements [33].

High movement speeds and high power outputs require the recoil of SEEs, so one of the main purposes of strength and power training is to improve muscle stiffness. It has been proposed that the influence of the facilitatory reflex which originates from the muscle spindles can be enhanced through training and can improve muscle stiffness. The role of the inhibitory force feedback component (from the GTOs) can be simultaneously decreased [15]. However, exercise selection and progression must be guided by training status, it has been reported that untrained subjects respond to the eccentric phase of a high stretch load with a period of inhibition [26]. The use of elastic energy is probably the key mechanism behind the increases in movement speed, power and efficiency that are observed in SSC movements.

ASSESSMENT OF THE SSC

Different approaches have been used to examine the effect of the SSC and its relationship to athletic ability [3]. Performance of the SSC is usually undertaken by adding a pre-stretch to a movement such as comparing a CMJ with a SJ performance. Both of these tests have been shown to be reliable and valid tests for estimating explosive muscular power [21]. Pre-stretch augmentation can be calculated as a percentage with % pre-stretch augmentation = [(CMJ – SJ)/SJ] x 100. Another approach is to measure the reactive strength index (RSI) (calculated as CMJ – SJ height) [22] which has been used in the practical strength and conditioning setting as a means to quantify SSC performance.

It has been suggested [27] that the SSC can be classified as either fast or slow. A fast SSC is characterised by short ground contact times (<0.25s) and small angular displacements of the hips, knees and ankles such as a depth jump. Slow SSCs involve longer ground contact times (>0.25s), larger angular displacements and can be observed when performing a maximal effort CMJ. Where a training stimulus is desired to improve performance in fast SSC movements, or to assess fast SSC function, the CMJ is not an appropriate modality [32, 17]. Therefore, appropriate exercise selections for training and assessment of the SSC should be guided by the principle of specificity and the demands of the sport.

CONCLUSION

The SSC is crucial for successful performance in many strength and ballistic activities. Plyometric exercises and sports that involve maximal sprinting and jumping are characterised by fast SSC movements. These techniques use rapid powerful movements that are preceded by a pre-loading countermovement that creates a SSC of the muscle [31]. Examples of plyometric exercises include in-depth jumps, box jumps, hopping, bounding and medicine ball throws.

Coaches should encourage fast, powerful movements that reduce the eccentric and concentric reversibility times and emphasise the importance of minimising ground contact times. Since strength and power training has been shown to increase muscle tendon stiffness which promotes effective use of the SSC, it is of benefit to both strength, power and endurance athletes.

Measuring the SSC of athletes will enable coaches to assess and monitor corresponding training adaptations. The principle of specificity determines the demands required in any sport, examining ground contact times allow coaches to assess the nature of the SSC (fast or slow) being utilised. Athletes wishing to increase maximum sprinting velocity (fast SSC) would require plyometric exercises that involve short contact times. Athletes involved in sports that demand fast and/or slower SSC movements (e.g., rugby union or powerlifting), may benefit from combining plyometric training with exercises such as back squats, squat jumps, box squats, box-squats on to foam, over-speed eccentric squats with resistance bands and snatch and clean variations. Combining exercises that demand variation in movement velocities, increase mechanical energy, and target different phases of the SSC, may provide superior performance results. Consideration should be given to exercise selection and variation, training intensity and volume throughout the periodised program as well as the training status of the athlete.

REFERENCES

[1]   Bobbert, M. F and Casius, L. (2005) Is the effect of a countermovement on jump height due to active state development? *Med Sci Sports Exerc*, 37, 440-446.

[2]   Bobbert, M. F., Gerritsen, K. G. M. Litjens, M. C. A. and van Soest, A. J. (1996) Why is countermovement jump height greater than squat jump height? *Med Sci Sports Exerc*, 28, 1402-1412.

[3]   Bosco, C., Mognoni, P. and Luhtanen, P. (1983) Relationship between isokinetic performance and ballistic movement. *Eur J Applied Phys Occ Phys*, 51, 357-364.

[4]   Brooks, G., Fahey, T. D., White, T. P. and Baldwin, KM. (2000) *Exercise Physiology: Human Bioenergetics and its Applications.* Mountain View, CA: Mayfield Publishing.

[5]   Butler, R. J., Crowell, H. P. and Davis, I. M. (2003) Lower extremity stiffness: Implications for performance and injury. *Clin Biomech*, 18, 511-517.

[6]   Dowling, J. J. and Vamos, L. (1993) Identification of kinetic and temporal factors related to vertical jump performance. *J App Biomech*, 9, 95-110.

[7]   Ebben, W. P., Simenz, C. and Jensen, R. L. (2008) Evaluation of Plyometric Intensity Using Electromyography. *J Strength Cond Res*, 22, 861-868.

[8]   Eloranta, V. (1996) Effect of postural and load variation on the coordination of the leg muscles in concentric jumping movement. *Electromyog Clin Neurophys*, 36, 59-64.

[9]   Ferris, D.P. and Farley, C.T. (1997) Interaction of leg stiffness and surface stiffness during human hopping. *J App Phys*, 82, 15-22.

[10] Flanagan, E.P. and Comyns, T.M. (2008) The use of contact time and the reactive strength index to optimize fast stretch-shortening cycle training. *Strength Cond J,* 30, 32-38.

[11] Fukunaga, T., Kawakami, Y., Kubo, K. and Kanehisa, H. (2002) Muscle and Tendon Interaction During Human Movements, *Exerc Sport Sci Rev,* 30, 106-110.

[12] Harrison, A.J., Keane, S. P. and Coglan, J. (2004) Force-Velocity Relationship and Stretch_Shortening Cycle Function in Sprint and Endurance Athletes. *J Strength Cond Res*, 18, 473-479.

[13] Helgeson, K. and Gajdosik, R. L. (1993) The stretch-shortening cycle of the quadriceps femoris muscle group measured by isokinetic dynamometry. *J Orth Sports Phys Ther*, 17, 17-23.

[14] Jensen, R.C., Warren, B., Lauresen, C. and Morrissey, M. C. (1991) Static pre-load effect on knee extensor isokinetic concentric and eccentric performance. *Med Sci Sports Exerc*, 23, 10-14.

[15] Komi, P.V. (1992) Stretch-Shortening Cycle. In: P.V. Komi, ed. *Strength and Power in Sport* (pp. 169-179) Blackwell Science

[16] Komi, P.V. (1986) The stretch-shortening cycle and human power output. In: N.L. Jones, N. McCartney and A.J. McComas, eds. *Human Muscle Power* (pp.27-39) Champaign, IL: Human Kinetics

[17] Komi, P.V. and Bosco, C. (1978) Utilization of Stored Elastic Energy in Leg Extensor Muscles in Men and Women. *Med Sci Sports Exerc*, 10, 261-265.

[18] Kryolainen, H. and Komi, P. (1995) The neuro-muscular system in maximal stretch-shortening cycle exercises: Comparison between power and endurance trained athletes. *J Electromyog Kines,* 5, 15-25.

[19] Kubo, K., Kawakami, Y. and Fukunaga, T. (1999) Influence of elastic properties of tendon structures on jump performance in humans. *J App Phys*, 87, 2090-2096.

[20] Latash, M.L and Zatsiorski V. (1993) Joint Stiffness: Myth or Reality? *Hum Mov Sci*, 12, 653-692.

[21] Markovic, G., Dizdar, D., Jukic, I. and Cardinale, M. (2004) Reliability and factorial validity of squat and countermovement jump tests. *J Strength Cond Res*, 18, 551-555.

[22] McGuigan, M. R., Doyle, T. L. A., Newton, M., Edwards, D. J., Nimphius, S. and Newton, R. (2006) Eccentric utilization Ratio: Effect of Sport and Phase Training. *J Strength Cond Res,* 20, 992-995.

[23] Miyaguchi, K. and Demura, S. (2008) Relationships between Stretch-Shortening Cycle Performance and Maximum Muscle Strength. *J Strength Cond Res*. 22, 19-24.

[24] Reiser, R.F., Rocheford, E. C. and Armstrong, C. J. (2006) Building a better understanding of basic mechanical principles through analysis of the vertical jump. *Strength Cond J*, 28, 70-80.

[25] Riemann, B and Lephart, S. (2002) The sensorimotor system, part 1: the physiologic basis of functional joint stability. *J Ath Train,* 37, 71-79.

[26] Sale, D.G. (1992) Neural Adaptations to Strength Training. In: P.V. Komi (ed). *Strength and Power in Sport.* (pp. 249-265) Blackwell Science.

[27] Schmitbleicher, D. (1992) Training for Power Events, In: P.V.Komi, ed. *The Encyclopedia of Sports Medicine, Vol 3: Strength and Power in Sport.* (pp. 169-179) Oxford, UK: Blackwell

[28] Spurrs, R.W., Murphy, A. J. and Watsford, M. (2003) The effect of plyometric training on distance running performance. *Eur J App Phys*, 89, 1-7.

[29] Van Ingen Schenau, G.J., Bobbert, M. F. and De Haan, A. (1997) Does elastic energy enhance work and efficiency in the stretch shortening cycle? *J App Biomech*, 13, 389-415.

[30] Walshe, A. D., Wilson, G. J. and Ettema, G. J. C. (1998) Stretch-shorten cycle compared with isometric pre-load: contributions to enhanced muscular performance. *J App Phys*, 84, 97-106.

[31] Wilk, K. E. (1993) Stretch-shortening drills for the upper extremities: theory and clinical application. *J Orth Sports Phys Ther*, 17, 225-234.

[32] Wilson, J. M and Flanagan, E. P. (2008) The role of elastic energy in activities with high force and power requirements: A brief review. *J Strength Cond Res*, 22, 1705-1715.

[33] Wilson, G. J., Murphy, A. J. and Pryor, J. F. (1994) Musculotendinous stiffness: its relationship to eccentric, isometric and concentric performance. *J App Phys*, 76, 2714-2719.

[34] Wilson, G. J., Elliott, B. C. and Wood, G. A. (1992) Stretch shorten cycle performance enhancement through flexibility training. *Med Sci Sports Exerc*, 24, 116-123.

[35] Wilson, G. J., Wood, G. A. and Elliott, B. C. (1991) Optimal stiffness of the series elastic component in a stretch shorten cycle activity. *J App Phys*, 70, 825-833.

[36] Zatsiorsky, V. M. and Kraemer, W. J. (2006) *Science and Practice of Strength Training. (2nd Edition)* Champaign, IL: Human Kinetics.

[37] Zatsiorsky, V.M. (1995) *Science and Practice of Strength Training*. Champaign, IL: Human Kinetics.

In: Advances in Strength and Conditioning Research
Editor: Michael Duncan and Mark Lyons

ISBN: 978-1-60692-909-4
© 2009 Nova Science Publishers, Inc.

Short Communication C

KNOWLEDGE, USE AND PERCEPTIONS OF SPORT PSYCHOLOGY IN BRITISH POWERLIFTERS

Rebecca Morris[1]
Nottingham Trent University, UK

ABSTRACT

The aim of the present study was to investigate British powerlifters' perceptions and use of sport psychology. Twenty-eight powerlifters ($n = 11$ male, $n = 17$ female, mean age $\pm$ S.D. $= 38.65 \pm 12.16$ years) completed a questionnaire comprising quantitative measures of their knowledge and use of 17 sport psychology topics, as well as the perceived importance of these topics for powerlifting. Participants also completed open-ended questions about their definition of sport psychology, barriers to using sport psychology in powerlifting and factors that may facilitate the use of sport psychology. Results indicated that participants had varying definitions of sport psychology. Quantitative responses revealed moderate to high knowledge, importance and use scores for the 17 topics. Positive within-cell correlations were also found among the knowledge, importance and use scores. While participants reported largely positive perceptions, a lack of knowledge or awareness of sport psychology was perceived as the most significant barrier to using sport psychology in powerlifting. The results indicate the need for greater education about and exposure to sport psychology. Coaches were identified as the most appropriate conduits for promoting the use of psychological skills in their athletes.

Keywords: Barriers, Importance

---

[1] Please address correspondence and requests for reprints to Rebecca L. Morris, School of Science and Technology, Nottingham Trent University, Clifton Campus, Nottingham, NG11 8NS, UK or e-mail rebecca.morris@ntu.ac.uk.

There is considerable evidence for the positive effects of psychological skills, such as imagery and goal-setting, on sport performance [1, 2]. However, research has indicated that athletes and coaches are less likely to embrace the psychological facets of their sport than other aspects of training and competition, such as physical practice. For example, Pain and Harwood [6] identified a lack of funding as one of the most important barriers to the use of sport psychology services in English soccer. Staff at youth football academies reported that limited budgets meant fitness training or other specializations were prioritized ahead of sport psychology.

Other key barriers to sport psychology use by athletes have been identified in the literature. These include negative perceptions of sport psychology, such as the perception that sport psychology is solely for problem athletes and involves an examination of weaknesses and vulnerabilities [4, 7]. Research has also shown that athletes and coaches do not always feel familiar with how psychology could be incorporated into their sport or its potential benefits for performance [7, 10]. Tied to this, professional sports organizations that have employed sport psychology services have reported that insufficient clarity regarding the role of the sport psychology consultant has prevented athletes from working effectively with them [6, 8].

Much of this research was conducted in the late 1980s and early 1990s when sport psychology was still a burgeoning area. The area of applied sport psychology has matured significantly over the past two decades. However, with the exception of work by Pain and Harwood [6], who contend that negative perceptions of sport psychologists continue to exist, there is little information about the current status of attitudes towards psychology in sport. It is not clear, therefore, whether perceptions and use of sport psychology have changed in this period. Furthermore, many of the studies were conducted in samples from the United States and in sports where athletes and coaches have had the opportunity to work with a sport psychologist.

The intention of the present investigation was to examine the current use of and attitudes towards of sport psychology in powerlifting. Powerlifting, a strength sport comprising three lifts (squat, bench press and deadlift), is a minority sport in Britain and does not have Olympic status. The level of funding the sport receives is limited and there is no formal provision of sport psychology services by the national governing bodies. Therefore, the current investigation provides an insight into the status of sport psychology in a sport that has no official structure for sport psychology support. This type of research is important in establishing the issues surrounding perceptions of sport psychology in a minority sport and identifying how the use of sport psychology can be better promoted.

A secondary purpose of the research was to examine gender difference in perceptions of sport psychology. Some research has suggested that perceptions of sport psychology vary according to gender. For example, a study of male and female college athletes found that female athletes had more positive attitudes towards sport psychology, a finding consistent across White and Black Americans [5]. The authors suggested that male athletes may be less willing to engage with sport psychology services because they viewed sport psychology as only for those with weaknesses.

METHOD

Participants

The sample consisted of 28 British powerlifters (n = 11 male, n = 17 female) ranging in age from 18 to 65 years (mean ± S.D. = 38.65 ± 12.16 years). On average, participants had competed in powerlifting for 8.49 years (S.D. = 12.90 years). Eighteen lifters reported competing in 'three lift' competitions, three reported competing in bench press-only competitions and seven lifters competed in both forms of powerlifting. Participants competed at national (n = 18) and international (n = 10) levels in weight categories from 52 kg to 125+ kg.

Measures

A questionnaire was developed to measure powerlifters' knowledge, use and perceptions of sport psychology. The first part of the questionnaire comprised items about demographic information. In the second part, participants were asked to define what sport psychology meant to them, using 5-10 keywords [see 9]. The third part contained 17 items about participants' *knowledge* of sport psychology, which were based on topics identified in existing literature [see 6, 9]. Items were rated on a Likert-type scale from 1 (*No knowledge*) to 7 (*Excellent knowledge*). Next, participants completed the 17 items with reference to the perceived *importance* of the topics to powerlifting (1 = *Not at all important, 7 = Extremely important*). Lifters also completed the 17 items about *how often they used* the topics in powerlifting (1 = *Never, 7 = Always*). Finally, participants indicated on a single item their interest in learning more about sport psychology (1 = *Not at all interested, 7 = Extremely interested*). The fourth part of the questionnaire comprised two open-ended questions regarding the factors that may make powerlifters less likely to use sport psychology and the factors that may encourage powerlifters to use sport psychology more.

Procedure

The organizer of a national powerlifting championships was contacted to seek their permission to approach potential participants at the championships. Questionnaires were distributed to powerlifters at the end of the competition and returned directly to the investigator. Participants were informed of the purpose of the study and were invited to give written informed consent before completing the questionnaire. It was emphasized that all information provided by participants would remain confidential and that data would only be presented at the group level.

Statistical Analysis

SPSS version 16.0 was used to calculate descriptive statistics for the sample. Pearson's product-moment correlations were calculated to examine relationships between powerlifters' knowledge of sport psychology topics, the perceived importance of the topics to powerlifting and participants' use of the topics. MANOVAs were used to investigate gender and competitive level differences in these variables.

RESULTS

Status of Sport Psychology

In response to the question 'Define what sport psychology means to you, using 5-10 key words', the most frequent keywords indicated by participants were: (a) mental preparation (n = 7), (b) attitude (e.g. mental toughness, n = 5), (c) concentration (n = 5), (d) confidence/positiveness (n = 3), (e) control (n = 3), (f) goal setting (n = 3), (g) mind associations (e.g., self-awareness, n = 3), (h) motivation (n = 2) and (g) imagery (n = 1).

Table 1. Mean ± S.D. for Knowledge, Importance and Use of Sport Psychology Topics

Topics	Knowledge		Importance		Use	
	Mean	S.D.	Mean	S.D.	Mean	S.D.
Motivation	5.52	1.47	6.67	0.44	6.29	0.92
Positive attitude	5.39	1.45	6.75	0.41	6.50	0.77
Concentration/Attention	5.29	1.73	6.57	0.60	6.21	0.86
Goal setting	5.26	1.35	6.17	0.83	5.92	1.24
Mental toughness	5.11	1.73	6.38	0.89	6.00	1.155
Pre-competition mental preparation	5.11	1.66	6.33	0.89	5.75	1.097
Confidence	5.25	1.67	6.63	0.46	5.96	1.07
Communication	4.96	1.71	5.29	1.29	5.04	1.26
Sportspersonship	4.79	2.15	5.46	1.54	4.75	2.04
Controlling your emotions	4.75	1.88	5.92	1.18	5.04	1.69
Dealing with anxiety/competitive stress	4.54	2.06	5.88	1.03	5.33	1.65
Relaxation	4.54	1.86	5.54	1.33	4.88	1.40
Imagery/Visualisation/Mental Practice	4.30	1.54	5.68	1.22	5.05	1.26
Psychological recovery from injury	4.14	2.07	5.43	1.58	4.26	1.52
Self-talk	4.07	1.94	4.92	1.18	4.04	1.52
Hypnosis	2.39	1.93	2.79	1.39	2.04	1.50
Biofeedback	2.18	1.89	3.38	1.82	2.96	1.84

Descriptive Statistics

The mean ± S.D. scores for powerlifters' knowledge, perceived importance and use of the sport psychology topics are presented in Table 1. Topics are ordered to indicate those with the greatest knowledge ratings. Motivation, positive attitude and concentration/attention were the most understood of the topics, while hypnosis and biofeedback were the least understood. Participants perceived positive attitude, motivation and confidence as the most important topics for performance in powerlifting, while biofeedback and hypnosis were rated as the least important. With regard to the use of sport psychology, positive attitude, motivation and concentration/attention were the most commonly employed topics. As with knowledge and importance ratings, hypnosis and biofeedback were the least used of the topics. The mean score for participants' interest in learning more about psychology was 4.76 ± 1.85.

Statistics Analyses

Pearson's product – moment correlations were calculated to examine the relationships between the respective knowledge, importance and use scores for each of the 17 topics (see Table 2). Significant, positive correlations were identified between knowledge and important ratings for mental toughness, communication, sportspersonship, emotional control, relaxation, psychological recovery from injury, self-talk, hypnosis and biofeedback. For knowledge and use scores, positive correlations were revealed for mental toughness, pre-competition mental preparation, communication, sportspersonship, emotional control, dealing with anxiety/competitive stress, relaxation, self-talk, hypnosis and biofeedback. Positive correlations also emerged between importance and use ratings for mental toughness, communication, sportspersonship, emotional control, relaxation, imagery, psychological recovery from injury, self-talk, hypnosis and biofeedback. Finally, MANOVAs revealed no significant gender or competitive level differences in the knowledge, importance and use scores for the 17 topics.

Qualitative Analyses

In the final section of the questionnaire, participants responded to open-ended questions. The first question addressed potential barriers to using sport psychology in powerlifting while the second question addressed the factors that may facilitate the use of sport psychology. The themes that emerged from these questions are presented in Table 3, including the frequency with which each theme was endorsed. The greatest barrier to using sport psychology perceived by the powerlifters was a lack of awareness and education about sport psychology. With regard to facilitating factors, the aspect perceived as most likely to encourage the use of sport psychology in powerlifting was evidence that sport psychology is effective in improving performance.

Table 2. Correlations among Knowledge, Importance and Use of Sport Psychology Topics

Topics	r between respective knowledge and importance	r between respective knowledge and use	r between respective importance and use
Motivation	.22	.20	.37
Positive attitude	-.02	.15	.22
Concentration/Attention	.22	.37	.35
Goal setting	.17	.07	.29
Mental toughness	.41*	.48**	.62**
Pre-competition mental preparation	.14	.39*	.18
Confidence	.02	.23	.30
Communication	.44*	.47*	.63**
Sportspersonship	.39*	.73**	.72**
Controlling your emotions	.48*	.49**	.65**
Dealing with anxiety/competitive stress	.29	.60**	.25
Relaxation	.48**	.51**	.38*
Imagery/Visualisation/Mental Practice	.30	.30	.62**
Psychological recovery from injury	.42*	.33	.60**
Self-talk	.60**	.39*	.58**
Hypnosis	.64**	.52**	.63**
Biofeedback	.54**	.51**	.68**

Table 3. Summary of Perceived Barriers and Facilitating Factors for Sport Psychology Use in Powerlifting

Barriers	Fre-quency	Facilitating Factors	Frequency
Lack of education about/awareness of sport psychology	8	Evidence that sport psychology improves performance	6
Physical aspects of powerlifting perceived as more important than the psychological aspects	5	Greater awareness of topics/Education/Greater exposure to sport psychology	4
Lack of funding	3	Knowledge that top lifters/peers use sport psychology (i.e., role models)	4
Applicability of sport psychology to powerlifting not clear/not sport-specific enough	1	Having access to sport psychology services	1
Powerlifters not capable of understanding it	1	Promoting a focus on performance enhancement rather than on 'fixing problems'	1

Perception that sport psychology is only for powerlifters with problems	1	Encouragement from fellow lifters and coach	1
Not encouraged by coach	1		
Not enough time	1		
No perceived need for it	1		

DISCUSSION

The open-ended questions regarding participants' definitions of sport psychology corroborates prior research which found athletes and coaches to have varying definitions of sport psychology [9]. In contrast, to work by Sullivan and Hodge [9], the most common definitions were mental preparation, attitude and concentration, which may reflect differing demands of powerlifting and other sports. Nevertheless, the categories identified in both pieces of research were very similar, suggesting that the athletes have a somewhat accurate definition of sport psychology at a general level.

With the exception of biofeedback and hypnosis, the descriptive statistics for athletes' knowledge about sport psychology suggest that they perceived themselves to have a moderate-to-good knowledge of the topics. Overall, powerlifters perceived the sport psychology topics to be important to powerlifting, with 14 of the 17 topics having a mean rating of five or above on a 7-point Likert-type scale. Use of the psychological topics was also high, with athletes' mean score for 15 of the topics above the mid-point of four. Correlations revealed strong links among the knowledge, importance and use of the skills. However, it is not clear as to the causality of relationships. For example, are athletes more likely to rate a topic as important for powerlifting when they are more familiar with that topic? Or are athletes more likely to make an effort to learn about a topic when they perceive it to be more important for their performance? Further research regarding the causal ordering of these variables is warranted and would contribute to our understanding of how psychological skills develop.

Although the quantitative analyses suggested that athletes had a good understanding of sport psychology topics, a lack of awareness or knowledge was the most common barrier to engaging with sport psychology. This raises a question as to whether powerlifters understand the sport psychology topics to have the same meaning as would a sport psychologist. In-depth analyses of the interpretation of sport psychology terminology was clearly beyond the scope of the current research, however, future research could consider providing an explanation of the sport psychology topics before assessing participants' familiarity with them.

In contrast with previous research that has found largely negative perceptions of sport psychology and sport psychology consultants [e.g., 3, 6], both the quantitative and qualitative data illustrate that sport psychology is generally perceived in a positive light by British powerlifters and that these attitudes are held equally across male and female participants. Overall, participants reported an openness to learning more about sport psychology but that greater education about and exposure to sport psychology is needed. Given the financial constraints present in minority sports and a lack of formal sport psychology provision in

British powerlifting, a more appropriate method of promoting sport psychology awareness might be via coaches who are well placed to encourage the use of sport psychology in their athletes. As highlighted by Ravizza [7] and by the most important facilitating factor identified in the current research, in order for sport psychology to be embraced, this education would need to be coupled with evidence of the benefits of sport psychology to powerlifting performance.

REFERENCES

[1]   Blair, A., Hall, C. & Leyshon, G. (1993). Imagery effects on the performance of skilled and novice soccer players. *Journal of Sports Sciences, 11,* 95-101.

[2]   Filby, W. C. D., Maynard, I. W. & Graydon, J. K. (1999). The effect of multiple-goal strategies on performance outcomes in training and competition. *Journal of Applied Sport Psychology, 11,* 230-246.

[3]   Gould, D., Tammen, V., Murphy, S., & May, J. (1989). An evaluation of the US Olympic sport psychology consultants and the services they provide. *The Sport Psychologist, 3,* 300–312.

[4]   Linder, D. E., Brewer, B. W., Van Raalte, J. L., & De Lange, N. (1991). A negative halo for athletes who consult sport psychologists: Replication and extension. *Journal of Sport & Exercise Psychology, 13,* 133-1455.

[5]   Martin, S.B., Wrisberg, C.A., Beitel, P.A., & Lounsbury, J. (1997). NCAA Division I athletes' attitudes toward seeking sport psychology consultation: the development of an objective instrument. *The Sport Psychologist, 11,* 201–218.

[6]   Pain, M. A. & Harwood, C. G. (2004). Knowledge and perceptions of sport psychology within English soccer. *Journal of Sports Sciences, 22,* 813-826.

[7]   Ravizza, K. (1988). Gaining entry with athletic personnel for season-long consulting. *The Sport Psychologist, 2,* 243-254

[8]   Ravizza, K. (1990). Sportpsych consultation issues in professional baseball. *The Sport Psychologist, 4,* 330–340.

[9]   Sullivan, J. & Hodge, K. (1991). A survey of coaches and athletes about sport psychology in New Zealand. *The Sport Psychologist, 5,* 140–151.

[10] Voight, M. & Callaghan, J. (2001). The use of sport psychology services at NCAA Division I Universities from 1998–1999. *The Sport Psychologist, 15,* 91–102.

RESEARCH ARTICLES

In: Advances in Strength and Conditioning Research
Editor: Michael Duncan and Mark Lyons

ISBN: 978-1-60692-909-4
© 2009 Nova Science Publishers, Inc.

Chapter 1

UPPER BODY ANAEROBIC AND AEROBIC CAPACITY IN PADDLERS: ASPECTS OF AGE AND GENDER

Jan Heller[1], Pavel Vodicka and Ivana Kinkorova
[1]Charles University, Prague, Czech Republic

ABSTRACT

Canoe and kayak flat water paddling are upper-body sports that make varying demands on upper body aerobic and anaerobic capacity. In order to evaluate the effect of age and gender on upper body aerobic and anaerobic capacity in flat water paddling, altogether 306 elite flat water paddlers (99 female kayak paddlers, 135 kayak and 72 canoe male paddlers) were tested by a 30-s Wingate anaerobic arm test at a resistance load 4 $W.kg^{-1}$ (=0.069 $kg.kg^{-1}$) in males and 3.3 $W.kg^{-1}$ (=0.057 $kg.kg^{-1}$) in females, and an incremental maximum aerobic arm-cranking test. The results were compared in canoe paddlers and in male and female kayak paddlers in four age categories 13 to 14 ("youngster"), 15 to 16 ("youth junior") and 17 to 18 and years of age (junior) and in seniors (19 years and older), respectively. Whereas maximum aerobic performance in male canoe and kayak paddlers increased from 13-14 to 15-16 age category and was not different in junior (17-18 years) and senior paddlers, in the anaerobic arm test, both peak power and mean power output increased with age from the youngest to the oldest age categories. These anaerobic capacity indices were strongly related to the amount of fat-free mass (PP: r= 0.69 and r= 0.62; MP: r= 0.72 and r= 0.71 for the canoe and kayak paddlers, respectively). In female kayak paddlers, the indices of upper body aerobic and anaerobic capacity also increased with age, however the differences among the age groups were smaller than in male paddlers. In contrast to male paddlers, in female kayak paddlers the upper body aerobic and anaerobic capacity indices (relative to body mass) were unrelated to the amount of fat free mass. The results had demonstrated the differences in evolution of upper body aerobic and anaerobic capacity in male and female flat water paddlers.

Keywords: Canoe, Kayak, Wingate, Arm-Cranking

Research interest in exercise physiology is focused on the development of specific exercise tests and testing procedures allowing to achieve greater understanding of the relationships among the components involved to various physical activities and sport performances. As many physical activities and sports are related partially and/or predominantly to upper body muscle work, various types of upper body exercise tests and testing procedures have been developed and introduced into practice. As canoeing and kayaking is typically a sport that places exceptional demands on the upper body and trunk musculature, upper body exercise testing had been introduced in paddlers in early seventeen's [5, 25]. The majority of studies in canoe and kayak paddlers has been focused on upper body aerobic capacity and its development because the paddlers spend the majority of their race at or around their VO$_2$peak [2, 7]. Methods and testing protocols to determine valid VO$_2$peak values using kayak and canoe ergometer protocols and/or arm cranking protocols are frequently discussed [8, 11, 16]. Tesch [26] suggested that elite paddlers exhibit not only well developed aerobic but also anaerobic capacity for upper body exercise, and later many studies had confirmed that anaerobic capacity may be one of the decisive predictors of the successful canoe and kayak performance [9, 13, 16, 27]. However, in contrast to aerobic exercise testing, there is an inconsistency in modes and protocols and test duration of anaerobic tests used in canoe and kayak paddlers. For example, Fry and Morton, [9] used a 60-s lasting all-out test, Bishop et al. [1] and van Someren and Palmer [28] have studied maximum accumulated oxygen deficit in a 2-min lasting all-out test, whereas Sitkowski [23] has tested kayak paddlers by a 40-s upper body exercise test, and/or van Someren and Dunbar [27] and Heller et al. [13, 14] used a 30-s lasting supramaximal test.

Gender differences in physical performance capacity have been investigated more extensively for lower body performance and less is known about the sex and age related differences in aerobic and anaerobic capacity as regards upper body exercise. In aerobic upper body exercise untrained females attain at about 60 to 70 % and specifically trained females at about 80 to 85 % of the performances (related to kg of body mass) of their male untrained and/or trained counterparts [12, 13]. There is only little evidence on the gender differences in upper body anaerobic arm performance. For the Wingate anaerobic arm test, Inbar et al. [15] has reported, in untrained females 64 % and 70 % of the mean power (MP) and peak power (PP) related to kg of body mass found in males. Similarly, in our previous study [13] we found that trained female junior kayak paddlers reached, on average, 69 % of MP and 66 of PP related to kg of body mass, found in trained male junior paddlers, and trained female senior kayak paddlers reached, on average, 63 % of MP and 62 % of PP related to kg of body mass found in trained male senior kayakists. Whereas biological maturation in females and males is different, the aspects of age and maturation should also be taken into account in the evaluation of upper body performance capacity.

In contrast to anthropometric studies [18] there is only little evidence on the upper body aerobic and anaerobic capacity in paddlers across the different age categories using the same methods and test protocols. Similarly, there are few comparative studies in young and adult female and male paddlers [13, 14]. Therefore, the aim of the present study was to evaluate the physiological parameters obtained in upper body aerobic and anaerobic exercise tests in

[1] Please address correspondence and requests for reprints to Jan Heller, Biomedical Laboratory, Faculty of Physical Education and Sport, Charles University in Prague, J.Martiho 31, 162 52 Prague, Czech Republic or e-mail Heller@ftvs.cuni.cz.

young (youngster, youth junior and junior) and adult (senior) trained male and female paddlers and evaluate the results from point of view of age and gender.

METHOD

Participants and Procedures

Altogether 306 elite flat water paddlers (99 female kayak paddlers, 135 kayak and 72 canoe male paddlers) participated in the study. All of them were competing at a high national and/or international level. The subjects were examined at the end of the preparatory period by two upper body exercise tests, in the asynchronous mode of cranking, in the same day. Anaerobic test was a 30-s Wingate anaerobic arm test, using a modified Monark ergometer, at a resistance load 4 $W.kg^{-1}$ (=0.069 $kg.kg^{-1}$) in males and 3.3 $W.kg^{-1}$ (=0.057 $kg.kg^{-1}$) in females. Power output in every revolution was computed on-line during the test, and 5-s peak power output (PP), mean power output (MP), total work or anaerobic capacity (AnC), and a power decrease, expressed as fatigue index (FI) were estimated. Peak heart rate was recorded at the end of the test (HRpeak). Peak blood lactate concentration was assessed at the 5th min of recovery [24].

After 2 hours of recovery, the athletes performed the aerobic progressive maximum arm-cranking ergometry test. The test started by a 6-min standardised warm-up at a cranking rate 60 rpm (first 3 min at 1.0 $W.kg^{-1}$ and next 3 min at 1.5 $W.kg^{-1}$ in males or 0.75 $W.kg^{-1}$ and 1.25 $W.kg^{-1}$ in females, respectively.) Thereafter, the subjects completed a continuous 1-min incremental test of 20-W increments, until exhaustion, which was defined as the inability to maintain the cranking rate 60 rpm despite strong verbal encouragement. Throughout the test, heart rate was continuously recorded by short-wave telemetry (Polar Electro, OY, Finland) and expired air was analysed throughout the test via on-line gas analysis system (Ergooxyscreen, Jaeger, Germany). Upper body VO_2max was determined as the highest values averaged over a 1-min period. The maximum blood lactate concentration was determined at the 3rd min of recovery [24]. Ventilatory threshold (T_{vent}) was assessed by means of a two-compartment linear model of the dependence of pulmonary ventilation on oxygen consumption with a computer algorithm to establish a two-line regression intersection point [3]. Body fat assessment and an amount of fat-free mass (FFM) calculation were based on the calliperation of 10 skinfolds [19]. Data are expressed as means and standard deviations.

Statistical Analysis

Correlation analysis was performed to assess the dependence of variables on the age of the athletes. Students' t-tests were used to identify the differences between the data obtained in the separate age groups of paddlers, and the statistical significance was set at $p<0.05$.

RESULTS

We found increases in body mass, body height and a fat-free mass from the youngest canoe paddlers' age category to the oldest senior category (Table 1), (correlation with age r= 0.55; r= 0.46; r=0.59, respectively, all p<0.01). Body mass index and body fat were also related with age (r= 0.53; r= - 0.41, respectively, all p<0.01), however the values were not significantly different across the groups. Aerobic upper body capacity and maximum power output increased with age (absolute values: r= 0,49; r= 0,64, respectively, all p<0.01), but difference in relative values of VO_2peak, maximum power output and pulse oxygen were relatively small and their increases were significant only between 13-14 and 15-16 year-old age category. Ventilatory threshold variables and maximum lactate concentrations were not substantially different across the age categories. Anaerobic performance capacity indices in canoe paddlers increased with age (peak power: r= 0.60; mean power: r= 0.67; anaerobic capacity r= 0.67; peak lactate concentration: r= 0.43, respectively, all p<0.01), whereas fatigue index, peak power/mean power ratio and a peak heart rate were not substantially different across the groups. As it could be expected, anaerobic performance variables were roughly dependent on the amount of fat-free mass (PP: r= 0.62, MP: r=0.73, anaerobic capacity: r= 0.73, all p<0.01), however, VO_2peak and maximum power relative to kg of body mass were independent on the amount of fat-free mass (r= 0.09, r= 0.09, respectively, not significant).

In a group of kayak paddlers (Table 2) the dependence of body mass, body height, body mass index and fat-free mass on age was well pronounced (r= 0,58; r= 0,38; r=0,54; r= 0,67, respectively, all p<0.01). Body fat in kayak paddlers was inversely related to age (r= - 0.38, p<0.01). Aerobic upper body capacity and maximum power output increased both in absolute and relative values increased with age (r= 0.53; r= 0.30; 0.67; r= 0.44, respectively, all p<0.01), and the differences were found among the younger groups of kayakists but not between 18-19 year-old juniors and senior kayak paddlers. The same was true for pulse oxygen but ventilatory threshold variables and maximum lactate concentrations were not substantially different across the age categories. Anaerobic performance capacity indices in kayak paddlers increased with age (peak power: r= 0.65; mean power: r= 0.70; anaerobic capacity r= 0.70; peak lactate concentration: r= 0.49, respectively, all p<0.01), whereas fatigue index, peak power/mean power ratio and a peak heart rate were not substantially different across the age groups. In kayak paddlers, the anaerobic performance variables were roughly dependent on the amount of fat-free mass (PP: r= 0.62, MP: r=0.71, anaerobic capacity: r= 0.70, all p<0.01) and also VO_2peak and maximum power relative to kg of body mass were dependent on the amount of fat-free mass (r= 0.39, r= 0.46, respectively, all p<0.01).

Table 1. Physical characteristics, upper body aerobic and anaerobic capacity in elite male canoe paddlers of different age categories [mean ± SD]

	13-14 yrs [n=20]	15-16 yrs [n=16]	17-18 yrs [n=20]	Seniors [n=16]
Age [years]	14.4±0.3	15.8±0.8*	17.7±0.5*	22.6±4.7*
Mass [kg]	60.7±11.0	67.4±10.1	75.1±5.3*	78.8±5.0*
Height [cm]	172±7	176±5	181±2*	182±3
BMI [kg.m^{-2}]	20.4±2.5	21.7±2.4	22.9±1.5	23.7±1.4
Fat [%]	9.8±2.8	8.3±2.1	7.7±2.3	7.2±2.8
Fat-free mass [kg]	54.6±8.9	61.7±9.1*	70.8±7.0*	73.1±5.2
VO$_2$peak [l.min^{-1}]	2.9±0.5	3.6±0.7*	4.1±0.3*	4.1±0.4
VO$_2$peak [ml.kg^{-1}.min^{-1}]	47.4±5.4	53.8±6.4*	54.8±5.6	52.1±5.8
Power output [W]	190±33	224±45*	247±21	270±24*
Power output [W.kg^{-1}]	3.2±0.3	3.3±0.4	3.3±0.3	3.4±0.3
HRmax [min^{-1}]	188±6	187±6	189±8	185±9
Oxygen pulse$_{max}$ [ml.kg^{-1}]	0.25±0.03	0.29±0.03*	0.29±0.03	0.28±0.03
T$_{vent}$ [%VO$_2$max]	73.3±6.7	67.2±5.8*	72.6±6.0*	73.2±4.4
T$_{vent}$ [%Power output$_{max}$]	73.5±5.2	71.7±5.4	75.7±4.9*	78.3±3.6
T$_{vent}$ [% HR$_{max}$]	90.3±2.8	89.7±2.5	89.8±2.5	90.6±2.8
LAmax [mmol.l^{-1}]	11.2±2.3	12.0±2.5	12.5±2.5	12.4±2.0
Peak power [W.kg^{-1}]	7.7±1.0	9.2±1.3*	9.9±1.0	10.5±1.1
Mean power [W.kg^{-1}]	5.8±0.7	6.8±0.9*	7.3±0.6	7.9±0.8*
Anaer. capacity [J.kg^{-1}]	175±20	204±28*	220±18	237±26*
Fatigue index [%]	42.1±6.9	45.8±5.2	46.1±6.5	45.4±6.7
MP/PP [%]	76.1±5.6	74.0±4.2	74.1±4.5	75.2±5.0
HRpeak [min^{-1}]	176±10	177±9	176±10	176±10
LApeak [mmol.l^{-1}]	10.2±1.4	11.6±2.6	12.4±2.1	12.8±2.1

* significantly different from the younger age group

Table 2. Physical characteristics, upper body aerobic and anaerobic capacity in elite male kayak paddlers of different age categories [mean ± SD]

	13-14 yrs [n=42]	15-16 yrs [n=53]	17-18 yrs [n=25]	Seniors [n=15]
Age [years]	14.1±0.3	15.9±0.5*	17.6±0.5*	22.1±3.6*
Mass [kg]	61.2±9.2	69.7±7.2*	75.8±8.4*	79.7±6.0
Height [cm]	173±8	180±5*	183±6	183±6
BMI [%]	20.4±2.0	21.4±1.7*	22.7±1.7*	23.8±1.3
Fat [%]	11.2±4.2	9.3±3.4*	8.8±3.2	5.9±2.6*
Fat-free mass [kg]	54.3±8.2	63.1±5.6*	69.0±7.1*	74.9±5.8*
VO$_2$peak [l.min^{-1}]	3.0±0.7	3.7±0.6*	4.4±0.6*	4.4±0.5
VO$_2$peak [ml.kg^{-1}.min^{-1}]	48.0±5.2	52.8±5.7*	57.3±4.3*	55.0±6.1
Power output [W]	194±33	240±31*	273±36*	301±28*
Power output [W.kg^{-1}]	3.2±0.3	3.5±0.3*	3.6±0.4*	3.8±0.3
HRmax [min^{-1}]	195±8	194±7	189±8*	188±7

Table 2. (Continued)

	13-14 yrs [n=42]	15-16 yrs [n=53]	17-18 yrs [n=25]	Seniors [n=15]
Oxygen pulse$_{max}$ [ml.kg^{-1}]	0.25±0.03	0.27±0.03*	0.30±0.02*	0.29±0.03
T$_{vent}$ [%VO$_2$max]	70.0±6.9	68.0±7.4	70.0±5.9	73.6±4.2
T$_{vent}$ [%Power output$_{max}$]	71.3±5.2	71.6±6.8	74.8±7.0	76.6±4.6
T$_{vent}$ [% HR$_{max}$]	88.6±3.3	88.5±3.1	89.3±3.6	89.8±2.3
LAmax [mmol.l^{-1}]	11.3±2.3	12.4±2.1*	13.2±2.0	13.9±2.2
Peak power [W.kg^{-1}]	7.8±1.2	9.2±1.1*	9.7±1.0*	11.1±0.7*
Mean power [W.kg^{-1}]	5.9±0.9	7.0±0.6*	7.3±0.7*	8.5±0.6*
Anaer. capacity [J.kg^{-1}]	177±28	209±19*	220±21*	257±19*
Fatigue index [%]	44.0±8.3	44.5±9.6	44.7±6.2	43.6±5.4
MP/PP [%]	75.2±6.1	76.1±6.1	75.8±3.8	77.0±3.3
HRpeak [min^{-1}]	182±10	183±8	177±9	178±9
LApeak [mmol.l^{-1}]	10.5±2.0	11.8±1.7*	12.2±1.7	14.2±1.7*

*significantly different from the younger age group

In the group of female kayak paddlers the most pronounced change in body mass, body height and a fat-free mass was observed between the 13-14 and the 15-16 year-old category. The dependence of anthropometric variables on age was found for mass, height, body fat, and fat-free mass (r= 0.28; r= 0.36; r= -0.44; r=0.59, respectively, all p<0.01) but not for body mass index. There was no difference in anthropometric variables between 18-19 year-old junior and senior female kayak paddlers except the lower body fat in senior kayakists. Similarly, the indices of the aerobic upper body capacity were not substantially different among the younger age groups but VO$_2$max both in absolute and relative values and pulse oxygen were significantly higher in senior female kayak paddlers than in 18-19 year-old junior kayakists. In female kayak paddlers there was also found the dependence of aerobic upper body capacity indices on age (r= 0,50; r= 0,35; r= 0,60; r= 0,38; r= 0,39; for the VO$_2$peak, VO$_2$peak/kg, power output, power output/kg, and pulse oxygen, respectively, all p<0.01). Ventilatory threshold variables and maximum lactate concentrations were not substantially different across the age categories. Anaerobic performance capacity indices in female kayak paddlers increased with age (peak power: r= 0.52; mean power: r= 0.52; anaerobic capacity r= 0.52; peak lactate concentration: r= 0.31, respectively, all p<0.01), whereas fatigue index, peak power/mean power ratio and a peak heart rate were not substantially different across the groups. Surprisingly, in female kayak paddlers, the anaerobic performance variables were not dependent on the amount of fat-free mass (PP: r= 0.06, MP: r=0.09, anaerobic capacity: r= 0.09, not significant) and also VO$_2$peak and maximum power relative to kg of body mass were not dependent on the amount of fat-free mass (r= 0.18, r= 0.04, respectively, not significant).

Table 3. Physical characteristics, upper body aerobic and anaerobic capacity in elite female kayak paddlers of different age categories [mean ± SD]

	13-14 yrs [n=18]	15-16 yrs [n=26]	17-18 yrs [n=30]	Seniors [n=25]
Age [years]	13.8±0.8	16.1±0.6*	17.9±0.6*	22.1±2.3*
Mass [kg]	59.7±5.8	64.3±5.8*	65.9±5.8	66.2±6.7
Height [cm]	165±5	170±4*	170±4	171±5
BMI [%]	21.9±2.4	22.3±1.6	22.7±1.7	22.6±1.7
Fat [%]	15.1±3.6	14.3±3.2	13.9±3.9	10.8±4.2*
Fat-free mass [kg]	50.6±4.8	55.0±4.1*	56.6±3.8	58.8±4.8
VO_2peak [$l.min^{-1}$]	2.6±0.5	2.8±0.4	2.9±0.3	3.2±0.4*
VO_2peak [$ml.kg^{-1}.min^{-1}$]	43.8±8.6	43.2±5.5	44.1±4.1	48.7±6.4*
Power output [W]	174±20	190±20*	204±16*	212±20
Power output [$W.kg^{-1}$]	2.9±0.4	3.0±0.3	3.1±0.3	3.2±0.3
HRmax [min^{-1}]	186±8	189±8	189±8	185±9
Oxygen pulse$_{max}$ [$ml.kg^{-1}$]	0.24±0.05	0.23±0.03	0.23±0.02	0.26±0.03*
T_{vent} [$\%VO_2max$]	72.7±7,6	74.2±6.8	73.8±6.2	73.1±5.3
T_{vent} [%Power output$_{max}$]	71.8±5.6	74.6±7.3	74.3±4.9	73.2±5.8
T_{vent} [% HR_{max}]	89.8±1.8	90.2±2.9	90.9±2.9	91.4±2.7
LAmax [$mmol.l^{-1}$]	10.7±1.4	12.4±2.0*	11.9±1.5	12.2±2.2
Peak power [$W.kg^{-1}$]	6.2±0.8	6.9±1.0*	7.2±0.9	7.8±0.8*
Mean power [$W.kg^{-1}$]	4.9±0.6	5.5±0.6*	5.6±0.6	5.9±0.6
Anaer. capacity [$J.kg^{-1}$]	146±20	164±19*	169±17	177±16
Fatigue index [%]	37.3±7.3	39.3±8.5	40.3±6.9	43.1±7.7
MP/PP [%]	78.7±5.5	79.4±5.3	78.0±4.0	76.0±4.5
HRpeak [min^{-1}]	171±13	177±8	179±11	176±6
LApeak [$mmol.l^{-1}$]	9.3±1.9	11.4±1.9*	11.2±1.8	11.9±1.8

* significantly different from the younger age group

Comparison of VO_2peak values obtained for canoe and kayak paddlers in various studies (Table 4) have to be done with caution due to various ergometers and protocols employed. As it has been evidenced by [8] specific kayak ergometers´ protocols may provide 7 to 8 % higher values of VO_2peak than arm cranking ergometry protocols. Values found young and adult canoeists and kayakists in this study based on the arm-cranking tests seem to be comparable with the previous reported data, being slightly higher in kayakists than in canoeists. Regardless of the high ability for upper body exercise, the aerobic capacity determined in upper body ergometry is lower than observed in treadmill testing. For example, Bunc et al. [3] reported 47 $ml.kg^{-1}.min^{-1}$ in female flat water paddlers. In male flat water paddlers, a treadmill value of VO_2max 62 $ml.kg^{-1}.min^{-1}$ has been described by many authors [3, 11, 17].

Table 4. Peak oxygen uptake values (VO₂peak) determined by arm ergometry in canoe (C) and kayak (K) paddlers (m. male, f. female athletes, WW. white water paddlers)

Reference	No. of subjects	Age [years]	Sample	VO$_2$peak [l.min^{-1}]	VO$_2$peak [ml.kg^{-1}.min^{-1}]
5	11	23±3	K, high perf (m)	3.4	42.1
25	5	22-28	C, nat. (m)	4.6	59.1
29	13	22±3	K, national (m)	5.1	60.2
29	11	16±1	K, national (m)	4.7	60.8
11	14	20±2	C+K, elite (m)	4.0	51.9
9	7	26±7	K, elite (m)	4.78	59.2
9	31	25±7	K, sub-elite (m)	3.87	54.8
10	9	22±2	K (m)	3.72	51.7
22	14	21±4	K, nat. (m)	5.2	64.2
28	13	26±5	K, internat.(m)	4.45	52.6
28	13	25±6	K, national (m)	4.25	54.5
2	16	22±4	K, high perf (m)	3.7	51.2
14	14	25±3	WW, nat. (m)	3.3	47.1
14	8	25±7	WW, hobby (m)	3.1	40.8
4	11	16±1	K, national (f)	2.9	44.6
21	-	21	K, high perf. (f)	3.5	-
21	-	17	K, high perf. (f)	2.9	-
1	9	27±5	K, high perf. (f)	3.1	44.8
13	15	22±3	K, national (f)	2.7	42.2
13	17	16±1	K, national (f)	2.8	42.7

As it has been previously discussed, the concept of anaerobic capacity and its testing in canoe and kayak paddlers is not consistent among studies. Table 5 summarizes the values from the Wingate anaerobic arm test and the force-velocity tests in canoe and kayak paddlers. The values of peak power obtained by the 30-s Wingate anaerobic arm test seem to be very close to those obtained in upper body force-velocity test reported by Peres et al. [20]. Comparison of the data should be done with caution due the various ergometers and different protocols employed. Values found young and adult canoeists and kayakists in this study based on the arm-cranking tests seem to be comparable with the previous reported data, and the age and gender differences in upper body anaerobic performance are consistent to the previous reported data. Comparative studies on anaerobic capacity in males and females had revealed that females have a capacity to use ATP similarly to males, however when glycolytic activity is required, their function is diminished, when compared to the response of males [6].

Table 5. Upper body anaerobic capacity determined by Wingate anaerobic arm test and/or force-velocity test in canoe (C) and kayak (K) paddlers (m. male, f. female athletes, WW. white water paddlers)

Reference	No. of Subjects	Age [years]	Sample	PP [W.kg^{-1}]	MP [W.kg^{-1}]	FI [%]
20 *	7	23	K, national (m)	13.4	-	-
20 *	5	23	C, national (m)	12.7	-	-
20 *	5	24	K, national (f)	9.5	-	-
20 *	22	17	K + C, high (m)	9.8	-	-
20 *	8	17	K + C, high (f)	7.8	-	-
20 *	6	17	WW, high (m)	9.5	-	-
13	15	22±3	K, national (f)	6.9	5.5	37.5
13	17	16±1	K, national (f)	5.8	4.8	33.2
23	13	26±5	K, internat.(m)	7.3	6.0	34.7
23	13	25±6	K, national (m)	6.0	5.1	32.6
14	24	23±4	K + C, elite, (m)	11.1	8.4	44.1
14	14	25±3	WW, nat. (m)	10.3	7.8	45.4
14	8	25±7	WW, hobby (m)	9.3	6.8	50.2
14	14	21±5	K, elite (f)	7.4	5.8	40.0
14	9	21±5	WW, nat. (f)	6.4	5.1	38.1

* .. force-velocity test

DISCUSSION

It could be summarized that, from the physiological point of view, the decisive predisposition for elite canoe and kayak performance is increasing fat-free mass and decreasing body fat during growth and maturation and improvements in upper body aerobic and anaerobic capacity, similarly in males and females. As biological maturation in females is earlier than in males, one may expect higher increases in 13-14 to 15-16 year-old category, from "youngsters" to "young juniors" or "cadets". Later, in female kayak paddlers, the junior and senior category seem to different in lower body fat, and a higher upper body VO$_2$peak and upper body anaerobic capacity indices in senior paddlers than in junior female kayak paddlers. In male kayak paddlers the junior and senior category seem to different in lower body fat, higher amount of the fat-free mass, and a higher upper body anaerobic capacity indices in senior paddlers than in junior kayak paddlers. Similar tendencies, but non significant differences were observed also in male canoe paddlers. In contrast to female paddlers, there were no significant differences in upper body neither absolute nor relative VO$_2$peak in male kayak and canoe paddlers and paddlers, whereas absolute maximum power output was significantly higher in senior than in junior paddlers.

In addition, in male kayak paddlers increases in upper body anaerobic capacity (PP, MP and anaerobic capacity) across the age categories were accompanied by higher responses in their peak blood lactate, corresponding to the previously reported data [16]. It could be concluded that aerobic upper body capacity in canoe and kayak paddlers is increasing from the youngster to the junior age category. Higher upper body anaerobic capacity, lower body fat and a higher amount of fat-free mass may account for the main physiological differences between senior and junior flat water paddlers.

ACKNOWLEDGEMENTS

This study was supported by grant of Czech Ministry of Education MSM 0021620864.

REFERENCES

[1]   Bishop, D., Lepianka, K. & Lehmann L. (1999) Physiological predictors of flat-water kayak performance in women. In: *4th Annual Congress of the European College of Sport Science,* July 14-17, Rome (p.311).

[2]   Bishop, D. (2000) Physiological predictors of flat-water kayak performance in women. *Eur J App Phys*, 82, 91-97.

[3]   Bunc, V., Heller, J., Leso, J, Sprynarova, S. & Zdanowicz, R. (1987) Ventilatory threshold in various groups of highly trained athletes. *Int J Sports Med*, 8, 275-280.

[4]   Bunc, V. & Heller, J. (1994) Ventilatory threshold and work efficiency during exercise on cycle and paddling ergometers in young female kayakists. *Eur J App Phys,* 68, 25-29.

[5]   Dal Monte, A. & Leonardi, M.L. (1975) Sulla specifita della valutazione funzionale negli atleti: esperienze sui canoisti. *Medicina dello Sport*, 28, 213-219.

[6]   Esbjornsson, M., Bodin, K. & Jansson, E. (1995) Muscle metabolism during a 30-s sprint test (Wingate test) in females and males. *Med Sci Sports,* 27, suppl, 448.

[7]   Fernandez, B., Perez-Landaluce, J., Rodriguez, M. & Terrados, N. (1995) Metabolic contribution in Olympic kayaking events. *Med Sci Sports,* 27, suppl, 24.

[8]   Forbes, S.C. & Chilibeck, P.D. (2007) Comparison of a kayaking ergometer protocol with an arm crank protocol for evaluating peak oxygen consumption. *J Strength Cond Res,* 21, 1282-1285.

[9]   Fry, R.W. & Morton, A.R. (1991) Physiological and kinanthropometric attributes of elite flatwater kayakists. *Med Sci Sports Exerc*, 23, 1297-1301.

[10] Garbutt, G. & Robinson, B. (1997) Prediction of 1000m flat water kayaking time from maximal oxygen uptake determined during a simulated kayaking ramp test. *J Sports Sci,* 15, 47.

[11] Heller, J., Bunc, V., Novak, J. & Kuta, I. (1984) A comparison of bicycle, paddling and treadmill ergometry in top paddlers. In: Löllgen, H. & Mellerowicz, H. (Eds.), *Progress in ergometry: Quality control and test criteria* (pp. 236-241). Berlin-Heidelberg, Springer.

[12] Heller, J, Pribanova, L. (2000) Asynchronous and synchronous arm ergometry in trained and untrained subjects. *Sci Sports*, 15, 333-334.

[13] Heller, J., Vodicka, P. & Pribanova, L. (2002) Upper body aerobic and anaerobic capacity in young and adult female kayak paddlers. In: Martos, E. (Ed.) *24th FIMS World Congress of Sports Medicine* (pp. 47-50). Bologna, Monduzzi Ed.

[14] Heller, J. & Vodicka, P. (2005) Upper body aerobic and anaerobic capacity in elite white-water slalom paddlers. *Acta Universitatis Carolinae, Kinanthropologica*, 41, 19-26.

[15] Inbar, O, Bar-Or, O. & Skinner, J.S. (1996) *The Wingate Anaerobic Test*. Champaign IL : Human Kinetics.

[16] Michael, J. S., Rooney, K. B. & Smith, R. (2008) The metabolic demands of kayaking. *J Sports Sci Med*, 7, 1297-1301.

[17] Misigoj-Durakovic, M. & Heimer S. (1992) Characteristics of the morphological and functional status of kayakers and canoeists. *J Sports Med Phys Fit*, 32, 45-50.

[18] Moreno, A.C., Morate Besuita, F.J., Serratosa Fernandez, L., Arnaudas Roy, C. & Rubio Gimeno, S. (1994) Caracteristicas morfologicas del piragüista español de alta competición: estudio por grupos de edad. *Medicina dello Sport*, 47, 19-26.

[19] Parizkova, J. (1977) Body fat and physical fitness. Hague: Nijhoff.

[20] Peres, G., Vandewalle, H. & Monod, H. (1988) Puissance maximale anaerobie des membres superieurs: etude comparee entre differentes populations de canoe-kayakistes. *Medicine du Sport (Paris) 62*, 134-139.

[21] Perez-Landaluce, J., Rodriguez, M., Fernandez, B., Garcia-Herrero, F. & Terrados, N. (1997) Aerobic and anaerobic capacity in junior and senior level women kayakers. In: *Proceedings of the 9th European Congress on Sports Medicine*, September 23-26, Porto (p.159).

[22] Santos, A.M.C., Fontes Ribeiro, C.A. & Silva, N.M.M. (2002) Physiological responses to a maximal kayak testing the laboratory an in the water. In: Koskolu, E., Geladas, N. & Klissuras, V. (Eds.), *Proceedings of the 7th Annual Congress of the ECCS, July 24-28,* Athens, University of Athens, (p. 231).

[23] Sitkowski, D. (2002) Some indices distinguishing Olympic or world championship medalists in sprint kayaking. *Biol Sport*, 19, 133-147.

[24] Smith, P.M., Davidson, R.C.R. & Price, M.J. (2002) Blood lactate profile after two different arm crank ergometry tests. *J Sport Sci,* 20, 58-59.

[25] Tesch, P., Piehl, K., Wilson, G. & Karlsson, J. (1976) Physiological investigations of Swedish elite canoe competitors. *Med Sci Sports*, 8, 58-59.

[26] Tesch, P.A. (1983) Physiological characteristics of elite kayak paddlers. *Can J App Sports Sci*, 8, 87-91.

[27] van Someren, K.A., & Dunbar G.M.J. (1997) Supramaximal testing on a kayak ergometer: Reliability and physiological responses. *J Sports Sci,* 15, 33-34.

[28] van Someren K.A., & Palmer, G.S. (2003) Prediction of 200-m sprint kayaking performance. *Can J App Phys*, 28, 505-517.

[29] Wojcieszak, I., Wojczuk, J., Czapowska, J. & Posnik, J. (1981) A specific test for determination of work capacity of kayak competitors. *Biol Sport*, 1, 7-18.

In: Advances in Strength and Conditioning Research
Editor: Michael Duncan and Mark Lyons

ISBN: 978-1-60692-909-4
© 2009 Nova Science Publishers, Inc.

Chapter 2

AGILITY TRAINING, AGILITY AND DRIBBLING SKILLS IN SOCCER PLAYERS: EFFECTS OF A 4-WEEK INTERVENTION

Julian Smith[1] and Andrew M. Lane
University of Wolverhampton, UK

ABSTRACT

The aim of this study was to examine the impact of a four-week training programme primarily designed to enhance agility, on changes in agility and dribbling performance. Forty-six volunteer male college soccer players (age-range 16-19 years) completed an agility T-test and a dribbling speed test. Participants were then randomly assigned to a control or experimental group, with the experimental group participating in a four-week agility-training programme, and the control group following their usual training programme for 4 weeks. Participants were then re-tested following the 4-week training period. A subsection of participants ($n = 25$) completed a questionnaire to assess pre-performance time goal and rated goal-confidence shortly before doing the agility T-test, repeated when participants were re-tested. Results showed the intervention was associated with participants setting more challenging goals and enhanced agility performance. No significant differences were found for dribbling skills and self-efficacy. It is suggested that factors underpinning improved performance could derive from a combination of physiological and psychological factors.

Keywords: stretch-shortening cycle (SSC), intervention, technical performance, goal setting.

Agility can be defined as the ability to maintain and control correct body position while quickly changing direction through a series of movements [48] and requires a combination of strength, speed, balance, and coordination [15]. Changes in speed and direction are required approximately once every 5 seconds throughout a soccer game [20]. Several studies have further highlighted the relevance of agility to soccer performance [12, 23, 26, 39, 41]. Whilst regular participation in soccer training and matches may enhance agility performance in comparison to non-activity, specificity of training is required for additional improvement [37]. It is suggested that in order to achieve specificity for soccer it is important that, in addition to changes of speed and direction, transitions between forward, backward, and lateral movement patterns are included [34, 40]. Rapid and frequent transitions between these movement patterns require the muscles to shorten in an elastic manner immediately after lengthening, and consequently incorporate the stretch-shortening cycle (SSC), which is key to agility training [8]. The performance of such activities requires the combination of many components including perceptual and decision-making factors, specific muscle characteristics, and sound technique [31].

Improvements in agility associated with specific training have been linked to concomitant developments in technical performance. Clearly, high levels of agility aid the development of athletic timing, rhythm and movement [18], and improve an athlete's ability to adjust to an external object such as a ball [47]. In particular, links between agility and dribbling have been suggested [40]. Dribbling ability has also been shown to distinguish elite under-16 players from players at a lower level to a greater degree than shooting, passing or ball control tests [41]. It therefore appears that agility and dribbling performance are important fitness and technical variables respectively for soccer performance, and that an improvement in agility may result in a concomitant improvement in dribbling performance. Given this evidence-base, sport scientists working in soccer should consider developing agility-specific training programmes.

The relationship between sport scientists and those athletes at the performance-end of sport is complex. Although sport scientists espouse the benefits of various factors on performance, these are not always readily taken up by athletes and coaches. For example, Thelwell [45] posits to an almost paradoxical scenario in which athletes attribute success and failure to psychological factors, but are cautious about engaging in psychological skills training, something that might address the very factor that could impinge performance. Athletes and coaches are always looking for methods to enhance performance, and evidence indicates that they are willing to experiment on potentially extreme methods, sometimes illegal, they require immediate effects. Lane [24] outlined the complex process though which credibility as a sport scientist can be hampered or enhanced in professional sport. It is clearly incumbent for sport scientists to develop credibility with athletes and coaches and to do this within the early stages of their work. If an agility training programme is to be seen as credible, then coaches and players would expect some discernible results almost immediately. Whilst athletes are prepared to experiment in their training, they will only do so if they believe positive effects will follow.

With this in mind, the present study was conducted with soccer players at an academy in which performance improvements were important. The intervention was kept deliberately short – 4 weeks in this case [42]. It is acknowledged that 8 weeks are needed for physiological changes to become apparent, but it was believed that players would not commit to changes in training for 8 weeks without sufficient improvements [38]. It was expected that performance would improve within 4 weeks, but this would be attributed to changes in the

---

[1] Please address correspondence and requests for reprints to Julian Smith, The University of Wolverhampton, Gorway Road, Walsall, England, WS1 3BD or e mail julian.smith@wlv.ac.uk

standard of performance set as a goal; that is specific training would lead to setting more challenging goals. Therefore, the aim of this study was to examine the impact of an intervention programme that focused on developing agility technique. We hypothesised that the anticipated improvements in agility performance would result in similar improvements in dribbling performance. We also hypothesised that improvements in performance would match increases the difficulty in performance set as a goal; that is players would set faster times as a goal.

METHOD

Background

The study was a quasi-experimental, repeated measures design, and compared a control with an experimental group. The participants performed separate tests designed to measure agility and dribbling skill (pre-test), and were then randomly assigned to the control or experimental group. The experimental group participated in supervised agility-training sessions twice a week for 4 weeks. Both the experimental and control groups also followed their usual training programme for 4 weeks. After the 4-week training period, participants were re-tested using the same standardised assessments (post-test). Whilst it is accepted that a four-week training programme is insufficient for many physiological adaptations, it has been suggested that this time period is sufficient for performance enhancement following Stretch-Shortening-Cycle (SSC) training [38]. The focus of the training programme was therefore the development of agility technique.

Although findings could be attributed to changes in physiological processes, it was worth exploring the extent to which improvements in performance could be explained by changes in psychological states. To this end, a subsection of participants completed measures of goal setting and self efficacy pertaining to performance goals at the two-agility testing times. Goal setting theory suggests that much of behaviour is motivated toward goal achievement [28]. It is suggested that goals enhance motivation through a cognitive process. The process of setting a goal identifies the standard of performance required for success. Once the perceived challenge of the goal is known, this leads to the activation of personal resources to increase effort and achieve success [1, 11, 29]. The rationale for setting challenging but attainable goals is based on the interaction between perceived goal difficulty and perceived personal resources to cope. Personal resources are seen as a function of ability and effort [1]. If personal resources outweigh perceived task difficulties, and provided the individual has sufficient interest in attaining the goal, this should be associated with confidence to achieve this goal [1]. Bandura [1] argues that confidence to achieve personal goal is associated with motivated behaviour. By contrast, where the difficulty of a goal outweighs personal ability, this is proposed to lead to poorly motivated behaviour. However, a very difficult goal will remain motivating provided the individual believes that this goal will be attained eventually [1].

Lane and Streeter [25] tested the relationship between self-set goals and goal confidence in a quasi-experimental study. They examined the effects of 'easy', 'difficult', and 'unrealistic' goals on improvements in basketball shooting performance. Results showed that participants continued to set difficult goals for themselves. They assessed self-efficacy to achieve these goals and found that efficacy estimates were relatively stable, whilst the standard of performance set as a goal increased. Therefore, it is speculated that if the performance standard remained constant, confidence would have increased. In relation to the present study, participants in the intervention group are likely to set more difficult goals as beliefs in the effectiveness of the specific agility intervention should inspire a belief that agility performance would improve. If participants set more difficult goals, and confidence to attain these goals is sustained, an argument for improved performance in the short term could be ascribed to changes in psychological factors rather than physiological adaptation.

Participants

Participants were 46 soccer players aged 16–19, and were classed as 'experienced' athletes as they had all been training for 1–5 years and were involved in a regular soccer programme [8]. They were heterogeneous in terms of playing ability with the standard ranging from involvement with professional clubs to playing for a college academy. The study was given ethical approval from the institute of the authors, and informed consent was obtained from all participants. In addition parental consent was obtained for those under 18 years of age.

A sub-section of 25 players completed a questionnaire to assess pre-performance time goal and rated goal-confidence (self-efficacy). Anticipated pre-performance time goal was indicated on a 9 point scale. In addition, participants indicated their goal confidence relative to all 9 points on the same scale. Participants completed measures shortly before completion of the agility T-test.

PROCEDURES

All testing and training sessions were conducted indoors in a college sports centre to maintain a consistent surface and environment. Before each testing or training session, participants performed a 5-minute standardised warm-up followed by 5-minutes of stretching, including ballistic exercises. The ballistic exercises were adapted from warm-up activities taken from previous research [32], and included stationary toe raises, side-to-side ankle hops, lunge walks, cross-over lateral steps, hurdle walks, arm swings across the chest, and arm circles. Each ballistic exercise was carried out for approximately thirty seconds in both forward and backwards, or left to right directions, and on both sides of the body.

Agility Testing Procedures

Agility was assessed using the agility T-test, which has demonstrated good reliability [33] and involves 4 changes of direction and 90/180° angles of directional change, which approximates previous recommendations for differentiating between linear sprinting and agility [49]. A detailed description of the procedure for the administration of the test can be found in the literature [44].

Dribbling Speed Testing Procedures

Dribbling speed was assessed by a test adapted from previous research [43]. It was adapted to include 4 changes of direction and 90° angles of directional change to relate to the agility T-test, and is shown in Figure 1.

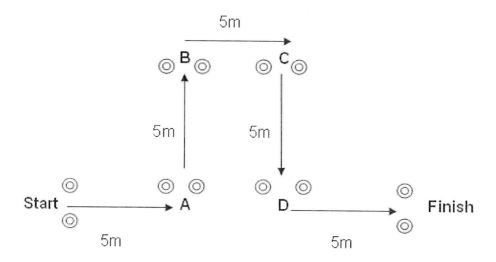

Figure 1. Dribbling Test.

Procedure for the Administration of the Dribbling Test

- The test administrator demonstrated the proper procedure of the test.
- Participants carried out a warm-up for approximately 10 minutes as described previously.

The participant starts with a stationary ball on a line in between the For both the agility and dribbling tests, two trials were allowed with a 3-minute rest between trials [5]. Scores were recorded to the nearest one-hundredth of a second and the best score was retained. The same individual administered each test.

Agility Training Programme

During the programme, all particiapants continued with their normal skill and fitness based training, whilst the exprimental group also participated in an agility specific intervention. The 7 drills chosen for the intervention related to movement patterns typically performed in soccer [14]. They consequently focused on minimising the loss of speed when changing direction forward, backward, and laterally. In order to reduce the influence of linear sprinting performance, drills with a maximum straight-line distance of 10 meters were selected. This corresponds closely with the average sprint distances during a soccer match [2]. The drills were programmable, where the participant knows in advance what the movement combinations will be, as opposed to reactive, where the participant is required to react to an external signal [18].

The intervention consisted of two sessions a week, separated by three full days [7]. One set, comprising of 5 repetitions was performed on each of the 7 drills, with each repetition taking approximately 5 seconds. The rest interval was 20 seconds which resulted in a work to rest ratio of 1:4, a ratio considered to provide sufficient rest to manage fatigue [14], and allow agility development [16]. A 1-minute rest was allowed between each drill, meaning the participants performed SSC activities over a 20-minute period during each session, which is in line with previous recommendations [17].

During the training sessions, coaching points were gradually introduced with a view to improving the participants' agility technique. The coaching points covered; the technique from a standing start [46]; centre of gravity and sideways movement [4]; head position, and initiating changes of direction [36].

A summary of the coaching points and training programme are shown in Table 1.

- two poles of the start gate.
- On a start command, the participant dribbles 5m with the ball, and dribbles through gate A.
- The participant then dribbles through gates B, C, and D in order. If a gate was missed, the participants were instructed to dribble back through the gate in the correct direction and then continue the course.
- The participant dribbles to the finish gate, and puts their foot on the ball.
- Poles were used to form the gates as opposed to cones.

Table 1. Coaching Points Given on the Training Programme

Coaching Points
<ul><li>Standing Start<ul><li>Hips back leaning slightly forward at the waist: shoulders and chest just over your knees.</li><li>Feet nearly flat and weight on the inside ball of your foot (feet may be staggered under the hips).</li><li>Upper body parallel with the forward angle of the shins.</li></ul></li><li>Centre of gravity low, knees slightly bent and the upper body relatively upright.</li><li>Moving sideways: knees slightly bent and your hips low. Point toes directly forward, keeping your body weight on the balls of the feet.</li><li>Head in a 'neutral position' eyes focused directly ahead.</li><li>Start changes of direction (Cutting) and movement patterns (transitions) by getting the head around quickly and finding a new focus.</li><li>Use 'explosive, punching/hammering' arm and knee actions to accelerate from a standing start and after changes of direction or movement pattern.</li></ul>

Statistical Analysis

Descriptive statistics (mean ± SD) were calculated for agility and dribbling speed, and the relationship between agility and dribbling was examined using the Pearson Product Moment correlation coefficient. Repeated measures multivariate analysis of variance (MANOVA) was used to analyse the effect of experimental group over time on agility and dribbling performance. Repeated measures MANOVA was also used to investigate changes in goal difficulty and goal efficacy over time between participants in the experimental and control groups. Statistical significance was set at $P < 0.05$.

RESULTS AND DISCUSSION: PERFORMANCE DATA

Results Descriptive statistics (mean ± SD) for agility and dribbling speed at test 1 and test 2 are shown in table 2 and depicted graphically in Figure 2. There were no significant differences ($P > 0.05$) in the agility or dribbling scores of the experimental and control groups at test 1. The mean agility score of the experimental group was significantly faster ($P = 0.003$) than the control group at test 2 following the agility training programme.

Agility was significantly ($P < 0.05$) correlated ($r = 0.51$) with dribbling at test 1, and this was still the case at test 2 ($r = 0.47$). However, the hypothesised interaction effect for differences in dribbling performance over time by group was not found ($P = 0.17$).

Table 2. Descriptive Statistics for Agility and Dribbling at Test 1 and Test 2

	Agility 1 (s)	Agility 2 (s)	Dribbling 1 (s)	Dribbling 2 (s)
Control	10.99 ± .53	11.10 ± .54*	9.60 ± .62	9.61 ± .64
Experimental	11.10 ± .65	10.75 ± .51*	9.68 ± .77	9.37 ± .51

* $p < 0.01$ for agility 2, control vs. experimental.

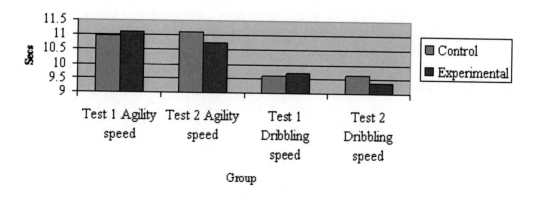

Figure 2. Agility and Dribbling scores over time in the experimental and control groups.

The results show that the agility-training programme was associated with improved the agility performance. Given that the control group maintained their usual training programme, this result demonstrates the importance of applying the principle of specificity when designing training programmes. It would also appear that the agility T-test is a sensitive measure of improvements in agility.

The findings demonstrate that agility performance can be improved over a relatively short time scale, and that the use of drills that focus on minimising the loss of speed when changing direction forward, backward, and laterally, is useful in the development of the agility of soccer players. This supports previous research that found that speed and agility training appears to be effective in the physical conditioning of female soccer players, and that it can be used during whole team training sessions without the need for specialised equipment [37].

Due to the combination of factors required for agility performance, it is difficult to specify which factors contribute to improved performance [10]. Although speculative, the observed training effects of the agility programme could be attributed to the improved agility technique of the participants. The period of four weeks used for the training programme may also have been sufficient to elicit certain neurological adaptations that occur in the early phases (2 – 8 weeks) of anaerobic training [22]. These include additional motor unit recruitment and an increase in the firing rate of the motor neurons [6], a reduction in the influence of the Golgi tendon organs [21], and enhanced influence of the stretch reflex.

The significant ($P < 0.05$) correlations observed between agility and dribbling at test 1 and test 2 were perhaps expected, because both tests involved acceleration, deceleration and changes of direction. It may not be surprising that an increased ability to perform these actions without a ball would be linked to an increased ability to perform them with a ball. Faster dribbling with a ball involves the co-ordination of sound technique with greater force at greater speed, which is related to elastic strength [14]. The physical ability to perform activities involving the SSC may therefore be a pre-requisite of fast dribbling performance. However, the hypothesised interaction effect for differences in dribbling performance over time by group was not found. This may be a result of the lack of sensitivity of the dribbling test.

It is worth noting that the training programme focused on agility technique. It might have been also worth strategies to enhance decision making skills. Perceptual skills involved in dribbling, such as reacting to the ball and decision-making could have been included in the agility training programme. Requiring a response to a directional order, which takes away the ability to anticipate the next move, would incorporate such perceptual skills. This improves the coordination between the CNS signal and the proprioreceptive feedback it receives [13], and may be useful when designing training programmes for, or testing, agility [49]. However, the addition of more variables in the intervention exacerbates identification of which variable was associated with the improvements in performance.

RESULTS AND DISCUSSION: PSYCHOLOGICAL DATA

Discussion

A repeated MANOVA was used to test differences in the time set as a goal, self-efficacy, and performance over time and between groups. The MANOVA results indicated a significant interaction effect for differences in goal and performance scores over time by group (Wilks' Lambda $_{3,16}$ = .53, p = .01, Eta^2 = .47). Univariate differences indicated that agility (F = 11.07, p = .004, Eta^2 = .38) and the difficulty of the goal (F = 6.54, p = .02, Eta^2 = .27) increased significantly more in the experiment group than the control group.

We examined the impact of a four-week training programme primarily designed on changes in self-set goals, self-efficacy and agility performance. The results indicate that agility training led to enhanced performance and setting difficult but achievable goals (Figure 2) in the experimental group; faster performance matched setting faster pre-performance time goals. Following the training programme, agility performance and the difficulty of the anticipated pre-performance goal increased significantly more in the experimental group than the control group. This increase in the difficulty of the anticipated pre-performance goal in the experimental group was thought to partly explain why self-efficacy did not significantly increase (Figure 3). It is suggested that the process of setting specific goals raises self-awareness of current ability, and that these anticipated pre-performance time goals are accurate predictors of performance.

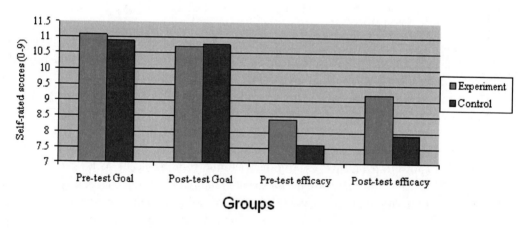

Figure 3. Changes in self-efficacy and goal difficulty in the experimental and control group.

Practical Applications

It is argued that specific agility training should be incorporated into the training programmes of soccer players, as general soccer training may not be sufficient to maximise agility performance. The use of functional drills that incorporate the stretch-shortening cycle and replicate the multiple, simultaneous joint movements of sports related/specific actions is suggested. These drills should focus on minimising the loss of speed when changing direction forward, backward, and laterally, and drills with a maximum straight-line distance of 10 meters, and a total distance of 20 meters are recommended. The use correct agility technique should be encouraged whilst performing such agility drills. Two 30-minute agility-training sessions per week, using a 5 seconds work to 20 seconds rest (1:4) ratio for each drill, are suggested. Based on a 10-minute warm-up, SSC activities should be performed over a 20-minute period during each session. It is worth noting that whilst this training programme might not be sufficient to illicit physiological adaptations, performance should improve through a combination of psychological factors such as increasing effort and being confident to perform to a higher standard. Alternatively, it is possible that participants in the intervention group focused attention on improving agility technique, and improved performance could be attributed to perceptual factors, a variable not assessed in the present study. With this potential limitation in mind, it should be noted that researchers are faced with a difficult decision when trying to account for all potentially confounding variables. The present study focused on agility performance, speed, the difficulty of the self-set goal and goal-confidence only, and clearly there are a multitude of factors that influence performance that were not assessed.

As indicated previously, applied sport scientists can struggle to develop credibility with clients if proposed enhancements in performance are not evidenced in the early stages of their work [45]. The present study sought to apply a theoretical sound intervention that required minimal equipment and time. Applied practitioners require an extensive evidence-base of ecologically valid studies from which they can draw upon to develop specific interventions for their clients. Whilst there is a plethora of scientific studies that seek to test the effects of selected variables, many of such studies involve one or more of the following issues. They use sophisticated equipment to which most practitioners do not have access and are not conducted in an ecologically valid setting. Therefore, applied practitioners might not readily see the application of such studies to their practice. Arguably, the present study addressed such a need by conducting an experiment in an ecologically valid setting, and provides practical guidelines for developing agility performance.

Future research should investigate the impact of different types of agility training, such as acceleration, and reactive agility drills, on both agility and dribbling performance. Whilst this study used drills involving the SSC and oblique angles of acceleration, the impact of improved acceleration should be examined, as this phase is considered especially important for speed and agility movements. Clearly, acceleration training needs to be carried out in conjunction with SSC training, not linear sprint training, if benefits in agility are to be achieved. The incorporation of perceptual skills into an agility training programme should be considered, as this more closely matches the demands of technical performance. Further research is also needed to examine methods of assessing technical performance.

ACKNOWLEDGEMENTS

Many thanks to Tony Lawes of Shrewsbury College for allowing the college academy players to participate in the training program, and to all the players who volunteered.

REFERENCES

[1]   Bandura, A. (1997). *Self-efficacy: The exercise of control*. New York: W. H. Freeman.

[2]   Bangsbo, J. (1994). The physiology of football with special reference to intense intermittent exercise. *Acta Phys Scand,* 151 (suppl 619), 1-156.

[3]   Barnes M. and Attaway J. (1996). Agility and conditioning of the San Francisco 49ers. *Strength Cond, 18*, 10-16.

[4]   Barnes, M. and Attaway, J. (1996). Agility and conditioning of the San Francisco 49ers. *Strength Cond, 18*, (4), 10-16.

[5]   Billeter, R. and Hoppeler, H. (1992). Muscular basis of strength. In: Komi, P. V. (Ed.), *Strength and power in sport*. (pp39-63), London: Blackwell Scientific Publications.

[6]   Bompa, T. O. (1996). *Power training for sports, plyometrics for maximum power development*. Mosiac Press.

[7]   Brown, L. E., Miller, J. M. and Roberts, J. (2000). Introduction To Saq Training. In: Brown, L. E., Ferrigno, V. A., Santana, J. C., (Eds.), *Training for speed agility and quickness*. (pp1-4), Champaign, Il: Human Kinetics.

[8]   Brown, L. E., Miller, J. M. and Roberts, J. (2005). How the training works. In: Brown, L. E., Ferrigno, V. A., Santana, J. C., (Eds.), *Training for speed agility and quickness*. (pp1-6), Champaign, Il: Human Kinetics.

[9]   Burton, D. (1989). Winning isn't everything: Examining the impact of performance goals on collegiate swimmers' cognitions and performance. *The Sport Psychologist, 3*, 105-132.

[10]   Buttifant, D., Graham, K. and Cross, K. (2002). Agility and speed in soccer players are two different performance parameters. In: Spinks, W., Reilly, T. and Murphy, A. (Eds.), *Science and football IV*. (pp329-332), London, Routledge.

[11]   Carron, A. V. (1984). Motivation: Implication for coaching and teaching. London, Sports Dynamics.

[12]   Cook, B. (2003). Combining exercises for football agility. *Nat Strength Cond Assoc*, 25(3), 45–47.

[13]   Craig, B. W. (2004). What is the scientific basis of speed and agility? *Nat Strength Cond Assoc., 26*, (3), 13–14.

[14]   Dick, F. W. (2002). *Sports training principles*. A & C Black, London.

[15]   Draper, J. A. and Lancaster, M. G. (1985). The 505 test, a test for agility in the horizontal plane. *Aus J Sci Med Sport, 17*, 15–18.

[16]   Ferrigno, V. A. and Santana, J. C. (2000). Sport-specific SAQ programs. In: Brown, L. E., Ferrigno, V. A., Santana, J. C., (Eds.), *Training for speed agility and quickness*. (pp219-224), Champaign, Il: Human Kinetics.

[17]   Giorgi, A. (1996). Speed and agility training for success in the game of touch. *Strength Cond coach*, 4, (2), 13-17.

[18]   Graham J. F. (2000). Agility training. In: Brown, L. E., Ferrigno, V. A., Santana, J. C., (Eds.), *Training for speed agility and quickness*. (pp80-143), Champaign, Il: Human Kinetics.

[19]   Kirkendall, D. (1985). The applied sport science of soccer. *Phys Sports Med, 13*, (4), 53–59.

[20] Komi, P. V. (1992). Stretch-shortening cycle. In: Komi, P. V. (Ed.), *Strength and power in sport.* (pp 169-179), London: Blackwell Scientific Publications.

[21] Kraemer, W. J. (2000). Physiological adaptations to anaerobic and aerobic endurance training programs. In: Baechle, T. R., Earle, R. W. (Eds.), *Essentials of strength training and conditioning.* (pp137-168), Champaign, Il: Human Kinetics.

[22] Kuhn, W. (1993). A comparative analysis of selected motor performance variables in American football, rugby union and soccer players. In: Reilly T, Clarys, J. and Stibbeet, A. (Eds.), *Science and Football II.* (pp 62-69), London: E and FN Spon Ltd.

[23] Lane, A. M. (2006). Reflections of professional boxing consultancy. Athletic Insight, 3, volume 8. http://www. athleticinsight. com/Vol8Iss3/Reflections. htm.

[24] Lane, A. M. and Streeter, B (2003). The effectiveness of goal setting as a strategy to improve basketball performance in adolescent club players. Int J Sport Psych, 34, 138-150.

[25] Little, T. and Williams, A. (2005). Specificity of acceleration, maximum speed, and agility in professional soccer players. In: Reilly, T., Cabri, J. and Araújo, D. (Eds.), *Science and Football V.* (pp276-283), London, Routledge.

[26] Locke, E. A. (1994). Comments on Weinberg and Weigand. *J Sport Ex Psych, 16*, 212-215.

[27] Locke, E. A. and Latham, G. P. (1990). *A theory of goal setting and task performance.* Eaglewood Cliffs, NJ: Prentice Hall.

[28] Locke, E. A., Shaw, K. N., Saari, L. M. and Latham, G. P. (1981). Goal setting and task performance. *Psych Bull, 90*, 125-152.

[29] Martens, R. (1987). *Coaches Guide to Sport Psychology.* Champaign, IL: Human Kinetics.

[30] Mero, A., Komi, P. V. and Gregor, R. J. (1992). Biomechanics of sprint running. *Sports Med*, 13, (6), 376-392.

[31] Parsons, L. S. and Jones, M. T. (1998). Development of speed, agility, and quickness for tennis athletes. *Strength Cond*, 20, 14–19.

[32] Pauole, K., Madole, K., Garhammer, J., Lacourse, M. and Rozenek, R. (2000). Reliability and validity of the T-test as a measure of agility, leg power and leg speed in college-aged men and women. *J Strength Cond Res, 14*, 443–450.

[33] Plisk S. S. (2000). Speed, agility and speed-endurance development. In: Baechle, T. R., Earle, R. W. (Eds.), *Essentials of strength training and conditioning.* (pp 472-491).

[34] Plisk, S. S. (2000). Needs analysis. In: Brown, L. E., Ferrigno, V. A. and Santana, J. C. (Eds), *Training for speed agility and quickness.* (pp 5-15), Champaign, Il: Human Kinetics.

[35] Polman, R., Walsh, D., Bloomfield, J. and Nesti, M. (2004). Effective conditioning of female soccer players. *J Sports Sci, 22*, 191–203.

[36] Potach, D. H. and Chu, D. A. (2000). Plyometric training. In: Baechle, T. R., Earle, R. W. (Eds.), *Essentials of strength training and conditioning.* (pp 427-470). Champaign, Il: Human Kinetics.

[37] Raven, P. B., Gettman, L. R., Pollock, M. L. and Cooper, K. H. (1976). A physiological evaluation of professional soccer players. *Br J Sports Med, 10*, 209–216.

[38] Reilly, T. (2005). An ergonomics model of the soccer training process. *J Sports Sci, 23*, 561–572.

[39] Reilly, T., Williams, A. M., Nevill, A. and Franks, A. (2000). A multidisciplinary approach to talent identification in soccer. *J Sports Sci, 18,* 695–702.

[40] Robinson, B. M. (2004). Five-week program to increase agility, speed, and power in the preparation phase of a yearly training plan. *Nat Strength Cond Assoc, 26,* 30–35.

[41] Rosch, D., Hodgson, R., Peterson, L., Graf-Baumann, T., Junge, A., Chomiak, J. and Dvorak, J. (2000). Assessment and evaluation of football performance. *Am J Sports Med,* 28, S29–S39.

[42] Semenick, D. (1990). The T-test. *Nat Strength Cond Assoc J, 12,* 36–37.

[43] Thelwell, R. (2008). Applied sport psychology: Enhancing performance using psychological skills training. In Lane, A. M. (Ed.), *Sport and Exercise Psychology: Topics in Applied Psychology.* (pp 1-6), London: Hodder-Stoughton.

[44] Verstegen, M. and Marcello, B. (2001). Agility and co-ordination. In: Foran, B. (Ed.), *High performance sports conditioning.* (pp 139-159), Champaign, Il: Human Kinetics.

[45] Weinberg, R. S. and Weigand, D. A. (1996). Let the discussion continue: A reaction to Locke's comments on Weinberg and Weigand. *J Sport Ex Psych, 18,* 89-93.

[46] Yap, C. W. and Brown, L. E. (2000). Development of speed, agility and quickness for the female soccer athlete. *Strength Cond J,* 22 (1), 9–12.

[47] Young, W. B., Mcdowell, M. H. and Scarlett, B. J. (2001). Specificity of sprint and agility training methods. *J Strength Cond Res,* 15, (3), 315–319.

In: Advances in Strength and Conditioning Research
Editor: Michael Duncan and Mark Lyons

ISBN: 978-1-60692-909-4
© 2009 Nova Science Publishers, Inc.

Chapter 3

PREDICTING PERFORMANCE IN WOMEN'S ICE HOCKEY

Christina A. Geithner[1]
Gonzaga University, Spokane, WA, USA

ABSTRACT

Performance prediction has been attempted in a wide variety of sports. The majority of research on predicting ice hockey performance has been focused on men, and has not included a combination of anthropometric and fitness variables as predictors. Thus, the purpose of this study was to determine if a combination of anthropometric parameters and off-ice fitness tests would predict on-ice skating performance in elite female hockey players. Pre-season data were collected on members of the women's ice hockey team at the University of Alberta (n=192 cases) over seven competitive seasons. Anthropometry included measures of body size, skeletal lengths and breadths, circumferences, and skinfolds; derived measures included BMI, leg length, estimated muscle circumferences, estimated percent body fat, and Heath-Carter anthropometric somatotypes. Off-ice fitness tests included vertical jump, 40-yard dash, push-ups, sit-ups, and the Leger test. Four on-ice skating tests served as the dependent variables: a 6.10 m acceleration test, a 44.8 m sprint test, a Cornering S-Turn agility test, and a Modified Repeat Sprint Skate (MRSS) test. Each dependent variable was regressed on 22 predictor variables, most of which had been previously identified in the literature as predictors of performance, with some additional variables never before utilized as predictors. On-ice acceleration, sprint, and MRSS tests were predicted by a combination of anthropometric and off-ice fitness variables: faster speed (40-yard dash); higher mesomorphy, biacromial breadth, and abdominal muscular endurance; and lower endomorphy and BMI. Anthropometric variables were the only significant predictors of on-ice agility. Significant predictors accounted for 22.3-34.2% of the variance in on-ice skating performance, indicating that there are other variables as yet unaccounted for that contribute to on-ice performance in women's ice hockey. Strength and conditioning coaches and hockey coaches might benefit from placing a greater emphasis on the development of speed and abdominal

---

[1] Please address correspondence and requests for reprints to Christina A. Geithner, Professor, Department of Exercise Science, Gonzaga University, 502 E. Boone Avenue, Spokane, WA 99258-0004, USA, or e mail geithner@gonzaga.edu.

muscular endurance, and on aerobic and resistance training in training programs and on-ice practices to achieve improvements in body composition, in order to help their athletes achieve high performance hockey.

Keywords: performance prediction, ice hockey, anthropometry, fitness

Performance prediction in sport is of specific interest to coaches, strength and conditioning practitioners, and athletes. If specific variables can be identified that are highly correlated with aspects of performance in a given sport, potential talent can be identified early on and training programs can be designed to more effectively develop these attributes or types of fitness and thereby improve performance in athletes already in a sport. Due to the long and relatively complicated process of identifying and selecting talented young athletes for development (Malina, 1997) and the mulitvariate factors and contingencies that affect performance, the validity of performance prediction has been questioned (Matsudo, 1996; Régnier et al., 1993; Rowland, 1998; see Sands and McNeal, 2000, for a theoretical perspective on and more recent review of performance prediction in athletes). However, in spite of being an imperfect science, the prediction of performance is of practical benefit when results are interpreted with caution and applied appropriately to efforts involving talent identification and to general and sport-specific training.

Studies dealing with performance prediction have been carried out for a variety of sports, with published studies existing for diving (Geithner, 2003), field hockey (Keogh et al., 2003; Reilly and Bretherton, 1986) gymnastics (Dotan et al., 1980), sprint kayaking (van Someren and Palmer, 2003), soccer (Hoare and Warr, 2000; Reilly et al., 2000), masters swimming (Zampagni et al., 2008), table tennis (Toriola and Toriola, 2004), and triathlon events (Burke and Jin, 1996). A number of additional studies have examined variables related to or predictive of performance in ice hockey (Bracko and Fellingham, 1997; Bracko and George, 2001; Diakoumis and Bracko, 1998; Farlinger et al., 2006; Farlinger et al., 2004, 2007; Gee et al., 2007; Green et al., 2006; McCarthy and Kelly, 1978; Mascaro et al., 1992; Vescovi et al., 2006; Voyer and Wright, 1998).

Relationships have been identified between off-ice tests and ice-skating performance in professional men's hockey (Farlinger et al., 2006; Mascaro et al., 1992; Voyer and Wright, 1998), female and male age group players (Bracko and Fellingham, 2001), female and male amateur players (Farlinger et al., 2004), male youth players (Bracko and Fellingham, 1997), male hockey players ages 15-22 years Farlinger et al., 2007), female age group players (Bracko et al., 2001), and elite and non-elite women hockey players (Bracko, 2001). Two approaches have been taken in research on ice hockey with regard to relationships between off-ice tests and other variables and skating performance. In the majority of studies, skating performance has been measured by on-ice skating tests including acceleration (6.10 m acceleration test developed by Naud and Holt, 1980; used by Bracko and Fellingham, 1997; Bracko and George, 2001; Diakoumis and Bracko, 1998; 22.3 m test - Farlinger et al., 2006) and sprint tests over specific distances (Bracko and Fellingham, 1997; Diakoumis and Bracko, 1998; Farlinger et al., 2004, 2006, 2007; Mascaro et al., 1992), the Reed Repeat Sprint Skate Test (developed by Reed et al., 1980; used by Farlinger et al., 2006) or the Modified Reed Repeat Sprint Skate (MRSS) test (developed by Bracko and George, 2001), and the Cornering S-turn agility test (developed by Greer et al., 1992; used by Farlinger et al.,

2004, 2007). Other studies have measured performance as reflected in game or career statistics, such as total minutes of playing time and net scoring chances (Green et al., 2006), or goals and assists in a collegiate hockey season (McCarthy and Kelly, 1978); NHL draft status (Vescovi et al., 2006); success in the National Hockey League (NHL, Gee et al., 2007); points scored per regular season game in NHL career and points per playoff game in NHL career (Voyer and Wright, 1998); and number of games played in a season; assists, goals, and points per game; net scoring chances; penalty minutes per game; and/or ice time in an NHL season (Farlinger et al., 2006). While both approaches are valid and in some cases suggest some relationship between a player's conditioning level and his/her on-ice performance (regardless of how it is assessed), the focus of this paper is on skating performance as measured in on-ice tests (speed, acceleration, agility, and anaerobic power and capacity as estimated from a repeat sprint skate test) rather than in game statistics.

Speed has been said to be at the top or near the top of every coach's wish list for hockey talent, but a player must be able to skate fast and handle a puck well (Brown, 2001). In his book, *Sports Talent: How to Identify and Develop Outstanding Athletes*, Brown (2001) indicates that ice hockey coaches agree that skating skills are probably the most important performance factor in the game, followed by skills related to puck-handling, and a conceptual understanding of the game.

Skating speed seems to be most easily predicted by off-ice variables, such as lower body muscular power as measured by vertical jump (Bracko and Fellingham, 1997, 2001; Bracko and George, 2001; Diakoumis and Bracko, 1998; Farlinger et al., 2004, 2007; Mascaro et al., 1992), broad jump and 3-hop jump (Farlinger et al., 2004) in both sexes and in young male hockey players 15-22 years of age (Farlinger et al., 2007). On-ice speed is also predicted by anaerobic power in amateur ice hockey players of both sexes (Farlinger et al., 2004), and by push-ups in male youth hockey players (Bracko and Fellingham, 1997).

On-ice speed, acceleration, and agility in women are all significantly related to off-ice sprint speed (Bracko and George, 2001); and off-ice sprint speed is the single strongest off-ice predictor of both on-ice speed and agility in female and male amateur players (Farlinger et al., 2004). Acceleration is predicted by push-ups and vertical jump in male youth hockey players (Bracko and Fellingham, 1997) and by vertical jump and 40-yard dash in deaf male hockey players (Diakoumis and Bracko, 1998). Agility seems less able to be predicted than skating speed. One study indicated that lower body muscular power is predictive of agility in amateur players of both sexes (Farlinger et al., 2004), but another found no off-ice fitness predictors of agility in male youth hockey players (Bracko and Fellingham, 1997). In contrast to the aforementioned findings, off-ice tests were not found to be accurate in predicting hockey playing ability or draft status in NHL players (Vescovi et al., 2006).

Only two full-length journal articles have been published on predicting performance in female ice hockey players (Bracko and George, 2001; Bracko et al., 2001), both of which examined age-group players. A combination of physical and performance characteristics has been found to be predictive of skating performance, and predictors varied with age (Bracko et al., 2001). In novice players (ages 8-10 years), ectomorphy and BMI were the strongest predictors of skating agility and speed, while estimated leg length and calf circumference best predicted the Modified Repeat Sprint Skate Test (MRSS). For peewee players (ages 11-13 years), skating agility and speed were best predicted by calf circumference and BMI, and MRSS was best predicted by stature and leg length (Bracko et al., 2001). Finally, for midget players (ages 14-18 years), skating agility and speed were best predicted by BMI and bicristal/biacromial ratio, while MRSS was predicted by BMI and thigh circumference (Bracko, 2001). For players of all levels and across a wide range of ages, skating speed was best predicted by 40-yard dash time (Bracko and George, 2001)

Little is currently known about performance prediction in elite women's ice hockey. In addition, many studies have examined the fitness tests as predictors of sport-specific performance; however, only a few have considered the combination of anthropometric and fitness variables for performance in female athletes in volleyball (Gabbett et al., 2007), soccer (Hoare and Warr, 2000), and field hockey (Keogh et al., 2003). Therefore, the purpose of this study was to determine if a combination of anthropometric parameters and off-ice fitness tests predict on-ice skating performance in elite female ice hockey players.

METHOD

Approach to the Problem

In order to predict sports performance using regression analyses, one needs a sufficient sample size of at least one group of highly skilled athletes. Most researchers have examined 20-70 athletes and usually over one season of play. The present study included 192 cases or pre-season observations of women's ice hockey players at the University of Alberta (Edmonton, Canada) and included 7 competitive seasons. During this period, the team had won 7 Canada West Conference titles and 4 Canadian Interuniversity Sports (CIS) National Championships and had a record of 148-12-5, which supports classification of the players as elite athletes. The team also established a 110-game winning streak in play during the regular conference season and play-offs in 2004-05.

Participants

Players on the University of Alberta's women ice hockey team (n=192 cases, age=20.9±2.5 years, range 17.6-37.5 years) participated in the study. Pre-season data were collected for seven years from 1999-2007, excluding 2001 and 2006. All participants provided informed consent and the study was approved by the Institutional Review Board at Gonzaga University.

PROCEDURES

Each player was measured with a full anthropometric battery by the same experienced anthropometrist (C.A. Geithner) following procedures consistent with Lohman et al. (1988) and using standard anthropometric equipment. Measurements taken included body mass, stature and four other skeletal lengths (sitting height, arm length, thigh length, and calf length; cm), four skeletal breadths (biacromial, bicristal, biepicondylar, and bicondylar; cm), six circumferences (two trunk: minimal waist and maximal hip, and four extremity: relaxed and flexed arm circumferences, mid-thigh, and maximal calf; cm), and nine skinfolds (subscapular, midaxillary, suprailiac, supraspinale, abdominal, triceps, biceps, mid-thigh, and medial calf; mm). A digital scale was used to measure each player's weight in pounds, which was then converted to kilograms. Derived measures included estimated leg length (stature – sitting height), BMI (kg/m^2), percent body fat (Withers et al., 1987), Heath-Carter anthropometric somatotypes (1990), androgyny [(3 x biacromial breadth) – bicristal breadth], estimated mid-arm muscle circumference [relaxed arm circumference – (π x triceps skinfold in cm)], and estimated mid-thigh muscle circumference [mid-thigh circumference – (π x thigh skinfold in cm)]. A detailed description of the physical measurements and methods used is provided in Geithner et al. (2006).

Five different tests were used to assess off-ice fitness: vertical jump, 40-yard dash, push-ups (maximum number performed in full body position with out breaking form in 1 minute), sit-ups (maximum number performed in 1 minute), and the Leger test (1988, predicted VO$_2$max) for each player. Four tests were used to assess on-ice skating performance: 6.10 m acceleration, 44.80 m speed, Cornering S-Turn agility, and Modified Repeat Sprint Skate (MRSS) tests (Figure 1). These tests have been described in detail previously (Bracko and George, 2001).

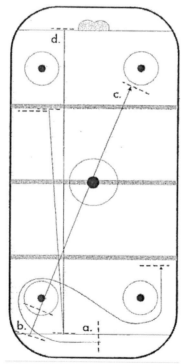

Adopted from Bracko and George, 2001.

Figure 1. On-ice skating tests: a) Cornering S-turn agility, b) 6.10 m acceleration, c) 44.80 m speed, d) Modified Repeat Sprint Skate (MRSS).

Statistical Analysis

Stepwise regression analyses were run using SPSS (Mac version 11.0, SPSS Inc. Chicago IL) with the significance level set *a priori* at $P<0.05$. Predictor variables were selected based on the significant predictors of on-ice performance found in the relevant literature, with four additional variables: arm length, estimated mid-arm muscle circumference, estimated and mid-thigh muscle circumference (substituted for thigh circumference), and mesomorphy. Each on-ice skating performance test (acceleration, agility, speed, and MRSS) was regressed separately from the others on a total of 22 predictor variables: 5 off-ice fitness tests, 5 skeletal lengths (4 measured and 1 derived), 7 circumferences (5 measured and 2 derived), and 3 somatotype components, and 2 ratios or proportions (BMI, androgyny).

All statistical analyses were run with and without one participant's data, because she was an outlier based on her chronological age of 37.5 years, and was playing on the University of Alberta team after having played on the Canadian national team. The results were not significantly different; thus, this player's data were retained in the analyses.

RESULTS

Descriptive statistics for anthropometric and performance characteristics are provided in Table 1, and the results of the stepwise regression analyses are provided in Table 2. On-ice acceleration was predicted by 40-yard dash, mesomorphy, and BMI (*Adj* $R^2=0.223$, $P=0.005$). Agility was predicted by endomorphy, biacromial breadth (shoulder width), and mesomorphy (*Adj* $R^2=0.247$, $P=0.022$). Speed was predicted by 40-yard dash, biacromial breadth, and sit-ups (*Adj* $R^2=0.289$, $P=0.030$). MRSS was predicted by endomorphy, biacromial breadth, and sit-ups (*Adj* $R^2=0.342$, $P=0.006$). Better on-ice skating performance was associated with greater off-ice speed, mesomorphy, biacromial breadth, and abdominal muscular endurance; and with lower endomorphy and BMI.

Table 1. Anthropometric and performance characteristics of the University of Alberta Women's Ice Hockey Team, 1999-2007

Variables	Mean ± sd
Age (yr)	20.9 ± 2.5
Weight (kg)*	66.7 ± 7.4
Stature (cm)*	168.1 ± 5.6
Body Mass Index (kg·m^{-2})	23.6 ± 2.4
Estimated Leg Length (cm)	78.1 ± 3.5
Arm Length (cm)	72.9 ± 3.3
Biacromial Breadth (cm)	38.3 ± 1.6
Bicristal Breadth (cm)	28.3 ± 1.5
Androgyny	86.5 ± 4.5
Hip Circumference (cm)	100.9 ± 5.2
Estimated Mid-Thigh Muscle Circumference (cm)	50.8 ± 4.4
Calf Circumference (cm)	36.3 ± 2.1

Estimated Mid-Arm Muscle Circumference (cm)	23.9 ± 1.7
% Fat (Withers et al., 1987)	20.5 ± 4.4
Endomorphy	4.0 ± 1.1
Mesomorphy	4.3 ± 1.0
Ectomorphy	4.1 ± 2.0
Vertical Jump (cm)	43.3 ± 4.8
40-Yard Dash (s)	5.81 ± 0.26
Push-Ups	36.4 ± 10.2
Sit-Ups	39.0 ± 9.9
Leger Test (predicted VO_{2max}, ml·kg^{-1}·min^{-1})	44.4 ± 5.1
6.10 m Acceleration (s)	1.48 ± 0.13
Cornering S-Turn Agility Test (s)	10.04 ± 0.84
On-Ice Speed Test (s)	7.09 ± 0.49
Modified Repeat Sprint Skate Test (MRSS, s)	48.83 ± 3.89

*Not used in stepwise regression analyses.

Table 2. Equations resulting from stepwise regression analyses using anthropometric variables and off-ice fitness tests to predict skating performance on acceleration, agility, speed, and MRSS tests

Variables	Regression Equations - Unstandardized Beta Coefficients, [Standardized Beta Coefficients]	*Adj R^2* (*P* Value)
Acceleration	$Y = 0.125$ (DASH) $- 7.624^{-2}$ (MESO) $+ 2.551^{-2}$ (BMI) $+ 0.476$ [$Y = 0.244$ (DASH) $- 0.601$ (MESO) $+ 0.458$ (BMI)]	0.223 (P=0.006)
Agility	$Y = 0.430$ (ENDO) $- 0.169$ (BIAC) $- 0.242$ (MESO) $+ 15.930$ [$Y = 0.448$ (ENDO) $- 0.291$ (BIAC) $- 0.254$ (MESO)]	0.247 (P=0.022)
Speed	$Y = 0.897$ (DASH) $- 0.817^{-2}$ (BIAC) $- 0.1.112^{-2}$ (SU) $+ 5.556$ [$Y = 0.421$ (DASH) $- 0.250$ (BIAC) $- 0.210$ (SU)]	0.289 (P=0.030)
MRSS	$Y = 1.338$ (ENDO) $- 1.051$ (BIAC) $- 0.116$ (SU) $+ 88.652$ [$Y = 0.329$ (ENDO) $- 0.389$ (BIAC) $- 0.264$ (SU)]	0.342 (P=0.006)

DASH: 40-yard dash, BMI: body mass index, MESO: mesomorphy, ENDO: endomorphy, BIAC: biacromial breadth (shoulder width), SU: sit-ups.

DISCUSSION

A combination of anthropometric variables and off-ice fitness tests were found to predict on-ice performance in women's hockey players. This finding is in agreement with findings for age group female ice hockey players (Bracko et al., 2001). It is also consistent with findings for female athletes in other sports in which players of different levels of performance of female athletes were distinguished from one another by a number of fitness variables (vertical jump, sprint speed, agility, and predicted maximal aerobic power in female soccer players - Hoare and Warr, 2000; knee extension and grip strength, vertical jump, sprint speed, agility, field distance covered in 2 min while dribbling, and predicted maximal power in female field hockey players - Reilly and Bretherton, 1986); or a combination of body composition, fitness variables, and skill (Keogh et al., 2003).

The somatotype components representing relative fatness and roundness or softness of physique (endomorphy) and relative muscularity and skeletal robusticity or sturdiness of build (mesomorphy) were consistent predictors of skating performance. For three of the four on-ice tests (agility, speed, and MRSS), lower endomorphy was associated with better/faster skating times. Similarly, a lower BMI (a weight-for-height ratio) was associated with lower times for the on-ice acceleration test. These findings are consistent with those for age group female ice hockey players (Bracko et al., 2001) in that certain aspects of physique are predictive of skating performance. Keogh et al. (2003) also found body composition to be one several factors that distinguished among different levels of play in female field hockey players. This finding is consistent with literature on the effect of body composition on sports performance in that greater fatness has a negative effect on performance in sports requiring participants to lift, project, or move their body mass quickly over distance.

Greater biacromial breadth was a predictor of faster times on the agility, speed, and MRSS tests, reflecting the role of body build, particularly broader shoulders or a more athletic (and, typically, more masculine) physique in conferring a performance advantage in sport. Greater shoulder width relative to hip width as assessed by bicristal breadth/biacromial breadth ratio and androgyny [(3 x biacromial breadth) – bicristal breadth] are also associated with later maturity status in females. The sample of elite women's ice hockey players in the current study had a median age at menarche of 13.5±1.4 years, approximately 0.6 years later than the median age at menarche of 12.9 years for Canadian girls and nearly 1 year later than that for U.S. girls (Whites) of 12.6 years reported in Malina et al. (200, p. 315) and consistent with a later-than-average age at menarche in female athletes (Malina et al., 2004, pp. 631-632).

Aside from BMI, endomorphy, mesomorphy, and biacromial breadth – variables reflecting weight-for-height, body composition, and physique; anthropometric variables were not predictive of on-ice performance in the present study. This finding is consistent with findings regarding body size (stature and weight) not distinguishing between different levels of play in female soccer players (Hoare and Warr, 2000) and anthropometric variables not discriminating between differences between regional representative female field hockey players and club players (Keogh et al., 2003), and elite and county level field hockey players (Reilly and Bretherton, 1986).

Two off-ice fitness tests or variables were identified as predictors of on-ice performance in the regression analyses: 40-yard dash and sit-ups. Off-ice speed as assessed by the 40-yard dash predicted acceleration and speed on the ice, which is consistent with the literature. Speed as measured in sprint tests is one of the two most common off-ice fitness variables consistently related to skating performance, particularly on-ice speed, in ice hockey. Speed in the 40-yard dash has been found to predict skating performance in age group female hockey players (Bracko and George, 2001), and speed in the 30-meter sprint was the single strongest off-ice predictor of both on-ice 35 m sprint skate test (*Adjusted R²*=0.845) and Cornering S-turn agility (*Adjusted R²*=0.706) in amateur male and female players (Farlinger et al., 2004). The other fitness variable found to be a predictor of on-ice performance in the present study was sit-ups, which predicted both speed on the ice and the MRSS. This most likely reflects the contribution of abdominal muscular endurance, even core muscular endurance or general fitness, to on-ice speed and power generation.

In the literature on ice hockey performance prediction, the other fitness test found to be predictive of skating performance in addition to sprint speed is lower body muscular power as measured with a vertical jump. Lower body power has been found to be a predictor of on-ice speed in age group females (Bracko and George, 2001); male youth hockey players (Bracko and Fellingham, 1997); on-ice speed and agility in amateur players of both sexes (Farlinger et al., 2004); and on-ice speed (Mascaro et al., 1992), on-ice acceleration and anaerobic capacity in men's hockey (Bracko et al., 1998). It is interesting to note that push-ups have also been found to predict on-ice speed and acceleration in male youth hockey players (Bracko and Fellingham, 2001), and push-ups and anaerobic power have been identified as predictors of on-ice speed in both male and female amateur players (Farlinger et al., 2004). These findings are in contrast to those of the present study in which neither vertical jump nor push-ups were predictive of on-ice performance. Differences among samples of ice hockey players studied may help to explain this inconsistency between findings of the present study and those of previous studies in that the present study is the only study to examine performance prediction in elite women's ice hockey players. Training programs may vary with age and level of play as well as between sexes in fitness components emphasized, which might also account for differences in findings. It is also possible that with the inclusion of somatotype components as independent variables or possible predictors in the present study which account are calculated using multiple anthropometric dimensions, that these factored in as more important predictors than some off-ice fitness tests.

In talent identification studies of female soccer and field hockey players of higher caliber tend to be faster, have greater lower body power, and have higher predicted maximal aerobic power (Hoare and Warr, 2000; Keogh et al., 2003; respectively). The specific predictors of athletic performance identified in the literature vary somewhat by study along with differences in samples studied, including age, sex, level of playing ability, and sport. However, speed, lower body muscular power, and muscular and cardiorespiratory endurance appear to be consistent predictors of performance and of playing level differences in women's soccer, field hockey, and ice hockey. Thus, fitness variables appear to be useful in performance prediction and talent identification in female athletes.

Strengths and Limitations

The strengths of the present study include the use of a larger sample size and longer study duration (seven pre-seasons' worth of data) than many other studies on prediction of performance in sport, and the inclusion of anthropometric variables in performance prediction, and notably somatotype components. Only one other study on female ice hockey has included anthropometric variables and that was on age group players (Bracko et al., 2001). Thus, this study provides a significant contribution to the literature on performance prediction in women's ice hockey.

Two of the limitations of the present study are shared by the majority of studies on ice hockey: information on skating technique is very limited, with the exception of Bracko et al. (1998), as is information puck handling skills and cognitive grasp of the game, in spite of the fact that coaches identify as the most important characteristics of a successful ice hockey player (Brown, 2001). Skill in puck handling would be simpler to assess then cognitive grasp of the game which may not translate easily into performance measures. The present study did assess on-ice skating performance; however, the tests used to assess it did not involve puck handling, nor did they involve novel, game-type situations that would require players to be creative in their responses and provide a glimpse into players' conceptual understanding of the game.

A third limitation is the limited ability to predict skating performance. Anthropometric variables and fitness tests accounted for low-to-moderate amounts of variance (22.3-34.2%) in the on-ice skating tests. Because performance is a multivariate phenomenon, predicting performance is a complex endeavor, the results of which must be interpreted with caution. Further research on predictors of skating performance is warranted, as is research on sport-specific skills and responses to game-specific situations in order to optimize the practical applications of the research.

Practical Applications

Previous studies on ice hockey suggest that speed, power, and muscular and cardiorespiratory endurance appear to be important predictors of on-ice skating performance, and are reflective of the anaerobic and aerobic demands of the sport. However, the best predictors of skating performance in acceleration, agility, speed, and MRSS tests in elite women's ice hockey players in the present study were physique, body composition, speed, and core endurance as assessed by endomorphy, mesomorphy, biacromial breadth, BMI, 40-yard dash, and sit-ups. Thus, the practical implications for hockey coaches and strength and conditioning coaches include a greater emphasis on aerobic and resistance training to help players become leaner, while avoiding the dangers of overemphasizing body composition and increasing the risk for the development of eating disorders in female athletes. In addition, coaches might focus more on speed and abdominal muscular endurance (or core endurance) in training programs and on-ice practices. The results of this study suggest that a combination of anthropometric and fitness variables predict skating performance, and that measures of physique (including biacromial breadth and somatotype components) and body composition should be considered in addition to speed and core endurance in player selection. Skating and puck handling skill, conceptual understanding of the game, and the ability to execute this understanding in game situations are critical components to performance and certainly should *not* be overlooked in talent identification and prediction of performance.

REFERENCES

[1] Bracko, M. R. (2001) On-ice performance characteristics of elite and non-elite women's ice hockey players. *J Strength Cond Res*, 15, 42-47.

[2] Bracko, M. R. & Fellingham, G.W. (2001) Comparison of physical performance characteristics of female and male ice hockey players. *Ped Exer Sci*, 13, 26-34.

[3] Bracko, M. R. & Fellingham, G.W. (1997) Prediction of ice skating performance with off-ice testing in youth hockey players [abstract]. *Med Sci Sports Exerc, Supplement* 29, S172.

[4]   Bracko, M. R., Fellingham, G. W., Hall, L. T., Fisher, A. G. and Cryer, W. (1998) Performance skating characteristics of professional ice hockey forwards. *Sports Med Training Rehab,* 8, 251 - 63.

[5]   Bracko, M., Geithner, C., and Fellingham, G. (2001) Prediction of ice skating performance and on-ice fitness with anthropometric testing in female hockey players [abstract]. *Pediatr Exerc Sci,* 13, 309.

[6]   Bracko, M. R. & George, J. D. (2001) Prediction of ice skating performance with off-ice testing in women's ice hockey players. *J Strength Cond Res,* 15, 116-122.

[7]   Brown, J. (2001) *Sports Talent: How to Identify and Develop Outstanding Athletes.* Champaign, IL: Human Kinetics.

[8]   Burke, S. T. and Jin, P. (1996) JIN. Predicting performance from a triathlon event. *Sport Behav,* 19, 272-287.

[9]   Carter, J. E. L. & Heath, H. (1990) *Somatotyping – Development and Applications.* Cambridge: Cambridge University Press.

[10] Diakoumis, K. and Bracko, M. R. (1998) Prediction of skating performance with off-ice testing in deaf ice hockey players [abstract]. *Med Sci Sports Exerc, Supplement* 30, S272.

[11] Dotan, R., Goldnourt. U. and Bar-Or, O. (1980) Kinanthropometric parameters as predictors for the success of young female and male gymnasts (Abstract). In: Ostyn, M., Beunen, G. and Simons, J. (Eds.), *Kinanthropometry II. International Series on Sports Sciences, Volume 9.* (pp. 212-213). Baltimore, MD: University Park Press.

[12] Farlinger, C. M., Kruisselbrink, D. and Fowles, J. R. (2004) Prediction of on-ice skating speed and cornering ability in amateur hockey players [abstract]. *Can J App Phys,* 21(Supplement), S45.

[13] Farlinger, C. M., Nichol. M. and Roy, B. D. (2006) Relationship between physiological profiles and on-ice performance of a National Hockey League (NHL) team [abstract]. *App Phys Nutr Metab,* 31 (Supplement), S25.

[14] Farlinger, C. M., Kruisselbrink, D. and Fowles, J. R. (2007) Relationships to skating performance in competitive hockey players. *J Strength Cond Res,* 21, 915 – 922.

[15] Gabbett, T., Georgieff, B. and Dowrow, N. (2007) The use of physiological, anthropometric and skill data to predict selection in a talent-identified junior volleyball squad. *Sports Sci,* 25, 1337 - 1344.

[16] Gee, C. J., Dougan, R. A., Marshall, J. C. and Dunn, L. A. (2007) Using a normative personality profile to predict success in the National Hockey League (NHL): A 15-year longitudinal study [abstract]. *J Sport Exerc Psych,* 29, S164-S165.

[17] Geithner, C. (2003) Profiling and talent identification in young divers: A summary of U.S. Diving's efforts 1991-2002. *Inside USA Diving,* 10, 7-8.

[18] Geithner, C., Lee, A. & Bracko, M. (2006) Physical and performance differences among forwards, defensemen and goalies in elite women's ice-hockey. *J Strength Cond Res,* 20, 500-505.

[19] Green, M. R., Pivarnik, J. M., Carrier, D. P. and Womack, C. J. (2006) Relationships between physiological profiles and on-ice performance of a National Collegiate Athletic Association Division I hockey team. *J Strength Cond Res* 20, 43 - 46.

[20] Greer, N., Serfass, R., Picconatto, W., and Blatherwick, J. (1992) The effect of hockey-specific training program on performance of bantam players. *Can J Appl Sport Sci,* 17, 65 - 69.

[21] Hoare, D.G., and Warr, C.R. (2000) Talent identification and women's soccer: An Australian experience. *J Sci Med Sport* 18, 751 - 758.

[22] Keogh, J. W. L., Weber, C.L. and Dalton, C. T. (2003) Evaluation of anthropometric, physiological, and skill-related tests for talent identification in female field hockey. *Can J App Phys,* 28, 397 - 409.

[23] Lohman, T, G., Roche, A. F. and Martorell, R. (1988) (Eds). *Anthropometric standardization reference manual*. Champaign, IL: Human Kinetics.

[24] McCarthy, J. F. and Kelly, B. R. (1978) Aggression, performance variables, and anger self-report in ice hockey players. *J Psych,* 99, 97 – 101.

[25] Malina, R. M. (1997) Talent identification and selection in sport. *Spotlight on Youth Sports,* 20, 1 – 3.

[26] Malina, R. M., Bouchard, C. and bar-Or, O. (2004) *Growth, Maturation, and Physical Activity*. Champaign, IL: Human Kinetics.

[27] Manners, T. W. (2004) Sport-specific training for ice hockey. *Strength Cond J,* 26, 16 – 21.

[28] Mascaro, T., Seaver, B. and Swanson, L. (1992) Prediction of skating speed with off-ice testing in professional hockey players. *J Orthop Sports Phys Ther,* 15, 92 - 98.

[29] Matsudo, V. K. R. (1996) Prediction of future athletic excellence. In: Bar-Or, O. (Ed.), *The Child and Adolescent Athlete*. (pp. 92-109). Oxford, UK: Blackwell Science.

[30] Naud, R.L., and Holt, L.E. (1980) A comparison of selected stop, reverse and start (SRS) techniques in ice hockey. *Can J Appl Sport Sci,* 5, 94 – 97.

[31] Regnier, G., Salmela, J. and Russell, S. J. (1993) Talent detection and development in sport. In: Singer, R. N., Murphey, M. and Tennant, L. K. (Eds.), *Handbook of Research on Sport Psychology* (pp. 290-313). New York, NY: MacMillan.

[32] Reilly, T. and Bretherton, S. (1986) Multivariate analysis of fitness of female field hockey players. In: Day, J. (Ed.), *Perspectives in Kinanthropometry* (pp. 135-142). Champaign, IL: Human Kinetics.

[33] Reilly, T., Williams, A. M., Nevill, A. and Franks, A. (2000) A multidisciplinary approach to talent identification in soccer. *J Sport Sci,* 18, 695 – 702.

[34] Rowland, T. (1998) Predicting athletic brilliancy, or the futility of training 'til the Salchow's come home. *Ped Exerc Sci,* 10, 197 – 201.

[35] Sands, W. A. and McNeal, J. R. (2000) Predicting athlete preparation and performance: A theoretical perspective. *J Sport Behav,* 23, 289 - 310.

[36] Toriola, A. I. and Toriola, O. M. (2004) Validity of specific motor skills in predicting table-tennis performance in novel players. *Percep Motor Skills,* 98, 584 – 586.

[37] van Someren K. A., & Palmer, G. S. (2003) Prediction of 200-m sprint kayaking performance. *Can J App Phys,* 28, 505-517.

[38] Vescovi, J. D., Murray, T. M., Fiala, K. A. and Vanheest, J. L. (2006) Off-ice performance and draft status of elite ice hockey players. *Int J Sports Phys Perf,* 1, 207 – 221.

[39] Voyer, D. and Wright, E. (1998) Predictors of performance in the national hockey league. *J Sport Behav,* 21, 456 - 473.

[40] Withers, R. T., Whittingham, N. O. and Norton, K. I., et al. (1987) Relative body fat and anthropometric prediction of body density of female athletes. *Eur J App Phys,* 56, 169-180.

[41] Zampagni, M. L., Casino, D., Benelli, P., Visani, A., Marcacci, M., and De Vito, G. (2008) Anthropometric and strength variables to predict freestyle performance times in elite master swimmers. *J Strength Cond Res,* 22, 1298 -1307.

In: Advances in Strength and Conditioning Research
Editor: Michael Duncan and Mark Lyons

ISBN: 978-1-60692-909-4
© 2009 Nova Science Publishers, Inc.

Chapter 4

MULTI-COMPONENT TRAINING FOR GAELIC GAMES: A CASE STUDY ON A COUNTY-LEVEL GAELIC FOOTBALL PLAYER

Mark Lyons[1] and *Michael J. Duncan[2]*
[1]Newman University College, UK
[2]University of Derby, UK

ABSTRACT

The purpose of this case study was to explore the effects of a 10-week multi-component training program on a number of anthropometric and physiological variables fundamental to success in Gaelic football. The training program comprised speed, agility and quickness training with a central plyometrics component. The study used a single-participant research design. Prior to commencement of the training program, a number of anthropometric (height, body mass and percent body fat) and physiological variables (upper and lower body strength, flexibility, agility, power, 10m and 30m sprint times with fatigue index) were measured. Compared to the (pre-training) baseline measures there was a slight decrease in body weight and percent body fat following the training program. In terms of the range of physiological measures however, there were large improvements with respect to repeated sprint ability over 30m, vertical jump performance and leg strength. Moderate improvements were also seen for 10m and 30m sprint time, upper body strength and agility. Flexibility remained relatively unchanged. It is acknowledged in the limited literature in Gaelic games that the various components of fitness should not be seen in isolation when devising training programs. The results of this case study show that combining SAQ and plyometric training holds some promise in terms of improving the multiple components of fitness fundamental in Gaelic football. Future studies employing randomized controlled designs are needed however, with respect to this topic, employing larger sample sizes so as to increase the statistical power of the study.

---

[*] Please address correspondence and requests for reprints to Mark Lyons, Department of Physical Education and Sports Studies, Newman University College, Bartley Green, Birmingham, England, B32 3NT or e mail m.lyons@newman.ac.uk.

Keywords: Gaelic football, speed, agility and quickness training, plyometric training

Gaelic football is one of a number of Gaelic games of Ireland. The Gaelic Athletic Association (GAA) governs the game and its rules (see [67] for history). The popularity of the game in more recent years has reached exceptional proportions with interest spreading to Canada, the USA and Australia. With this increased popularity, there has also been an increase in scientific research relating to selected aspects of the game. A thorough review of the science of the game was published in 2001 [67]. However, since then two further reviews have been published [68, 66] both of which include Gaelic football. Peer-reviewed journal articles have also been published with respect to physiological profiling [16, 29, 48, 50, 64, 74, 78, 79], match demands [22, 29, 38, 47, 53] and injuries [18, 33, 42, 55, 56, 80-85] in Gaelic football. Many chapters within the series of 'Science and Football' textbooks are also devoted to scientific research on Gaelic football and abstract publications from conference presentations are numerous. However, while scientific publications relating to the sport are undoubtedly increasing, there is still a distinct lack of published work relating to training methods in Gaelic football.

Empirical research relating to Gaelic football specifically, has identified that multiple components of fitness are important within the game. These include speed and speed endurance [48, 67], strength [48, 49, 67] and power [75]. Speed over short distances is also particularly influential in beating an opponent to the ball and escaping tackles [67]. Anecdotal evidence also confirms that explosive bursts of speed, acceleration and quickness to out-maneuver or evade an opposing player are all fundamental to success in Gaelic football. However, while speed is essential, it is also important to recognize that it is a "start and stop" sport involving repetitive sprint situations. Consequently, maximal speed will rarely, if ever, be reached in a game. As a result of this, a preferable method of performance enhancement may be to increase acceleration. It has been also been identified [19] that the various components of fitness should not be seen in isolation when devising training programs in Gaelic games. The following case study describes a multi-component training program conducted with a Gaelic football player over a 10-week period in preparation for the start of her competitive season. The training was requested as part of ongoing scientific support (following a needs analysis) in an effort to improve a number of physiological components. The main weaknesses identified by the participant in their needs analysis were as follows: (1) sprint speed but more importantly sprint recovery, (2) agility and (3) jumping ability. These components were all deemed as weaknesses of the player in her playing position in Gaelic football (centre back). Because of the need here to train multiple fitness components, a speed, agility and quickness (SAQ) training program with plyometric exercises as a central component of the program was agreed.

Since the 1960's speed and quickness programs have been a large part of performance enhancement programs. Research has found that a properly executed speed and quickness program will increase acceleration and speed [17], two components fundamental to the aims of this training program. Within the scientific literature there are also a plethora of studies demonstrating that plyometric-type training enhances jumping performance [5, 9, 31, 35, 41, 43, 46, 62, 87] and muscle power output [36]. In addition, many studies have demonstrated that plyometric training improves running velocity or speed development [2, 20, 30, 40, 69, 70] and a limited number of studies suggest scope for improving agility [51]. Plyometric training however, is not intended to be a stand-alone exercise program [6, 13] and greater gains have been demonstrated when it is combined with other types of training. For example, when plyometric training is combined with resistance type training (termed complex training) significantly greater gains have been found [1, 3, 4, 21, 27, 58, 59, 86] (for a brief review see [25]). It is not surprising therefore, that training methods are now being combined in an effort to achieve even greater performance gains. In team sports combining training methods is now common as it enables fitness coaches, trainers and strength and conditioning experts alike to achieve their multiple fitness training goals.

With respect to multi-component training, past research has found that a 6-week training program including resistance training, plyometric training and speed training led to significantly better 9.1m sprint performance times in adolescent female athletes compared to a control group [52]. It was decided in the context of this case study to combine SAQ training with plyometrics in an effort to yield the best improvements in the multiple components of fitness identified by the participant. The aim of this case study therefore, is to document the impact of a 10-week combined SAQ and plyometric training program on a range of anthropometric and physiological variables.

METHOD

Participant

The participant was a senior female Warwickshire Gaelic football player who also represented Great Britain in international Gaelic football tournaments. The participant's age, height and body mass were 24 years, 1.6 m and 63.5 kg respectively. Written informed consent and a medical history questionnaire were completed by the participant in advance of the baseline testing session.

Anthropometric Variables

A number of anthropometric measurements were taken pre- and post-intervention. Height and body mass were assessed using a Seca stadiometer and weighing scales (Seca Instruments Ltd, Germany). Percent body fat was assessed using skinfold measurements at four sites using Harpenden skinfold callipers (Harpenden Instruments Ltd, England). The skinfold equation employed was that of Durnin and Womersley [24]. All anthropometric measures were completed by an ISAK accredited anthropometrist who's TEMs for the sites involved was no greater than 2%.

Physiological Variables

A number of physiological measurements were also conducted pre- and post-intervention. All measurements were conducted on the same day and to account for any time-of-day effects both testing sessions were performed within a time difference of ± 2 hours. A

10 minute standardized dynamic warm-up was also performed prior to the testing. Lower back and hamstring flexibility was assessed using the modified sit and reach test (Acuflex 1, Novel Products Inc, USA). Leg and trunk strength was assessed using a leg dynamometer (Takei Instruments Ltd, Japan). Upper body strength was measured using the Dyno push test (Concept II, England). Vertical jump performance was measured using a vertical jump meter (Takei, 5106-Jump MD, Tokyo). A counter movement jump with arm swing (CMJA) was employed here. With all tests the participant was instructed to give an all-out maximal effort. Three trials were completed on each test with the best test score used for analysis.

Agility was measured using a standard T-test with photoelectric speed gates (Brower wireless speed system, USA). The t-test has demonstrated high reliability across trials with a reliability coefficient of 0.98 [57]. The authors however, accept the points outlined by Sheppard and Young [73] with respect to tests of agility that do not include a cognitive component in particular. Two trials were completed here with the best score used for analysis. Three minutes rest was given between trials so as to eliminate any effects from the previous test. The test was set up as shown in Figure 1.

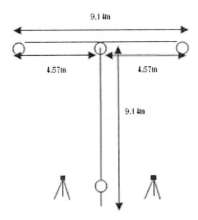

Figure 1. Diagrammatic representation of the T-test.

Test Instructions:

- Participant starts at the base of the "T" behind the first marker (sequencing spot).
- Examiner gives signal to go and when the participant crosses the photocell the time begins.
- Participant sprints to middle marker touching it with her foot, then side steps to the left and touches the marker with her foot, side steps 9.14m to the right and touches the marker with her foot.
- The participant then side steps back into the middle cone and back pedals 9.14m through the starting sequencing spot.
- Time stops when the participant crosses the photocell.

Speed over 10m and 30m was recorded to within one hundredth of a second using the photoelectric speed gates. In accordance with the published guidelines [65], the participant was required to start in front of the first set of speed gates (Figure 2). Additional speed gates were set up at 10m and 30m as shown in Figure 2 with the time at each of these distances recorded as the participant's body breaks through the beam. They were instructed to then slow down over the course of the 10m deceleration zone and jog back to the start again to perform the next sprint. Both 10m and 30m times were then recorded before the start of the next sprint. 7 sprints were completed in total with 25 seconds recovery time between each sprint. Again this was agreed based on published recommendations [88]. Peak acceleration (10m) and speed (time over 30m) was then ascertained from the results collated. A fatigue index was calculated both for acceleration (10m) and speed over 30m, based on the drop off in performance over the 7 sprints. This was calculated by expressing the slowest time recorded over the fastest time recorded, converting this to a percentage and then subtracting 100. It is generally regarded that the lower the fatigue index the better conditioned the participant is to reproduce high-intensity sprints. Despite some criticism of this calculation method [54], there is nevertheless merit in this fatigue index in intervention-type studies or for monitoring training effectiveness. All testing procedures used for this study were approved by the institutional ethics committee.

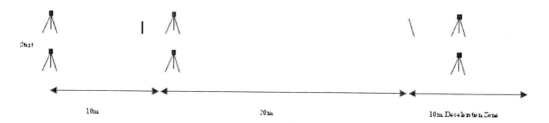

Figure 2. Diagrammatic representation of the repeated sprint test.

SAQ / Plyometric Training

The participant agreed not to change or increase her current exercise habits over the 10-week period. Careful consideration was also given to the well documented risks and stresses associated with plyometric training [10, 70, 14, 32, 72]. Broadly speaking, these link to the fact that this form of training places large stresses on the body and is often associated with delayed onset of muscle soreness [70]. More recently, it has been demonstrated that high intensity plyometric training can even impair unilateral balance [76]. With these points in mind, progression within the training program was imperative and so two training sessions per week were agreed with the participant. This is also consistent with published guidelines [1]. Training sessions were always conducted on non-consecutive days. All training sessions were directly supervised and the participant was instructed on how to perform each exercise or new exercises in advance. The initial training sessions were aimed at ensuring and reinforcing the correct technique using agility ladders, gradually progressing to 16cm hurdles and finally 30cm hurdles. The initial sessions also emphasized double leg movements and progressively a greater number of single leg movements were introduced. After the initial training sessions (weeks 1-2) the volume of training was increased as technique was perfected (weeks 3-6). Following this period (weeks 3-6) the volume of training was then decreased again to allow for increased training intensity (weeks 7-10). In weeks 7-10 a number of combination drills were performed (see Figures 3 & 4) emphasizing speed, agility and power with sport-specific elements also. Prior to each training session, the participant performed a 10-15 minute low intensity dynamic warm up consisting typically of the exercises listed below. This was then followed by a number of dynamic stretches:

- Jogging (2 x 15m)
- Jogging with 'butt kickers' – (2 x 15m)
- Backpedalling (2 x 15m)
- Lateral running (2 x 15m)
- Alternate skips with low knee raise (2 x 15m)
- Alternate skips with high knee raise (2 x 15m)
- Carioca (2 x 15m)
- Jog (5m), fast feet (5m) and jog (5m)
- Walking lunges (2 x 15m)
- Rope skipping (one and two foot combinations - 2 minutes)

To increase the specificity of the program, Gaelic football-specific actions were completed where possible. This included fielding exercises (with and without an opponent), hand-passing exercises, kick-passing and low impact contact work using cushioned tackle bags. Solo running at maximum speed was also included in some of the drills. The importance of using the ball in designing training drills in Gaelic football has been documented [66, 68]. A number of cutting exercises were also used over the course of the training sessions. The importance of including cutting movements in multidirectional sports has been recognized by past authors [34, 35]. These authors emphasize not just potential improvements in sports performance but also a decreased risk of lower extremity injury in female athletes specifically. A summary of the training program is provided in Table 1. As is evident from this table, the main body of the training session began with lower body plyometric exercises and this was then followed by upper body plyometric exercises. This allowed the participant to recover from the predominant lower body exercises within this program. The training session then finished with speed, agility and quickness drills which were completed with a ball where possible. The participant was provided with adequate time for recovery between exercises and sets. With all exercises, correct technique was emphasized and in the event that the participant was unable to perform and exercise with correct technique, the exercise was stopped. Each session was reviewed post training and where appropriate adjustments in sets and reps were made accordingly. A summary of the exercise program is outlined below in Table 1. More detailed descriptions and demonstrations of the drills and components here can be found in selected resources [8, 12, 61, 63].

Table 1. Summary of Training Program

Weeks 1-2 1-2 Sets / 8 repetitions	Weeks 3-6 1-2 Sets / 10 Repetitions	Weeks 7-10 1-2 Sets / 8 Repetitions
15 minute warm up	15 minute warm up	15 minute warm up
*Single leg run through / step overs (16cm hurdles) Bunny jumps (16cm hurdles)	*Single leg run through / step overs (16cm hurdles) Bunny jumps (16cm hurdles)	Bunny jumps (30cm hurdles) *Single leg hop (30cm hurdles)
Hop scotch (16cm hurdles) Run through (16cm hurdles)	Run through with high knees (16cm hurdles) *Lateral barrier alternate feet (16cm hurdles)	Run through (high knees) (30cm hurdles) Alternate leg bounds (10m)
*Lateral barrier alternate feet (16cm hurdles) Run through (2.5m agility ladder)	* Single leg hop (5.5m agility ladder) Quick feet (16cm hurdles) (forward & lateral)	Depth jump (30cm height) (8-10 reps) Depth jump (30cm) to second box (30cm) (8-10 reps)
Quick feet (2.5m agility ladder) (forward & lateral)	Icky shuffle (5.5m agility ladder)	Depth jump (30cm) followed by 2 double leg barrier (64cm) jumps – 5 reps
Icky shuffle (2.5m agility ladder)	Double leg barrier (64cm) jumps 3 sets x 3 barriers	
**Medicine ball half twist (2 sets x 8 reps) **Medicine ball wall chest pass (2 sets x 8 reps) **45° sit up with medicine ball (2 sets x 15 reps)	**Medicine ball half twist (2 sets x 10 reps) **Medicine ball wall chest pass (2 sets x 12 reps) **Medicine ball release sit ups with a partner (2 sets x 15 reps)	**Medicine ball half twist (2 sets x 10 reps) **Medicine ball wall chest pass (2 sets x 12 reps) **Medicine ball release sit ups with a partner (2 sets x 20 reps)
**Medicine ball scoop throw, bounce and catch (2 sets x 8 reps)	Medicine ball upper body shuffles (20-30 second period) **Medicine ball scoop throw, bounce and catch (3 sets x 8 reps)	**Medicine ball scoop throw, bounce and catch (3 sets x 8 reps)
5m x 5m box drill (run, side to side, backpedal, side to side) – 2 sets	5m x 5m box drill (sprint, side to side, backpedal, side to side) – 1 set	7m x 7m box drill (sprint, side to side, backpedal, side to side) – 2 sets

Table 1. (Continued)

Weeks 1-2 1-2 Sets / 8 repetitions	Weeks 3-6 1-2 Sets / 10 Repetitions	Weeks 7-10 1-2 Sets / 8 Repetitions
10m x 5m square drill (run, side to side, backpedal, side to side) - 2 sets	5m x 5m box drill (sprint, side to side, backpedal, side to side) x 2 - 2 sets	5m x 5m box drill followed by 10m zig-zag cone drill – 2 sets
Zig-zag cone drill (20m)	Zig-zag cone drill (10m) – 2 sets	Double leg barrier (64cm) jumps (x 3) followed by cut and sprint 5m
Mirror drill (side shuffle / lateral quick feet) (20 seconds)	Double leg hexagon drill 6 x 16cm hurdles - 3 sets	Partner resisted sprints with let go (high resistance - 20m x 3 sprints) (cutting movement included at 10m)
Double leg hexagon drill (6 x 16cm hurdles – 2 sets)	Partner resisted sprint with let go (medium resistance - 20m x 3 sprints) (cutting movement included at 10m)	Harness pull with let go (high resistance - 15m x 2 sprints)
Partner resisted let-go's (light resistance - 10m x 2 sprints)	Harness pull with let go (medium resistance - 10m x 2 sprints)	Combined exercise 1 (see Figure 3) x 1 Combined exercise 2 (see Figure 4) x 2
15 minute cool down	15 minute cool down	15 minute cool down

* All single leg exercises were performed on the left and right leg   **All exercises performed
   with a 3kg medicine ball

The combination drill in Figure 3 contains the following elements in order:

- Run through (2.5m agility ladder)
- Sprint forwards (7m)
- Side to side movement (3m)
- Backpedaling (3m)
- Side to side shuffle (3m)
- Sprint forwards (7m)
- Laterals (alternate feet) (5.5m)
- Light shoulder tackle against padded tackle bag
- Sprint forward to receive a hand pass and the ball

- Cut right and solo ball towards cone (6m)
- Perform cutting movement around the cone
- Solo ball to the finish line (6m)

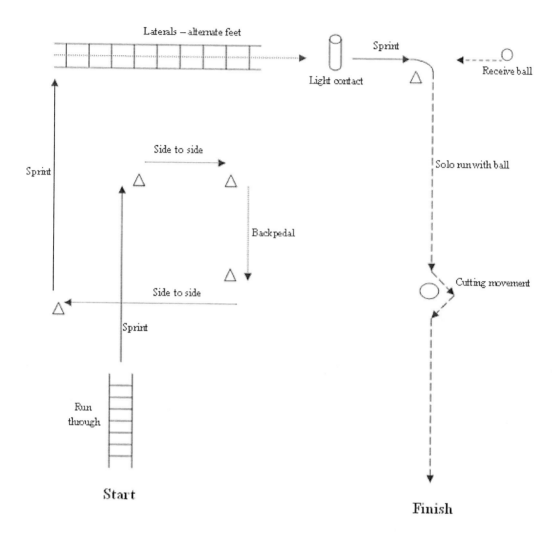

Figure 3. Combination Drill 1.

The combination drill in figure 4 again contained the following elements in order:

- Start with double leg hurdle jumps (hurdle height 63cm)
- Run through (2.5m agility ladder)
- Light shoulder tackle against padded tackle bag
- Sprint forwards into hexagon drill (with command – 20 seconds)
- Mirror drill (20 seconds) (participant finishes on far left / far right cone)
- Sprint forwards (4m)
- Side to side movement (3m)

- Backpedaling (3m) with a 180 degree turn and then fields the ball from the air
- Solo ball towards cone
- Perform cutting movement around the cone
- Solo ball to the finish line

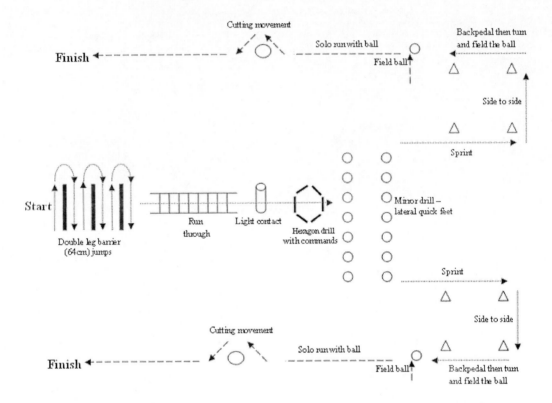

Figure 4. Combination Drill 2.

RESULTS

The pre- and post-intervention results are illustrated below in Tables 2 and 3:

Table 2. Anthropometric Results

Measure	Pre-intervention value	Post-intervention value
Height (m)	1.60	1.60
Body mass (kg)	63.5	62.1
Body fatness (%)	30.7	28.4

Table 3. Physiological Results

Measure	Pre-intervention value	Post-intervention value
Sprint speed, 10m fastest time (s)	2.38	2.20
Sprint speed, 10m mean time (s)	2.51	2.39
Sprint speed, 30m fastest time (s)	5.35	4.98
Sprint speed, 30m mean time (s)	5.66	5.19
Fatigue index, 10m (%)	8.8	9.7
Fatigue index, 30m (%)	13.83	9.23
Vertical Jump (cm)	40	46
Leg and trunk strength (kgF)	98	115
Upper body strength (kgF)	41	45
Flexibility (cm)	25	26
T-test (s)	12.80	11.32

DISCUSSION

The aim of this case study was to document the impact of a 10-week combined SAQ and plyometric training program on a range of anthropometric and physiological variables in a county standard female Gaelic football player. To reiterate, the main weaknesses highlighted in the participant's needs analysis were (1) sprint speed and repeated sprint ability, (2) jumping ability and (3) agility. It was hypothesized here that the combinatory effects of SAQ training with plyometrics would yield greater improvements in the performance variables outlines above as opposed to any other single mode of training. This study was also partly exploratory and other physiological measures (flexibility, upper body strength and leg and trunk strength) were evaluated pre and post intervention in an effort to ascertain if this program of training would impact on these components of fitness.

In terms of the range of fitness components measured here, the greatest improvement was evident with repeated sprint ability over 30m. There was a decrease of 4.6% in the calculated fatigue index over 30m. The results demonstrate therefore, that combining SAQ training with plyometric training could prove very effective indeed in reducing a participant's fatigue index over 30m. Concomitant with improved repeated sprint ability was an 8.3% improvement in the average sprint time over 30m and a 6.9% improvement in the fastest time over 30m. The values here are also higher than those reported by Tucker and Reilly [75] for British University Gaelic football players. The program of training therefore, was effective in terms of improving a number of variables related to 30m sprinting ability. The improvements in performance found here are difficult to compare with other past research however, as few studies with the specific focus of this study have been conducted to date. The research articles cited here often differ in terms of the design of the training program, focus of the program, participant characteristics and methods of testing the physiological components. The findings therefore, must be interpreted with these differences in mind.

It is clear from the 30m sprint variables that the improvements pre- and post-intervention are greater than those found in previous studies [23, 60] similar to this in terms of the number of sessions, period of the training program and the nature of the participants. In a study by Polman et al. [60] SAQ training led to a 4.8% improvement in 25m sprint time while Duncan [23] found that plyometric training led to a 2.5% increase in 30m sprint time. Duncan [23] also examined repeated sprint performance over 30m and found a 0.9% decrease in fatigue index following a 10-week plyometric training program. While existing information regarding the effectiveness of plyometric training on running velocity is conflicting [40], it does seem from the results found here that combining SAQ training with plyometric training may lead to greater improvements in 30m sprint times and repeated sprint performance, compared to plyometric training or SAQ training alone. Improvements in 30-40m sprint times of 2.5% and 1.24% respectively have been found in similar studies of this nature [40, 69]. There are however, a select number of studies [70] within the scientific literature where improvements above those found here in female participants have been found with plyometric training alone.

With respect to sprint speed over 10m, again there was a 12% decrease in the mean time over the 7 sprints, concurrent with a decrease of 7.6% in the fastest time. This led to a fatigue index which was 0.9 % higher than that at baseline or prior to the training intervention. The latter finding here is not surprising given the improvements with respect to mean time and the fastest time over the 7 sprints. The fact that each of the 7 sprint times were better than those at baseline shows that sprinting ability over shorter distances again improved with the multi-component training conducted here. In Gaelic football, player's that possess speed and acceleration over short distances should in essence, have an increased capability to out-react and out-accelerate their opponent. This is important in terms of match performance therefore. It is interesting also that the improvement in sprint performance over 10m in more recent studies ranges from 2.2% [40, 26] to 2.55% [69]. The same 10m sprint variables have been measured in past work [23] but smaller improvements were found following a plyometric training program. Duncan [23] however, found that fatigue index over 10m actually improved by 2.4% which does contrast with the findings here. This may be due, in part to the differing nature of the training programs. Despite the points here the results show that combining SAQ training with plyometric training is very effective in terms of improving acceleration or 10m sprint performance. The results also indicate that improvements in performance may be greater when both SAQ and plyometric training is combined, compared to plyometric or sprint training alone.

Jumping to catch the ball has been identified as an important skill in Gaelic football irrespective of playing position [75]. Jumping ability was deemed a key weakness by the participant in this study and the plyometric elements of the program were aimed at improving jumping ability or power. Game-specific fielding (catching) of the ball in the air was also included in the program and progressed to fielding the ball against an opponent. The results of this training program revealed a 15% increase in CMJA with the post-intervention value (Table 3) greater than that reported for similar level players [75]. It is interesting here that the improvement with respect to CMJA is very similar to other studies [23, 37] structured over a 10-week period. This is also similar to programs where a combination of training methods were adopted [52]. However, the improvement in CMJA is much greater than that reported in several plyometric training studies [e.g. 11] as well as multi-component training studies [44, 26] conducted over shorter time periods (4-6 weeks). The 15% improvement found here is also much higher than the 7.5% mean effect of plyometric training on CMJA highlighted by Markovic [45] in his review paper. The findings here reinforce again that there may be merit in combining SAQ training with plyometric training in terms of improving CMJA or power. Future research needs to consider whether 4-6 weeks is a sufficiently long training period to see significant improvements in vertical jump performance beyond those mediated by neural factors [28].

In terms of the effects of the training program on agility again the findings of this study show that agility improved by 11.6%. In selected studied SAQ training has led to improvements in agility in the range of 4-5% [60] while other studies [51] have found that plyometric training improved agility (as measured using the t-test) by 4.86%. These findings again indicate that the multi-component training here over a period of 10 weeks may prove more beneficial in terms of improving agility above other single modes of training. The relationship between plyometric exercise and increased performance in agility tests may be due to their similar patterns of movement to facilitate power and improved movement efficiency by the immediate change in direction upon landing [71]. Decreased ground contact time is also a possible explanation for the improved performance here although kinetic analyses would be needed here to substantiate this point.

The importance of muscular strength in Gaelic football has again been confirmed by different authors [67, 48]. Muscular strength is required in many game contexts (e.g. tackling, kicking and jumping). Additionally, the physical contact associated with playing mean that upper body and lower body strength is imperative for each player regardless of position. The need for training programs in Gaelic games to consider upper body, lower body and trunk strength has also been documented [19]. This was carefully considered in this training program (Table 1). The inclusion of the upper body plyometric components also enabled the participant to recover from the high volume of lower body plyometric exercises. Although improving strength was not a key focus here, the results show that there was a 9.76% improvement in upper body strength following the training program. These results concur with past research work [52, 77] where upper body plyometric exercise led to increases in a female athlete's upper body strength. Additionally, leg and trunk strength increased by 17.3% and the value for leg and trunk strength following the training program (Table 3) is in fact higher than values reported for county standard female Gaelic football players in Ulster [7]. The results combined, provide some evidence that this type of multi-component training may be effective in terms of developing both lower body strength and upper body strength.

The final physiological component that will be addressed here is that of flexibility and this was measured pre- and post-intervention for exploratory purposes. The findings here show that lower back and hamstring flexibility remained relatively unchanged following the training program here. This has also been found in other studies of this nature [23], while some studies in the literature found significant improvements in flexibility with combined training methods [26]. The nature of the participants in both studies varies considerably here and warrants consideration. It is noteworthy however, that in the study by Polman et al [60] which arguably most closely resembles the work here, no significant changes in flexibility were found. It may be therefore, that combining SAQ training with plyometric training does little to enhance flexibility levels and that this needs specific training.

In terms of the limited number of anthropometric variables measured here again the results reveal some intriguing changes. For example, body mass decreased by 1.4kg and concomitant with this was a 2.3% decrease in overall percent body fat. The values reported here for body mass and percent body fat (following the training program) are less than those reported for junior county standard female Gaelic players [7]. It has been highlighted also that player's with low skinfold thicknesses are likely to be more mobile on the pitch [67]. The improvements with respect to some of the variables already examined therefore, may be linked (in part) to this decrease in body mass/percent body fat. The 2.3% drop in percent body fat found here is also greater than the 1% decrease reported by Polman et al. [60] in their study.

In summary, the restrictions in practice time that are a feature of any amateur sport augment the need to train multiple components of fitness within the same training session. This study has demonstrated that it is possible to train and improve multiple components of fitness in the same Gaelic football training session. This study has shown that when SAQ training is combined with plyometric training simultaneous improvements across a range of physiological variables can be achieved. The most notable found here was the improvement in repeated sprint ability over 30m, improved vertical jump performance and leg strength. There were also moderate improvements in 10m and 30m sprint variables as well as moderate improvements in agility. Some positive changes in the anthropometric profile of the participant were also found here which could prove to be significant in terms of match performance or outcome. As an example, the improvement with respect to acceleration or 10m sprint time could determine which player gets to the ball first, thereby dictating subsequent play or the final result of a match. There are shortcomings in this work however, that should be acknowledged and addressed by future researchers where possible. Firstly, future empirical work of this nature needs to use randomized controlled designs. In the case of this work but more importantly its context, it was not possible to employ such a design. This study instead used a single-participant research design in order to examine the extent to which the regimen worked for the individual [39]. Larger sample sizes are needed however, in future studies so as to increase the statistical power of the study. Improvements also need to be evaluated with effect sizes provided so that the practical significance of the findings can be ascertained. We concur with recommendation of some past authors [70, 43] that future research is needed to determine more specifically, the optimal plyometric training length. While 10-16 weeks is recommended by some authors [9, 15], many past studies in the literature have been conducted over shorter time periods (<10 weeks). The impact of these programs on performance varies considerably across studies as a result. As with any form of training it is important with multi-component training to understand the necessary duration to employ in order to elicit peak athletic performance. In Gaelic games this issue is particularly important as a task force in 2007 found compelling empirical evidence of player burnout within the game. Future research therefore, needs to carefully examine the optimal length, volume and progression of this type of combined or multi-component training so as to avoid injuries and player burnout.

Currently in the scientific literature, published work relating to training methods or strength and conditioning in Gaelic games is lacking. Such work is needed however, in order to advance knowledge and understanding of strength and conditioning in Gaelic games. The results of this case study may be of some benefit to those engaged with Gaelic football teams in developing scientifically-based training protocols and improving performance. It is hoped however, that this study at least will generate further questions, debate or prompt further investigation along varying lines of inquiry. Short-term such investigation will greatly enhance the scientific knowledge base on Gaelic football and long-term one would hope that this knowledge will facilitate trainers, sport scientists, fitness coaches and strength and conditioning experts working with Gaelic games players at all levels of the game.

REFERENCES

[1]   Adams, K., O'Shea, J.P., O'Shea, K.L. & Climstein, M. (1992) The effect of six weeks of squat, plyometrics and squat-plyometrics training on power production. *J Strength Cond Res*, 6, 36-41.

[2]   Adams, T.M., Worley, D. & Throgmartin, D. (1984) An investigation of selected plyometric training exercises on muscular leg strength and power. *Track Field Q Rev*, 84, 36-40.

[3]   Anderst, W.J., Eksten, F. & Koceja, D.M. (1994) Effects of plyometric and explosive resistance training on lower body power. *Med Sci Sports Exerc*, 26: S31.

[4]   Arabatzi, F. (2007) Effects of plyometric, weight lifting and plyometric plus weight lifting combination training on jumping performance. In: *Proceedings of 12th Annual Congress of the European College of Sport Science* (pp. 344-345), Jyvaskyla, Finland.

[5]   Blattner, S.E. & Noble, L. (1979) Relative effects of isokinetic and plyometric training on vertical jump performance. *Res Q*, 50, 583-588.

[6]   Bompa, T. (2000) *Total Training for Young Champions.* Champaign IL: Human Kinetics.

[7]   Boyle, P., Mulligan, D. & O'Donoghue, P.G. (2002) Fitness profile of junior county female Gaelic football players. *J Sports Sci*, 20, 32-33.

[8]   Brown, L.E. & Ferrigno, V. (2005) *Training for speed, agility, and quickness.* Champaign IL: Human Kinetics.

[9]   Brown M.E., Mayhew, J.L. & Boleach, L.W. (1986) Effects of plyometric training on vertical jump performance in high school basketball players. *J Sports Med Phys Fit*, 26, 1-4.

[10]   Burgess, K.E., Connick, M.J., Graham-Smith, P., Pearson, S.J. (2007) Plyometric vs. isometric training influences on tendon properties and muscle output. *J Strength Cond Res*, 21 (3), 986-989.

[11]   Chimera, N.J., Swanik, K.A., Swanik, C.B. & Straub, S.J. (2004) Effects of plyometric training on muscle-activation strategies and performance in female athletes. *J Athl Train*, 39 (1), 24-31.

[12]   Chu, D.A. (1998) *Jumping into Plyometrics* (2nd Edition). Champaign Ill: Human Kinetics.

[13]   Chu, D., Faigenbaum, A. and Falkel, J. (2006) *Progressive plyometrics for kids.* Monterey, CA: Healthy Learning.

[14]   Clarkson, P.M., Nosaka, K. & Braun, B. (1992) Muscle function and exercise-induced muscle damage and rapid adaptation. *Med Sci Sports Exerc*, 24, 512-520.

[15]   Clutch, D., Wilton,, B., McGown, M, & Byrce, G.R. (1983) The effect of depth jumps and weight training on leg strength and vertical jump. *Res Q Exerc Sport*, 54, 5-10.

[16]   Conneely, P. Kehoe, B. & Gormley, J. (2004) Physical fitness as a predictor of playing time in Gaelic footballers. *Br J Sports Med*, 38 (5), 652.

[17] Craig, B.W. (2004) What is the science basis of speed and agility? *Strength and Cond J*, 26 (3), 13-14.

[18] Cromwell, F., Walsh, J. & Gormley, J. (2000) A pilot study examining injuries in elite Gaelic footballers. *Br J Sports Med*, 34, 104-108.

[19] Daly, P. (1993) *The complete coaching guide to hurling and football*. Dublin: Techman.

[20] Diallo, O., Dore, E., Duche, P. & Van Praagh, E. (2001) Effects of plyometric training followed by a reduced training program on physical performance in prepubescent soccer players. *J Sports Med Phys Fit*, 41, 342-348.

[21] Dodd, D.J. & Alvar, B.A. (2007) Analysis of acute explosive training modalities to improve lower-body power in baseball players. *J Strength Cond Res*, 21, 1177-1182.

[22] Donnelly, J.P., Doran, D.A. & Reilly, T. (2003) Kinanthropometric and performance characteristics of Gaelic games players. *J Sports Sci*, 21 (4), 296-297.

[23] Duncan, M.J. (2006) Plyometric training in Gaelic games: A case study on a county level hurler. *Intl J Sports Phys Perf*, 1, 361-364.

[24] Durnin, J. V. G. A. & Womersley, J. (1974) Body fat assessed from total body density and its estimation from skinfold thickness: Measurements on 481 men and women aged from 16 to 72 years. *B J Nut*, 32, 77-97.

[25] Ebben, W.P. (2002) Complex training: a brief review. *J Sports Sci and Med*, 1, 42-46.

[26] Faigenbaum, A.D., McFarland, J.E., Keiper, F.B., Tevlin, W., Ratamess, N.A., Kang, J. & Hoffman, J.R. (2007) Effect of a short-term plyometric and resistance training program on fitness performance in boys age 12 to 15 years. *J Sports Sci Med*, 6, 519-525.

[27] Fatouros, I.G., Jamurtus, A.Z., Leontsini, D., Kyriakos, T., Aggelousis, N., Kostopoulos, N. & Buckenmeyer, P. (2000) Evaluation of plyometric exercise training, weight training, and their combination on vertical jump performance and strength. *J Strength Cond Res*, 14, 470-476.

[28] Fleck, S.J. & Kraemer, W.J. (2004) *Designing Resistance Training Programs* (3rd Edition). Champaign IL: Human Kinetics.

[29] Florida-James, G. & Reilly, T. (1995) The physiological demands of Gaelic football. *Br J Sports Med,* 29, 41-45.

[30] Ford, H.T., Puckett, J.R., Drummond, J.P., Sawyer, K., Gantt, K. & Fussell, C. (1983) Effects of three combinations of plyometric weight training programs on selected physical fitness test items. *Percept Motor Skills*, 56: 919-922.

[31] Gehri, D.J., Ricard, M.D., Kleiner, D.M. & Kirkendall, D.T. (1998) A comparison of plyometric training techniques for improving vertical jump ability and energy production. *J Strength Cond Res*, 12, 85-89.

[32] Gullick, D.T., Kimura, I.F., Silter, M., Paolone, A. & Kelly, J.D. (1996) Various treatment techniques on signs and symptoms of delayed onset muscle soreness. *J Athl Train*, 31, 145-`52.

[33] Hennessy, L. & Watson, A.W.S. (1993) Flexibility and posture assessment in relation to hamstring injury. Br *J Sports Med*, 27 (4), 243-246.

[34] Hewett, T.E., Riccobene, J.V., Lindenfeld, T.N., Noyes, F.R. (1999) The effect of neuromuscular training on the incidence of knee injury in female athletes: A prospective study. *Am J Sports Med*, 27, 699-706.

[35] Hewett, T.E., Stroupe, A.L., Nance, T.A. & Noyes, F.R. (1996) Plyometric training in female athletes. Decreased impact forces and increased hamstring torques. *Am J Sports Med*, 24, 765-773.

[36] Holcomb, W.R., Lander, J.E., Rutland, R.M. & Wilson, G.D. (1996) The effectiveness of a modified plyometric program on power and the vertical jump. *J Strength Cond Res*, 10, 89-92.

[37] Hunter, J.P. & Marshall, R.T. (2002) Effects of power and flexibility training on vertical jump technique. *Med Sci Sports Exerc*, 34 (3), 478-486.

[38] Keane, S., Reilly, T. and Hughes, M. (1993) Analysis of work-rates in Gaelic football. *Aus J Sci Med Sport,* 25 (4), 100-102.

[39] Kinugasa, T., Cerin, E., Hooper, S. (2004) Single-subject research designs and data analyses for assessing elite athletes' conditioning. *Sports Med*, 34, 1035-1050.

[40] Kotzamandis, C. (2006) Effect of plyometric training on running performance and vertical jumping in prepubertal boys. *J Strength Cond Res*, 20, 441- 445.

[41] Lachance, P.F. (1995) Plyometric exercise. *J Strength Cond Res*, 8, 16-23.

[42] Lenehan, B., Fleming, P., Walsh, S. & Kaar, K. (2003) Tibial shaft fractures in amateur footballers. Br *J Sports Med*, 37 (2), 176-178.

[43] Luebbers, P.E., Potteiger, J.A., Hulver, M.W. Thyfault, J.P., Carper, M.J. & Lockwood, R.H. (2003) Effects of plyometric training and recovery on vertical jump performance and anaerobic power. *J Strength Cond Res*, 17 (4), 704-709.

[44] Maffiuletti, N.A., Dugnani, S., Folz, M., Di Pierna, E. & Mauro, F. (2002) Effect of combined electrostimulation and plyometric training on vertical jump height. *Med Sci Sports Exerc*, 34 (10), 1638-1644.

[45] Markovic, G. (2007) Does plyometric training improve vertical jump height? A meta-analytical review. Br *J Sports Med*, 41, 349-355.

[46] Matavulj, D., Kukolj, M., Ugarkovic, J., Tihanyi, J. & Jaric, S. (2001) Effects of plyometric training on jumping performance in junior basketball players. *J Sports Med Phys Fit*, 41, 159-164.

[47] McErlean, C., Murphy, M., & O'Donoghue, P. (1998) Time-motion analysis of work-rate within various positional roles of elite ladies' Gaelic football. *J Sports Sci*, 16, 21-22.

[48] McIntyre, M.C. (2005) A comparison of the physiological profiles of elite Gaelic footballers, hurlers and soccer players. *Br J Sports Med,* 39, 437-439.

[49] McIntyre, M.C. & Hall, M. (2002) Isokinetic knee strength of elite inter-varsity Gaelic footballers. *J Sports Sci*, 20 (1), 32.

[50] McIntyre, M.C. & Hall, M. (2005) Physiological profile in relation to playing position of elite college Gaelic footballers. *Br J Sports Med,* 39, 264-266.

[51] Miller, M.G., Herniman, J.J., Ricard, M.D., Cheatham, C.C. & Michael, T.J. (2006) The effects of a 6-week plyometric training program on agility. *J Sports Sci Med*, 5, 459-465.

[52] Myer, G., Ford, K., Palumbo, J. & Hewitt, T. (2005) Neuromuscular training improves performance and lower extremity biomechanics in female athletes. *J Strength Cond Res*, 19, 51-60.

[53] O'Donoghue, P. & King, S. (2005) Activity profile of men's Gaelic football. In T. Reilly, J. Cabri, & D. Araujo (Eds.) *Science and football V* (pp.205-210). London: Routledge.

[54] Oliver, J.L. (in press) Is a fatigue index a worthwhile measure of repeated sprint ability. *J Sci Med Sport*.

[55] O'Sullivan, M.E. & Curtin, J. (1989) Hand injuries in Gaelic games. *Ir J Med Sci*, 158 (4), 79-81.

[56] O'Sullivan, K., O'Ceallaigh, B., O'Connell, K., & Shafat, A. (2008) The relationship between previous hamstring injury and the concentric isokinetic knee muscle strength of Irish Gaelic footballers. *BMC Musculoskeletal Dis*, 9, 30.

[57] Pauole, K., Madole, K. and Lacourse, M. (2000) Reliability and validity of the T-test as a measure of agility, leg power and leg speed in college aged men and women. *J Strength and Cond Res*, 14, 443-450.

[58] Perez-Gomez, J., Olmedillas, H., Delgado-Guerra, S., Royo, I.A., Vincente-Rodriguez, G., Ortiz, R.A., Chavarren, J. & Calbet, J.A.L. (2008) Effects of weight lifting training combined with plyometric exercises on physical fitness, body composition, and knee extension velocity during kicking in football. *Appl Phys Nutr Met,* 33 (3), 501-509.

[59] Polhemus, R., Burkhart, E., Osina, M. & Patterson, M. (1981) The effects of plyometric training with ankle and vest weights on conventional weight training programs for men and women. *Strength Cond Assoc J*, 2, 13-15.

[60] Polman, R., Walsh, D., Bloomfield, J. & Nesti, M. (2004) effective conditioning of female soccer players. *J Sports Sci*, 22, 191-203.

[61] Potach, D.H. & Chu, D.A. (2000) Plyometric training. In: Baechle TR, Earle RW, (Eds.) *Essentials of strength training and conditioning.* (pp.427-470). Champaign IL: Human Kinetics.

[62] Potteiger, J.A., Lockwood, M.D., Haub, M.D., Dolezal, B.A., Alumzaini, K.S., Schroeder, J.M. & Zebas, C.J. (1999) Muscle power and fiber characteristics following 8 weeks of plyometric training. *J Strength Cond Res*, 13, 275-279.

[63] Radcliffe, J.C. & Farentinos, R.C. (1999) *High-powered plyometrics.* Champaign IL: Human Kinetics.

[64] Reeves, S. & Collins, K. (2003) the nutritional and anthropometric status of Gaelic football players. *Intl J Sports Nut Exerc Meta*, 13, 535-548.

[65] Reilly, T. (2001) Assessment of performance in team games. In: Eston, R. Reilly, T. (Eds.), *Kinanthropometry and Exercise Physiology Laboratory Manual, Volume 1. Anthropometry.* (pp. 171-182). London: Routledge Publishers.

[66] Reilly, T. & Collins, K. (2008) Science and the Gaelic sports: Gaelic football and hurling. *Eur J Sports Sci*, 8 (5) 231-240.

[67] Reilly, T. & Doran, D. (2001) Science and Gaelic football: a review. *J Sports Sci*, 19, 181-193.

[68] Reilly, T. & Gilbourne, D. (2003) Science and football: a review of applied research in the football codes. *J Sports Sci*, 21, 693-705.

[69] Rimmer, E. & Sleivert, G. (2000) Effects of a plyometrics intervention program on sprint performance. *J Strength Cond Res*, 14 (3), 295-301.

[70] Robinson, L.E., Devor, S.T., Merrick, M.A. & Buckworth, J. (2004) The effects of land vs. aquatic plyometrics on power, torque, velocity, and muscle soreness in women. *J Strength Cond Res*, 18 (1), 84-91.

[71] Roper, R.L. (1998) Incorporating agility training and backward movement into a plyometric program. *Strength and Cond*, 20 (4), 60-63.

[72] Saxton, J.M., Clarkson, P.M., James, R., Miles, M., Westerfer, M., Clark, S. & Donnelley, A.E. (1995) Neuromuscular dysfunction following eccentric exercise. *Med Sci Sports Exerc*, 27, 1185-1193.

[73] Sheppard, J.M. & Young, W.B. (2006) Agility literature review: Classifications, training and testing. *J Sports Sci,* 24 (9): 919-932.

[74] Strudwick, A., Reilly, T. & Doran, D. (2002) Anthropometric and fitness profiles of elite players in two football codes. *J Sports Med Phys Fit*, 42 (2), 239-242.

[75] Tucker, L. & Reilly, T. (2005) Physiological and anthropometric characteristics of female Gaelic football players. In T, Reilly, J. Cabri, & D. Araujo, (Eds.) *Science and football V* (pp. 172-175). London: Routledge.

[76] Twist, C., Gleeson, N. & Eston, R. (2008) The effects of plyometric exercise on unilateral balance performance. *J Sports Sci*, 26 (10), 1037-1080.

[77] Vossen, J.F., Burke, D.G. & Vossen, D.P. (2000) Comparison of dynamic push-up training and plyometric push-up training on upper body power and strength. *J Strength Cond Res*, 14, 248-253.

[78] Watson, A. (1977) A study of the physical working capacity of Gaelic footballers and hurlers. *Br J Sports Med*, 11, 133-137.

[79] Watson, A. (1995a) Physical and fitness characteristics of successful Gaelic footballers. *Br J Sports Med,* 29, 229-231.

[80] Watson, A. (1995b) Sports injures in footballers related to defects of posture and body mechanics. *J Sports Med Phys Fit*, 35 (4), 289-294.

[81] Watson, A. (1997) Injuries in schoolboy players of basketball, field-hockey, hurling Gaelic football, rugby and soccer. *NZ J Sports Med*, 25 (2), 22-24.

[82] Watson, A. (1998) Sports injuries related to intrinsic factors. *NZ J Sports Med*, 26 (2), 18-20.

[83] Watson, A. (1999) Ankle sprains in players of the field games Gaelic football and hurling. *J Sports Med Phys Fit*, 39, 66-70.

In: Advances in Strength and Conditioning Research
Editor: Michael Duncan and Mark Lyons

ISBN: 978-1-60692-909-4
© 2009 Nova Science Publishers, Inc.

Chapter 5

CAFFEINE: IS IT ERGOGENIC FOR ATHLETES?

Todd A. Astorino[1]

California State University – San Marcos, CA, USA

ABSTRACT

Caffeine is the most widely-used drug in the world whose ergogenic properties are well-established. Early studies demonstrated that glycogen sparing was responsible for the enhanced performance observed after caffeine ingestion, yet more recent work has identified adenosine antagonism and decreased exertion and sensation of pain as the primary mechanisms explaining its ergogenic effects. As a component in coffee or in capsule form, caffeine in doses ranging from 1.3 – 13 mg/kg ingested one hour pre-exercise is ergogenic for endurance exercise, resistance training, and short-term, high intensity activity, with this effect lasting for up to six hours after ingestion. However, the caffeine-mediated change in performance widely varies across individuals. Repeated dosing appears to maintain the ergogenic effect of acute caffeine intake. Compared to recreationally-active individuals, it is plausible that athletes may experience a greater ergogenic effect during short-term, high-intensity exercise due to a direct effect of caffeine upon skeletal muscle, although further study is merited. Potential side effects of acute caffeine ingestion include increases in blood pressure, which may be exacerbated with exercise and in persons with hypertension. Furthermore, alterations in blood glucose control have been demonstrated after caffeine intake, although coffee may exert a protective effect.

Keywords: adenosine, strength training, endurance exercise, muscle pain

Both prolonged endurance exercise and repeated, high-intensity efforts require continued delivery of substrates to maintain exercise performance. This is especially critical as the primary substrates degraded to supply adenosine triphosphate (ATP), carbohydrate from

---

[1] Please address correspondence and requests for reprints to Todd A. Astorino, Department of Kinesiology, California State University – San Marcos, 333 S Twin Oaks Valley Road, MH 352, San Marcos, CA 92096-001, USA or e mail astorino@csusm.edu

muscle and liver glycogen and phosphocreatine, are limited, and cannot be resynthesized during exercise. In the absence of proper nutrition, fatigue is imminent, with the source of fatigue being peripheral (glycogen depletion, hypoglycemia, dehydration, and acidosis) as well as central (in the brain). This emphasizes the importance of proper nutrition before and during exercise to sustain performance in these activities. This is of utmost importance for competitive athletes in whom small changes in performance can differentiate winners from losers.

Above and beyond dietary manipulation is the use of ergogenic aids to enhance performance. One of the most widely-consumed ergogenic aids is caffeine, which has been used since the Stone Age [29] and whose capacity to enhance muscular work was first identified over 100 years ago [76]. It is found naturally in the leaves, fruits, or seeds of various plants, and is a constituent of various foods, drinks, and medicinal products. It has been reported [61] that 90 % of adults in the United States consume caffeine daily, in the form of coffee, tea, soft drinks, and energy drinks. It is also widely-used by athletes, as data [32] report that 27 % of young athletes ingest caffeine to enhance performance. In addition, approximately 66 % of 2000 college athletes surveyed regularly consumed caffeine, although they reported it was not to augment performance [89]. Previously, two world-class athletes were stripped of international medals after a positive caffeine test [4], although the status of caffeine as a banned stimulant was lifted by the World Anti-Doping Agency in 2004.

Due to the widespread availability and use of caffeine, it is important to examine in detail how caffeine enhances performance in a wide range of athletic activities. Its multiple actions on the body, time course of responses, dosing regimens, and effects on exercise performance in athletic populations will be discussed. Attention will also be given to documented side effects of acute and chronic caffeine ingestion, and areas of research that remain unexplored. Results obtained in athletes and studies in which protocols mimic competition or training will be emphasized, with less attention given to data obtained in untrained or recreationally-active populations or exercise protocols that do not simulate the demands of sport.

MECHANISMS EXPLAINING ERGOGENIC EFFECT OF CAFFEINE

Seminal studies from Costill's lab in the 1970s [28, 47] showed that increased lipolysis and a sparing of muscle glycogen explained the ergogenic effect of caffeine during endurance exercise. This finding was corroborated by more recent investigation [28, 88], yet a growing body of evidence [36, 48] revealed that caffeine does not spare glycogen during endurance exercise. Alternatively, increased intracellular calcium concentration [26] and/or altered excitation-contraction coupling [14] have been postulated. Moreover, Davis et al. [23] reported that caffeine delays fatigue through its stimulation of the central nervous system by acting as an adenosine antagonist. Adenosine is a normal component of the cell whose concentration increases with muscular contraction. Its primary role is to inhibit neuron excitability and synaptic transmission of the brain via binding to its receptors [58], leading to decreased arousal and increased sleep [75]. In male rats, run time to fatigue was 60 % longer with caffeine versus an adenosine agonist [23].

Besides these physiological mechanisms, caffeine ingestion also modifies perceptual responses that may alter performance. In a meta-analysis of 21 studies in 202 active to trained subjects using a placebo-controlled, double-blind design, the effect of caffeine on performance and exertion during exercise was examined [25]. Data revealed that caffeine intake decreased rating of perceived exertion (RPE) by 5.6 % during prolonged exercise, a result that explained approximately 33 % of improved performance. It was speculated that caffeine may augment performance by masking the perception of fatigue and recruiting additional motor units during exercise. However, these findings may not apply to the high-intensity, intermittent nature of team-sports or explosive exercise such as sprinting and/or resistance training in which recording RPE during a brief, intense bout is almost impossible. An analgesic effect of caffeine has also been documented. In college-aged men [67] and women [34] completing 30 min of submaximal cycle ergometry, caffeine in doses from 5 – 10 mg/kg body weight ingested 1 h before exercise significantly reduced leg pain (assessed with a visual scale) versus placebo. A higher systolic blood pressure, a direct effect upon the CNS, and enhanced motor unit activation were identified as potential mechanisms explaining the attenuated pain sensation with caffeine. However, high doses may not be practical as a pre-exercise intervention. In addition, constant-load exercise may mimic day-to-day training, yet does not simulate the demands of competition, so further study is merited to examine the analgesic effect of caffeine when lower doses are administered, and when trials simulating competitive sports are used.

The effect of caffeine on psychological status cannot be discounted, as it alters the central nervous system by promoting serotonin release, increasing sympathetic activity, and decreasing the activity of inhibitory neurons due to adenosine antagonism [81]. As a result, reduced tiredness, improved mood, and enhanced alertness and reaction time occur with acute caffeine ingestion. In one study [80], repeated small doses of caffeine (1.5 mg/kg) were administered to 60 caffeine consumers who completed prolonged testing in the evening. Caffeine improved mood and performance on various tasks versus placebo. It also enhanced vigilance and running performance during sustained operations in soldiers [64]. The magnitude of these effects depends upon the dose and timing of caffeine as well as the individual's tolerance to caffeine.

In summary, the ergogenic effects of caffeine are likely multifactorial, with central factors such as adenosine antagonism the most accepted mechanism, yet enhanced performance may also be related to cognition and mood, especially in activities that are sustained and/or require repetitive execution of simple tasks.

RECOMMENDED DOSING, TIMING AND FORM OF CAFFEINE INGESTION

Caffeine can be consumed in capsule form, dissolved in water, or contained in beverages such as soft drinks, coffee, or energy drinks. Typically, caffeine is ingested in a single bolus before exercise, yet in a recent study, multiple doses improved performance versus placebo [21]. It appears that all of these regimens of caffeine ingestion increase performance, although one study [37] in young men revealed that pure caffeine in capsule form enhanced time to exhaustion, yet coffee did not.

The optimal means to provide caffeine to individuals is according to body weight, as this leads to expected changes in plasma caffeine levels [38]. In contrast, an absolute dose does not account for differences in body weight between subjects and provides smaller subjects with higher doses. Doses from 3 – 9 mg/kg body weight were shown to be ergogenic in a variety of studies [13, 37, 62, 91], with a 6 mg/kg dose used in the majority of studies. For a 70 kg male, this dose equates to approximately four brewed cups of coffee. However, lower doses are also ergogenic. In combination with a carbohydrate/electrolyte beverage, a 2.1 mg/kg caffeine dose enhanced time-trial performance compared to placebo, although higher doses had a greater effect upon performance [56]. Cox et al. [21] revealed that 1.5 mg/kg of caffeine in the form of Coca-Cola increased time-trial performance similar to a 6 mg/kg dose. Yet, doses greater than 9 mg/kg do not improve performance more than doses ranging from 3 - 6 mg/kg. Because of the wide range of ergogenic doses, it is important for the individual athlete to determine his/her minimal dose of caffeine needed to elicit an ergogenic effect, and use that prior to competition.

A typical dosing regimen for caffeine includes drug ingestion followed by a 60 min rest period before exercise. This allows caffeine concentration to peak in plasma [35] and elicit its ergogenic effects. Caffeine has a half-life of 4 – 6 hr [1] which may vary depending upon the size of the ingested dose, as doses above 300 mg elicit a longer half-life, although this response may be altered in users versus non-users. In one study [9], alterations in performance (cycling at 80 %VO$_2$max until exhaustion) were examined 1, 3, and 6 hr post-caffeine or placebo ingestion. Data showed that performance was significantly augmented at all time points in the non-users, yet only at 1 and 3 hr in the users. These results emphasize that exercise should be completed within 6 hr of caffeine ingestion to experience its ergogenic effects, with this duration shorter in persons habituated to caffeine.

Whether repeated doses of caffeine are superior than a single bolus remains to be determined. Data from Bell and McLellan [10] revealed no additional ergogenic effect of a second dose of caffeine ingested 6 hr after a morning dose. Repeated, small doses of caffeine (1 mg/kg) ingested 20 and 40 min before a mental challenge enhanced vigilance and alertness in 120 subjects [43]. These findings may support ingestion of small doses of caffeine in subjects whose mood or vigilance may be reduced during prolonged exertion or activity, such as soldiers, ultraendurance athletes, hospital personnel, and firefighters. However, further study is needed in this area.

Typically, caffeine is administered in capsule form, in coffee/decaffeinated coffee or soft drinks, and as an ingredient in supplements. Data [37] revealed that pure caffeine in capsule form improved performance; whereas, no significant effect was observed with coffee or decaffeinated coffee plus caffeine. These findings were furthered by a recent study [63] in which prior coffee intake did not negate the effect of caffeine on time to exhaustion at 80 %VO$_2$max. The widespread availability and popularity of caffeine-containing energy drinks including RedBull™ have initiated research into the ergogenic properties of these beverages. Improved aerobic/anaerobic performance [1] and muscular endurance [31] have been demonstrated in randomized, placebo-controlled studies, although subjects were recreationally-active and not athletes. Because of the limited data pertaining to various products containing caffeine, further investigation is merited.

TOLERANCE AND WITHDRAWAL TO CAFFEINE

Repeated ingestion of caffeine does promote a tolerance to its multiple effects by altering the individual's caffeine sensitivity. Caffeine tolerance is related to an upregulation of adenosine activity and a decrease in adrenergic activity [57]. Typically, tolerance requires 5 – 6 days of repeated use for its effects to be maintained. In one study [27], 32 healthy subjects were subjected to 18 d of chronic caffeine consumption. Results showed that caffeine 'choosers' reported positive subjective effects of caffeine (300 mg/d) and negative subjective effects of placebo, thus establishing a tolerance to the CNS effects of caffeine. Nevertheless, caffeine-mediated changes in running performance [90] and muscular force development [85] were similar in users versus non-users. At this time, it seems that differences in performance due to caffeine habituation appear minimal.

Withdrawal is related to headaches, irritability, anxiety, and fatigue and can occur within 12 – 24 hr, peaks at 3 – 4 days, and lasts approximately 7 days [45]. A recent study [55] revealed that caffeine withdrawal adversely affected abstract reasoning and concept formation in sleep-deprived individuals versus placebo. Various lengths of withdrawal (0, 2, and 4 days) did not affect time to exhaustion at 80 %VO2max compared to no withdrawal [87]. As magnitude of dependence varies across individuals, symptoms of withdrawal may vary.

CAFFEINE AND ENDURANCE EXERCISE

One of the first studies to investigate caffeine to augment endurance performance was by Costill et al. [20]. In this study, cyclists exercised until exhaustion at 80 % VO2max after ingestion of decaffeinated coffee or coffee including 330 mg of caffeine. Results demonstrated a 20 % increase in endurance, which was explained by enhanced fat oxidation as well as lower RPE. A follow-up study [47] revealed 7 % increases in work production when 250 mg of caffeine was ingested before and during 2 hr of cycling. In distance runners, a 10 mg/kg dose of caffeine increased time to exhaustion compared to placebo and control [33], although the protocol consisted of sustained running at 75 %VO2max followed by 2 mph increases in treadmill speed until exhaustion. Compared to placebo, Pasman et al. [69] demonstrated significant increases in time to exhaustion (11 – 12 min) when various caffeine doses (5, 9, and 13 mg/kg) were administered to cyclists 1 hr pre-exercise, yet there was no dose-related response. When combined with a carbohydrate/electrolyte beverage, 2.1 and 3.2 mg/kg of caffeine increased cycling time trial performance compared to placebo or carbohydrate drink alone [56]. Furthermore, these results occurred with no alteration in fat metabolism, as revealed in another investigation [35]. In cyclists initially completing 2 hr of submaximal exercise [21], Coca-Cola administered in concentrations of 1.3 and 1.9 mg/kg augmented cycling time trial performance by about 3 %. A similar low dose of caffeine (3 mg/kg) increased 8 km run performance by 1.2 % in trained runners [12], and other findings [54] revealed that caffeine doses of 2 and 3 mg/kg increased performance in male cyclists by 4 % and 3 %, respectively, yet a lower dose equal to 1 mg/kg did not alter performance versus placebo. However, there was large interindividual variability in caffeine's ergogenic properties. This suggests that caffeine doses above 1.3 mg/kg body weight seem to be ergogenic for endurance exercise, yet lower doses may not benefit endurance performance.

Overall, the preponderance of data supports the ingestion of caffeine to enhance endurance performance versus placebo (Table 1). However, a few studies [15, 46] fail to demonstrate caffeine-mediated improvements in performance during prolonged exercise. It is clear that there is a large amount of subject variability in the magnitude of response to caffeine, with future study merited to better explain these differences. Furthermore, it is unknown if regular intake of caffeine enhances performance during sustained training.

Table 1. Change in endurance exercise performance in athletes after acute caffeine ingestion

Study	Subjects	Dose	Protocol	Findings
20	9 cyclists	330 mg in coffee	Exercise to exhaustion at 80 %VO$_2$max	↑ performance by 14.7 min
47	9 cyclists	250 mg + 250 mg every 15 min of exercise	2 hr of isokinetic cycling	↑ work production by 7.4 %
21	20 endurance athletes	1.3 – 1.9 mg/kg	2 hr cycling + time trial	3.1 – 3.3 ↑ in performance
37	9 runners	4.45 mg/kg	Running at 85 %VO$_2$max until exhaustion	7.5 – 10 min ↑ in exercise time
13	8 rowers	6 and 9 mg/kg	2000 m rowing trial	1.2 % ↑ in performance
62	11 swimmers	6 mg/kg	1,500 m swim	23 s ↑ in performance
30	15 endurance athletes	150, 225, and 320 mg/L	1 hr cycling time trial	9 – 17 Watt ↑ power output; ↑ time trial performance
33	6 distance runners	10 mg/kg	45 min at 75 %VO$_2$max + exercise to exhaustion	↑ time to exhaustion
71	9 cyclists	0, 5, 9, and 13 mg/kg	Cycling to exhaustion at 80 %Wmax	11 – 12 min ↑ duration of exercise
12	8 male distance runners	3 mg/kg	8 km outdoor run	23.8 s ↑ in performance
54	13 cyclists	1, 2, and 3 mg/kg	15 min performance ride	3 – 4 % ↑ performance
46	8 cyclists	6 mg/kg	100 km time trial	No effect on performance
15	7 endurance athletes	0, 5, and 9 mg/kg	21 km outdoor road race in hot conditions	No effect on performance
74	6 elite swimmers	6.2 mg/kg	Two 200 m time trials	No effect on performance

Table 1. (Continued)

Study	Subjects	Dose	Protocol	Findings
16	10 endurance athletes	6 mg/kg	30 min of isokinetic cycling	12 % ↑ in total work; ↓ perception of effort
39	7 trained runners	9 mg/kg	Running and cycling at 85 %VO$_2$max	20 – 22 min ↑ in time to exhaustion

CAFFEINE AND SHORT-TERM, HIGH-INTENSITY EXERCISE

Compared to endurance exercise, fewer investigations have examined ergogenic properties of caffeine during short-term, high-intensity exercise in which fatigue is mediated by acidosis, phosphocreatine depletion, and central factors (Table 2). Early studies failed to reveal any benefits of caffeine for short-term exercise. During 15 s of all-out cycling, no change in power, work, or fatigue was revealed [92], similar to maintenance of cycling time to exhaustion in another study [17]. Collomp et al. [18] revealed enhanced anaerobic power during a force-velocity test, yet no changes in anaerobic capacity via the Wingate test. One year later in swimmers, Collomp et al. [19] demonstrated significant improvements in 2 X 100 m swim performance in trained swimmers with 250 mg of caffeine ingested 1 hr before exercise versus placebo. End-exercise blood lactate concentration was increased in both groups, which may reflect a potentiation of glycogenolysis and thus enhanced high-intensity exercise performance. In 14 young adults, cycling time to exhaustion was increased by almost 20 % (4.12 to 4.93 min) after a 6 mg/kg dose of caffeine [48]. In nine active men completing four Wingate tests separated by 4 min of recovery [41], caffeine ingestion (6 mg/kg) did not alter peak or mean power versus placebo. In fact, in bouts 3 and 4, mean/peak power was lower ($p < 0.05$) with caffeine. A detrimental effect on time to peak power was also revealed in men and women during repeated 60 s cycling efforts [22]. A follow-up study by Greer et al. [42] also revealed no change in power output as well as neuromuscular drive during the Wingate test. However, a recent study [93] revealed significantly higher peak power, but not mean power or fatigue index, when male athletes naïve to caffeine completed the Wingate test after ingesting caffeine (5 mg/kg) or placebo. Collectively, data indicate that caffeine may be ergogenic for high-intensity activities greater than 4 min duration, but is less effective when bouts are repeated or less than 4 min duration. However, the majority of data were acquired in physically active persons, and not athletes, so further study is needed. An increased sensitivity to caffeine has been revealed in human slow-twitch fibers (65), and it has been reported that adenosine receptors exist primarily in type I fibers (40), so a potential ergogenic effect of caffeine in activities depending upon fast-twitch motor unit recruitment may be unexpected.

Table 2. Change in short-term, high-intensity exercise performance in athletes after acute caffeine ingestion

Study	Subjects	Dose	Protocol	Findings
48	14 endurance athletes	6 mg/kg	2 min bouts of maximal cycling	43 s ↑ in endurance at 100 %VO_2max
91	8 male cyclists	5 mg/kg	1 km time-trial	3.1 % ↑ in performance; 3.6 – 8.8 % ↑ in power output
19	7 trained swimmers; 7 untrained swimmers	250 mg	Two 100 m sprint swims	↑ swimming velocity in bout 1 only in trained swimmers
22	17 team sport athletes	6 mg/kg	Two 60 s maximal cycling bouts	No effect on performance
93	18 male athletes	5 mg/kg	Leg/bench press to fatigue + Wingate test	↑ peak power and total weight lifted for bench press
6	10 male team-sport athletes	6 mg/kg	18 4-s sprints on a cycle ergometer	6.6 – 8.5 % ↑ in total work and mean power
82	9 male rugby players	6 mg/kg	Tests of sprint speed, drive power, and passing accuracy	↑ performance in all tests
64	16 male team-sport athletes	6 mg/kg	Ten 20 m sprints	No effect on performance
11	12 male track sprinters	5 mg/kg	6-RM of knee extension and flexion at three speeds	No effect on performance
50	20 male football players	7 mg/kg	3 – 15 reps of knee extension and flexion	4 – 8 % ↑ in peak torque
49	13 strength-trained men	4 mg/kg	Superset of leg press and bench press	No effect on performance
5	16 strength-trained men	6 mg/kg	1-RM bench/leg press and endurance testing	No effect on performance
91	9 strength-trained men	300 mg	1-RM bench press, lat-pull down, and Wingate test	No effect on performance
8	37 strength-trained men	2.5 mg/kg in a supplement	Wingate test, muscle strength and endurance tests	2.1 % ↑ in bench press 1-RM; no effects on other parameters

Table 2. (Continued)

Study	Subjects	Dose	Protocol	Findings
7	24 male rugby players	0, 200, 400, or 800 mg	10 m sprints + resistance exercise	1.7 % ↑ in sprint performance
74	7 cyclists	6 mg/kg	120 min of cycling + MVC efforts in warm environment	↑ MVC and maximal power

More recent investigations have demonstrated an ergogenic effect of caffeine in protocols that simulate sport, such as cycling and team sports. In eight male cyclists, ingestion of 5 mg/kg caffeine increased 1 km time-trial performance by 2 s and augmented mean and peak power compared to placebo and control (91). However, no mechanisms for these results were identified. In team sport athletes, total sprint work and mean power were enhanced by 6 – 8 % in the first and second half when repeated sprinting (4 s) separated by active recovery was performed on a cycle ergometer after caffeine (6 mg/kg) or placebo ingestion [79]. The transfer of laboratory cycling to on-the-field performance is questionable, though. In rugby players, caffeine (6 mg/kg) increased parameters of repeated, intermittent, high-intensity performance mimicking 80 min of competitive rugby, including sprint speed, power, and passing accuracy, compared to placebo [82]. These data are in contrast to the failure of caffeine (6 mg/kg) to enhance performance of ten 20 m sprints, interspersed with 10 s of recovery, in male team-sport athletes [72]. The relatively short duration of this bout compared to those used in previous studies [79, 82] may explain the lack of an ergogenic effect of caffeine. Caffeine also does not alter agility [60], so its ingestion to enhance performance in sports characterized by quick movements and/or brief sprints of short duration is not warranted.

CAFFEINE AND RESISTANCE TRAINING

Due to the reduced pain and exertion elicited by caffeine ingestion, its use may benefit athletes who actively participate in resistance training. However, this area of study is relatively unexplored. In sprinters [11], caffeine ingested 1 hr before isokinetic knee flexion and extension exercise did not alter peak torque, power, or fatigue index at three contraction velocities compared to placebo. Six years later, a similar study [50] was completed in collegiate football players, but the caffeine dose was increased to 7 mg/kg, and subjects were required to fast for 8 hr pre-trial. Results showed significant improvements in muscle torque and power after caffeine administration. One study [49] required strength-trained men to complete supersets of leg press and bench press at 70 – 80 % 1-RM after ingestion of placebo or caffeine (4 mg/kg). No effect of caffeine was revealed on repetitions completed or total weight lifted between treatments. Similarly, others reported no effect of acute caffeine ingestion on 1-RM bench press and leg press [5] or bench press and lat pull down in strength-trained men [91]. In contrast, Beck et al. [8] reported a significant increase in 1-RM bench press in men ingesting a caffeine-containing (201 mg) supplement, although the magnitude of this increase was small (+ 2.0 %), and other parameters of muscular strength and power were unaltered. Similarly, bench press performance was augmented in response to acute caffeine intake (5 mg/kg) in elite male athletes, but leg press performance was unaffected [93]. This result was explained by subjects' low daily caffeine intake (40.8 mg/day) and large muscle mass, which may promote a direct effect of caffeine on skeletal muscle, which is a potential mechanism postulated for its ergogenic properties. Further research is necessary to examine the effect of caffeine habituation on strength training performance in athletes.

Muscle hypertrophy as a result of chronic resistance training is mediated by testosterone, the primary anabolic hormone in skeletal muscle. A recent study [7] examined changes in testosterone in rugby players performing resistance training after various doses of caffeine (0, 200, 400, and 800 mg) or placebo. Results showed a consistent increase in testosterone levels with increasing caffeine dose, yet cortisol concentration was also augmented. In recovery, catabolism was marked as shown by a negative testosterone:cortisol ratio, especially in the 800 mg caffeine condition. A long-term training study is warranted to further elucidate the effect of chronic caffeine intake on muscle anabolism in response to chronic resistance training.

Overall, the benefits of caffeine to augment dynamic resistance training performance appear limited. The majority of data show minimal alterations in 1-RM strength, repetitions completed at a given load, peak torque, or power. The only studies reporting significant increases in performance are characterized by higher doses (7 mg/kg) that may be impractical to ingest pre-exercise, or caffeine combined with other constituents that may alter metabolism. Despite its anti-fatigue properties, caffeine alone may not be ergogenic during resistance training due to the intermittent nature of this exercise mode that is dissimilar from endurance exercise.

In regards to the ergogenic potential of caffeine, one factor that cannot be ignored is training status. Of the studies revealing a significant benefit of caffeine for short-term, high-intensity exercise, the majority included trained athletes. This may be explained by their more consistent performance day-day, which may reduce variability and thus increase statistical power. Furthermore, trained muscle may respond better to acute ingestion of caffeine than untrained muscle, and their familiarity with intense, fatiguing exercise may make them more likely to benefit from any caffeine-mediated improvement in performance. However, further study is needed to elucidate these explanations.

POTENTIAL SIDE EFFECTS OF CAFFEINE INGESTION

One long-believed side effect of caffeine is dehydration, which may be deleterious to performance. However, Falk et al. [30] revealed no alterations ($p > 0.05$) in plasma volume, water loss, sweat rate, heat storage, or rectal temperature in trained men completing treadmill exercise to exhaustion after ingestion of caffeine or placebo. In another study [3], healthy men initially ingested 3 mg/kg caffeine for six days, followed by 0, 3, or 6 mg/kg per days for five days. Results showed no changes in markers of hydration or electrolyte status as a result of caffeine intake versus placebo. Overall, this study and others [77] support the notion that caffeine is not a diuretic, and athletes should not refrain from consuming it pre-exercise for fear of dehydration.

Over 70 years ago, data revealed that caffeine increased blood pressure in young men [68]. A meta-analysis of 11 studies including 522 participants (median dose = 5 cups/day) revealed that chronic coffee drinking increased systolic and diastolic blood pressure by 2.4 and 1.2 mm Hg, respectively [53]. This pressor response via acute caffeine ingestion was also demonstrated in response to submaximal exercise [83], intense resistance training [6], and in persons with hypertension [84]. However, other studies [2, 93] showed no relationship between coffee intake and blood pressure. It has been reported that caffeine in capsule form or soft drinks elicits larger changes in blood pressure than coffee, which may exert a protective effect [70]. To date, there is no clear evidence linking intake of caffeinated coffee with hypertension, and factors such as genetics and lifestyle factors mediate this relationship. Based on the increased health risks observed with only small increases in blood pressure [51], this remains an important public health question for future study to elucidate.

Insulin action is an important component of monitoring risk of obesity and type II diabetes. However, there is some evidence that caffeine intake may alter insulin sensitivity in diverse populations. Over 40 years ago, the effect of caffeine and coffee on glucose and insulin concentration and glucose tolerance was investigated [52]. In a placebo-controlled study, Pizziol et al. [73] observed a significant rise in blood glucose concentration in response to a glucose tolerance test when 200 mg of caffeine was administered to subjects who had abstained from caffeine for four weeks. Recently, caffeinated coffee ingestion (5 mg/kg) combined with a high or low glycemic index meal reduced blood glucose management and insulin sensitivity versus decaffeinated coffee [66]. Yet, these findings oppose data from a series of cohort studies that demonstrate an inverse relationship between coffee intake and risk for type II diabetes [78, 86]. It may be that impaired glucose tolerance is only observed in short-term laboratory studies, and that chronic caffeine consumption helps to assuage this response. Considering the widespread use of caffeine across the world as well as the growing epidemic of type II diabetes, further study to clarify this relationship using longitudinal, placebo-controlled studies is necessary.

CONCLUSION

1. The most likely mechanisms for the ergogenic action of caffeine appear to be adenosine antagonism and reduced sensations of pain and exertion during exercise. Furthermore, enhanced mood may improve performance during activities that require sustained exertion.
2. Caffeine, preferably in capsule form, should be ingested approximately 1 hr before exercise to optimize its ergogenic effects, and multiple doses act to maintain these effects during prolonged exercise. Doses ranging from 1.3 – 13 mg/kg have been shown to be ergogenic in a wide range of studies.
3. It appears that tolerance and withdrawal do not alter the magnitude of performance improvement after acute caffeine ingestion.
4. Endurance exercise is clearly benefited by acute caffeine ingestion in doses as low as 1.3 - 2 mg/kg, and can be ingested in the form of Coca-Cola or capsules. It seems that higher doses do not provide a greater ergogenic advantage. The exact

mechanism for this improved performance is unknown, although more than likely it is not related to glycogen sparing.

5. For short-term, high-intensity exercise such as resistance training and sprinting, data supporting the ingestion of caffeine are equivocal. Compared to recreationally-active individuals, trained athletes may be more responsive to the effects of caffeine for this exercise mode.

6. Ingestion of caffeine does not elicit dehydration, as multiple studies have revealed no change in urine loss or fluid balance with caffeine versus placebo.

7. Acute caffeine ingestion significantly increases blood pressure in both normotensive and hypertensive individuals due to enhanced peripheral resistance. However, most longitudinal studies do not show a relationship between caffeine intake and hypertension.

8. Caffeine ingestion may alter insulin sensitivity and blood glucose. The effect of chronic caffeine intake on diabetes risk in athletes is unknown and requires further study.

REFERENCES

[1]   Alford, C., Cox, H. & Wescott, R. (2001) The effects of red bull energy drink on human performance and mood. *Amino Acids*, 21 (2), 139-150.

[2]   Andersen, J.F., Jacobs, D.R., Carlsen, M.H. & Blomoff, R. (2006) Consumption of coffee is associated with reduced risk of death attributed to inflammatory and cardiovascular diseases in the Iowa Women's Health Study. *Am J Clin Nutr*, 83, 1039-1046.

[3]   Armstrong, L.E., Pumerantz, A.C., Roti, M.W., Judelson, D.A., Watson, G., Dias, J.C., Sokmen, B., Casa, D.J., Maresh, C.M., Lieberman, H. & Kellogg, M. (2005) Fluid, electrolyte, and renal indices of hydration during eleven days of controlled caffeine consumption. *Int J Sports Nutr Exerc Metab*,15, 252-265.

[4]   Associated Press. Revised banned list will be in force for Athens. ESPN Internet Ventures, 2003 [online]. Available from URL: http://espn.go.com/oly/news/2003/0917/1617822.html.

[5]   Astorino, T.A., Firth, K. & Rohmann, R.L. (2008) Effect of caffeine ingestion on one-repetition maximum muscular strength. *Eur J Appl Physiol*, 102 (2), 127-132.

[6]   Astorino, T.A., Rohmann, R.L., Firth, K. & Kelly, S. (2007) Caffeine-induced changes in cardiovascular function during resistance training. *Int J Sports Nutr Exerc Metab*, 17 (5), 468-477.

[7]   Beaven, C.M., Hopkins, W.G., Hansen, K.T., Wood, M.R., Cronin, J.B. & Lowe, T.E. (2008) Dose effect of caffeine on testosterone and cortisol responses to resistance exercise. *Int J Sports Nutr Exerc Metab*, 18, 131-141.

[8]   Beck, T.W., Housh, T.J., Schmidt, R.J., Johnson, G.O., Housh, D.J., Coburn, J.W. & Malek, M.H. (2006) The acute effects of a caffeine-containing supplement on strength, muscular endurance, and anaerobic capabilities. *J Strength Cond Res*, 20(3), 506-510.

[9]   Bell, D.G. & McLellan, T.M. (2002) Exercise endurance 1, 3, and 6 h after caffeine ingestion. *J Appl Physiol*, 93 (4), 1227-1234.

[10] Bell, D.G. & McLellan, T.M. (2003) Effect of repeated caffeine ingestion on repeated exhaustive exercise endurance. *Med Sci Sports Exerc*, 35 (8), 1348-1354.

[11] Bond, V., Gresham, K., McRae, J. & Tearney, R.J. (1986) Caffeine ingestion and isokinetic strength. *Br J Sports Med*, 20 (3), 135-137.

[12] Bridge, C.A. & Jones, M.A. (2006) The effect of caffeine ingestion on 8 km run performance in a field setting. *J Sports Sci*, 24, 433-439.

[13] Bruce, C.R., Anderson, M.E., Fraser, S.F., Stepto, N.K., Klein, R., Hopgins, W.G. & Hawley, J.A. (2000) Enhancement of 2000-m rowing performance after caffeine ingestion. *Med Sci Sports Exerc*, 32 (11), 1958-1963.

[14] Clausen, T. (2003) Na+-K+ pump regulation and skeletal muscle contractility. *Physiol Rev*, 83, 1269-1324.

[15] Cohen, B.S., Nelson, A.G., Prevost, M.C., Thompson, G.D., Marx, B.D. & Morris, G.S. (1996) Effects of caffeine ingestion on endurance racing in heat and humidity. *Eur J Appl Physiol*, 73 (3-4), 358-363.

[16] Cole K.J., Costill, D.L., Starling, R.D., Goodpaster, B.H., Trappe, S.W. & Fink, W.J. (1996) Effect of caffeine ingestion on perception of effort and subsequent work production. *Int J Sports Nutr*, 6, 14-23.

[17] Collomp, K., Caillaud, M., Audran, M., Chanal, J.L. & Prefaut, C. (1990) Influence of acute and chronic bouts of caffeine on performance and catecholamines in the course of maximal exercise. *Comptes Rendes des Seances de la Societe de Biologie et de ses Filiales*, 184, 87-92.

[18] Collomp, K., Ahmaidi, S., Audran, M., Chanal, J.L. & Prefaut, C. (1991) Effects of caffeine ingestion on performance and anaerobic metabolism during the Wingate test. *Int J Sports Med*, 12, 439-443.

[19] Collomp, K., Ahmaidi, S., Chatard, J.C., Audran, M. & Prefaut, C. (1992) Benefits of caffeine ingestion on sprint performance in trained and untrained swimmers. *Eur J Appl Physiol*, 64, 377-380.

[20] Costill, D.L., Dalsky, G.P. & Fink, W.J. (1978) Effects of caffeine on metabolism and exercise performance. *Med Sci Sports*, 10, 155-158.

[21] Cox, G.R., Desbrow, B., Montgomery, P.G., Anderson, M.E., Bruce, C.R., Macrides, T.A., Martin, D.T., Moquin, A., Roberts, A., Hawley, J.A. & Burke, L.M. (2002) Effect of different protocols of caffeine intake on metabolism and endurance performance. *J Appl Physiol*, 93, 990-999.

[22] Crowe, M.J., Leicht, A.S. & Spinks, W.L. (2006) Physiological and cognitive responses to caffeine during repeated, high-intensity exercise. *Int J Sports Nutr Exerc Metab*, 16, 528-544.

[23] Davis, J.M., Zhao, Z., Stock, H.S., Mehl, K.A., Buggy, J. & Hand, G.A. (2003) Central nervous system effects of caffeine and adenosine on fatigue. *Am J Physiol*, 284, R399-R404.

[24] Del Coso, J., Estevez, A. & Mora-Rodriguez, R. (2008) Caffeine effects on short-term performance during prolonged exercise in the heat. *Med Sci Sports Exerc*, 40(4), 744-751.

[25] Doherty, M. & Smith P.M. (2005) Effects of caffeine ingestion on rating of perceived exertion during and after exercise: a meta-analysis. *Scand J Med Sci Sports*, 15, 69-78.

[26] Doherty, M., Smith, P.M., Hughes, M., Davison, R. (2004) Caffeine lowers perceptual response and increases power output during high-intensity cycling. *J Sports Sci*, 22, 637-643.

[27] Evans, S.M. & Griffiths, R.R. (1992) Caffeine tolerance and choice in humans. *Psychopharmacol (Berl.)*, 108 (1-2), 51-59.

[28] Engels, H.J., Wirth, J.C., Celik, S. & Dorsey, J.L. (1999) Influence of caffeine on metabolic and cardiovascular functions during sustained light intensity cycling and at rest. *Intl J Sports Nutr*, 9, 361-370.

[29] Escohotado, A. & Symington, K. (1999) *A Brief History of Drugs: From the Stone Age to the Stoned Age*. Park Street Press.

[30] Falk, B., Zylber-Katz, E. & Bashan, N. (1990) Effects of caffeine ingestion on body fluid balance and thermoregulation during exercise. *Can J Physiol Pharmacol*, 68, 889-892.

[31] Forbes, S.C., Candow, D.G., Little, J.P., Magnus, C. & Chilibeck, P.D. (2007) Effect of Red Bull energy drink on repeated Wingate cycle performance and bench-press muscle endurance. *Intl J Sports Nutr Exerc Metab*, 17 (5), 433-444.

[32] Forman, E.S., Dekker, A.H., Javors, J.R. & Davison, D.T. (1995) High-risk behaviors in teenage male athletes. *Clin J Sports Med*, 5 (1), 36-42.

[33] French, C., McNaughton, L.R., Davies, P. & Tristram, S. (1991) Caffeine ingestion during exercise to exhaustion in elite distance runners. *J Sports Med Phys Fitness*, 31, 425-432.

[34] Gliottoni, R.C. & Motl, R.W. (2008) Effect of caffeine on leg-muscle pain during intense cycling exercise: possible role of anxiety sensitivity. *Intl J Sports Nutr Exerc Metab*, 18, 103-115.

[35] Graham, T.E. (2000) Caffeine and exercise: Metabolism, endurance, and performance. *Sports Med*, 31 (11), 785-807.

[36] Graham, T.E., Helge, J.W., MacLean, D.A., Kiens, B. & Richter, E.A. (2000) Caffeine ingestion does not alter carbohydrate or fat metabolism in human skeletal muscle during exercise. *J Physiol*, 529, 837-847.

[37] Graham, T.E., Hibbert, E. & Sathasivam, P. (1998) Metabolic and exercise endurance effects of coffee and caffeine ingestion. *J Appl Physiol*, 85, 883-889.

[38] Graham, T.E. & McLean, C. (1999) Gender differences in the metabolic responses to caffeine. In: Tarnopolsky, M, (Ed.) *Gender differences in metabolism: practical and nutritional applications* (pp. 301-327). Boca Raton: CRC Press.

[39] Graham, T.E. & Spriet, L.L. (1992) Performance and metabolic responses to a high caffeine dose during prolonged exercise. *J Appl Physiol*, 71 (6), 2292-2298.

[40] Greer, F., Graham, T.E. & Nagy, L.E. (1997) Characterization of adenosine receptors in rat skeletal muscle. *Can J Appl Physiol*, 22, 23P.

[41] Greer, F., McLean, C. & Graham, T.E. Caffeine, performance, and metabolism during repeated Wingate exercise tests. *J Appl Physiol*, 85 (4), 1502-1508.

[42] Greer, F., Morales, J. & Coles, M. (2006) Wingate performance and surface EMG frequency variables are not affected by caffeine ingestion. *Appl Phys Nutr Metab*, 31, 597-603.

[43] Hewlett, P. & Smith, A. (2007) Effects of repeated doses of caffeine on performance and alertness: new data and secondary analyses. *Hum Psychopharmacol*, 22 (6), 339-350.

[44] Horst, K., Buxton, R.E. & Robinson, W.D. (1934) The effect of the habitual use of coffee or decaffeinated coffee upon blood pressure and certain motor reactions of normal young men. *J Pharmacol Exp Ther*, 53, 322-337.

[45] Hughes, J.R., Higgins, S.T., Bickel, W.K., Hunt, W.K., Fenwick, J.W., Gulliver, S.B. & Mireault, S.B. (1991) Caffeine self-administration, withdrawal, and adverse effects among coffee drinkers. *Arch Gen Psychiatry*, 48 (7), 611-617.

[46] Hunter, A.M., St Clair Gibson, A., Collins, M., Lambert, M. & Noakes, T.D. (2002) Caffeine ingestion does not alter performance during a 100-km cycling time-trial performance. *Int J Sports Nutr Exerc Metab*, 12 (4), 238-252.

[47] Ivy, J.L., Costill, D.L., Fink, W.J. & Lower, R.W. (1979) Influence of caffeine and carbohydrate feedings on endurance performance. *Med Sci Sports*, 11, 6-11.

[48] Jackman, M., Wendling, P., Friars, D. & Graham, T.E. (1996) Metabolic, catecholamine, and endurance responses to caffeine during intense exercise. *J Appl Physiol*, 81, 1658-1663.

[49] Jacobs, I., Pasternak, H. & Bell, D.G. (2003) Effects of ephedrine, caffeine, and their ombination of muscular endurance. *Med Sci Sports Exerc*, 35 (6), 987-994.

[50] Jacobson, B.H., Weber, M.D., Claypool, I. & Hunt, L.E. (1992) Effect of caffeine on maximal strength and power in elite male athletes. *Br J Sports Med*, 26 (4), 276-280.

[51] James, J.E. (2004) Critical review of dietary caffeine and blood pressure: a relationship that should be taken more seriously. *Psychosom Med*, 66 (1), 63-71.

[52] Jankelson, O.M., Beaser, S.B., Howard, F.M. & Mayer, J. (1967) Effect of coffee on glucose tolerance and circulating insulin in men with maturity-onset diabetes. *Lancet*, 1, 527-529.

[53] Jee, S.H., He, J., Whelton, P.K., Suh, I. & Klag, M.J. (1999) The effect of chronic coffee drinking on blood pressure. *Hypertension*, 33, 647-652.

[54] Jenkins, N.T., Trilk, J.L., Singhal, A., O'Connor, P.J. & Cureton, K.J. (2008) Ergogenic effects of low doses of caffeine on cycling performance. *Int J Sports Nutr Exerc Metab*, 18 (3), 328-342.

[55] Killgore, W.D., Kahn-Greene, E.T., Killgore, D.B., Kamimori, G.H. & Balkin, T.J. (2007) Effects of acute caffeine withdrawal on Short Category Test performance in sleep-deprived individuals. *Percept Mot Skills*, 105 (3) 2, 1265-1274.

[56] Kovacs, E.M.R., Stegen, J.H.C.H. & Brouns, F. (1998) Effect of caffeinated drinks on substrate metabolism, caffeine excretion, and performance. *J Appl Physiol*, 85, 709-715.

[57] Lane, J.D. & Philips-Bute, B.G. (1998) Caffeine deprivation affects vigilance, performance, and mood. *Phys Behav*, 65, 171-175.

[58] Latini, S. & Pedata, F. (2001) Adenosine in the central nervous system: release mechanisms and extracellular concentrations. *J Neurochem*, 79, 463-484.

[59] Leonard, T.K., Watson, R.R. & Mohs, M.E. (1987) The effects of caffeine on various body systems: a review. *J Am Diet Assoc*, 1048-1053.

[60] Lorino, A.J., Lloyd, L.K., Crixell, S.H. & Walker, J.L. (2006) The effects of caffeine on athletic agility. *J Strength Cond Res*, 20 (4), 851-854.

[61] Lovett, R. (2005) Coffee: The demon drink? New Scientist (2518) Retrieved on 2007-11-19.

[62] MacIntosh, B.R. & Wright, BM. (1995) Caffeine ingestion and performance of a 1,500-metre swim. *Can J Appl Physiol*, 20 (2), 168-177.

[63] McLellan, T.M. & Bell, D.G. (2004) The impact of prior coffee consumption on the subsequent ergogenic effect of anhydrous caffeine. *Intl J Sports Nutr Exerc Metab*, 14 (6), 698-708.

[64] McLellan T.M., Kamimori G.H., Voss D.M., Bell D.G., Cole K.G. & Johnson D. (2005) Caffeine maintains vigilance and improves run times during night operations for Special Forces. *Aviat Space Environ Med*, 76, 647-654.

[65] Mitsumoto, H.G., DeBoer, G.E., Bunge, G., Andrish, J.T., Tetzlaff, J.E., Cruse, R.P. (1990) Fiber-type specific caffeine sensitivity in normal human skinned muscle fibres. *Anesthesiology*, 72, 50-54.

[66] Moisey, L.L., Kacker, S., Bickerton, A.C., Robinson, L.E. & Graham, T.E. (2008) Caffeinated coffee consumption impairs blood glucose homeostasis in response to high and low glycemic index meals in healthy men. *Am J Clin Nutr*, 87 (5), 1254-1261.

[67] Motl, R.W., O'Connor, P.J. & Dishman, R.K. (2003) Effect of caffeine on perceptions of leg muscle pain during moderate intensity cycling exercise. *J Pain*, 4 (6), 316-321.

[68] Noordzij, M., Uiterwal, C.S., Arends, L.R., Kok, F.J., Grobbee, D.E. & Geleijnse, G.M. (2005) Blood pressure response to chronic intake of coffee and caffeine: a meta-analysis of randomized controlled trials. *J Hypertens*, 23, 921-928.

[69] Pasman, W.J., van Baak, M.A., Jeukendrup, A.E. & de Haan A. (1995) The effects of different dosages of caffeine on endurance performance time. *Int J Sports Med*, 16, 225-230.

[70] Paton, C.D., Hopkins, W.G. & Vollebregt, L. (2001) Little effect of caffeine ingestion on repeated sprints in team-sports athletes. *Med Sci Sports Exerc*, 33 (5), 822-825.

[71] Pizziol, A., Tikhonoff, V., Paleari, C.D., Russo, E., Mazza, A., Ginocchio, G., Onesto, C., Pavan, L., Casiglia, E. & Pessina, A.C. (1998) Effects of caffeine on glucose tolerance: a placebo-controlled study. *Eur J Clin Nutr*, 52, 846-849.

[72] Prescino, C.L., Ross, M.L.R., Gregory, J.R., Savage, B. & Flanagan, T.R. (2008) Effects of sodium bicarbonate, caffeine, and their combination on repeated 200-m freestyle performance. *Intl J Sports Nutr Exerc Metab*, 16, 116-130.

[73] Porkka-Heiskanen, T. (1999) Adenosine in sleep and wakefulness. *Ann Med*, 31, 125-129.

[74] Rivers, W.H.R. & Webber, H.N. (1907) The action of caffeine on the capacity for muscular work. *J Physiol*, 36, 33-47.

[75] Roti, M.W., Casa, D.J., Pumerantz, A.C., Watson, G., Judelson, D.A., Dias, J.C., Ruffin, K. & Armstrong L.E. (2006) Thermoregulatory responses to exercise in the heat: chronic caffeine intake has no effect. *Aviat Space Environ Med*, 77 (2), 124-129.

[76] Salazar-Martinez, E., Willett, W.C., Ascherio, A., Manson, J.E., Leitzmann, M.F., Stampfer, M.J. & Hu, F.B. (2004) Coffee consumption and risk for type 2 diabetes mellitus. *Ann Intern Med*, 140, 1-8.

[77] Schneiker, K.T., Bishop, D., Dawson, B. & Hackett, L.P. (2006) Effects of caffeine on prolonged intermittent-sprint ability in team-sport athletes. *Med Sci Sports Exerc*, 38 (3), 578-585.

[78] Smith, A., Sutherland, D. & Christopher, G. (2005) Effects of repeated doses of caffeine on mood and performance of alert and fatigued volunteers. *J Psychopharmacol*, 19 (6), 620-626.

[79] Sokmen, B., Armstrong, L.E., Kraemer, W.J., Casa, D.J., Dias, J.C., Judelson, D.A. & Maresh, C.M. (2008) Caffeine use in sports: Considerations for the athlete. *J Strength Cond Res*, 22 (3), 978-986.

[80] Stuart, G.R., Hopkins, W.G., Cook, C. & Cairns, S.P. (1995) Multiple effects of caffeine on simulated high-intensity team-sport performance. *Med Sci Sports Exerc*, 37 (11), 1998-2005.

[81] Sung, B.H., Lovallo, W.R., Pincomb, G.A. & Wilson, M.F. (1990) Effects of caffeine on blood pressure response during exercise in normotensive healthy young men. *Am J Cardiol*, 65 (13), 909-913.

[82] Sung, B.H., Lovallo, W.R., Whitsett, T. & Wilson, M.F. (1995) Caffeine elevates blood pressure response to exercise in mild hypertensive men. *Am J Hypertens*, 8 (12)1, 1184-1188.

[83] Tarnopolsky, M.A. & Cupido, C. (2000) Caffeine potentiates low-frequency skeletal muscle force in habitual and nonhabitual caffeine consumers. *J Appl Physiol*, 89, 1719-1724.

[84] van Dam, R.M. & Feskens, E.J. (2002) Coffee consumption and risk of type II diabetes mellitus. *Lancet*, 360, 1477-1478.

[85] Van Soeren, M.H. & Graham, T.E. (1998) Effect of caffeine on metabolism, exercise endurance, and catecholamine responses after withdrawal. *J Appl Physiol*, 85 (4), 1493-1501.

[86] Van Soeren, M.H., Sathasivam, P., Spriet, L.L. & Graham, T.E. (1993) Caffeine metabolism and epinephrine responses during exercise in users and nonusers. *J Appl Physiol*, 75, 805-812.

[87] Wagner, J.C. (1991) Enhancement of athletic performance with drugs: an overview. *Sports Med*, 12 (4), 250-265.

[88] Wiles, J.D., Bird, S.R., Hopkins, J. & Riley, M. (1992) Effect of caffeinated coffee on running speed, respiratory factors, blood lactate, and perceived exertion during 1500 m treadmill running. *Br J Sports Med*, 26, 116-120.

[89] Wiles, J.D., Coleman, D., Tegerdine, M. & Swaine, I.L. (2006) The effects of caffeine ingestion on performance time, speed, and power during a laboratory-based 1 km cycling time-trial. *J Sports Sci*, 24 (11), 1165-1171.

[90] Williams, A.D., Cribb, P.J., Cooke, M.B. & Hayes, A. (2008) The effect of ephedra and caffeine on maximal strength and power in resistance-trained athletes. *J Strength Cond Res*, 22 (2), 464-470.

[91] Williams, J.H., Signorile, J.F., Barnes, W.S. & Henrich, T.W. (1988) Caffeine, maximal power output, and fatigue. *Br J Sports Med*, 22, 132-134.

[92] Winkelmayer, W.C., Stampfer, M.J., Willett, W.C. & Curhan, G.C. (2005) Habitual caffeine intake and the risk for hypertension in women. *J Am Med Assoc*, 294, 2330-2335.

[93] Woolf, K.W., Bidwell, W.K. & Carlson, A.G. (2008) The effect of caffeine as an ergogenic aid in anaerobic exercise. *Int J Sports Nutr Exerc Metab*, 18 (4), 412-429.

In: Advances in Strength and Conditioning Research
Editor: Michael Duncan and Mark Lyons

ISBN: 978-1-60692-909-4
© 2009 Nova Science Publishers, Inc.

Chapter 6

ERGOGENIC AIDS IN TRAINING: WHAT CAN IT HELP?

Stéphane Perrey[1]
University of Montpellier, France

ABSTRACT

As external influences, ergogenic aids can positively affect locomotor, physiological and psychological functions in human. Ergogenic aids may remove some constraints, which impact performance and related fatigue, and increase the speed of recovery from training and competition. Are ergogenic aids really helpful? This chapter presents research-supported evidence of four types of ergogenic aids commonly used by experienced and recreational exercisers during training. First, physiological (energy expenditure and locomotor-respiratory coupling) and biomechanical (muscle activation and kimematics patterns) benefits of poles during walking practice are discussed. Recent findings suggest that adapting differently breathing and mechanics of locomotion with the use of poles may alleviate increased exertion and muscle fatigue during walking. Then, compression garments in aiding recovery (stockings) and preventing fatigue (sleeves) are described in two case studies. Second, music as a psychophysiological ergogenic aid is shown to be effective during aerobic and anaerobic exercises. The music would help runners to maintain an efficient and regular running rhythm, and allow them to distract from the negative bodily sensations associated with fatigue and to tolerate better the training load as studied during an 8-week training period. Finally, two nutritional aids (branched chain amino acid and minerals supplement) for enhancing performance and delaying fatigue are presented and studied. Significant evidence indicates various positive benefits during aerobic and anaerobic exercises of branched chain amino acid for athletes. As well ingestion of minerals supplement studied during three weeks of training for alkalinization purpose in rugby players allow them to decrease acid loads and increase anaerobic performance. Overall, the effectiveness of the mechanical (equipment), psychophysiological (music) and nutritional (supplementation)

---

[1] Please address correspondence and requests for reprints to Stephane Perrey, EA2991 Motor Efficiency and Motor Deficiency Laboratory, University of Montpellier I, Faculty of Sports Sciences, 700 Avenue du Pic Saint Loup, 34090 Montpellier, France or e mail stephane.perrey@univ-montpl.fr

ergonegic aids presented in this review suggests that it can help. These new ways to improve the quality and quantity of athletes' training need however to be further studied.

Keywords: Compression Garments, Music, Hiking Poles, Nutritional Aids

The limits of human performance are continually being pushed in keeping wth the Olympic motto "stronger, higher, faster". World-best sport performances appear to plateau for short periods of time before being taken to new levels. This has been achieved by several factors including more sophisticated coaching, better equipment and advanced knowledge of training methodologies. Also, for thousands of years people have been using substances to improve their physical performance. Substances that are used to improve physical performance are collectively referred to as "ergogenics," a term derived from a Greek phrase meaning "work production". Ergogenic aids may directly influence the physiological capacity of a particular body system thereby improving performance during competition or to increase the speed of recovery during training: this enables athletes to endure higher training loads. An ergogenic aid is considered as a performance enhancing device or substance. Hopefully, they are tools or means that can be used to improve the performance of an athlete without resorting to any illegal methods. Ergogenic aids may be divided into the following categories: mechanical, physiological and psychological and nutritional.

The purpose of this chapter, which is divided into three main sections, is to analyze the physiological, psychological and biomechanical responses of some ergogenic aids that should be addressed for the conditioning practitioner. Many coaches, athletes and trainers are using them but we may wonder whether it can help? The first section addresses two mechanical ergogenic aids (equipment), in particular their benefits on biomechanical and physiological responses. The second section looks at one psychophysiological ergogenic aid (music), overviewing its different impacts on athletic performance and training tolerance. The third section synthesizes research on the relationship between two common nutritional aids and performance outcomes. Case studies are presented to illustrate each section.

1. EQUIPMENT AS A MECHANICAL ERGOGENIC AID

Any kind of tool or equipment that can be used to help an athlete train a specific targeted area of their fitness can be described as a mechanical ergogenic aid. Among mechanical aids, we chose to discuss two common pieces of equipment (walking poles and compression garments) used extensively by experienced and recreational exercisers during their workouts, and that have both anecdotal and research supported evidence of enhancing exercise performance.

1.1. Physiological and Biomechanical Benefits of Poles during Practice

Regular participation in aerobic endurance sports seems to be an appropriate stimulus to maintain or enhance physical fitness and health. Walking is a widely practiced form of moderate-intensity health-enhancing physical activity [48]. Due to the simplicity of walking, the technique is easy to practice even for beginners in endurance sports [58]. In Nordic walking, the exerciser uses poles, which resemble those for cross-country skiing. The essential physiological difference of Nordic walking versus walking is the use of upper body musculature. The use of poles has been justified by reducing stress on the lower limbs and spine, as well as by increasing balance, ease of walking, reduced fatigue and additional exercising of the shoulders and arms musculature [14, 60]. In spite of the importance of these factors, some questions regarding the physiological and biomechanical effects of hiking poles remain. Recent investigations gave some interesting results and consideration for training purposes in assisting fatigue and performance and injury prevention.

First, as often claimed pole walking do not systematically increase energy expenditure when compared to regular walking [25, 51]. One of the main issues is the self-chosen walking speed by practitioners. Energy expenditure as appreciated by metabolic rate (i.e., VO_2) and energy cost (as the quotient of steady-state VO_2 divided by the displacement velocity) and perceived exertion during uphill and level does not change significantly with the use of poles at self-selected walking speed [51]. The use of hiking poles (equipment weighing less than 500 g) during uphill walking does not lead to an increased energy cost but redistributes muscular activity from lower to upper limbs [25]. At preferred movement frequency, poles reduce the activation of lower limb muscles by 15% and increase upper limb muscle activation by 95%. And walking at low frequency (- 20% than preferred speed) redistributed the muscular work from thigh muscles to calf and upper limbs muscles, but this does not lead to an increased VO_2. Thus, during uphill walking, repeatedly changing the frequency from preferred to low frequency could be a useful strategy to lessen fatigue [25]. As well, reducing the frequency of arm movements separately from legs (i.e., one pole planted every two steps) could also provide physiological and biomechanical benefits. When the poles are used without excessive motor movements, no additional energy expenditure occurs during uphill and flat sections [51]. Also, strategy for optimizing energy expenditure for users when using poles is likely to link up to a modification of the locomotor rhythm. Thus, stride rate appears an important determinant for optimal energetic speed in Nordic walking. In the same way, breathing frequency that governs the respiratory system may play a role during activities using arm propulsion. Entrained breathing during exercise has been assumed to be due to synchronization of the respiratory and locomotive musculature, the so-called locomotor-respiratory coupling. The latter has been observed and described in human locomotion such as running or walking, cycling, rowing, hand-rim wheelchair propulsion and cross-country skiing [15, 24, 53]. The theoretical advantages of entrainment of breathing (that is locomotion that drives ventilation) during rhythmic exercise are a possible enhancement in efficiency of stride mechanics, a decrease in the energy cost and the rate of perceived exertion. This response pattern may increase the mechanical work efficiency between breathing and locomotive activity, leading to a decreased overall metabolic rate [4, 30]. Some authors [42] proposed that such a benefit of the locomotor respiratory coupling on metabolic rate might require months to years of training. Learning the appropriate breathing pattern with arm propulsion during training would be relevant for some people to increase the degree of coordination between respiratory and locomotor rhythms in order to observe any physiological and/or biomechanical benefits during Nordic walking, cross-country skiing, or rowing.

Concerning the influence of hiking poles, the proximity of the respiratory and locomotor muscles during the walking exercise with poles can explain the significantly higher average ratio of leg movement per breath with poles than without [51]. The propulsive forces or the simple grip of the poles by the upper body would allow an increase in the mechanical constraints of the locomotor and respiratory muscles (intercostal, abdominal muscles and diaphragm, pectoral, etc.). Interestingly, downhill walking induces higher energy expenditure and ventilatory responses with than without poles on treadmill at self-selected speed [51]. The higher breathing frequency during downhill walking may suggest that the propulsive action of the upper body could interact with the control of the ventilatory rhythm due to the proximity of the respiratory and locomotor muscles [1, 24]. According to different respiratory responses observed with grade, mechanics of downhill walking may be different from the uphill and flat sections. As proposed [51], walkers who want to use poles during downhill at self-selected walking speed should adapt differently breathing and mechanics of locomotion to lower energy expenditure.

Second, it is often stated that Nordic walking does not aggravate joints of the lower extremity and that it reduces the load on the knee joints. Recent study [31] does not support the statement that Nordic walking reduces the load on especially the knees joints compared with walking without poles for experienced Nordic walking instructors. In the same way, experienced Nordic Walkers showed higher vertical and horizontal ground reaction forces during landing for Nordic walking compared with normal walking [36]. They concluded that none of the kinematic parameters suggest a physiological benefit of Nordic walking compared with walking. For recreational users, Nordic walking is rarely introduced for hill walking but rather for level walking and thus the loadings on the joints have different physiological benefit. In novice and healthy people, walking with poles could result in a load reduction of the lower extremities [70]. In healthy subjects, uphill walking with poles using the alternate stride technique, but relieving knee extensor muscles, measured by EMG activity, could alleviate knee joint forces and, during long walks, lessen fatigue of the lower limb muscles [24]. Overall, literature seems to indicate that poles significantly relieve the muscles implicated in propulsion but would have a lesser influence on the muscles involved in leg swing or to face gravitational forces.

1.2. Influence of Compressive Clothing in Sport and Exercise

Combining clothing functions with wear comfort is a growing market trend, and for all active sportsmen this constitutes one of the vital factors for achieving a high level of performance. The physiological comfort of sportswear can affect not only a wearer's well being but also his performance. The role of elastic clothing can also play a part in providing comfort, through minimizing the garment's resistance to the wearer's movements. Athletes search for the key to improving their maximum performance, endurance and recovery. A relatively new product to the sporting scene, compression garments could be the answer to help enhance performance in training, competing and accelerate recovery. The use of compression clothing, such as elastic undergarments and tights, is showing more popularity among athletes. Over recent years, compression and their use in sport and exercise have increased exponentially. As with most new products, injury prevention and improved performance is purported to be a benefit from using such garments. While a significant body of research evidence exists describing the role of compression garments on vascular function in diseased patients, less evidence exists for athletic sport performance. Compression garments are a relatively simple mechanical modality, which may have the potential to enhance sport performance and recovery from exercise or training. Compression garments represent a way of safely and legally manipulating human physiology to produce an internal environment that is more conducive to high performance and faster recovery. Exciting new research is emerging from numerous sports science laboratories around the world as to the multitude of beneficial effects that compression garments can provide the athlete. The underlying mechanism is attributed to enhanced blood flow to muscle, which is similar to the effect of active recovery. In healthy subjects, aerobic training is known to increase lower limb venous compliance and would predispose to varicose veins, venous insufficiency and orthostatic intolerance. Garments (elastic bandages or compression stockings), as massages post-exercise represent a mechanical manipulation of body tissues increasing deep venous flow, decreasing superficial venous flow and preventing cutaneous venous stasis [16, 39, 45]. Improvements in microcirculation whilst wearing compression garments may be judged beneficial for such persons.

Regarding performance, improvements in maximal aerobic performance with compression garments have been reported in repeated 5-min maximal cycle efforts separated by an 80-min recovery [18]. It has been suggested that excess oscillatory displacement of a muscle during a dynamic movement may contribute to fatigue and interfere with neurotransmission and optimal muscle recruitment patterns. Recent research reported that compression garments were able to significantly reduce longitudinal and anterior- posterior muscle oscillation by 0.32 and 0.40 cm respectively upon landing from a maximal vertical jump. Explosive muscular power is highly correlated with success in most sports. Research in track and field athletes has reported a significant increase in maximal vertical jump height when vertical jumps are measured wearing compression garments but without significant improvement in 10-, 20- or 60-min sprint time [6, 22]. High intensity exercise produces lactic acid, which presents a challenge to the body's ability to maintain pH within the narrow physiological range. This in turn can negatively impact the force generating capacity of the muscle, which results in muscle fatigue and impaired athletic performance. Data published [7] showed a 14% decrease in blood lactate concentrations 15 minutes following high intensity exercise when compression garments were worn during and after exercise. Recent research [44] on fatigue recovery reported compression garments did not increase fatigability during ankle dorsi-flexion and did not improve force recovery between repeated fatiguing static efforts. In contrast, faster recovery of force production in single arm bicep curls has been reported following heavy eccentric exercise when wearing compression sleeves [37]. Muscle damage is an inevitable consequence of high intensity exercise and any technique that can facilitate muscle repair and faster recovery is of large benefit to the athlete. Overall, the previous findings tend to suggest that compression garments may be benefits for their use as a recovery intervention tool rather than for improving physical performance.

CASE STUDIES: EQUIPMENT IN AIDING RECOVERY AND PREVENTING FATIGUE

Case 1 describes the impact of compressive stockings on muscle recovery time course in 8 young males. Case 2 focuses on the influence of compressive sleeves during sustained heavy forearm exercise in 4 healthy subjects. The first case shows that recovery from unaccustomed eccentric exercise is a process that may be speeded up by the use of external mechanical compression on impaired muscle. The second case exemplifies how an ergogenic interplay (e.g. sleeve over the forearm muscles) can lower the muscle fatigue.

Case Study 1: Efficacy of Compression Garment as a Recovery Intervention

Delayed onset muscle soreness (DOMS) is a common experience following unaccustomed eccentric exercise. DOMS and associated force deficits may limit optimal performance in subsequent days. The cause of DOMS remains poorly understood, thus there is no effective treatment. Compression stockings are a commonly used intervention believed to diminish DOMS. The purpose of this case study was to determine if compression stockings after eccentric walking exercise minimizes DOMS and associated deficits (e.g. muscle force capacity). Eight healthy subjects (age 26 ± 4 yrs, height 175 ± 8 cm, weight 70 ± 5 kg) volunteered to perform a single bout of backward downhill walking exercise (duration 30 min, velocity 1 m.s^{-1}, negative grade -25%, load 12% of body weight). The subjects were fully accustomed to the testing procedures before giving informed consent to participate. The experimental procedure was performed in accordance with the declaration of Helsinki and was approved by the local committee of human research. Following walking exercise, subjects were required to wear 5 hours per day for 3 consecutive days compression stockings on one leg while the second was used as control. Muscle soreness and neuromuscular measures (M-wave, peak twitch, maximal voluntary force) were taken pre and post-walk, then 2, 24, 48 and 72 hours post-walking exercise for the two legs. There was a 28% reduction in DOMS 72 h after exercise when wearing compression stockings ($P < 0.05$) than in the control leg. Immediately after exercise there was a 15% decrease in maximal voluntary force of the plantar flexors in both legs partly attributable to an alteration in contractile properties (-22% in electrically evoked mechanical twitch).

In leg wearing compression stockings, maximal voluntary force starts to recover while the contractile properties had significantly recovered within 24 h (figure 1) but not in the control leg. In the current case study, compression stockings might have had the effect of compressing the muscle tissue to such an extent that less structural damage occurred relative to a control condition. Compression stockings accelerated the recovery of the muscle force capacity at 24 hours beyond that achieved by the control condition. This could have important implications not only for cross-country runners and trailers, but also for individuals who wish to embark on exercise regimes with associated pain following exercise in the management of the muscle function impairment associated with DOMS.

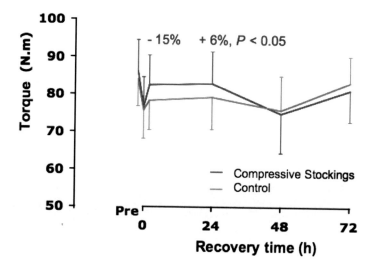

Figure 1. Mean ± SD of maximal voluntary torque following the walking exercise protocol for compressive stockings and control conditions during different epochs of recovery. In post-exercise, a similar decrease of about 15 % in maximal torque produced by calf muscle was observed. At 24 h some difference was noted between conditions but not thereafter.

Case Study 2. Compressive Sleeve and Fatigue during Forearm Exercise

The effects of compressive sleeves on haemodynamics and muscle fatigue during and after a fatiguing forearm exercise was tested during a pilot study in 4 healthy young males (age of 28 ± 3 years). This study aimed to evaluate continuously haemodynamic changes and muscle oxygenation with Near-InfraRed Spectroscopy (NIRS) during a fatiguing task of handgrip. The subjects were familiarized to the testing procedures before giving consent to participate. The experimental procedure was performed in accordance with the declaration of Helsinki and was approved by the local committee of human research. EMG and forearm flexor muscle force were measured to assess fatigue. The fatigue protocol consisted in a sustained isometric contraction of wrist flexors until exhaustion (i.e., task of handgrip). The workload was fixed at 60% of the maximal voluntary force measured at the beginning of the experiment. Visual feedback was projected on a computer screen to allow subjects to control their force level. Subjects had to continue the fatigue task until exhaustion, when they were unable to maintain the workload for at least 5 s. The main result of this study was that the use of compressive sleeves during the sustained forearm exercise significantly diminished muscle fatigue without improving significantly endurance performance (+8 %). The decrease of force was less pronounced with the compressive sleeves than without (-12%, $P < 0.05$) and neuromuscular efficiency (Force/EMG) was higher by 22% ($P < 0.05$).

The use of compressive sleeves may counteract muscle fatigue by an enhanced O_2 delivery to the working muscle. In the present study tissue oxygenation was measured by NIRS method. At the beginning of exercise oxy-hemoglobin and blood volume were greatly enhanced with the compressive sleeves. This can explain why subjects with the sleeves increased their endurance times (+8%) because more oxygen was available. When O_2

availability decreases, time of endurance decreases, because fast twitch fibers are recruited preferentially [47]. External compression pressure increases tissue pressure and consequently decreases transmural vascular pressure [12]. This may trigger a myogenic response resulting in vessel relaxation and in turn lead to a flow rise in small arteries and arterioles. With different applications of pressures from 20 to 30 mmHg during a task of handgrip (5-10% maximal force, 1 s contraction / 2 s relaxation duty cycle for nearly 70 min), the arterial flow increased significantly [12]. Using compressive sleeves appears a legitimate tool for enhancing the efficiency of the muscle function during heavy physical activity when O_2 delivery is compromised.

2. MUSIC AS A PSYCHOPHYSIOLOGICAL ERGOGENIC AID

Examples of psychological aids include, but are not limited to hypnosis, relaxation activities and music. Many health and fitness instructors regard the addition of music to exercise similarly to an ergogenic aid. Listening to a rock song may appear no more than a welcome distraction from aching muscles on a run bout. But it could also significantly enhance performance. Many sports stars have taken to listening to music, including the long-distance runner Haile Gebreselassie. In recent years, many reports in music and psychology have cited the anxiolytic effects of music. These effects have been examined for different music types and for self-selected versus experimenter-selected music. Perceived relaxation is elicited by sedative music, which is characterized as melodious, delicate, harmonic, and romantic [33], and by self-selected music [65]. On the other hand, stimulative and excitative music, is characterized as loud, dynamic, rhythmic and elicits tension and excitement [33]. It appears that sedative music may actually decrease a person's muscular fitness potential training ability. Listening to sedative music decreased grip strength significantly when compared to stimulative music and silence, but with no statistical significant difference between stimulative music and silence [50]. This suggests that trainers would be well advised in surveying their athletes as to their perceived best workout environment (with or without music accompaniment). To take the use of music to a high level, program components of training should coincide with segments of music. That way, work time and recovery time can be punctuated by music so that delicate/slow music will follow loud/dynamic music. This approach is especially suited to highly structured sessions such as circuit or interval training. It is also imperative that athletes are involved in the selection of music, as this is likely to increase the potency of music-related effects.

It is important to consider what types of activity the sportsmen are engaged in, and what is the desired purpose of the music. A particularly effective strategy is to get each athlete to list her/his favorite music selection for different types of training (e.g., anaerobic interval training, strength training, recovery, etc.). The Brunel Music Rating Inventory-2 [34] is a useful tool in this regard as various activities can be substituted into the generic item structure in order to select music that is context-specific. It was found that a switch from slow to fast tempo music produced an ergogenic effect during cycle ergometry [63]. The practical implication of this finding is that a change of music tempo from slow to fast may enhance participants' motivation and work output, especially when work level plateaus or in the latter stages of an exercise bout. Similarly, it has been indicated that the careful application of music during a simulated 10 km cycle time-trial could be used to regulate work output [3]. The music was particularly effective in the early stages of the trial when perceived exertion was relatively low. Precisely, music with a tempo of 142 beats/min improved 10-km cycling time by about 2 % compared to a no-music condition. This improvement was explained mostly by an increase in speed in the first 3 km of the time trial. The characteristic U-shaped profile of speed during the time trial was observed in the music condition only, with the participants apparently choosing relatively high starting speeds, which could not be maintained until the final effort was made.

The benefits of motivational music are dependent on intensity of exercise. In an investigation of the physiological processes underlying the benefits of music, music was associated with reduced heart rate, exercise lactate and the rate of perceived exertion (RPE) during treadmill running at 70% VO_2 max [64]. They suggested that music allowed participants to relax, reducing muscle tension, and thereby increasing blood flow and lactate clearance while decreasing lactate production in working muscle. However, there appears to be no benefit of music on performance of a Wingate anaerobic test (a supramaximal effort over 30-s) [52]. So, music engenders an ergogenic effect during submaximal endurance exercise but not during very high intensity activities.

It is relevant to note that music may also be used during training or competition consciously by trying to synchronize repetitive movements in time with the tempo of the music. Humans have the tendency to respond to the rhythmical qualities of music by synchronizing movement patterns to tempo. This is called synchronous music and it has been reliably shown to produce an ergogenic effect. Therefore, if athletes or exercisers work in time to music, they will likely work harder for longer. In the context of physical training, it has been suggested that music may significantly influence patterns of exercise compliance [61]. In the latter study, music exhibited no significant influence on any physiological variable measured (aerobic capacity, ventilation, respiratory exchange ratio, heart rate, and blood lactate) during submaximal cycling in untrained college men and women. In addition, the psychological perception of effort was not altered with or without the music stimulus, although subjects felt they performed better with the music [61]. Another investigation of submaximal intensity (walking/jogging on a treadmill) showed that subjects had longer times to exhaustion when listening to slow music as compared to loud music [20]. The efficacy of synchronous music as an ergogenic aid in aerobic activities has been demonstrated (e.g., [2]). Typically, synchronous music has been used to extend exercise duration among non-highly trained participants. Concerning performance, synchronous music during 400 m track running elicited faster times than no music [62]. In sum, it appears that synchronous music can be applied to aerobic and anaerobic performance among non-elite athletes and exercise participants with considerable effect. For more experienced users, effect is likely more difficult to get.

Case Study 3: Music Accompaniment during Heavy Endurance Training

Case 3 describes the impact of music during an 8-week training period in trained marathoners. It focuses on the possible impact of music tempo during interval-training workouts. This case study emphasizes that music appears to provide a motivational construct for exercise, positively affecting the mental attitude during some heavy workouts and a better tolerance to training.

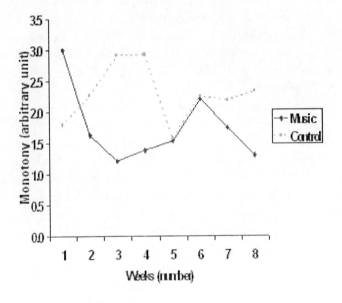

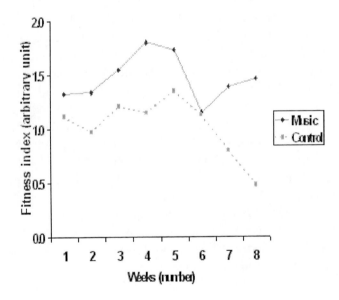

Figure 2. Mean changes in monotony (upper graph) and fitness (lower graph) indices during the course of an 8-week training period for the music and control groups.

Although performance may be enhanced by the addition of music to the workout, athletes regularly report that they feel their performance is better with the music accompaniment. Music exposure during physical exercise influences RPE. However, most of these studies, often in a laboratory context, pointed out an acute impact of music on exercising. Therefore, we decided to assess the effect of music during a prolonged training period (2 months) on the

RPE and training load responses. Two groups were constituted: one group with self-chosen music associated to coach's instructions with MP3 player (in two out of five training bouts per week, n=8) and one control group without music (n=8). The experimental procedure was performed in accordance with the declaration of Helsinki for research in humans. Both the athlete and the coach agreed to standardize and keep the physical training load equal during the eight weeks. Training load was rated after each workout, with the help of the 6-20 RPE scale. From the session RPE method, the accessory indices of training, monotony and strain were calculated, potentially providing an index of the training outcomes [26]. Monotony was defined as the variability of practices for the entire training period, while strain was defined as the overall stress demanded on the athlete for a period of a week. Monotony was calculated by dividing the mean daily load over each week by the standard deviation of load. Strain was calculated by multiplying monotony by the weekly load.

The results presented no significant differences of RPE between both groups during the eight weeks. However, the indices of the training seem to bring out some tendencies underlining the positive effects of the music on the training program tolerance. For a similar training load in the two groups, the group with music showed a lower monotony and higher fitness indices in weeks 3 and 4 (figure 2). The music would help runners to maintain an efficient and regular running rhythm and allow them to distract from the negative bodily sensations associated with fatigue during heavy workouts.

3. Nutritional Aids for Enhancing Performance and Delaying Fatigue

Athletes often use a variety of nutritional supplements in order to enhance recovery processes. Most nutritional supplements can be categorized as potential energy sources, anabolic enhancers, or recovery aids. Research has consistently shown that supplementation with iron and magnesium, which is involved in some biochemical processes, may prevent the decline in iron and magnesium status associated with training loads [17]. In addition, dietary antioxidants, such as vitamins A, C and E [19] and trace-elements like selenium, zinc, and manganese, may prevent the oxidative stress that occurs with intense exercise, training and over-training. Others supplements for athletes include various protein and branched chain amino acid (BCAA) products. These various foods and drink substances are legal to use and can be used to aid an athlete in some way. They usually work as stimulants or as short-term replenishment of things the body goes through quickly (such as various electrolytic ions). Two examples of nutritional aids are presented and studied below (case study 4): Branched-Chain Amino Acids (BCAA) and minerals supplement.

Branched chain amino acids (leucine, isoleucine, and valine), or BCAA's, are a group of essential amino acids that play important roles in protein synthesis and energy production. Researchers have expended a considerable amount of effort on evaluating the effects of supplementation of branched-chain amino acids (BCAAs: leucine, isoleucine, and valine) on physiological and psychological responses to exercise (see [69]). The use of supplemental BCAA's has been tested as a means to improve exercise performance. BCAA's may serve as anabolic agents by optimizing muscle mass - crucial in strength-related sports, but also as a potential energy source during aerobic exercise [67]. BCAA's may have benefits for the athlete, especially when taken during or before workout. Several studies have also pointed out that BCAA uptake and oxidation increase with increasing plasma concentrations [29] due to pre-exercise BCAA ingestion during exercise [67] and during recovery [5]. First, BCAA's may spare muscle and liver glycogen stores and increase fuel supply. BCAA supplementation increases alanine production during exercise and also decreased plasma lactate with chronic supplementation (30 minutes before exercise) to triathletes, presumably by increasing the conversion rate of pyruvate to alanine [21]. Studies in humans have found that BCAA's have a glycogen sparing effect during exercise, although in some cases it is not statistically significant [10, 11]. However, other studies indicate that BCAA supplementation prior to exercise does not alter plasma glucose [46]. Nutritional supplementation during 28 days with protein hydrolysate enriched in BCAA and antioxidants, trace and mineral elements, and vitamins did not improve significantly time to fatigue at VO_2max or supramaximal exercise performance, but induced a delayed fatigue appearance in two types of anaerobic exercise potentially explained by adaptations in oxidant/antioxidant status at rest and changes in lactate metabolism [66]. These results confirm the results of previous studies that have shown no effect of antioxidants [32] or BCAA supplementation [68] on physical anaerobic performance. Decrease in fatigue indices was in accordance with those of Vukovich et al. [68] who reported a small delayed fatigue during a 30-s Wingate test, but after only one week of protein treatment in untrained subjects. Consequently, changes in antioxidant potential and metabolic adaptations induced by 28 days of treatment in [66] could explain the delayed fatigue. Given the information above, there is significant evidence indicating various benefits of BCAA ingestion for athletes during aerobic and anaerobic exercises.

Case Study 4. The Effects of a Commercial Dietary Mineral Supplement on Net Acid Excretion and Anaerobic Performance During Training in an Elite Rugby League Player

This next section provides typical scenario of supplementation during a training period aimed at maximizing the training responses to training load while minimizing fatigue for an optimal performance outcome.

During high intensity activities acidosis is thought to be responsible for fatigue and exhaustion in working muscles. The ingestion of sodium bicarbonate or sodium citrate results in a metabolic alkalosis and has been reported to increase performance of intense exercise lasting between 30 s and 4 min [8, 49]. The evidence for any ergogenic effect resulting from ingestion of alkalinizers is, however, equivocal. Several authors [53, 38] found no improvement in the performance of high-intensity exercise following the ingestion of either sodium bicarbonate or sodium citrate. The variation in findings may partially be explained by differences in the dosages of alkalinizing agents and in the exercise intensity and duration that were employed.

Today, there is a general consensus that diet can markedly affect acid-base status [23, 27 54, 55, 56, 57]. To compensate for the acid-base disequilibrium, the body draws on its mineral reserves, which leads to a urinary loss of minerals. Large extrarenal bicarbonate losses must be compensated by alkali supplements. Acid production can be neutralized by sources of bicarbonate in the diet or endogenous sources [43]. However, there is still limited scientific justification for the widespread use of mineral supplements by athletes. Therefore, we aimed to investigate whether commercial dietary minerals supplement (195 mEq of alkalinization potential weekly during 3 weeks) would lower acid loads (quantified as urinary net acid excretion, NAE in 24-h urine samples) and affect anaerobic performance in a group of 12 highly trained rugby league players.

The subjects gave informed consent before to participate. The experimental procedure was performed in accordance with the declaration of Helsinki and was approved by the local committee of human research. The study utilized a double-blind, placebo-controlled 2-group design with random assignment. Baseline testing was conducted prior to supplementation and included assessment of sprint performance and NAE. Following baseline testing, both groups of subjects followed the same 3-week strength and conditioning program, which was prescribed by the head strength and conditioning coach of the professional rugby league team to which the subjects were contracted. Subjects were retested post-supplementation in a manner identical to baseline testing.

The supplement and placebo was in powder form and provided in individual packets. The contents of each packet were mixed with 50 g of a commercially available sport drinks (Carbo Energizer, NUTRICO, Belgium) in 1 L of water to prevent dehydration and hypoglycemia during exercise frequently used in daily practice. During training, the experimental group received a 16.5 g stick of a commercial dietary minerals supplement (Enabiane®, Pileje, Saint Laurent Des Autels, France) to consume three times weekly for 3 weeks. Enabiane® takes the form of a 16.5 g stick to be diluted in 1 to 1.5 L of water, and it provides: 65 mEq of alkalinization potential, due to the citrate salts of minerals (150 mg of magnesium, 400 mg of calcium and 1 g of potassium), and 5 g of fructo-oligosaccharides to facilitate the absorption of minerals. The control group received an equivalent amount of placebo containing 50 g of a commercially available sport drinks (Carbo Energizer, Nutrico, Belgium) in 1 L of water identical in appearance and prepared at a laboratory in bottles. The experimental and placebo drinks were similar in color and taste and indistinguishable for the subjects. We did not choose a water placebo, since this is not used in sports practice. The subjects were asked to record food and fluid intake on the day of the first test and to follow the same intake protocol on the days of the following test to minimize variation in output parameters.

The 5-m repeat-sprint test (5-m RST, see [13]) was chosen to evaluate in Rugby players their anaerobic capacity. Six beacons were placed 5 m apart in a straight line to cover a total distance of 25 m. Subjects were instructed to avoid pacing and perform with a maximal effort throughout the whole test. Each subject started the test in line with the first beacon and on an auditory signal sprinted 5 m to a second beacon, touched the ground adjacent to the beacon with a hand, and returned back to the first beacon, again touching down on the ground adjacent to the beacon with a hand. The subject then sprinted 10 m to the third beacon, back to the first beacon, and so on, until an exercise period of 30 seconds had elapsed. The subjects performed 3 repeat bouts of this protocol with a 35-second rest between bouts. The total distance (anaerobic performance) covered in the 3 bouts was recorded.

A single urine sample was collected from each athlete at a standardized time of day during week 0 and week 5 of the experimental period. Subjects consumed their usual diets, which they reported for 24 h, during which time they made a 24 h- urine collection. Subjects were instructed to begin collecting after rising (after discarding first void). Acid-base status was determined in the freshly thawed 24-h samples. Urine pH, titratable acid (TA), ammonium (NH_4), and bicarbonate (HCO_3) were measured according to the method of

Lüthy et al. [41]. NAE (mEq) was calculated from the analytic data in the conventional manner as the sum of TA plus NH4 minus HCO3. To ensure compliance in the 24-h urine collection the rugby players were carefully instructed in the collection procedure and also received written guidance. Urine specimens were stored below -20 °C. Acid-base status was determined in the freshly thawed and thoroughly pooled 24-h samples. Urine pH, titratable acid (TA), NH4, and bicarbonate were measured according to Lüthy et al. [41].

The present study revealed that ingestion of 49.50 g per week for 3 weeks of Enabiane significantly reduces NAE and enhances lactic capacity performance (figure 3) by increasing the number of meters traveled on 5-m RST in professional rugby league players.

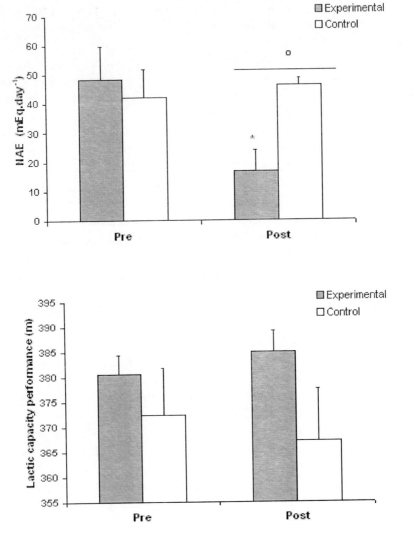

Figure 3. Mean ± SE of changes in net acid excretion (NAE) and lactic capacity performance as appreciated by the number of meters traveled on 5-m RST after a 3 weeks supplementation period of a commercial dietary minerals supplement for the two groups (experimental and control) of professional rugby league players. $ P < 0.05, significantly different between groups. * P < 0.05, significantly different from pre.

Our study provides additional support for a previous study [28] that reported that alkalizing complementation of potassium bicarbonate for two weeks allowed reducing strongly NAE to - 38mEq/day. In addition, this finding provides additional support for Bishop et al. [9], who reported recently that chronic alkalizing supplementation was allowed to improve performance significantly. The mechanisms by which chronic alkalizing ingestion elicits its performance-enhancing in these shuttle sprint repeated suggest mechanisms including increased recovery, enhanced buffer capacity [40] and attenuation of the magnesium loss [59].

CONCLUSION

Training and competition creates an overload to stress the body, which in turn produces fatigue followed by improved performance. Depending on the nature of the training or activities, physiological, biomechanical, psychological and nutritional components are stressed in different ways that result in fatigue. Despite the popularity of some ergogenic aids for helping aiding recovery and preventing fatigue, too little research has been conducted so far. The effectiveness of some mechanical (equipment), psychophysiological (music) and nutritional (supplementation) has been the focus of this overview accompanied with some case studies. Overall, most experimental evidence suggests that some components of proposed ergogenic aids may help. These new ways to improve the quality and quantity of athletes' training need however to be further studied before conclusions and guidelines can be drawn.

ACKNOWLEDGMENTS

In the preparation of this review, efforts of the following individuals in collecting some experimental data should be acknowledged: Thibaud Thedon, Aurélien Bringard, Joël Alibert and Benoît Albert.

REFERENCES

[1] Amazeen, P.G., Amazeen, E.L. & Beek, P.J. (2001) Coupling of breathing and movement during manual wheelchair propulsion. *J Exp Psych: Hum Percep Perf*, 27, 1243-1259.

[2] Anshel, M.H., & Marisi, D.Q. (1978) Effects of music and rhythm on physical performance. *Res Q*, 49, 109-113

[3] Atkinson, G., Wilson, D., & Eubank, M. (2004) Effects of music on work-rate distribution during a cycle time trial. *Int J Sports Med*, 62, 413-419.

[4] Bechbache, R.R., & Duffin, J. (1977) The entrainment of breathing frequency by exercise rhythm. *J Phys*, 272, 553-561.

[5] Bergman, B.C., Horning, M.A., Casazza, G.A., Wolfel, E.E., Butterfield, G.E., & Brooks, G.A. (2000) Endurance training increases gluconeogenesis during rest and exercise in men. *Am J Phys*, 278, E244-254.

[6]   Bernhardt, T., & Anderson, G.S. (2005) Influence of moderate prophylactic compression on sport performance. *J Strength Cond Res*, 19, 292-297.

[7]   Berry, M.J., & McMurray, R.G. (1987) Effects of graduated compression stockings on blood lactate following an exhaustive bout of exercise. *Am J Phys Med*, 66, 121-132.

[8]   Bird, S.R., Wiles, J., & Robbins, J. (1995) The effect of sodium bicarbonate ingestion on 1500-m racing time. *J Sports Sci*, 13, 399-403.

[9]   Bishop, D., Edge, J., Davis, C., & Goodman, C. (2004) Induced metabolic alkalosis affects muscle metabolism and repeated-sprint ability. *Med Sci Sports Exerc*, 36, 807-813.

[10] Blomstrand, E., & Saltin, B. (2001) BCAA intake affects protein metabolism in muscle after but not during exercise in humans. *Am J Phys. Endocrin Met*, 281, E365-E374

[11] Blomstrand, E., Ek, S., & Newsholme, E.A. (1996) Influence of ingesting a solution of branched-chain amino acids on plasma and muscle concentrations of amino acids during prolonged submaximal exercise. *Nutrition*, 12, 485-490.

[12] Bochmann, R.P., Seibel, W., Haase, E., Hietschold, V., Rödel, H., & Deussen, A. (2005) External compression increases forearm perfusion. *J of Appl Phys*, 99, 2337-2344.

[13] Boddington, M.K., Lambert, M.I., St Clair Gibson, A., & Noakes, T.D. (2001) Reliability of a 5-m multiple shuttle test. *J Sports Sci*, 19, 223-238.

[14] Bohne, M., & Abendroth-Smith, J. (2007) Effects of hiking downhill using trekking poles while carrying external loads. *Med Sci Sports Exerc*, 39, 177-183.

[15] Bramble, D.M., & Carrier, D.R. (1983) Running and breathing in mammals. *Sci*, 219, 251-256.

[16] Bringard, A., Denis, R., Belluye, N., & Perrey, S. (2006) Effects of compression tights on calf muscle oxygenation and venous pooling during quiet resting in supine and standing positions. *J Sports Med Phys Fit*, 46, 548-554.

[17] Brotherhood, J.R. (1984) Nutrition and sports performance. *Sports Med*, 1, 350-389.

[18] Chatard, J.C., Atlaoui, D., Farjanel, J., Louisy, F., Rastel, D., & Guézennec, C.Y. (2004) Elastic stockings, performance and leg pain recovery in 63-year-old sportsmen. *Eur J Appl Physiol*, 93, 347-352.

[19] Clarkson, P.M., & Thompson, H.S. (2000) Antioxidants: what role do they play in physical activity and health? *Am J Clin Nut*, 72, 637S-646S.

[20] Copeland, B. L., & Franks, B. D. (1991) Effects of types and intensities of background music on treadmill endurance. *J Sports Med Phys Fit*, 31, 100-103.

[21] De Palo, E.F., Gatti, R., Cappellin, E., Schiraldi, C., De Palo, C.B., & Spinella, P. (2001) Plasma lactate, GH and GH-binding protein levels in exercise following BCAA supplementation in athletes. *Amino Acids*, 20, 1-11.

[22] Duffield, R., & Portus, M. (2007) Comparison of three types of full-body compression garments on throwing and repeat-sprint performance in cricket players. *Br J Sports Med*, 41, 409-414.

[23] Dwyer, J., Foulkes, E., Evans, M., & Ausman, L. (1985) Acid/alkaline ash diets: time for assessment and change. *J Am Dietetic Assoc*, 85, 841-845.

[24] Fabre, N., Perrey, S., Arbez, L., & Rouillon, J.D. (2007) Neuro-mechanical and chemical influences on locomotor respiratory coupling in humans. *Resp Phys Neurobiology, 155*, 128 -136.

[25] Foissac, M.J., Berthollet, R., Seux, J., Belli, A., & Millet, G.Y. (2008) Effects of hiking pole inertia on energy and muscular costs during uphill walking. *Med Sci Sports Exerc*, 40, 1117-1125.

[26] Foster, C. (1998) Monitoring training in athletes in reference to overtraining syndrome. *Med Sci Sports Exerc*, 30, 1164-1168.

[27] Frassetto, L.A., Todd, K.M., Morris, R.C. Jr, & Sebastian, A. (1998) Estimation of net endogenous noncarbonic acid production in humans from diet potassium and protein contents. *Am J of Clin Nut*, 68, 576-583.

[28] Frassetto, L., Nash, E., Moris, RC Jr., & Sebastian, A. (2000) Comparative effets of potassium chloride and bicarbonate on thiazide-induced reduction in urinary calcium excretion. *Kidney Intl*, 58,748-752.

[29] Freund, H.R., & Hanani, M. (2002) The metabolic role of branched-chain amino acids. *Nut*, 18, 287-288.

[30] Garlando, F., Kohl, J., Koller, E.A., & Pietsch, P. (1985) Effect of coupling the breathing- and cycling rhythms on oxygen uptake during bicycle ergometry. *European Journal of Appl Physiol Occup Physiol*, 54, 497-501.

[31] Hansen, L., Henriksen, M., Larsen, P., & Alkjaer, T. (in press) Nordic Walking does not reduce the loading of the knee joint. *Scan J Med Sci Sports.*

[32] Ihara, H., Shino, Y., Morita, Y., Kawaguchi, E., Hashizume, N., & Yoshida, M. (2001) Is skeletal muscle damaged by the oxidative stress following anaerobic exercise? *J Clin Lab Anal*, 15, 239-243.

[33] Iwanaga, M., & Moroki, Y. (1999) Subjective and physiological responses to music stimuli controlled over activity and preference. *J Music Ther*, 36, 26-38.

[34] Karageorghis, C.I., Priest, D.L., Terry, P.C., Chatzisarantis, N.L.D., & Lane, A.M. (2006) Redesign and initial validation of an instrument to assess the motivational qualities of music in exercise: The Brunel Music Rating Inventory-2. *J Sports Sci*, 24, 899-909.

[35] Katz, A., Costill, D.L., King, D.S., Hargreaves, M., & Fink, W.J. (1984) Maximal exercise tolerance after induced alkalosis. *Intl J Sports Med*, 5, 107-110.

[36] Kleindienst, F.L., Michel K.J., Schwartz, J., & Krabbe, B. (2006) Comparison of kinematic and kinetic parameters between the locomotion patterns in nordic walking, walking and running. *Sportverletz Sportschaden*, 20, 25-30.

[37] Kraemer, W.J., Bush, J.A., Wickham, R.B., Denegar, C.R., Gómez, A.L., Gotshalk, L.A., Duncan, N.D., Volek, J.S., Putukian, M., & Sebastianelli, W.J. (2001) Influence of compression therapy on symptoms following soft tissue injury from maximal eccentric exercise. *J of Orthop Sports Phys Ther*, 31, 282-290.

[38] Lambert, C.P., Greenhaff, P.L., Ball, D., & Maughan, R.J. (1993) Influence of sodium bicarbonate ingestion on plasma ammonia accumulation during incremental exercise in man. *Eur J Appl Phys Occup Physiol*, 66, 49-54.

[39] Lawrence, D., & Kakkar, V.V. (1980) Graduated, static, external compression of the lower limb: a physiological assessment. *Br J Surgery*, 67, 119-121.

[40] Linderman, J.K., & Gosselink, K.L. (1994) The effects of sodium bicarbonate ingestion on exercise performance. *Sports Med*, 18, 75-80.

[41] Lüthy, C., Moser, C., & Oetliker, O. (1977) Acid-base determination of urine in 3 steps. *Das Medizinische Laboratorium*, 30, 174-181. [Article in German]

[42] Maclennan, S.E., Silvestri, G.A., Ward, J., & Mahler, D.A. (1994) Does entrained breathing improve the economy of rowing? *Med Sci Sports and Exerc*, 26, 610-614.

[43] Maton, B., Thiney, G., Dang, S., Tra, S., Bassez, S., Wicart, P., & Ouchene, A. (2006) Human muscle fatigue and elastic compressive stockings. *Eur J Appl Phys*, 97, 432-442.

[44] Manz, F., Schmidt, H., Scharer, K., & Bickel, H. (1977) Acid-base status in dietary treatment of phenylketonuria. *Ped Res*, 11, 1084-1087.

[45] Remer, T. (2000) Influence of diet on acid-base balance. *Seminars in Dialysis*, 13, 221-226.

[46] Mayrovitz, H.N., & Larsen, P.B. (1997) Effects of compression bandaging on leg pulsatile blood flow. *Clin Physiol*, 17, 107-117.

[47] Mittleman, K.D., Ricci, M.R., & Bailey, S.P. (1998) Branched-chain amino acids prolong exercise during heat stress in men and women. *Med Sci Sports Exerc*, 30, 83-91.

[48] Moritani, T., Sherman, W.M., Shibata, M., Matsumoto, T., & Shinohara, M. (1992) Oxygen availability and motor unit activity in humans. *Eur J Appl Phys*, 64, 552-556.

[49] Morris, J.N., & Hardman, A.E. (1997) Walking to health. *Sports Med*, 23, 306-332.

[50] Parry-Billings, M., & MacLaren, D.P. (1986) The effect of sodium bicarbonate and sodium citrate ingestion on anaerobic power during intermittent exercise. *Eur J Appl Phys Occup Physiol*, 55, 524-529.

[51] Pearce, K.A. (1981) Effects of different types of music on physical strength. *Percept Mot Skills*, 53, 351-352.

[52] Perrey, S., & Fabre, N. (2008) Exertion during uphill, level and downhill walking with and without hiking poles. *J Sports Sci Med*, 7, 32-38.

[53] Pujol, T.J., & Langenfeld, M.E. (1999) Influence of music on Wingate anaerobic test performance. *Percept Mot Skills*, 88, 292-296.

[54] Rassler, B., & Kohl, J. (1996) Analysis of coordination between breathing and walking rhythms in humans. *Resp Physiol*, 106, 317-327

[55] Remer, T., & Manz, F. (1995) Potential renal acid load of foods and its influence on urine pH. *J Am Dietetic Assoc*, 95, 791-797.

[56] Remer, T., & Manz, F. (1994) Estimation of the renal net acid excretion by adults consuming diets containing variable amounts of protein. *Am J Clin Nut*, 59,1356-1361.

[57] Remer, T., & Manz, F. (1995) Dietary protein as a modulator of the renal net acid excretion capacity: evidence that an increased protein intake improves the capability of the kidney to excrete ammonium. *J Nut Biochem*, 6, 431-437.

[58] Rippe, J.M., Ward, A., Porcari, J.P., & Freedson, P.S. (1988). Walking for health and fitness. *J Am Med Assoc*, 259, 2720-2724.

[59] Rylander, R., Remer, T., Berkemeyer, S., & Vormann, J. (2006) Acid-base status affects renal magnesium losses in healthy, elderly persons. *J Nut*, 136, 2374-2377.

[60] Schwameder, H., Roithner, R., Muller, E., Niessen, W., & Raschner, C. (1999) Knee joint forces during downhill walking with hiking poles. *J Sports Sci*, 17, 969-978.

[61] Schwartz, S.E., Fernhall, B., & Plowman, S.A. (1990) Effects of music on exercise performance. *J Cardiopul Rehab,* 10, 312-316.

[62] Simpson, S.D., & Karageorghis, C.I. (2006) The effects of synchronous music on 400-m sprint performance. *J Sports Sci*, 24, 1095-1102.

[63] Szabo, A., Small, A., & Leigh, M. (1999) The effects of slow- and fast-rhythm classical music on progressive cycling to voluntary physical exhaustion. *J Sports Med Phys Fit*, 39, 220-225.

[64] Szmedra, L., & Bacharach, D.W. (1998) Effect of music on perceived exertion, plasma lactate, norepinephrine and cardiovascular hemodynamics during treadmill running. *Intl J Sports Med*, 19, 32-37.

[65] Thaut, M.H., Davis, W.B. (1993) The influence of subject-selected versus experimenter-chosen music on affect, anxiety, and relaxation. *J Music Ther*, 30, 210–223.

[66] Thomas, C., Perrey, S., Ben Saad, H., Delage, M., Dupuy, A.M., Cristol, J.P., & Mercier, J. (2007) Effects of a supplementation during exercise and recovery. *Intl J Sports Med,* 28, 703-712.

[67] van Hall, G., MacLean, D.A., Saltin, B., & Wagenmakers, A.J. (1996) Mechanisms of activation of muscle branched-chain alpha-keto acid dehydrogenase during exercise in man. *J Phys*, 494, 899-905.

[68] Vukovich, M.D., Sharp, R.L., King, D.S. & Kershishnik, K. (1992) The effect of protein supplementation on lactate accumulation during submaximal and maximal exercise. *Intl J Sport Nut*, 2, 307-316.

[69] Wagenmakers, A.J. (1998) Muscle amino acid metabolism at rest and during exercise: role in human physiology and metabolism. *Exerc Sport Sci Rev*, 26, 287-314.

[70] Willson, J., Torry, M.R., Decker, M.J., Kernozek, T., & Steadman, J.R. (2001) Effects of walking poles on lower extremity gait mechanics. *Med Sci Sports and Exerc*, 33, 142-147.

In: Advances in Strength and Conditioning Research
Editor: Michael Duncan and Mark Lyons

ISBN: 978-1-60692-909-4
© 2009 Nova Science Publishers, Inc.

Chapter 7

POWER IN RESISTANCE EXERCISE

James L. Nuzzo[1], Prue Cormie[2] and Jeffrey M. McBride[3]*
[1]Slippery Rock University, Slippery Rock, PA, USA
[2]Edith Cowan University, Perth, Australia
[3]Appalachian State University, Boone, NC, USA

ABSTRACT

The ability of an athlete to generate high power outputs appears to be related to athletic performance and success in athletics. Additionally, improvements in power output as a result of resistance training have been found to coincide with improvements in measures of athletic performance. Thus, determining the optimal way to train for increased power has been of interest to many sports scientists. However, due to the various methodologies employed in investigations which assess the load-power relationships for various multi-joint resistance exercises, the optimal way to train for increased power has recently been debated. The purposes of this review are to: (1) discuss methodological considerations when quantifying power, (2) discuss recent findings regarding the load-power relationships and the optimal loads for maximal power in various multi-joint exercises, (3) discuss effective ways to train for increased power, and (4) discuss future considerations for studying power.

Keywords: kinetics, kinematics, force, velocity, jump squat

The desire of strength and conditioning professionals to improve power output (power = force × velocity) in athletes most likely stems from evidence which has (1) discovered that power is an important attribute in determining athletic ability and predicting success in athletics [5, 12, 22, 71, 76], and (2) demonstrated that improvements in power output occur concurrently with improvements in measures of dynamic athletic performance such as vertical jump height [17, 41, 62] and sprint times [41, 62]. Much recent scientific

---
* Please address correspondence and requests for reprints to James L. Nuzzo, Department of Exercise and Rehabilitative Science, Slippery Rock University, Slippery Rock, PA 16057, USA or e mail james.nuzzo@sru.edu.

investigation has been focused on defining the load-power relationships of various resistance exercises with hopes of providing insight as to the optimal way to train for improved power. A recent infatuation in the literature regarding power output in resistance exercise has been to identify the load which elicits maximal power. However, due to components of study methodology such as the loading spectrums used, the methods used for load determination, the different kinetic and kinematic tools used in quantify power, the influence of body mass on calculations of power, the specific resistance exercises assessed, and the training histories and maximal strength levels of the subjects studied, debate still exists regarding the load-power relationships and the optimal load for power in resistance exercise. Furthermore, debate also exists regarding the most effective ways to train for improved power production.

The purposes of this review are to: (1) discuss the methodological considerations when quantifying power, (2) discuss recent findings regarding the load-power relationships and the optimal loads for maximal power in various multi-joint exercises, (3) discuss effective ways to train for increased power, and (4) discuss future considerations for studying power.

METHODOLOGICAL CONSIDERATIONS FOR ASSESSING POWER

The Loading Spectrum

Power must be assessed across a spectrum of loads in order to properly identify the load that maximizes power production (i.e. the optimal load), to identify appropriate load intensities for power training, and to assess the effectiveness of training programs on power enhancement. A complete loading spectrum would require subjects to perform an exercise at a zero load condition (i.e. high velocity and low force), a maximal load condition (i.e. low velocity and high force), and various loading conditions between the zero and maximal load conditions. An example loading spectrum may consist of the following loads: 0 (i.e. no external load), 20, 40, 60, 80, and 100 % of a one-repetition maximum (1RM) [18].

The implementation of a complete loading spectrum is essential when attempting to identify the optimal load for maximal power production. In previous investigations, some researchers have identified the optimal load for power as the lightest load which was studied [37, 47, 80, 82]; however, the absence of lighter loads in these studies leads to speculation as to whether the true optimal load was actually identified. Implementing a complete loading spectrum can also be important for identifying appropriate load intensities for power training. Incomplete loading spectrums, which typically involve the absence of loads at either the high velocity or high force portions of the load-power relationship, may not properly identify loads in which power production is significantly reduced from the optimal load. The absence of this data may fail to provide practitioners with valuable information regarding a range of loads which may be used in training sessions to elicit moderate to high power outputs.

When creating an athlete profile or assessing the effectiveness of training programs on power, assessing power across a complete loading spectrum can provide valuable information regarding the strengths and weaknesses of the athlete or program. For the individual athlete, deficiencies in power with lighter loads may indicate a need for more high velocity training, while deficiencies in power at heavier loads may indicate a need for more high force, heavy resistance training. Such data can be extremely valuable for subsequent training prescriptions as previous studies have found that different portions of the load-power relationship are trainable based on the loading intensity used in training [17, 50, 65, 83, 84] (Figure 1). Similarly, groups of athletes can be averaged together to assess pre- and post-training power output [17] and these data may inform strength and conditioning coaches about the strengths and weaknesses of their training programs.

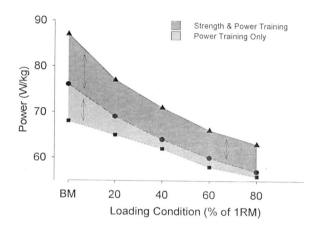

Figure 1. A theoretical load-power relationship in comparison to baseline testing (■ –dotted line) after strength and power training (▲-solid line) or power training only (●-dashed line).

Load Determination

When determining the loading spectrum for the load-power relationship of multi-joint exercises, studies have implemented loads based on a dynamic 1RM [4, 6, 18, 40, 47, 51, 59, 61, 65, 68, 75, 76, 80, 82]. In exercises such as the bench press and bench press throw, load determination based on a 1RM appears to be appropriate because of the relatively small limb masses (i.e. forearm + upper-arm mass) which, in addition to the 1RM load, are moved during the 1RM test. However, in exercises such as the back squat and jump squat, loads which are calculated based solely on a 1RM may not be appropriate because the majority of the body mass must also be lifted during the 1RM and subsequent squat and jump squat power tests. Ultimately, the resulting force, velocity, and power measurements are determined by an athlete's ability to accelerate the total system mass (i.e., external load + body mass). Thus, calculating loads from an individual's maximal dynamic strength (MDS) (MDS = 1RM + [body mass - shank mass]), as opposed to a 1RM, appears to be more applicable for the squat and jump squat [18-20, 69]. Recently, the question has been posed as to whether to include the entire body mass in the MDS calculation for load determination, or if the body mass minus the shank and foot mass (a portion equivalent to 12% of body mass [15] should be utilized [19, 31]. It is theorized that excluding the shank and foot mass is the most valid practice due to the fact that the shanks and feet remain in a relatively static position during the concentric phase of most athletic movements and especially during the squat and jump squat [31]. Therefore, the MDS calculation is appropriate for the squat and jump squat, and subsequently, loading conditions can be determined as a percentage of MDS [18-20, 69].

MDS derived loads can later be expressed as a percentage of a 1RM to provide comparable loading spectrums with previous investigations [18, 69]. Additionally, it should be noted that initial calculations based on MDS are also important because they help to establish comparable loading spectrums for subjects with varied squat 1RM-to-body mass ratios [69].

Data Collection and Analysis Techniques

Throughout the literature the identification of the load that maximizes power output in investigations involving *in vitro* study of muscle fibers [8, 85] and single-joint movements [50] has been rather consistent. However, investigations of dynamic, multi-joint exercises have reported considerably different results (e.g. the optimal load in the jump squat has been reported to range from 0% [18] to 59% of a 1RM [4]). The discrepancies between these previous investigations may be associated with various factors but the most predominant factor appears to be the data collection and analysis techniques utilized when assessing such movements.

The methods commonly used in strength and power research to examine power output involve: (1) a force plate (FP), (2) a position transducer (PT), or (3) the combination of force plate and position transducer(s) (FP+PT). The use of a FP to calculate power from vertical ground reaction forces is a method commonly utilized in strength and power research to compare various types of body weight jumps or monitor vertical jump performance following an intervention [13, 25, 27, 29, 36, 37, 44, 51, 57, 61, 62, 74]. Several investigations have utilized this methodology to examine the load-power relationship in the squat [72], jump squat [62], and the power clean [37, 43, 51]. The FP methodology relies on the impulse-momentum relationship to determine velocity and thus allows for power to be calculated through a forward dynamics approach. Previous research has also utilized equipment that measures displacement to determine power output, the most common of which is the linear position transducer but also includes rotary encoders, chronoscopic light systems, infrared light systems (all referred to as 'PT' for the purpose of this review) [2, 4, 5, 7, 9, 23, 32, 33, 40, 47-49, 72, 75, 76, 77, 81, 86, 87] The PT systems utilize inverse dynamics in order to determine power output solely from kinematic data. Specifically, velocity is calculated through the differentiation of displacement data with respect to time (velocity = displacement/time). Double differentiation of the displacement data allows for the determination of acceleration (acceleration = velocity/time), which is in turn utilized to determine force (force = system mass [acceleration + acceleration due to gravity]). Additionally the combination of a FP and PT (or similar device) is commonly used throughout the literature to examine power output during jumping movements [9, 16-21, 55, 61, 62, 88], weightlifting movements [18, 20, 42, 89] and bench press movements [66-68]. The majority of research involving the combination of a FP and PT incorporates information obtained from a FP and a single PT [55, 66-68, 61-62, 88] but more recently a FP and two PTs have been utilized to assess both vertical and horizontal displacement during multi-dimensional movements [16-21, 60, 63, 69]. This measurement system is typically arranged to collect displacement and force data simultaneously at equal frequencies allowing for the determination of power output (power = force · [displacement/time]).

Recent investigations have compared the validity of the primary data collection and analysis methodologies [14, 16, 20, 24, 42, 43] and their impact on the load-power relationship in various movements [16, 20]. Some comparisons between displacement based modalities (i.e. PT) and a FP have reported no difference in force data during jumping movements [14, 24] or power data during concentric half squats [72]. However, these investigations are in contrast to more comprehensive analyses which have examined differences throughout a loading spectrum and compared the PT and FP methodologies to the FP+PT technique [16, 20, 43]. The most comprehensive analysis to date has established that significant and meaningful differences in power values (both peak and mean power) exist depending on the methodological procedures utilized and that these differences affect the load-power relationship in the squat, jump squat, and power clean [20]. Specifically, PT methodologies relying solely on kinematic data consistently elevate power output across various loads in the squat, jump squat, and power clean in comparison to the FP+PT methodologies [20]. Furthermore, when compared to the FP+PT method, the FP technique under-represents velocity and power output during the squat, jump squat, and more prominently during movements involving the bar traveling independently of the body such as the power clean [20]. The practical importance of this research is that differences in power output were calculated by the different data collection techniques, and as a result, the load-power relationships in the squat and the power clean were defined incorrectly [20].

The large discrepancies in the identification of an optimal load for power in resistance exercises such as the jump squat [5, 7, 13, 18, 25, 29, 40, 57, 61, 69, 76, 82] and the impact of various collection and analysis techniques on the load-power relationship [20] highlight the need for a standardization of methodological procedures used to assess power output. In applied strength and power research the use of a data collection and analysis procedures which measure both kinematic and kinetic components (i.e. PT+FP) are the most appropriate for determining power output in exercises that involve synchronous movement the bar and the body [20, 31]. This is based on the fact that the production of muscular power involves both kinematic (velocity of shortening) and kinetic (force of concentric contraction) components. It is important to note that care must be taken when considering movements involving the bar moving independently of the body (e.g. weightlifting movements), and researchers and practitioners need to consider the aspect of the movements they are most interested in examining and/or monitoring when examining these exercises (e.g. velocity of the barbell versus velocity of the system center of mass in the power clean).

Influence of Body Mass on Power Calculation

A further methodological concern involved with the measurement of power output in dynamic, lower body exercises is the decision to include or exclude the mass of the body in power calculations [31]. Body mass is a primary component of the force contributing to the calculation of power during dynamic, lower body movements. Muscle force must be generated to accelerate the entire system mass (external load + body mass) during lower body movements such as the squat, jump squat, and power clean. Therefore, there is no plausible reason to exclude body mass from the calculation of force and power during the squat, jump squat, and power clean. A recent investigation identified the underestimation of peak power and the misrepresentation of the load-power relationship during the squat, jump squat, and power clean when body mass was excluded from force calculations [19]. With the minimal external load encountered at low intensities, the body mass constitutes a larger relative proportion of the system mass than it does with heavy loads. Therefore, neglecting the contribution of body mass results in a greater reduction in power at light loads simply because the majority of the load and thus force produced was not accounted for [19, 31]. Consequently, if body mass is excluded a proportionally larger error in the force data is evident at lower intensities in comparison with heavy loading conditions. This results in a tendency towards maximal power production occurring at heavier loads regardless of the nature of the movement [19].

THE LOAD-POWER RELATIONSHIP

In order to gain a broader understanding of power training and how it can be utilized to increase athletic performance, information concerning the most effective type of loading to be used for power training is required. Furthermore, information pertaining to power output during various types of exercises as well as how the load-power relationship differs between exercises is necessary. Power output across a series of loads has been evaluated in both single muscle fibers [8] and single sarcomeres [85]. Investigation of single muscle fiber function *in vitro* has demonstrated that a force level equivalent to approximately 26% of maximal isometric force elicited maximal power output in fast twitch muscle fibers (type IIb as classified by myosin heavy chain isoforms) [8]. Furthermore, study of individual muscle fibers in both human and animal models indicate that peak power is obtained at loads considerably below 50% of maximal isometric strength and is correlated with the percentage of fast twitch fibers [26, 30, 35, 73]. Kaneko and associates [50] performed one of the initial studies investigating the load-power relationship during a dynamic movement, the bicep curl. It was reported that using a resistance equal to 30% of maximum isometric strength of the elbow flexors optimized power output. This finding was supported by further investigation of single joint movements examining bicep curls [64, 84] and knee extensions [70]. While consistency regarding the identification of the optimal load exists in investigations involving *in vitro* study of muscle fibers and in single-joint movements, investigations of the optimal load for dynamic, upper- and lower-body resistance exercise have reported differing results.

The Optimal Load for Power

Bench Press and Bench Press Throw

Investigations of power output across a series of loads in the bench press and bench press throw have observed load-power relationships similar to that previously established in single joint movements. Although differences in power output exist between the bench press and bench press throw due to the nature of the movement (i.e. traditional versus ballistic movements [67], a similar range of optimal loads has been observed. The optimal load for power has been observed to be between 30 to 45% of 1RM in the bench press (Table 1) and between 15 to 55% 1RM in the bench press throw (Table 2). As previously discussed, a range in the optimal loads reported throughout the literature could be due to the methodological procedures utilized to collect and analyze power output. Furthermore, the training history of the subjects studied may also be a contributing factor as Izquierdo and associates [47] have reported that different types of athletes maximize bench press power with different loads. Weightlifters and handball players were found to maximize power at 30% of a 1RM while road cyclists, middle-distance runners, and control subjects were found to maximize power at 45% of a 1RM [47]. While a range of optimal loads has been reported for the bench press and bench press throw throughout the literature, the general shape of the load-power relationship in these movements has been established [47, 59, 68, 75, 82]. Further study is required to clarify precisely how the load-power relationship differs between the two movements.

Table 1. Summary of studies regarding the optimal load for power in the bench press

Study	Subjects	Methodology	Loading Spectrum	Optimal Load
Izquierdo et al. [47]*	Male weightlifters (n=11)	PT (Rotary encoder) PT (Rotary encoder)	30 - 100% 1RM	30% 1RM (MP)
	Male handball players (n=19)	PT (Rotary encoder) PT (Rotary encoder)	30 - 100% 1RM	30% 1RM (MP)
	Male road cyclists (n=18)	PT (Rotary encoder)	30 - 100% 1RM	45% 1RM (MP)
	Male middle-distance runners (n=10)		30 - 100% 1RM	45% 1RM (MP)
	Male controls (n=12)		30 - 100% 1RM	45% 1RM (MP)
Mayhew et al. [59]	College-aged males (n=24)	PT (Digital timing system with infrared lights)	30 - 80% 1RM	40% 1RM (PP)
Siegel et al. [75]	College-aged males (n=25)	PT (Chronoscopic timing light system)	30 - 90% 1RM	40% 1RM (PP)

*Concentric phase-only bench press; PT = position transducer; 1RM = one-repetition maximum; MP = mean power; PP = peak power.

Table 2. Summary of studies regarding the optimal load for power in the bench press throw

Study	Subjects	Methodology	Loading Spectrum	Optimal Load
Baker [4]	Professional male rugby players (n=22) College-aged male rugby players (n=27)	PT PT	30 - 59% 1RM 36 - 72% 1RM	51% 1RM (MP) 55% 1RM (MP)
Baker et al. [6]	Professional and semi-professional male rugby players (n=31)	PT	31 - 62% 1RM	55% 1RM (MP)
Newton et al. [68]	Resistance trained males (n=17)	FP + PT	15 - 100% 1RM	30 & 45% 1RM (MP) 15 & 30% 1RM (PP)
Thomas et al. [82]	Male Division I soccer players (n=19) Female Division I soccer players (n=14)	PT PT	30 - 70% 1RM 30 - 70% 1RM	30% 1RM (PP) 30% 1RM (PP)

PT = position transducer; 1RM = one-repetition maximum; PP = peak power; MP = mean power.

Back Squat

The optimal load for power in the back squat has consistently been observed to be between 45 to 60% of a squat 1RM (**Table 3**). Again, this range in the load that maximizes power output may be attributable to a number of factors including the training status of the athlete, methodological procedures utilized and the type of instruction given. Similar to the bench press, Izquierdo and associates [47] have reported that different types of athletes maximize power with different loads in the back squat. Weightlifters and road cyclists were found to maximize power at 45% 1RM while team handball players, middle-distance runners, and control subjects maximized power at 60% 1RM. Using the most valid and reliable assessments of power, Cormie and colleagues [20] demonstrated that back squat power was maximal at approximately 56% of 1RM. In an investigation addressing the issues involved with using different data collection and analysis procedures, Cormie and colleagues [20] discovered that different methodological procedures resulted in the identification of various optimal loads (i.e. 0 - 71% 1RM). Furthermore, different optimal loads were also observed when comparing mean power output and peak power output [20].

Table 3. Summary of studies regarding the optimal load for power in the back squat

Study	Subjects	Methodology	Loading Spectrum	Optimal Load
Cormie et al. [18]	Collegiate male football and track athletes (n=12)	FP + 2-PTs	0 - 85% 1RM	56% 1RM (PP)
Izquierdo et al. [47]*	Male weightlifters (n=11)	PT (Rotary encoder)	30 - 100% 1RM	45% 1RM (MP)
	Male handball players (n=19)	PT (Rotary encoder)	30 - 100% 1RM	60% 1RM (MP)
	Male road cyclists (n=18)	PT (Rotary encoder)	30 - 100% 1RM	45% 1RM (MP)
	Male middle-distance runners (n=10)	PT (Rotary encoder)	30 - 100% 1RM	60% 1RM (MP)
	Male controls (n=12)	PT (Rotary encoder)		60% 1RM (MP)
Siegel et al. [75]	College aged-males (n=25)	PT (Chronoscopic timing light system)	30 - 90% 1RM	60% 1RM (PP)

FP = force plate; PT = position transducers; 1RM = one-repetition maximum; *Concentric phase-only hack squat.
It should be noted that 0% 1RM represents a back squat with no external load (i.e. body mass only).

Jump Squat

Considerable research has been undertaken examining the load-power relationship in jumping movements [5, 7, 13, 18, 25, 29, 40, 57, 61, 69, 76, 80, 82] with these studies reporting conflicting data (Table 4). Loads ranging from 0% of a back squat 1RM (i.e. jumping with no external load, just the load applied by athletes own body mass) [13, 18, 25, 29, 57, 61, 69] up to 59% [4] of a back squat 1RM have been reported to maximize power in the jump squat. The inconsistent results found when studying the jump squat appear to be primarily attributed to the different methodologies used when measuring power output (i.e.

the range of loads examined, how the loading was determined, and the different collection and analysis procedures) but may also be influenced by the training status of the athletes investigated. In the most comprehensive analyses of the jump squat load-power relationship, the optimal load has consistently been reported to occur at 0% 1RM [13, 18, 25, 29, 57, 61, 69] which equates to approximately 30% MDS [18]. These results indicate that the load applied by the mass of the body provides an optimal match between force and velocity such that maximal power is generated. The finding that power is maximized at 0% 1RM is further supported by studies involving the examination of power output at loads lighter than an individual's body mass [13, 57, 69].

Table 4. Summary of studies regarding the optimal load for power in the jump squat

Study	Subjects	Methodology	Loading Spectrum	Optimal Load
Baker & Nance [5]	Professional rugby players (n=20)	PT	40 - 100kg	100kg (MP)
Baker et al. [7]	Professional and semi-professional male rugby players (n=32)	PT	24 - 75% 1RM	55 - 59% 1RM (MP)
Cavagna et al. [13]	Untrained male adults (n=2)	FP	0.15 - 1.77g	1.00g (MP)
Cormie et al. [18]	Collegiate male football and track athletes (n=12)	FP + 2-PTs	0 - 85% 1RM	0% 1RM (PP)
Davies & Young [25]	Male and female children (n=10) Male adults (n=4)	FP FP	0 - 30% BM 0 - 40% BM	0% BM (MP & PP) 0% BM (MP & PP)
Driss et al. [29]	Sedentary male and female adults (n=20) Elite male volleyball players and Olympic weightlifters (n=20)	FP FP	0, 5, and 10kg 0, 5, and 10kg	0kg (MP & PP) 5kg (MP & PP)
Harris et al. [42]	National-level male rugby players (n=18)	PT	10 - 100% 1RM	22% 1RM (PP) 39% 1RM (MP)
Markovic & Jaric [57]	Recreationally-trained college students (n=15)	FP	0.70 - 1.30g	1.00g (MP) 0.70g (PP)
McBride et al. [61]	Male powerlifters (n=8) Male Olympic weightlifters (n=6) Male sprinters (n=6) Male controls (n=8)	FP & FP + PT FP & FP + PT FP & FP + PT FP & FP + PT	0 - 90% 1RM 0 - 90% 1RM 0 - 90% 1RM 0 - 90% 1RM	9% 1RM (PP) 8% 1RM (PP) 0 % 1RM (PP) 12% 1RM (PP)
Nuzzo [69]	Strength-power trained males (1RM/BM = 1.96) (n=14) Untrained males (1RM/BM = 0.94) (n=6)	FP + 2-PTs FP + 2-PTs	-31 - 42% 1RM -77 - 21% 1RM	0% 1RM (MP & PP) 0% 1RM (MP & PP)

Sleivert & Taingahue [76]	College-aged rugby and basketball athletes (n=30)	Accelerometer	30 - 70% 1RM	40% 1RM (MP) 60% 1RM (PP)
Stone et al. [80]	College-aged males (n–20) Strongest (1RM/BM = 2.00) (n=5) Weakest (1RM/BM = 1.21) (n=5)	V-scope V-scope V-scope	10 - 100% 1RM 10 - 100% 1RM 10 - 100% 1RM	10% 1RM (PP) 40% 1RM (PP) 10% 1RM (PP)
Thomas et al. [82]	Collegiate male soccer players (n=19) Collegiate female soccer players (n=14)	PT PT	30 - 70% 1RM 30 - 70% 1RM	30% 1RM (PP) 40% 1RM (PP)

PT = position transducer; MP = mean power; 1RM = one-repetition maximum; FP = force plate; BM = body mass; PP = peak power. It should be noted that 1.00g, 0% 1RM, 0% BM, and 0kg all represent jump squats with no external load (i.e. body mass only).

Variations of the Clean Exercise

The power clean, hang clean, and mid-thigh pull are all variations of the clean exercise in which the load-power relationship has been previously studied (Table 5). The load which maximizes power output in variations of the clean has consistently been reported at 70 to 80% of a 1RM [18, 37, 51, 89]. In contrast, Thomas et al. [82] observed power to be maximal at 40 to 50% of a 1RM. Based on the findings of Cormie et al. [20] which compared the power clean load-power relationship between different data collection and analysis techniques, this contrasting evidence may be attributable to the methodology employed.

Table 5. Summary of studies regarding the optimal load for power in variations of the clean exercise

Study	Subjects	Methodology	Loading Spectrum	Optimal Load
Cormie et al. [18] (PC)	Collegiate male football and track athletes (n=12)	FP + 2-PTs	0 - 90% 1RM	80% 1RM (PP)
Haff et al. [37] (MTP)	Resistance-trained males (n=8)	FP	80 - 100% 1RM	80% 1RM (PP)
Kawamori et al. [51] (HC)	Division II male athletes (n=15)	FP	30 - 90% 1RM	70% 1RM (PP & MP)
Thomas et al. [82] (MTP)	Collegiate male soccer players (n=19) Collegiate female soccer players (n=14)	PT PT	30 - 70% 1RM 30 - 70% 1RM	40 - 50% 1RM (PP) 40 - 50% 1RM (PP)
Winchester et al. [89] (PC)	Division III male athletes (n=18)	FP + Videography	50 - 90% 1RM	70% 1RM (PP)

PC = power clean; FP = force plate; PT = position transducer; BM = body mass, 1RM = one-repetition maximum; PP = peak power; MTP = mid-thigh pull; HC = hang clean; MP = mean power.

Maximal Strength and the Load-Power Relationship

Recently it has been suggested that training histories and levels of maximal strength may change the shape of the load power relationship and further specify the load which maximizes power during various exercises [3, 4, 29, 47, 80]. It has been observed that athletes who have high 1RM-to-body mass ratios as a result of extensive strength and power training, may be able to generate maximal power output under conditions of external loading [80]. It has been demonstrated by Stone and colleagues [80] that subjects with back squat 1RM-to-body mass ratios of 2.00 produced peak power at a load equal to 40% of 1RM while subjects with a back squat 1RM-to-body mass ratio of 1.21 produced peak power at the lightest load studied (i.e. 10% of 1RM). In addition, when comparing competitive power-trained athletes to sedentary individuals, the power-trained athletes did not exhibit any significant decrements in power output as they were loaded from body mass to body mass + 5kg and body mass + 10kg [29]. The sedentary individuals, however, produced significantly less power when they were loaded with an additional 5 and 10kg [29]. Thus, these data suggest that increased maximal strength levels, as a result of the neuromuscular adaptations which occur from previous strength-power training, may help in attenuating the decrease in jump squat velocity which typically occurs as a result of external loading. However, data opposing these results have been reported in regard to the effects of maximal strength on jump squat power output [3, 40, 69]. Both Baker et al. [3] and Harris et al. [40] have reported that stronger athletes produced maximal power at lighter loads when compared to subjects with lower levels of maximal strength. However, numerous issues regarding the validity of the methodological procedures utilized in these two investigations have been raised in the literature [20, 31, 42]. In a more recent investigation, which utilized methodological procedures widely accepted throughout the literature, Nuzzo [69] reported that the optimal load was the same for strength-power trained subjects (back squat 1RM-to-body mass ratio of 1.96 ± 0.24) and untrained subjects (back squat 1RM-to-body mass ratio of 0.94 ± 0.18). Further study is required to clarify the role of maximal strength levels and training backgrounds on the load-power relationship in various resistance exercises.

TRAINING FOR POWER

Several investigations have demonstrated strong relationships between power production and athletic ability [4, 5, 12, 22, 71, 76], and other investigations have demonstrated concurrent improvements in power output and measures of athletic performance after training [17, 41, 62]. Thus, training to improve power output in athletes has been the desire of many sport scientists and coaches. However, due to the debate regarding the load which maximizes power output in multi-joint exercises, and the exercises which elicit the greatest power outputs, a consensus on the optimal way to train for improved power has yet to be reached. While an entire book could be dedicated to the topic of training for power, a brief discussion of the literature pertaining to the impact of training loads and exercise selection will be raised in this review. The role of plyometrics in training for improved power will also be briefly discussed.

Load Selection

Training at the Optimal Load

In one of the first investigations examining the effect of specific-load power training, Kaneko and associates [50] discovered that training at the load that maximized power output in the biceps curl (30% of maximal force) had the greatest training effect on maximal power output when compared to training at 0, 60, or 90% of maximal force. Consequently, Wilson and associates [88] applied this data to a jump squat model and compared programs involving jump squat training at 30% of back squat 1RM, traditional resistance training using loads equivalent to a 6 - 10RM, and plyometric training involving drop jumps. It was observed that subjects who trained at 30% of a 1RM had the best overall results in dynamic athletic performance (vertical jump height, 30-m sprint time, 6-s cycle peak power, and isokinetic leg extension peak torque). However, due to the methodological considerations discussed earlier, a load equal to 0% 1RM (i.e. body mass) and not 30% of a 1RM has subsequently been identified as the optimal load for maximal power in the jump squat [13, 18, 25, 29, 57, 61, 69]. Cormie and colleagues [17] later observed that jump squat training at body mass was also effective in significantly improving dynamic athletic performance as measured by vertical jump height. Although the exact mechanisms underlying superior adaptations after training with a specific load remain unidentified, it is theorized that the optimal load provides a unique stimulus due to specific adaptations in neural activation patterns [39, 50, 62]. Since adaptations are most pronounced at the load used in training, the optimal load provides the best stimulus to elicit the physiological changes necessary to increase maximal power output. While the scientific evidence illustrates that training at the optimal load does appear to be the most effective for improving maximal power output over short-term interventions, this does not necessarily mean that training at that the optimal load is the best way or the only way to increase power over a long-term training program. Furthermore, this research has been conducted using homogenous groups of moderately trained subjects and does not take into consideration the training histories of the athletes, their individual strengths and weaknesses, or the specific requirements of their sports.

Training with a Spectrum of Loads

Power output can be improved through improvements in either force or velocity as well as a combination of both (power = force × velocity). Thus, it seems logical that combined strength and power training programs, which incorporate training intensities across a spectrum of forces and velocities, would be effective for improving power output. Investigations using the biceps model have demonstrated that when two combined training methods were compared (0 + 30% max force training vs. 30 + 90% max force training), the 30 + 90% group received the greatest overall improvements in power production across the loading spectrum [84]. Furthermore, when comparing three combined training groups (30 + 60% max force vs. 30 + 100% max force vs. 30 + 60 + 100% max force), it was demonstrated that the 30 + 60 + 100% max force group had the greatest overall improvements in power output across the loading spectrum [83]. Similar to studies using the biceps model, combined strength-power training has been observed to be effective in multi-joint exercises [17, 41]. Harris and associates [41] compared three training programs over a period of 9 weeks: high force (80-85% of back squat 1RM), high power (30% of back squat 1RM), and a combined high force-high power group. After 9 weeks, the combined training group demonstrated significant improvements in various measures of maximal strength and lower-body power, as well as vertical jump height and 10 meter sprint time. Both the high-force group and high-power group, on the other hand, only improved significantly in a select number of tests. Similarly, Cormie and associates [17] compared a power training group (jump squats at 0% 1RM) and a combined strength-power training group (jump squats at 0% 1RM + back squats at 90% of a 1RM) over a 12 week training program which was equated for work. It was discovered that the combined strength-power training program was the most effective in improving performance across the entire load-force, load-velocity, load-power, and load-jump height relationships. This research indicates that utilizing a variety of loads during power training or combined strength and power training produces all-round improvements across the load-power relationship as well as improving maximal power output. However, these findings are limited to recreationally and/or moderately trained individuals and short training interventions (i.e. 9 – 12 weeks), thus it is unclear how power training with a spectrum of loads influence performance improvements in athletes with various strength levels and training histories.

Specific Load Selection

Prior to the prescription of a training program designed to improve power, the training status and the individual strengths and weaknesses of the athlete should be taken into consideration. As mentioned earlier, it has been demonstrated that velocity-specific adaptations to the load-power relationship occur following power training [17, 50, 62, , 65, 83, 84]. Therefore, specific areas of the load-power curve can be trained (e.g. Figure 1). Consideration should also be given to the specific velocities and loads which are encountered by the athlete during sport competition.

Resistance Exercise Selection

The ability to produce power in multi-joint exercises is dependent on the nature of the movement involved; thus, the exercises selected for power training may influence the type and magnitude of performance improvements and physiological adaptations observed. It is well established throughout the literature that the bench press throw is the upper-body movement that elicits the greatest power outputs [6, 7, 68, 67, 68, 82] and is therefore a very effective exercise to utilize to improve muscular power of the upper-body. However, a number of movements can be utilized for improving muscular power in the lower-body. The back squat, jump squat, and variations of the clean exercise all elicit large power outputs due to the nature of the movements and the involvement of several large muscle groups.

Back Squat

While the back squat has been shown to elicit high power outputs, both the jump squat and the power clean elicit significantly greater power output throughout the loading spectrum [18]. Therefore, power training at the optimal load in the squat would not be the most effective use of this exercise. However, the back squat, in addition to other traditional knee extensor exercises, has been found to increase muscle cross-sectional area and muscular strength of the quadriceps when moderate to heavy loads ($\geq$ 70% 1RM) are used in training [11]. Thus, the role of the back squat in a training program may not be for the direct benefit in eliciting high power outputs, but instead for its ability to indirectly increase power through improvements in muscle cross-sectional area and force output.

Jump Squat

Unlike the back squat, the jump squat is a ballistic movement that requires athletes to accelerate the load throughout the entire concentric phase in order to attain maximal jump height. As a result, high forces can be generated under light loads in the jump squat. When the high forces are coupled with the high movement velocities achievable under light loading conditions, the ballistic nature of the jump squat allows for very high power outputs which are almost double that of the back squat [18]. This is supported by comparisons between lower-body exercises which have reported that the greatest maximal power outputs are elicited by the jump squat [18, 51, 52, 37]. Thus, the jump squat may be the most specific power training exercise for athletes who are required to produce high velocities against light loads (e.g. sprinters and jumpers). Furthermore, examination of the load-power relationship reveals that high power outputs are sustainable throughout the loading spectrum [18, 61, 69, 80, 82]. Therefore, jump squats are an ideal exercise to include in power training programs to improve maximal power output as well as power output across a variety of loads.

Power Clean

The inherent high force, high velocity nature of weightlifting exercises creates the potential for these movements to produce large power outputs across a variety of different loading conditions. Weightlifting movements such as the power clean have been previously suggested to elicit the highest power outputs of all lower body movements [38, 79]. However, comparison of the load-power relationship between the power clean and jump squat have illustrated a trend in which power output is greater for weightlifting movements under heavy loading conditions only (i.e. 80-90% 1RM [18]). Based on these findings, weightlifting movements such as the power clean are ideal power training exercises for athletes who are required to generate high velocities against heavy loads (e.g. football linemen). Thus, the nature of weightlifting movements coupled with the specificity of their movement patterns to numerous athletic activities, creates the potential for the power clean and other weightlifting movements to be very effective power training exercises when heavy loads (i.e. $\geq$ 70% 1RM) are utilized [18, 37, 51].

Plyometrics

A plyometric exercise consists of an explosive movement pattern which involves some level of pre-stretch or pre-load of the muscle and ultimately results in a stretch-shortening cycle of the muscle-tendon unit [45, 46]. The drop or depth jump has been a popular lower-body plyometric exercise included in power training programs [1, 28, 53, 54, 58, 78]. This exercise requires an individual to drop to the ground surface from a fixed box height, and upon making ground contact, immediately perform a vertical jump. The drop jump, at a box height equal to maximal countermovement jump height, has been found elicit significantly greater power outputs when compared to both static jumps and regular countermovement jumps [60]. Increased power outputs in the drop jump may be attributed to the unique role of muscle pre-activation which occurs prior to ground contact [46, 60, 63]. It appears that this preparatory activation of the muscle is used to stiffen the muscle upon ground contact, and subsequently cause an increase in the use of stored elastic energy in the tendon [45, 46].

Plyometric training programs which have included the drop jump, in addition to other plyometric exercises (e.g. hopping, bounding, hurdle jumps, and split squat jumps), have been successful at significantly improving lower-body power output [54] and vertical jump height [1, 28, 53, 54, 58, 78] after 6 to 12 weeks of training. Additionally, it appears that the effect of plyometric training on vertical jump height is augmented when lower-body resistance training is performed concurrently [1]. Adams and associates [1] implemented three training programs with recreationally-active male subjects: squat training (periodized back squat training with loads of 50 to 100% 1RM), plyometric training (drop jumps, double leg hops, and split squat jumps), and squat + plyometric training. After the interventions, the squat + plyometric group demonstrated a 10.7cm improvement in vertical jump height, while the squat and plyometric groups demonstrated improvements of 3.3 and 3.8cm, respectively [1].

The exact physiological and biomechanical mechanisms which cause improvements in power and jump height after plyometric training are still being studied. It seems plausible that improvements in jump height after plyometric training could be the result of increased pre-activation of the agonist muscle groups and/or changes in the mechanical properties of the actual muscle-tendon complex. One recent investigation has discovered that increased jump height after 12 weeks of unilateral plyometric training was not the result of increased pre-activation but instead was the result of enhanced mechanical properties of the muscle-tendon unit and joint stiffness [53]. Other studies have discovered increased power outputs of single skeletal muscle fibers [56] and increased tendon stiffness [10] after plyometric training programs. Although there is not yet a consensus regarding the mechanisms behind improved performance after plyometric training, recent advancements with *in vivo* measurement techniques in the field of biomechanics (e.g. ultrasonography and optic fiber) now give scientists the opportunity to quantify changes in muscle fascicle length and tendon length during plyometric exercises [34, 45, 46], as well as tendon stiffness after the completion of plyometric training programs [10, 53]. Ultimately, these measurement techniques may help to answer questions regarding the role of plyometrics in training programs and their subsequent role in training for power and improved athletic performance.

FUTURE CONSIDERATIONS

To date, most investigations regarding power have reported either peak or mean power. Peak power represents the single greatest data point of power production on the power-time curve, and the mean or average power would represent the total power created divided by the time with which it took to create that power. Typically, mean power is calculated over the concentric phase of an exercise. While these variables are important indicators of power output, they are limited in their ability to delineate the exact nature and timing of changes following training interventions, differences between subject populations, and/or loading conditions *throughout the entire movement*. The most recent advancement in the analysis of power output has been temporal phase analysis of power output throughout entire movements [21]. This technique uses custom-designed computer programs, to combine all individual power-time curves into one representative average power-time curve. Typically, the absolute time it takes for a group of individuals to complete a jump is different, and thus, their power-time curves cannot be added together and later expressed as an average. However, through a re-sampling procedure which interpolates 500 samples of data from each of the original power-time curves (i.e. from the start of the eccentric phase to the point at which the individual leaves the ground), all subjects' re-sampled power-time curves can be expressed on the same relative time scale (0-100% normalized time). Subsequently, since all individual power-time curves are on the same relative time scale, they can be added together and averaged to produce a single average curve for that group of individuals. Statistical analysis can then be used to detect significant differences in power in specific portions of the movement. Comparisons can be made before and after training interventions, between loading conditions, and also across different groups of subjects. Research using average curve analysis in the field of strength and conditioning is limited [21]; however, the analysis of power output throughout the entire movement may provide novel insights into the differences between athletic populations, the nature of adaptations to power training, and the mechanisms involved in improving power output.

While much research has previously examined power output in strength and conditioning applications, there are still many questions that remained unanswered. Specifically, further investigation is required to elucidate if and how the load-power relationship of various movements changes between athletes with different training histories, across different phases of training and competition, and in response to various training interventions. Additionally, the mechanisms which elicit performance changes as a result of power training should be expanded upon. Furthermore, it is imperative that future research, which is designed to answer these questions, is conducted with appropriate methodology for assessing power in light of the current issues which have been presented in the literature.

CONCLUSION

Improving power output in athletes is a training goal of strength and conditioning coaches because of the relationships between power production and athletic ability [4, 5, 12, 22, 71, 76], and the concurrent improvements in power output and athletic performance after training [17, 41, 62]. Numerous investigations have attempted to determine the optimal load for maximal power in various multi-joint exercises; however, many of these studies suffer from methodological flaws when measuring power across the loading spectrum. Recent evidence has clearly demonstrated that power should be evaluated across a complete loading spectrum and that the measurement of power in scientific investigations should include both kinetic and kinematic measurement devices in order to attain valid and reliable data [16, 20, 42]. In order to further advance the study of power output it will be necessary for scientists to standardize methodology when measuring power.

Based on the current literature it appears that bench press power is maximal at a load equal to 30-45% of a bench press 1RM, bench press throw power is maximal at 30-55% of a bench press 1RM, back squat power is maximal at 45-60% of a back squat 1RM, jump squat power is maximal 0% of back squat 1RM (i.e. at body mass), and variations of the clean exercise elicit maximal power at 70-80% of a 1RM. However, the identification of an optimal load should be viewed from a biomechanical perspective and not necessarily a training perspective. The optimal load demonstrates an acute situation in which the neuromuscular system is most efficient at developing power. This does not necessarily indicate that training at the optimal load is the most beneficial way or the only way to train for increased power output for various types of athletes over long-term training periods. Recent investigations have demonstrated that overall improvements in power output are a result of combined strength and power training programs which involve multi-joint exercises across a complete loading spectrum including body mass jumping activities and heavy resistance training. Future research should attempt to understand the specific physiological and biomechanical mechanisms which affect the production of power and the adaptations demonstrated after participation in power training programs. Furthermore, future research regarding power in resistance exercise should attempt to use both the standard load-power relationship and temporal phase analysis techniques to assess specific strengths and weaknesses amongst athletes with different training histories and on-field demands, as well as to evaluate the adaptations to power training.

REFERENCES

[1]   Adams, K., O'Shea, J.P., O'Shea, K.L. & Climstein, M. (1992) The effect of six weeks of squat, plyometric and squat-plyometric training on power production. *J of Appl Sport Sci Res*, 6, 36-41.

[2]   Alemany, J. A., Pandorf, C.E., Montain, S.J., Castellani, J.W., Tuckow, A.P., & Nindl, B.C. (2005) Reliability assessment of ballistic jump squats and bench throws. *J Strength Cond Res*, 19, 33-38.

[3]   Baker, D. (2001a) A series of studies on the training of high-intensity muscle power in rugby league football players. *J Strength Cond Res*, 15, 98-209.

[4]   Baker, D. (2001b) Comparison of upper-body strength and power between professional and college-aged rugby league players. *J Strength Cond Res*, 15, 30-35.

[5]   Baker, D., & Nance, S. (1999) The relation between running speed and measures of strength and power in professional rugby players. *J Strength Cond Res*, 13, 230-235.

[6]   Baker, D., Nance, S. & Moore, M. (2001a) The load that maximizes the average mechanical power output during explosive bench press throws in highly trained athletes. *J Strength Cond Res*, 15, 20-24.

[7]   Baker, D., Nance, S. & Moore, M. (2001b) The load that maximizes the average mechanical power output during jump squats in power-trained athletes. *J Strength Cond Res*, 15, 92-97.

[8]   Bottinelli, R., Pellegrino, M.A., Canepari, M., Rossi, R. & Reggiani, C. (1999) Specific contributions of various muscle fibre types to human muscle performance: an in vitro study. *J Electromyogr Kinesiol, 9*, 87-95.

[9]   Bourque, P. J. Determinants of load at peak power during maximal effort squat jumps in endurance and power trained athletes. Doctoral Dissertation, University of New Brunswick, Fredericton, Canada.

[10] Burgess, K.E., Connick, M.J., Graham-Smith, P. & Pearson, S.J. (2007) Plyometric vs. isometric training influences on tendon properties and muscle output. *J Strength Cond Res*, 21, 986-989.

[11] Campos, G.E.R., Luecke, T.J., Wendeln, H.K., Toma, K., Hagerman, F.C., Murray, T.F., Ragg, K.E., Ratamess, N.A., Kraemer, W.J. & Staron, R.S. (2002) Muscular adaptations in response to three different resistance-training regimens: specificity of repetition maximum training zones. *Eur J Appl Physiol*, 88, 50-60.

[12] Carlock, J.M., Smith, S.L., Hartman, M.J., Morris, R.T., Ciroslan, D.A., Pierce, K.C., Newton, R.U., Harman, E.A., Sands, W.A. & Stone, M.H. (2004) The relationship between vertical jump power estimates and weightlifting ability: a field-test approach. *J Strength Cond Res*, 18, 534-539.

[13] Cavagna, G.A., Zamboni, A., Faraggiana, T. & Margaria, R. (1972) Jumping on the moon: power output at different gravity values. *Aerospace Med*, 43, 408-414.

[14] Chiu, L. Z. F., Schilling, B.K., Fry, A.C. & Weiss, L.W. (2004) Measurement of resistance exercise force expression. *J Appl Biomech*, 20, 204-212.

[15] Clauser, C. E., McConville, J.T. & Young, J.W. (1969) Weight, volume, and center of mass of segments of human body. (Report No. AMRL-TR-69-70). Dayton, OH: Wright-Patterson Air Force Base, Aerospace Medical Research Laboratory.

[16] Cormie, P., Deane, R. & McBride, J.M. (2007a) Methodological concerns for determining power output in the jump squat. *J Strength Cond Res*, 21, 424-430.

[17] Cormie P., McCaulley, G.O. & McBride, J.M. (2007b) Power versus strength-power jump squat training: Influence on the load-power relationship. *Med Sci Sports Exerc*, 39, 996-1003.

[18] Cormie, P., McCaulley, G.O., Triplett, N.T. & McBride, J.M. (2007c) Optimal loading for maximal power output during lower-body resistance exercises. *Med Sci Sports Exerc,* 39, 340-349.

[19] Cormie, P., McBride, J.M. & McCaulley, G.O. (2007d) The influence of body mass on calculation of power during lower-body resistance exercises. *J Strength Cond Res, 21,* 1042-1049.

[20] Cormie, P., McBride, J.M. & McCaulley, G.O. (2007e) Validation of power measurement techniques in dynamic lower body resistance exercises. *J Appl Biomech*, 23, 103-118.

[21] Cormie, P., McBride, J.M. & McCaulley, G.O. (2008) Power-time, force-time, and velocity-time curve analysis during the jump squat: impact of load. *J Appl Biomech*, 24, 112-120.

[22] Cronin, J.B. & Hansen, K.T. (2005) Strength and power predictors of sports speed. *J Strength Cond Res*, 19, 349-357.

[23] Cronin, J. B. & Henderson, M.E. (2004) Maximal strength and power assessment in novice weight trainers. *J Strength Cond Res*, 18, 48-52.

[24] Cronin, J.B., Hing, R.D. & McNair, P.J. (2004) Reliability and validity of a linear position transducer for measuring jump performance. *J Strength Cond Res*, 18, 590-593.

[25] Davies, C.T. & Young, K. (1984) Effects of external loading on short term power output in children and young male adults. *Eur J Appl Physiol Occup Physiol*, 52, 351-354.

[26] de Haan, A., Jones, D.A. & Sargeant, A.J. (1989) Changes in velocity of shortening, power output and relaxation rate during fatigue of rat medial gastrocnemius muscle. *Pflugers Archive: Eur J Physiol*, 413, 422-428.

[27] Delecluse, C., Roelants, M., Diels, R., Koninckx, E. & Verschueren, S. (2005) Effects of whole body vibration training on muscle strength and sprint performance in sprint-trained athletes. *Intl J Sports Med*, 26, 662-668.

[28] de Villarreal, E.S.S., Gonzalez-Badillo, J.J. & Izquierdo, M. (2008) Low and moderate plyometric training frequency produces greater jumping and sprinting gains compared with high frequency. *J Strength Cond Res*, 22, 715-725.

[29] Driss, T., Vandewalle, H., Quievre, J., Miller, C. & Monod, H. (2001) Effects of external loading on power output in a squat jump on a force platform: A comparison between strength and power athletes and sedentary individuals. *J Sports Sci*, 19, 99-105.

[30] Duchateau, J. & Hainaut, K. (1984) Isometric or dynamic training: differential effects on mechanical properties of human muscle. *J Appl Physiol*, 56, 296-3001.

[31] Dugan, E.L., Doyle, T.L.A, Humphries, B., Hasson, C.J. & Newton, R.U. (2004). Determining the optimal load for jump squats: a review of methods and calculations. *J Strength Cond Res*, 18, 668-674.

[32] Esliger, D. W. (2003) The neuromechanics of maximal effort squat jumps. Fredericton: University of New Brunswick.

[33] Falvo, M., Moore, C., Weiss, L., Schilling, B., Ermert, R.C., Fry, A., Wendell, M., Chiu, L., Kumar, S. & LeRoux, C. (2005) Reliability and precision of force, power, and velocity measures obtained during jump squats. In: NSCA National Conference and Exhibition. *Proceedings of the National Strength and Conditioning Association National Conference* (p. 793). Las Vegas, Nevada.

[34] Finni, T., Komi, P.V. & Lepola, V. (2000) In vivo human triceps surae and quadriceps femoris muscle function in a squat jump and countermovement jump. *Eur J Appl Physiol*, 83, 416-426.

[35] Fitts, R. H., McDonald, K.S. & Schluter, J.M. (1991) The determinants of skeletal muscle force and power: their adaptability with changes in activity pattern. *J Biomech*, 24, 111-122.

[36] French, D. N., Gomez, A.L., Volek, J.S., Rubin, M.R., Ratamess, N.A., Sharman, M.J., Gotshalk, L.A., Sebastianelli, W.J., Putukian, M., Newton, R.U., Häkkinen, K., Fleck, S.J. & Kraemer, W.J. (2004) Longitudinal tracking of muscular power changes of NCAA Division I collegiate women gymnasts. *J Strength Cond Res*, 18, 101-107.

[37] Haff, G.G., Stone, M., O'Bryant, H.S., Harmann, E., Dinan, C., Johnson, R. & Han, K. (1997) Force-time dependent characteristics of dynamic and isometric muscle actions. *J Strength Cond Res*, 11, 269-272.

[38] Haff, .G.G., Whitley, A. & Potteiger, J.A. (2001) A brief review: explosive exercise and sports performance. *Strength Cond J*, 23, 13-20.

[39] Häkkinen, K., Komi, P.V. & Alen, M. (1985) Effect of explosive type strength training on isometric force- and relaxation-time, electromyographic and muscle fibre characteristics of leg extensor muscles. *Acta Physiol Scand*, 125, 587-600.

[40] Harris, N.K., Cronin, J.B. & Hopkins, W.G. (2007) Power outputs of a machine squat-jump across a spectrum of loads. *J Strength Cond Res*, 21, 1260-1264.

[41] Harris, G.R., Stone, M.H., O'Bryant, H.S., Proulx, C.M. & Johnson, R.L. (2000) Short-term performance effects of high power, high force, and combined weight-training methods. *J Strength Cond Res*, 14, 14-20.

[42] Hori, N., Newton, R.U., Andrews, W.A., Kawamori, N., McGuigan, M.R. & Nosaka, K. (2007) Comparison of four different methods to measure power output during the hang power clean and the weighted jump squat. *J Strength Cond Res*, 21, 314-320.

[43] Hori, N., Newton, R.U., Nosaka, K. & McGuigan, M.R. (2005) Comparison of system versus barbell force, velocity and power in the hang snatch. *J Strength Cond Res*, 19, e19.

[44] Iossifidou, A., Baltzopoulos, V. & Giakas, G. (2005) Isokinetic knee extension and vertical jumping: are they related? *J Sports Sci*, 23, 1121-1127.

[45] Ishikawa, M., Finni, T. & Komi, P.V. (2003) Behaviour of vastus lateralis muscle-tendon during high intensity SSC exercises *in vivo*. *Acta Physiol Scand*, 178, 205-213.

[46] Ishikawa, M. & Komi, P.V. (2003) Effects of different dropping intensities on fascicle and tendinous tissue behavior during stretch-shortening cycle exercise. *J Appl Physiol*, 96, 842-852.

[47] Izquierdo, M., Hakkinen, K., Gonzalez-Badillo, J.J., Ibanez, J. & Gorostiaga, E.M. (2002) Effect of long-term training specificity on maximal strength and power of the upper and lower extremities in athletes from different sports. *Eur J Appl Physiol*, 87, 264-271.

[48] Izquierdo, M., Häkkinen, K., Ibanez, J., Garrues, M., Anton, A., Zuniga, A., Larrion, J.L. & Gorostiaga, E.M. (2001) Effects of strength training on muscle power and serum hormones in middle-aged and older men. *J Appl Physiol*, 90, 1497-1507.

[49] Izquierdo, M., Ibanez, J., Gorostiaga, E., Garrues, M., Zuniga, A., Anton, A., Larrion, J.L. & Häkkinen, K. (1999) Maximal strength and power characteristics in isometric and dynamic actions of the upper and lower extremities in middle-aged and older men. *Acta Physiol Scand*, 167, 57-68.

[50] Kaneko, M., Fuchimoto, T., Toji, H. & Suei, K. (1983) Training effect of different loads on the force-velocity relationship and mechanical power output in human muscle. *Scand J Sports Sci*, 5, 50-55.

[51] Kawamori, N., Crum, A.J., Blumert, P.A., Kulik, J.R., Childers, J.T., Wood, J.A., Stone, M.H. & Haff, G.G. (2005) Influence of different relative intensities on power output during the hang power clean: identification of the optimal load. *J Strength Cond Res*, 19, 698-708.

[52] Kawamori, N., Rossi, S.J., Justice, B.D., Haff, E.E., Pistilli, E.E., O'Bryant, H.S., Stone, M.H. & Haff, G.G. (2006) Peak force and rate of force development during isometric and dynamic mid-thigh clean pulls performed at various intensities. *J Strength Cond Res*, 20, 482-491.

[53] Kubo, K., Morimoto, M., Komuro, T., Yata, H., Tsunoda, N., Kanehisa, H. & Fukanaga, T. (2007) Effects of plyometric and weight training on muscle-tendon complex and jump performance. *Med Sci Sports Exerc*, 39, 1801-1810.

[54] Luebbers, P.E., Potteiger, J.A., Hulver, M.W., Thyfault, J.P., Carper, M.J. & Lockwood, R.H. (2003) Effects of plyometric training and recovery on vertical jump performance and anaerobic power. *J Strength Cond Res*, 17, 704-709.

[55] Lyttle, A. D., Wilson, G.J. & Ostrowski, K.J. (1996) Enhancing performance: maximal power versus combined weights and plyometrics training. *J Strength Cond Res*, 10, 173-179.

[56] Malisoux, L., Francaux, M., Nielens, H. & Theisen, D. (2006) Stretch-shortening cycle exercises: an effective training paradigm to enhance power output of human single muscle fibers. *J Appl Physiol*, 100, 771-779.

[57] Markovic, G. & Jaric, S. (2007) Positive and negative loading and mechanical output in maximum vertical jumping. *Med Sci Sports Exerc*, 39, 1757-1764.

[58] Markovic, G., Jukic, I., Milanovic, D. & Metikos, D. (2007) Effects of sprint and plyometric training on muscle function and athletic performance. *J Strength Cond Res*, 21, 543-549.

[59] Mayhew, J.L., Ware, J.S., Johns, R.A. & Bemben, M.G. (1997) Changes in upper body power following heavy-resistance strength training in college men. *Intl J Sports Med*, 18, 516-520.

[60] McBride, J.M., McCaulley, G.O. & Cormie, P. (2008) Influence of preactivity and eccentric muscle activity on concentric performance during vertical jumping. *J Strength Cond Res*, 22, 750-757.

[61] McBride, J.M., Triplett-McBride, T., Davie, A. & Newton, R.U. (1999) A comparison of strength and power characteristics between power lifters, Olympic lifters, and sprinters. *J Strength Cond Res*, 13, 58-66.

[62] McBride, J.M., Triplett-McBride, T., Davie, A. & Newton, R.U. (2002) The effect of heavy- vs. light-load jump squats on the development of strength, power, and speed. *J Strength Cond Res*, 16, 75-82.

[63] McCaulley, G.O., Cormie, P., Cavill, M.J., Nuzzo, J.L., Urbiztondo, Z.G. & McBride, J.M. (2007) Mechanical efficiency during repetitive vertical jumping. *Eur J Appl Physiol*, 101, 115-123.

[64] Moritani, T., M. Muro., Ishida, K. & Taguchi, S. (1987) Electro-physiological analyses of the effects of muscle power training. *Res J Phys Ed*, 1, 23-32.

[65] Moss, B.M., Refnes, P.E, Abildgaard, A., Nicolaysen, K. & Jensen, J. (1997) Effects of maximal effort strength training with different loads on dynamic strength, cross-sectional area, load-power, and load-velocity relationships. *Eur J Appl Physiol Occup Physiol*, 75, 193-199.

[66] Newton, R. U. & Kraemer, W.J. (1994) Developing explosive muscle power: Implications for a mixed methods training strategy. *Strength Cond J*, 16, 20-31.

[67] Newton, R. U., Kraemer, W.J., Häkkinen, K., Humphries, B.J. & Murphy, A.J. (1996) Kinematics, kinetics and muscle activation during explosive upper body movements. *J Appl Biomech*, 12, 31-43.

[68] Newton, R.U., Murphy, A.J., Humphries, B.J., Wilson, G., Kraemer, W.J. & Hakkinen, K. (1997) Influence of load and stretch shorten cycle on the kinematics, kinetics and muscle activation that occurs during explosive upper-body movements. *J Appl Physiol Occup Physiol*, 75, 333-342.

[69] Nuzzo, J. (2008) Jump squat power during deloading. Master's Thesis, Appalachian State University, Boone, NC.

[70] Perrine, J. J. & Edgerton, V.R. (1978) Muscle force-velocity and power-velocity relationships under isokinetic loading. *Med Sci Sports*, 10, 159-166.

[71] Peterson, M.D., Alvar, B.A. & Rhea, M.R. (2006) The contribution of maximal force production to explosive movement among young collegiate athletes. *J Strength Cond Res,* 20, 867-873.

[72] Rahmani, A., Viale, F., Dalleau, G. & Lacour, J.R. (2001) Force/velocity and power/velocity relationships in squat exercise. *Eur J Appl Physiol*, 84, 227-232.

[73] Rome, L. C., Funke, R.P., Alexander, R.M., Lutz, G., Aldrige, H., Scott, F. & Freadman, M. (1988) Why animals have different fiber types. *Nature*, 335, 824-827.

[74] Sands, W. A., Smith, L.S., Kivi, D.M., McNeal, J.R., Dorman, J.C., Stone, M.H., & Cormie, P. (2005). Anthropometric and physical abilities profiles: US national skeleton team. *Sports Biomech*, 4, 197-214.

[75] Siegel, J.A., Gilders, R.M., Staron, R.S. & Hagerman, F.C. (2002) Human muscle power output during upper-body and lower-body exercises. *J Strength Cond Res*, 16, 173-178.

[76] Sleivert, G. & Taingahue, M. (2004) The relationship between maximal jump-squat power and sprint acceleration in athletes. *Eur J Appl Physiol*, 91, 46-52.

[77] Smith, W. A., Weiss, L., Moore, C., Schilling, B., Ermert, R.C., Fry, A., Chui, L., Wendell, M. & LeRoux, C. (2005) Reliability and precision of multiple expressions of hang power clean external power. In: NSCA National Conference and Exhibition. *Proceedings of the National Strength and Conditioning Association National Conference*, (p. 804). Las Vegas, Nevada.

[78] Spurrs, R.W., Murphy, A.J. & Watsford, M.L. (2003) The effect of plyometric training on distance running performance. *Eur J Appl Physiol*, 89, 1-7.

[79] Stone, M. H. (1993) Position statement and literature review: Explosive exercises and training. *Nat Strength Cond Assoc J*, 15, 7-15.

[80] Stone, M.H., O'Bryant, H.S., McCoy, L., Coglianese, R., Lehmkuhl, M. & Schilling, B. (2003) Power and maximum strength relationships during performance of dynamic and static weighted jumps. *J Strength Cond Res*, 17, 140-147.

[81] Thomas, M., Fiatarone, M.A. & Fielding, R.A. (1996) Leg power in young women: Relationship to body composition, strength and function. *Med Sci Sports Exerc*, 28, 1321-1326.

[82] Thomas, G.A., Kraemer, W.J., Spiering, B.A., Volek, J.S., Anderson, J.M. & Maresh, C.M. (2007) Maximal power output at different percentages of one repetition maximum: Influence of resistance and gender. *J Strength Cond Res*, 21, 336-342.

[83] Toji, H. & Kaneko, M. (2004) Effect of multiple-load training on the force-velocity relationship. *J Strength Cond Res*, 18, 792-795.

[84] Toji, H., Suei, K. & Kaneko, M. (1997) Effect of combined training loads on relations among force, velocity, and power development. *Can J Appl Physiol*, 22, 328-336.

[85] van Leeuwen, J.L. (1991) Optimum power output and structural design of sarcomeres. *J Ther Biol*, 149, 229–256.

[86] Weiss, L. W., Fry, A.C., Magu, B., Moore, C., Chiu, L., Buchanan, K., Scates, C., Bondurant, B.W., Schilling, B.K. & Henderson, S. (2004) Relative external loads eliciting maximal concentric force and power during non-countermovement squats. In: NSCA National Conference and Exhibition. *Proceedings of the National Strength and Conditioning Association National Conference* (p. 566). Minneapolis, Minnesota.

[87] Weiss, L. W., Moore, C., Schilling, B., Ermert, R.C., Fry, A., Chiu, L., Wendell, M. & LeRoux, C. (2005) Reliability and precision of multiple expressions of hang power

clean bar velocity. In: NSCA National Conference and Exhibition. *Proceedings of the National Strength and Conditioning Association National Conference* (p. 827). Las Vegas, Nevada.

[88] Wilson, G.J., Newton, R.U., Murphy, A.J. & Humphries, B.J. (1993) The optimal training load for the development of dynamic athletic performance. *Med Sci Sports Exerc*, 25, 1279-1286.

[89] Winchester, J.B., Erickson, T.M., Blaak, J.B. & McBride, J.M. (2005) Changes in bar-path kinematics and kinetics after power-clean training. *J Strength Cond Res*, 19, 177-183.

In: Advances in Strength and Conditioning Research   ISBN: 978-1-60692-909-4
Editor: Michael Duncan and Mark Lyons   © 2009 Nova Science Publishers, Inc.

Chapter 8

USING RATINGS OF PERCEIVED EXERTION TO REGULATE EXERCISE INTENSITY DURING RESISTANCE EXERCISE TRAINING IN APPARENTLY HEALTHY ADULTS

Kristen M. Lagally[1]
Illinois State University, IL, USA

ABSTRACT

A growing body of evidence suggests that ratings of perceived exertion (RPE) are related to various physiological markers of resistance exercise intensity, including muscle activity, blood lactic acid concentration, total weight lifted and contraction intensity. The relationship between ratings of perceived exertion and these physiological variables suggests that ratings of perceived exertion can be used to prescribe and monitor resistance exercise intensity. Ratings from the Borg RPE and CR-10 scales are appropriate for regulating resistance exercise intensity, as are ratings from the newer OMNI-Resistance Exercise scale (OMNI-RES). Ratings from these scales can be used as an adjunct or alternative to traditional methods of resistance exercise intensity prescription. Research indicates that differentiated ratings, or ratings made specific to the active muscle, are more appropriate to use during resistance exercise than undifferentiated, or overall body, ratings. To ensure accuracy in rating, participants should be provided with scaling instructions prior to using ratings of perceived exertion to regulate resistance exercise intensity.

Keywords: RPE, OMNI, Weight Training

---

[1] Please address correspondence and requests for reprints to Kristen M. Lagally, Illinois State University, School of Kinesiology and Recreation, Horton Fieldhouse, Campus Box 5120, Normal IL, 67190-5120, USA or e mail kmlagal@ilstu.edu.

Establishing, prescribing and monitoring exercise intensity are the most challenging aspects of exercise programming. The goal is to ensure an intensity that provides a stimulus that is adequate for improving physical fitness, minimizes injury and promotes compliance. During resistance exercise, exercise intensity is typically prescribed as a percentage of the one-repetition maximum (% 1RM) or by selecting a resistance that allows a certain number of repetitions to be performed prior to fatigue (the Repetition Maximum, or RM method). These methods work reasonably well but do have limitations. For recreational exercisers, it is not common for a maximal test to be performed for each resistance exercise. In these cases, it is impossible to prescribe resistance exercise intensity using a percentage of the 1RM. With the RM method, an exerciser has to perform at least one full set of each exercise to know whether or not the weight they have selected is appropriate. This method of intensity selection would need to be repeated whenever strength changes occur.

An alternative to the %1RM and RM methods is to use ratings of perceived exertion (RPE) to prescribe and regulate resistance exercise intensity. Ratings of perceived exertion are commonly used to prescribe and monitor exercise intensity for aerobic exercise, although it is only recently that researchers have begun to investigate the use of ratings of perceived exertion during resistance exercise. Ratings of perceived exertion have been shown to be positively related to various indices of resistance exercise intensity, such as blood lactic acid concentration [10, 11, 21], total weight lifted [20], contraction intensity [12, 18], and muscle activity [6, 9, 12]. For example, Lagally et al. [13] examined perceived exertion responses and muscle activity during the biceps curl exercise performed at 30%, 60% and 90% 1RM. Total work was held constant by varying the number of repetitions performed (i.e. 12, 6 and 4 repetitions, respectively). Perceived exertion increased significantly as intensity increased, even though the total work was the same across all three conditions, indicating a relation between ratings of perceived exertion and contraction intensity (i.e. % 1RM). Furthermore, muscle activity, as measured by electromyography, demonstrated corresponding increases with perceptual responses as resistance exercise intensity increased from 30% to 60% to 90% 1RM.

The links that have been found between ratings of perceived exertion and the aforementioned variables indicate that ratings of perceived exertion provide an assessment of resistance exercise intensity. In Borg's Effort Continua [1], he postulates that when ratings of perceived exertion are shown to be related to physiological variables that provide information about intensity, it follows that ratings of perceived exertion provide similar information about intensity as do the physiological variables. Once a corresponding and interdependent link has been demonstrated between physiological and perceptual responses, ratings of perceived exertion can be considered a valid method of prescribing exercise [1]. The analogy with aerobic exercise would be that ratings of perceived exertion are strongly related to heart rate and oxygen uptake [17], and so ratings of perceived exertion can be used to subjectively monitor aerobic exercise intensity in place of these objective physiological variables. Based on Borg's Effort Continua model and the research that has examined ratings of perceived exertion during resistance exercise, ratings of perceived exertion can be used to regulate and prescribe resistance exercise intensity.

Further evidence supporting the use of ratings of perceived exertion as a method of prescribing intensity during resistance exercise comes from estimation-production protocol research. In perceived exertion research, an estimation-production protocol is the recommended method of examining the validity of using ratings of perceived exertion to prescribe intensity [17]. Lagally & Amorose [16] used a traditional estimation-production protocol, modified for resistance exercise. During estimation, subjects performed a graded resistance exercise test using the knee extension exercise and rated perceived exertion throughout the test. Subjects then returned for a separate production session during which they were asked to select weights that elicited the feelings of exertion associated with a 9, 13, and 17 on the Borg RPE scale. Subjects were unaware of the weight lifted during all sessions. The results indicated that subjects selected weights during the production session that were similar to weights they had lifted in the earlier estimation session at the target rating of perceived exertion values. The conclusion from this study is that ratings of perceived exertion from an estimation session can be used to produce a target intensity during a training session, which provides further support for the use of ratings of perceived exertion to prescribe resistance exercise intensity.

CONSIDERATIONS FOR USING RATINGS OF PERCEIVED EXERTION DURING RESISTANCE EXERCISE

The most commonly researched and used RPE scale for both aerobic and resistance exercise is the Borg RPE 6-20 category scale [2]. Ratings from this scale have been validated for use during resistance exercise in a number of studies [12, 13]. The Borg CR-10 scale [3] has also been examined and shown to be a valid tool for regulating resistance exercise intensity [21]. Recently, a new set of RPE scales has been introduced by Robertson from the University of Pittsburgh. These scales, called OMNI scales, range in numbers from 0 to 10 and have both verbal and pictorial descriptors that may facilitate perceived exertion measurement in health/fitness settings [19]. Each scale has a different set of pictures that is specific to a mode of exercise. Concurrent validity of the OMNI-Resistance Exercise Scale (OMNI-RES) (Figure 1) has been established by demonstrating a positive correlation between ratings of perceived exertion and both blood lactic acid and the total weight lifted during resistance exercise for men and women [20]. Construct validity of the OMNI-RES has been established using the Borg RPE scale as the criterion measure [15]. The specificity of the OMNI-RES to resistance exercise may make it preferable to the Borg RPE and CR-10 scales in resistance exercise settings, although it would be appropriate to use any of the scales to measure perceived exertion during resistance exercise.

Regardless of scale choice, in order to ensure accurate perceived exertion responses, scaling instructions and anchoring procedures should be provided for participants who use an RPE scale to regulate resistance exercise intensity. Scaling and anchoring instructions for resistance exercise have been published by Gearhart [7] and Robertson [20]. Scale instructions should define perceived exertion, explain the use of the scale, explain differentiated ratings, and explain correctness of responses [17]. Scale anchoring can be accomplished using exercise anchoring, memory anchoring or a combination of both. The purpose of anchoring is to provide the participant with an understanding of the low and high points on an RPE scale. During resistance exercise, exercise anchoring requires the participant to perform one repetition with no weight and one with maximal weight to understand the feelings of exertion associated with the low and high points on the scale. Although this is appropriate for research settings, in other settings, memory anchoring may be preferable because it provides an understanding of the low and high points by simply asking clients to recall the least and greatest effort they have experienced while lifting weights.

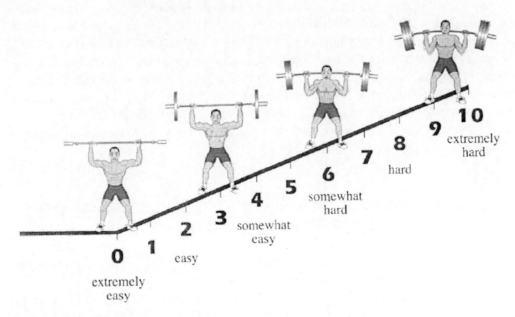

Reprinted with permission by Robert J. Robertson. Robertson, R. J. et al. (2003). Concurrent validation of the OMNI perceived exertion scale for resistance exercise. *Medicine and Science in Sports and Exercise*, *35*, 333-341.

Figure 1. OMNI-Resistance Exercise Scale (OMNI-RES).

Ratings of perceived exertion responses can be used to describe how the body feels as a whole during resistance exercise (i.e. overall body RPE or undifferentiated ratings) or can be made specific to the muscles that are active during a particular resistance exercise (i.e. active muscle RPE or differentiated ratings) [17]. The research examining ratings of perceived exertion during resistance exercise indicates that ratings of perceived exertion provide a valid assessment of differences in the intensity of differentiated and undifferentiated signals [12, 13]. Furthermore, the studies that have examined both overall body and active muscle ratings of perceived exertion have shown that active muscle RPE is consistently higher than overall body RPE at a given intensity [6, 12, 13, 15]. These consistent findings suggest that differentiated RPE may be more appropriate than undifferentiated RPE to use for regulation of resistance exercise intensity. As such, it is important that participants are provided with an explanation of overall body and active muscle ratings of perceived exertion, which is included in the scaling instructions mentioned above.

USING RATINGS OF PERCEIVED EXERTION FOR RESISTANCE EXERCISE PRESCRIPTION

Robertson (2004) has proposed a method of using ratings of perceived exertion from the OMNI-RES for resistance exercise prescription, called the OMNI Sliding Zone System. This method requires that the initial weight for a resistance exercise be selected using an appropriate rating (i.e. a "3" for muscular endurance training, a "6" for hypertrophy training, a "9" for muscular strength training). These values roughly correspond to the ratings of 9, 13 and 17 from the Borg RPE scale [15], which have been associated with resistances of approximately 42%, 66%, and 82% of the 1RM, respectively [16]. Once the initial weight is selected, the exerciser performs repetitions at the selected weight. Exertion will increase as the number of repetitions increases. If muscle failure is the goal, then the exerciser would continue until a "failure" rating of perceived exertion is reached (i.e. for the OMNI scale, a "10"). The number of repetitions performed will decrease as the rating of perceived exertion used to select the initial weight increases from a 3 to a 6 to a 9. Thus, a participant who begins at a "3" will perform more repetitions to reach a "10" than a participant who begins at a "9". After the first set, the participant would stop, rest and repeat the same exercise or begin a new exercise set using the target rating of perceived exertion as a guide in selecting the resistance. Used in this way, the Sliding Zone System provides a protocol for using ratings of perceived exertion to guide resistance exercise training [19]. While the Sliding Zone System focuses on the use of the OMNI-RES, it would be appropriate to use ratings from any of the RPE scales as an adjunct or an alternative to traditional methods of resistance exercise intensity prescription.

Another option for regulating resistance exercise intensity is to use the Session RPE, which is a global assessment of the intensity of an entire resistance exercise training session [4]. Day et al. [4] asked participants to provide overall body ratings of perceived exertion after each of five resistance exercises and then again thirty minutes following the training session (Session RPE). The five exercises were performed for 15 repetitions at 50% 1RM, 10 repetitions at 70% 1RM and 4-5 repetitions at 90% 1RM in three separate sessions. Session RPE increased significantly as the intensity of the exercises increased. Additionally, when the ratings of perceived exertion from the five exercises were averaged and compared to the Session RPE, there was no significant difference between the two values at any of the three intensities examined. This suggests that a single Session RPE can be used to monitor the intensity of an entire training session.

The benefits of using ratings of perceived exertion include that it allows participants to use the same method to regulate intensity for both aerobic and resistance exercise, and to perform training programs that they have personally selected and prefer, which may improve compliance [5]. In addition, the Sliding Zone System inherently recognizes improvements in muscular strength and/or endurance made through training. As strength increases, the selected weight needed to produce a given rating of perceived exertion value will increase, thereby providing a progressive stimulus for training. What felt like a "3" pre-training, will feel like a "1" or "2" when muscle fitness increases. Thus, the participant would need to increase the weight to continue to experience the effort associated with the target rating of perceived exertion.

Ratings of perceived exertion could be useful for regulating intensity in non-traditional resistance exercise settings as well as traditional resistance exercise settings. Examples of non-traditional settings would include group resistance exercise classes, work settings in which lifting and loading are common or mind/body classes where the intensity of the strength activities is not related to repetitions. Currently, there is no ideal method for regulating intensity in these settings. Using ratings of perceived exertion would provide a method of quantifying what the activity should (or shouldn't) feel like and could be used to assist participants with selecting appropriate resistances. For example, in group resistance exercise settings where participants perform the same exercise for extended periods of time, instructors might suggest that the initial lift should not feel more effortful than a "3"on the OMNI-RES or a "9" on the Borg RPE scale if the participant wants to complete the entire set with good form.

In summary, the research thus far indicates that ratings of perceived exertion provide an index of resistance exercise intensity, as ratings of perceived exertion are related to variables such as contraction intensity, muscle activity and blood lactic acid concentration. The research also indicates that ratings of perceived exertion are a valid method of regulating and prescribing resistance exercise intensity, and may be used as an alternative or adjunct to traditional methods of resistance exercise intensity prescription. While any of the RPE scales are appropriate to use during resistance exercise, the specificity of the OMNI-RES for resistance exercise may make it a preferable scale to use in that setting. It is important to note that the majority of the research has used recreationally-trained young men and women. Little is known about the use of ratings of perceived exertion during resistance exercise with novice lifters [14], clinical populations and older adults [8]. These may be ideal populations for using ratings of perceived exertion during resistance exercise because traditional methods of resistance exercise intensity prescription require maximal testing and/or maximal performance (i.e. exercise to muscle fatigue), which is not the best approach for those with minimal experience, hypertension or bone and joint conditions. Because resistance exercise is an important component of a comprehensive exercise program for all individuals, future research in the area should examine ratings of perceived exertion during resistance exercise with these populations.

REFERENCES

[1]   Borg, G. (1970) Perceived exertion as an indicator of somatic stress. *Scand J Rehab Med*, 2-3, 92-98.

[2]   Borg, G. (1971) The perception of physical performance. *Frontiers of fitness*. Springfield, IL: Charles C. Thomas.

[3]   Borg, G. (1982) Psychophysical bases of perceived exertion. *Med Sci Sports Exerc, 14*, 377-381.

[4]   Day, M. L., McGuigan, M. R., Brice, G. & Foster, C. (2004) Monitoring exercise intensity during resistance training using the session RPE scale. *J Strength Cond Res*, 18, 353-358.

[5]   Dishman, R. K. (1994) Prescribing exercise intensity for healthy adults using perceived exertion. *Med Sci Sports Exerc*, 26, 783-790.

[6]   Duncan, M. J., Al-Nakeeb, Y. & Scurr, J. (2006) Perceived exertion is related to muscle activity during leg extension exercise. *Res Sports Med*, 14, 179-189.

[7]   Gearhart, R.F., Goss, F. L., Lagally, K. M., Jakicic, J. M., Gallagher, J. & Robertson, R. J. (2001) Standardized scaling procedures for rating perceived exertion during resistance exercise. *J Strength Cond Res*, 15, 320-325.

[8]   Gearhart, R. F., Lagally, K. M., Riechman, S. E., Andrews, R. D. & Robertson, R. J. (2008) RPE at relative intensities after 12 weeks of resistance exercise training by older adults. *Percep Mot Skills*, 106, 893-903.

[9]   Hasson, S. M., Signorile, J. F. & Williams, J. H. (1989) Fatigue-induced changes in myoelectric signal characteristics and perceived exertion. *Can J Sport Sci*, 14, 99-102.

[10]   Hollander, D. B., Durand, R. J. Trynicki, J. L., Larock, D., Castracane, V. D., Hebert, E. P. & Kraemer, R. R. (2003) RPE, pain, and physiological adjustment to concentric and eccentric contractions. *Med Sci Sports Exerc,* 35, 1017-1025.

[11]   Kraemer, W. J., Noble, F. J. Clark, M. J. & Culver, B. W. (1987) Physiologic responses to heavy-resistance exercise with very short rest periods. *Int J Sports Med*, 8, 247-252.

[12]   Lagally, K. M., Robertson, R. J., Gallagher, K. I., Goss, F. L., Jakicic, J. M., Lephart, S. M., McCaw, S. T., & Goodpaster, B. (2002) Perceived exertion, electromyography, and blood lactate during acute bouts of resistance exercise. *Med Sci Sports Exerc*, 34, 552-559.

[13]   Lagally, K. M., Robertson, R. J., Gallagher, K. I., Gearhart, R. F., & Goss, F. L. (2002) Ratings of perceived exertion during low- and high- intensity resistance exercise by young adults. *Percep Mot Skills*, 94, 723-731.

[14]   Lagally, K. M., McCaw, S. T., Young, G. T., Medema, H. C., & Thomas, D. Q. (2004) Ratings of perceived exertion and muscle activity during the bench press exercise in recreational and novice lifters. *J Strength Cond Res*, 18, 359-364.

[15]   Lagally, K. M. & Robertson, R. J. (2006) Construct validity of the OMNI resistance exercise scale. *J Strength Cond Res*, 20, 252-256.

[16]   Lagally, K. M. & Amorose, A. J. (2007) The validity of using prior ratings of perceived exertion to regulate resistance exercise intensity. *Percep Mot Skills*, 104, 534-542.

[17]   Noble, B. J., & Robertson, R. J. (1996) *Perceived exertion.* Champaign, IL: Human Kinetics.

[18]   Pincivero, D. M., Coelho, A. J., Campy, R. M. Salfetnikov, Y. & Bright, A. (2001) The effects of voluntary contraction intensity and gender on perceived exertion during isokinetic quadriceps exercise. *Eur J App Phys*, 84, 221-226.

[19]   Robertson, R. J. (2004) *Perceived exertion for practitioners.* Champaign, IL: Human Kinetics.

[20]   Robertson, R. J., Goss, F. L., Rutkowski, J., Lenz, B., Dixon, C., Timmer, J., Frazee, K., Dube, J. & Andreacci, J. (2003) Concurrent validation of the OMNI Perceived Exertion Scale for resistance exercise. *Med Sci Sports Exerc*, 35, 333-341.

[21]   Suminski, R. R., Robertson, R. J., Arslanian, S., Kang, J., Utter, A. C., DaSilva, S. G., Goss, F. L. & Metz, K. F. (1997) Perception of effort during resistance exercise. *J Strength Cond Res*, 11, 261-265.

In: Advances in Strength and Conditioning Research   ISBN: 978-1-60692-909-4
Editor: Michael Duncan and Mark Lyons   © 2009 Nova Science Publishers, Inc.

Chapter 9

PLYOMETRIC TRAINING EFFECTS ON MUSCLE FUNCTION AND RAPID MOVEMENT PERFORMANCE: A REVIEW

Goran Markovic[1] and Pavle Mikulic
[1]University of Zagreb, Croatia

ABSTRACT

Plyometric (or stretch-shortening cycle) training has experienced a surge of popularity among coaches and sports scientists over the past few decades, and the purpose of this paper was to review the available literature on the effects of lower-body plyometric training (PT) on muscle function and rapid movement performance. Thirty-three studies that matched the inclusion criteria were analyzed, and our findings include the following: PT improves maximal strength of lower-limb muscles by an average of 6.6%, with these PT-induced changes specific to the muscle group being trained. The mean PT-related change in contractile rate of force development was 0.9%, with a wide range of changes from -22.7% to 31.3%. In terms of the effects of PT on lower-body power, a relatively vast range of changes, from -5.2% to 25.9%, was again observed, with a mean change of 6.0%. Furthermore, PT may improve vertical jump height, with PT effects seemingly more dramatic in vertical jumps containing either slow (countermovement jump: 6.9% and 10%) or fast stretch-shortening cycles (drop jump: 8.1%) than in concentric-only vertical jumps (squat jump: 4.3%). The PT-induced improvement in horizontal jump performance was found to be smaller, amounting to 2.7%. The average effect of PT on sprint performance was only 1.6%, with the observed effect of PT appearing to decrease as the sprint distance increased. Agility performance following a PT training intervention improved on average by 4.8%. We conclude that appropriate forms of PT may be recommended as a way to improve various types of muscle function and rapid movement performance in healthy individuals.

Keywords: muscle/skeletal, stretch-shortening cycle, athletic performance

---

[1] Please address correspondence and requests for reprints to Goran Markovic, School of Kinesiology, University of Zagreb, Horvacanski Zavoj 15, 10000 Zagreb, Croatia or e mail gmarkov@kif.hr

Since its introduction in the Western professional literature in the 1960s, plyometric (or stretch-shortening cycle; SSC) training has gained a remarkable popularity among coaches and scientists. Indeed, it is one of the most often used and studied training paradigms in the area of physical conditioning and sports and exercise sciences. Despite this popularity, relatively little is known about the effects of plyometric training (PT) on muscle strength and power, as well as on rapid movement performance. Available reviews of literature in this area were mainly focused on PT effects on vertical jump performance [5, 31], as well as on neurophysiological basis of stretch-shortening cycle muscle contraction [25, 49]. The purpose of this paper is to review the available literature regarding PT effects on muscle function and rapid movement performance. Since the vast majority of scientific studies were focused on lower-body PT, we decided to review only the effects of PT on lower-body muscular performance.

METHOD

The present literature review includes studies published in journals that have presented original research data on healthy human subjects. Abstracts and unpublished theses/dissertations were excluded from this review. Inclusion criteria applied in this study were as follows: 1) randomized or non-randomized controlled trials that included a comparable control group; 2) land-based PT studies which lasted ≥ 4 weeks; 3) studies that used at least one of the following measures as dependent variables: muscle force or torque, muscle power, rate of force/torque development, vertical jump height, horizontal jump distance, sprint running performance and agility performance; 4) studies published in a peer-reviewed journal. Studies that combined PT with other forms of physical training like weight training, sprint training, electro stimulation training etc., were excluded.

The size of the effect of PT on each dependent variable (Δ_{tot}) is given by the difference between the mean change in performance of subjects in the plyometric group (Δ_{plyo}) and the control group (Δ_{con}). In order to be able to compare the effects of PT on different muscular and performance characteristics, we expressed Δ_{tot} relative to the mean value of the control group – that is, in percentage values.

RESULTS

Plyometric Training Effects on Muscle Strength and Power

This section reviews the effects of PT on lower-body muscle strength and power. Altogether, 17 studies matched our inclusion criteria and were analyzed. Note, however, that a number of included studies had more than one experimental group. Therefore, the total number of effect sizes (Δ_{tot}) exceeded the number of studies included in this section. The studies included had an intervention duration ranging from 5 to 15 weeks, a total number of training sessions ranging from 7 to 30, and a total number of foot contacts ranging from 360 to 7800.

Maximal Muscle Strength

Maximal muscle strength is usually defined as the peak force or torque developed during a maximal voluntary contraction (MVC) under a given set of conditions, and is measured using isometric, isokinetic or isoinertial (i.e., weight lifting) dynamometry [2]. Numerous studies have evaluated the effects of PT on lower-body muscle strength (Table 1). Fifteen studies were focused on leg extensor muscles, 4 studies were focused on knee extensor and plantar flexor muscles, and 2 studies were focused on hip extensor muscles. When we considered all studies together, the mean change in maximum muscle strength as a result of PT was 6.6% and ranged from small negative values of -3.2% to moderate positive values of 16%.

However, a clearer picture of PT effects on lower-body muscle strength can be seen when a particular muscle or muscle groups are analyzed separately. In that case, the mean change in maximal strength as a result of PT was 4.9% for the leg extensor muscle, 0.1% for the knee extensor muscles, 11.1% for the hip extensor muscles and 14.9% for the plantar flexor muscles. These data suggest that PT produces the greatest positive effects on strength of the hip and ankle extensor muscles, but not on the knee extensor muscles. These findings could be the result of specific plyometric exercises used in training. Specifically, it has been hypothesized that horizontal jumps (e.g., standing long and triple jumps, single-leg or alternate leg bounding, etc.) are particularly suited for training the hip musculature. In contrast, vertical jumps are more suitable for activating the knee and ankle musculature. In case of the most popular vertical jump exercise – drop jump (DJ), there exist at least two jumping techniques that change the activation of the leg muscles. The first DJ technique, known as bounce DJ, emphasizes the activation of the ankle musculature, while the second, known as countermovement DJ, emphasizes the activation of the knee musculature [6]. Since most of the studies used DJ as a training exercise but did not specify the particular DJ technique applied, we speculate that most of the evaluated PT studies used the bounce DJ as training exercise.

Explosive Muscle Strength

'Explosive' muscle strength or contractile rate of force development (RFD) is a term used to describe the ability to rapidly develop muscular force [1]. In a number of sports involving explosive movements, the time allowed to exert force is typically very limited (~50-250 ms). Thus, in certain sports a high contractile RFD exerted during the initial phase of muscular contraction may be of vital importance for successful performance [3]. Since PT involves performance of explosive exercises, it is generally believed that PT improves contractile RFD. However, our literature review does not support this hypothesis. Specifically, in 10 studies included in this review, the mean change in contractile RFD as a result of PT was only 0.9%, with a wide range of changes from -22.7% to 31.3% (Table 2). When we performed separate analyses for particular muscle groups, the results became more informative. Specifically, three experiments [27, 43] revealed very large positive effects (mean effect: 24%; range: 17.6% to 31.3%) of PT on RFD of plantar flexor muscles. In contrast, considerably smaller positive effects of PT on RFD were observed for the leg extensor muscles (mean effect: 4.3%, range: -6.9% to 15.4%), while there was a negative effect of PT on RFD of hip (mean effect: -4.8%; range: -6.6 to -3.0%) and knee extensor muscles (mean effect: -20.5%; range: -22.7% to -18.2%). These findings together with the results obtained for maximal muscle strength (see previous text) suggest that PT produces changes in muscle strength that are specific to the muscle group involved. Although more studies are needed, it appears that PT is well suited for increasing the maximal and explosive strength of ankle plantar flexors and (to a lesser degree) hip extensors, but not for the knee extensors.

Muscle Power

Muscle power can be defined as the rate at which mechanical work is performed or as the product of force and velocity, and is commonly perceived to be critical for the performance of many athletic tasks [2]. Consequently, the development of power has been the subject of much research. In that regard, most researches and coaches agree that PT is particularly well suited physical conditioning method for the development of muscular power [31, 34, 51]. In this review, we analyzed 13 experimental studies that evaluated the effects of PT on lower-body power (Table 3). The results show that the mean change in lower-body power as a result of PT is 6.0%, with the relatively wide range of changes from -5.2% to 25.9%. Since the reviewed studies used different settings for power assessment (cycle ergometry, squat jump, countermovement jump, or repetitive jumps), it is likely that the observed heterogeneity of effects in muscle power could be partly explained by the differences in power testing methods applied. This is an important methodological issue due to the well known effect of contraction-type on muscle power output [32, 33]. More studies are needed before any firm conclusion regarding PT effects on muscle power could be drawn.

At the end of this section, several general issues need to be addressed. First, we should point out that almost all studies included in this review (see Tables 1-3) were performed on male subjects. Thus, our knowledge about PT effects on muscle strength and power in women is rather limited. However, several PT studies that did not match our inclusion criteria and were performed on female subjects, suggest that these effects could be similar to the one observed in males [19]. More well-designed PT studies that use women as subjects are needed to clarify this issue. Second, most of the reviewed studies used non-athletes as subjects. It is, therefore, possible that the observed effects of PT on muscle strength and power could be lower when applied on trained athletes. Finally, an important question related to strength and power changes as a result of PT is related to the possible sites of adaptation. At this point, we may only speculate about the possible adaptive mechanisms responsible for the PT-induced increase in leg muscle strength and power. However, given that PT produces only small changes in muscle and/or fiber size, it is expected that strength and power gains resulting from PT have neural, rather than structural (i.e., hypetrophic) origin.

Summary

Summarizing the findings of PT effects on muscle strength and power, the present review demonstrated the following:

- On average, PT improves maximal strength of lower-limb muscles by 6.6%. However, these PT-induced changes in maximal strength were specific to the muscle group trained; the largest positive effects of PT on maximal strength were observed for plantar flexor muscles (mean effect: 14.9%), followed by hip extensor muscles (mean effect: 11.1%), leg extensor muscles (mean effect: 4.9%), and knee extensor muscles (mean effect: 0.1%).

- The mean change in contractile RFD as a result of PT was 0.9%, with a wide range of changes from -22.7% to 31.3%. Separate analyses for particular muscle groups revealed large positive effects (mean effect: 24%) of PT on RFD of plantar flexor muscles, while a considerably smaller positive effects were observed for the leg extensor muscles (mean effect: 4.3%). Finally, there was a negative effect of PT on RFD of hip (mean effect: -4.8%) and knee extensor muscles (mean effect: -20.5%).

- The results of 13 reviewed studies show that the mean change in lower-body power as a result of PT is 6.0%, with the relatively wide range of changes from -5.2% to 25.9%. An important methodological limitation of the reviewed studies is related to the differences in methods used for power assessment. Specifically, some authors applied concentric, while others applied slow SSC or rapid SSC movements for the assessment of muscle power. Therefore, no firm conclusion regarding PT effects on lower-body power can be drawn at present.

Plyometric Training Effects on Rapid Movement Performance

Altogether, 32 published studies were included in this review assessing the effects of PT on rapid movement performance, and the effects were analyzed from the aspects of vertical and horizontal jump performance as well as from the aspects of sprint running and agility performance. As was the case in previous section, a number of included studies had more than one experimental group. Therefore, the total number of effect sizes (Δ_{tot}) exceeded the number of studies included in this section. The studies included had an intervention duration ranging from 4 to 24 weeks, a total number of training sessions ranging from 7 to 60, and a total number of foot contacts ranging from 420 to 7500.

Vertical Jump

PT has been extensively used for augmenting jumping performance in athletes. Many previous research studies have shown that PT improves vertical jump height in healthy individuals, and the recently published meta-analytical study by the first author, evaluating the effects of PT on vertical jump performance [2], was the first to provide precise estimates of the magnitude of effects of PT on different types of vertical jumps. The present review includes additional relevant studies that have since been published and that have satisfied the inclusion criteria as stated in the Methods.

Twenty-eight studies were included in this review evaluating the effects of PT on vertical jump performance. Vertical jump performance was assessed using all four types of standard vertical jumps: squat jump (SJ), countermovement jump (CMJ), countermovement jump with the arm swing (CMJA) and drop jump (DJ). Tables 4 - 7 summarize the characteristics of the included studies. Note that we excluded 3 studies (1 for SJ and 2 for DJ) from this review owing to the unrealistically large positive effects [26, 27, 28]. Although these 3 studies satisfied our inclusion criteria, their findings in terms of overwhelmingly large positive effects presented outliers from the rest of data, and including them in calculation of the overall means may have produced misleading results.

The results of this review suggest that PT considerably improves vertical jump height and the estimated improvements could be considered as practically relevant. The improvements range from 4.3% for SJ to 10.0% for CMJ (Tables 4 – 7). An improvement in vertical jump height of ~5-10% (i.e. ~2-6 cm, depending on the type of the vertical jump) could be of high importance for trained athletes in sports such as volleyball, basketball, or high jump. Increased vertical jump ability in mentioned sports can directly increase one's overall athletic performance, because athletes in the above mentioned sports rely heavily on vertical jump performance (for example, spiking and blocking in volleyball and rebounding in basketball). In addition to these improvements in vertical jump performance, it is important to note that two studies [5, 29] demonstrated that significant improvements in vertical jump performance of ~10% were accompanied by similar improvements in sport-specific jumping, following a PT intervention. Obviously, there appear to be a positive transfer of PT effects on vertical jumping ability to sport-specific vertical jumping performance.

Our results also suggest that the effects of PT are likely to be higher in slow stretch-shortening cycle vertical jumps (CMJ and CMJA) and in fast stretch-shortening cycle vertical jump (DJ) than is the case for concentric-only vertical jump (SJ). These findings are largely in accord with previous suggestion [51] that PT is more effective in improving vertical jump performance in the stretch-shortening cycle jumps as it enhances the ability of participants to use the elastic and neural benefits of the stretch-shortening cycle. It should be stressed that the observed effect of PT in the present review was, on average, more than twice as high in CMJ (10.0%) than in SJ (4.3%).

The results of the present review offer further evidence to support previous narrative reviews [1, 19] which concluded that PT intervention is effective in improving vertical jump performance. In addition to the recently published meta-analytical study [2], an estimate of the magnitude of the effects of PT intervention is a valuable contribution of the present review.

Horizontal Jump

The effects of PT on horizontal jump performance have been sparsely investigated; we were able to obtain only three studies that satisfied our inclusion criteria. The mean effect calculated from the findings of the included studies indicated an improvement in horizontal jump performance of 2.7%, with a relatively narrow range of improvement of 1.4% - 3.9%. This finding suggests smaller effects following a PT intervention in comparison to the effects on vertical jump performance. Of course, due to the low number of studies for the horizontal jump performance the results need to be interpreted with caution. Another point that suggests caution in the interpretation of the results is the fact that two out of three studies we were able to obtain used 13- and 16-year-old adolescents as participants (Table 8).

It is generally assumed that the transfer of PT effects to athletic performance likely depends on the specificity of plyometric exercises performed. Therefore, athletes who require power for moving in the horizontal plane (i.e. sprinters, long jumpers etc.) mainly engage in bounding plyometric exercises, as opposed to high jumpers, basketball or volleyball players, who require power to be exerted in vertical direction, and who perform mainly vertical jump exercises. This corresponds to the well-known principle of training specificity [41].

However, the findings of Hortobagy et al. [21] could not support this assumption, as the two experimental groups that performed two distinctly different PT routines did not yield specific gains in performance. On the contrary, the improvement for both groups was virtually equal in vertical and horizontal jumping tests. The authors state that these unexpected findings may be explained by the high degree of generality among the jumping tests performed, as the vertical and horizontal jumping tests were highly correlated. A large degree of generality between vertical and horizontal tests refutes the notion that the different stretch-shorten tests would measure different physical ability components. In addition, in their subsequent study [22], the authors observed an improvement in vertical jumping velocity despite the fact that PT routine had been executed entirely in the horizontal plane. Finally, the authors state that 'it is possible that it is not direction of the movement but its complexity what influences the commonality of the various jumping tests'.

In a study conducted by Markovic et al. [34], two groups of subjects performed two different 10-week training routines: sprint training (ST) routine and PT routine. No significant training effects for standing long jump between ST and PT groups were observed, and the improvements in both groups were significantly higher compared with the control group. The PT routine had been performed in vertical plane.

Additional well-designed studies evaluating the effects of PT on horizontal jump performance are needed before the magnitude of effect can be established more accurately. Also, the issue of specificity of plyometric exercises in improving the horizontal jump performance needs to be clarified.

Sprint Performance

Sprint running, in varying degrees, is essential for successful performance in many sports. It represents a multidimensional movement skill consisting of three different phases: a) initial starting phase, b) acceleration phase, and c) maximum running speed phase [12]. Various training regimes have commonly been used in order to improve sprinting performance, and those regimes include sprint drills, over-speed training, sprinting against resistance, weight training, and PT [39]. Similar to PT, sprint running also represents an explosive-type training method commonly used in athletic training. However, unlike PT in which the leg extensor muscles operate solely in stretch-shortening cycle, sprint running involves both concentric and stretch-shortening cycle muscle function [11]. Moreover, sprint running involves an activation of much greater proportion of muscles compared to PT, thereby increasing the metabolic demands of such training.

The use of PT to increase speed is widely accepted and utilized by coaches and athletes. Such PT includes various types of jumping, hopping and bounding. The transfer of PT effects to sprinting performance is believed to depend on the specificity of plyometric exercises performed. Therefore athletes who require power for moving in the horizontal plane (i.e. sprinters) engage primarily in bounding plyometric exercises. However, for all the anecdotal support, there are relatively few scientific studies cited in the literature that clearly define PT as a viable mechanism for increasing speed. Given the limited findings in this area and the several studies that suggest real benefits from PT, it is clear that further well-controlled studies are needed to clarify the role of PT when aiming to improve sprinting performance.

As stated above, whether PT improves sprinting performance is not altogether clear. Also, if PT does improve sprint performance, the exact magnitude of effect remains to be determined. In the present review, 12 studies assessing the effects of PT on sprinting performance were included (Table 9).

The calculated average main effect was 1.6%, with a range of -0.6% - 3.7%. Based on the results of the present study, it can generally be concluded that PT results in the slight improvement of sprint performance, and that the magnitude of improvement is likely to be smaller compared to the improvement in horizontal jumping performance, and considerably smaller compared to the improvement in vertical jumping performance.

One of the major questions in everyday training practice is the following: if PT is an effective method of speed improvement, can it improve speed more so than the conventional speed training? In that regard, Rimmer and Sleivert [24] compared the effects of sprint-specific PT against traditional sprint training on 10 m and 40 m sprint times. The PT group showed significant decreases in both 10 m and 40 m sprint times, however, these improvements weren't significantly different from the improvements achieved by the group who underwent traditional sprint training routine. In their conclusion, the authors state that sprint-specific PT can improve 40 m sprint times by the same extent as traditional sprint training possibly through decreasing ground contact times. These findings are not supported by the only other study that compared the effects of sprint and PT on human muscular performance. Namely, a recent study by Markovic et al. [34] found sprint training to be significantly superior to PT in improving the 20 m sprint time. It should be noted that PT exercises used in this study were not sprint-specific, possibly making the power transfer from PT to sprint performance somewhat more difficult.

It has been suggested that the greatest effects of PT on sprinting performance occur in the acceleration phase [39]. The rationale behind this suggestion is that the velocity of muscle action in bounding plyometric exercises the most closely approximates the velocities of muscle action in the acceleration phase of the sprint. An indirect measure of the rate at which the forces are produced in the concentric and eccentric actions during sprinting and in plyometric exercises is obtained from contact time data. In the acceleration phase the body is accelerated primarily through an explosive concentric force production of knee and hip extensor muscles [12]. The ability to produce a great concentric force/power and to generate high velocity during acceleration is of primary importance in this phase of sprint running [38].

The results of the present review partly support the above-mentioned theory, as the greatest effects of PT were observed for 10 m sprint performance (average improvement 2.2%), reducing to the average improvement of 2.1% for 12 m sprint performance, further reducing to the average improvement of 1.5% for 20 m sprint performance and finally reducing to the average improvement of 1.3% for 30 m sprint performance. However, the effect for 40 m sprint performance was 2.2% and for 50 m sprint performance averaged 1.5%. It should be noted that performance times for 50 m sprint performance time were measured manually, possibly contributing to less accurate results.

Overall, although our results demonstrate that PT does improve sprint running in healthy individuals, its superiority in that regard to the conventional speed training remains debatable. Further work is also required to determine the exact mechanisms behind speed improvement as a result of PT.

Agility Performance

Agility is the ability to maintain or control body position while quickly changing direction during a series of movements [47]. Ground contact time when preparing to change direction is a major component of agility, and it has been suggested [40] that PT program can decrease ground reaction test times through the increase in muscular power and movement efficiency, which directly positively affects agility performance. However, little scientific information is available to determine if PT actually enhances agility. Despite that, plyometric activities have been used in sports such as soccer, basketball, handball, tennis, or other sporting events that agility may be useful for their athletes.

Four very recently published studies assessing the effects of PT on agility performance matched our inclusion criteria (Table 10). The overall magnitude of improvement in agility performance was 4.8%, with a relatively wide range of 1.5% - 10.2%. While additional well-designed studies are needed before we can draw any firm conclusions regarding the effect of PT on agility performance, this finding is certainly promising for athletes who require quick movements and quick changes of direction while performing their sport.

Agility tasks are complex tasks, certainly more complex than jumping or sprinting. Tricoli et al. [45] speculate that this complexity makes power transfer from plyometric exercises to the tasks requiring agility difficult. The authors found that 6-week PT intervention consisting of plyometric exercises executed in vertical direction (hurdle hops and drop jumps) improved agility performance, but the magnitude of improvement was no different from the group that underwent Olympic weightlifting training intervention. Young et al. [52] suggested that agility tasks could be more influenced by motor control factors than by muscle strength or power capacity.

Miller et al. [37] employed two agility tests (T-test and Illinois agility test) to assess the effects of a 6-week PT intervention on agility performance. An additional Force-plate test was used to measure ground contact time while hopping. PT intervention consisted of various tasks performed in both vertical and horizontal direction. The participants improved their performance times in both agility tests and the authors conclude that PT improved times in agility test because of either better motor recruitment or neural adaptations. Ground contact times as measured by Force-plate test were also reduced supporting the suggestion of Roper [40] that PT program can decrease ground reaction test times through the increase in muscular power and movement efficiency, which directly positively affects performance times in agility tests.

Somewhat contrary to the findings of Miller et al. [37], Markovic et al. [34] found improvements in 20-yard shuttle run performance times following a 10-week PT intervention, however, these improvements were not statistically significant and were statistically smaller to the improvements obtained by the group engaged in a 10-week sprint training intervention. It should be noted that this study was conducted on a sample size that considerably exceeded the usual sample size in studies evaluating training intervention programs. Sample size is one of the factors directly influencing the power of detecting the real and meaningful effect in treatment studies.

At the end of this section, we would like to address the following: Although widely discussed, it remains debatable whether the improvements in rapid movement performance following a PT training intervention are a result of improvement in strength and power of the lower extremities, or are they a result of the improved muscle coordination, or both? A straightforward answer to this question can not be provided at this point; however, based on the results of the present study, it can carefully be assumed that rapid movement performance is at least partly influenced by the improvements in strength and power characteristics of the lower extremities. These PT-induced changes, particularly in maximal strength, seem to be specific to the muscle group trained.

Table 1. Chronological summary of investigations that studied the effects of plyometric training on maximal muscle strength

Study (first author)	Age (yrs)	Fitness level	SS EXP M/F	SS CON M/F	Duration (wk)	Session (n)	Type of exercise	Foot contacts (n)	Δ_{tot} (%)
Force/torque									
Hortobagyi [22]	16	N-A	11/0	8/0	10	30	COMB	2280	-3.2
Wilson [51]	23	N-A	13/0	14/0	5	10	DJT	360	3.3
Wilson [51]	23	N-A	13/0	14/0	10	20	DJT	720	0.2
Cornu [10]	24	N-A	14/0	5/0	7	14	COMB	n/a	14.3
Young [53]	26	N-A	5/0	9/0	6	18	DJT	468	6.1
Young [53]	26	N-A	11/0	9/0	6	18	DJT	468	0.8
Matavulj [35]	15	A	11/0	11/0	6	18	DJT	540	11.5
Matavulj [35]	15	A	11/0	11/0	6	18	DJT	540	10.7
Matavulj [35]	15	A	11/0	11/0	6	18	DJT	540	2.0
Matavulj [35]	15	A	11/0	11/0	6	18	DJT	540	-1.8
Spurrs [43]	25	A	8/0	9/0	6	15	COMB	2064	13.3
Spurrs [43]	25	A	8/0	9/0	6	15	COMB	2064	15.4
Kyrolainen [27]	24	N-A	13/0	10/0	15	30	COMB	7800	16.0
Kyrolainen [27]	24	N-A	13/0	10/0	15	30	COMB	7800	4.2
Herrero [18]	21	N-A	9/0	10/0	10	20	COMB	1580	-0.3
Markovic [34]	20	N-A	30/0	33/0	10	30	COMB	1800	2.5
de Villarreal [13]	23	N-A	10/0	10/0	7	7	DJT	420	-2.9
de Villarreal [13]	23	N-A	12/0	10/0	7	14	DJT	840	11.5
de Villarreal [13]	23	N-A	10/0	10/0	7	28	DJT	1680	14.9
1 RM									
Wilson [50]	22	N-A	14/0	13/0	8	16	DJT	900	-2.4
Fatouros [16]	21	N-A	11/0	10/0	12	36	COMB	5480	8.2
Fatouros [16]	21	N-A	11/0	10/0	12	36	COMB	5480	11.4
de Villarreal [13]	23	N-A	10/0	10/0	7	7	DJT	420	1.6
de Villarreal [13]	23	N-A	12/0	10/0	7	14	DJT	840	2.4

| de Villarreal [13] | 23 | N-A | 10/0 | 10/0 | 7 | 28 | DJT | 1680 | 13.1 |
| *Overall mean* | *22* | *-* | *~12/0* | *~11/0* | *12* | *17* | *-* | *1971* | *6.6* |

Legend. A – athletes; CMJT – countermovement jump exercise; COMB – combination of various jump exercises; DJT – drop jump exercise; N-A – non-athletes; n/a – not applicable; SS EXP – sample size for the experimental (plyometric) group; SS CON – sample size for the control group; Δ_{tot} –size of the effect of plyometric training (in percentage).

Table 2. Chronological summary of investigations that studied the effects of plyometric training on explosive muscle strength (i.e., rate of force development)

Study (first author)	Age (yrs)	Fitness level	SS EXP M/F	SS CON M/F	Duration (wk)	Sessions (n)	Type of exercise	Foot contacts (n)	Δ_{tot} (%)
Wilson [51]	23	N-A	13/0	14/0	5	10	DJT	360	2.4
Wilson [50]	22	N-A	14/0	13/0	8	16	DJT	900	-6.9
Matavulj [35]	15	A	11/0	11/0	6	18	DJT	540	-6.6
Matavulj [35]	15	A	11/0	11/0	6	18	DJT	540	-3.0
Matavulj [35]	15	A	11/0	11/0	6	18	DJT	540	-22.7
Matavulj [35]	15	A	11/0	11/0	6	18	DJT	540	-18.2
Spurrs [43]	25	A	8/0	9/0	6	15	COMB	2064	21.0
Spurrs [43]	25	A	8/0	9/0	6	15	COMB	2064	31.3
Irmischer [23]	24	N-A	0/14	0/14	9	18	COMB	2952	15.4
Kyrolainen [27]	24	N-A	13/0	10/0	15	30	COMB	7800	17.6
Overall mean	*20*	*-*	*~10/2*	*~9/2*	*7*	*18*	*-*	*1830*	*0.9*

Legend: for details, see Table 1.

Table 3. Chronological summary of investigations that studied the effects of plyometric training on muscle power

Study (first author)	Age (yrs)	Fitness level	SS EXP M/F	SS CON M/F	Duration (wk)	Sessions (n)	Type of exercise	Foot contacts (n)	Δ_{tot} (%)
Dvir [15]	24	N-A	8/0	8/0	8	24	DJT	720	6.4
Dvir [15]	24	N-A	8/0	8/0	8	24	CMJT	720	5.7
Wilson [51]	23	N-A	13/0	14/0	10	20	DJT	720	1.1
Holcomb [20]	20	N-A	10/0	9/0	8	24	DJT	1728	4.6
Holcomb [20]	20	N-A	10/0	9/0	8	24	DJT	1728	3.1
Holcomb [20]	20	N-A	10/0	9/0	8	24	CMJT	1728	-0.9
Holcomb [20]	20	N-A	10/0	9/0	8	24	DJT	1728	10.2
Holcomb [20]	20	N-A	10/0	9/0	8	24	DJT	1728	7.7
Holcomb [20]	20	N-A	10/0	9/0	8	24	CMJT	1728	7.5
Fatouros [16]	21	N-A	11/0	10/0	12	36	COMB	5480	25.9
Diallo [14]	13	A	10/0	10/0	10	30	COMB	7500	16.6
Canavan [8]	20	N-A	0/10	0/10	6	18	COMB	n/a	-5.2
Lehance [28]	23	N-A	10/0	10/0	6	12	DJT	640	-5.1
Overall mean	*21*	*-*	*~9/1*	*~9/1*	*28*	*24*	*-*	*2179*	*6.0*

Legend: for details, see Table 1.

Table 4. Chronological summary of investigations that studied the effects of plyometric training on squat jump performance

Study (first author)	Age (yrs)	Fitness level	SS EXP M/F	SS CON M/F	Duration (wk)	Sessions (n)	Type of exercise	Foot contacts (n)	Δ_{tot} (%)
Wilson [51]	23	N-A	13/0	14/0	10	20	DJT	720	6.7
Holcomb [20]	20	N-A	10/0	9/0	8	24	DJT	1728	7.3
Holcomb [20]	20	N-A	10/0	9/0	8	24	DJT	1728	3.3
Holcomb [20]	20	N-A	10/0	9/0	8	24	CMJT	1728	6.4
Gehri [17]	20	N-A	5/6	5/5	12	24	DJT	704	10.8
Gehri [17]	20	N-A	4/3	5/5	12	24	CMJT	704	5.1
Young [53]	26	N-A	5/0	9/0	6	18	DJT	468	-1.7
Young [53]	26	N-A	11/0	9/0	6	18	DJT	468	-3.7
Diallo [14]	13	A	10/0	10/0	10	30	COMB	7500	14.3
Turner [46]	29	A	4/6	4/4	6	18	COMB	1599	0.0
Tricoli [29]	20	N-A	8/0	7/0	6	12	DJT	2028	3.6
Herrero [18]	21	N-A	9/0	10/0	10	20	COMB	1580	-3.8
Kotzamanidis* [26]	11	N-A	15/0	15/0	10	20	COMB	1520	39.3
Markovic [34]	20	N-A	30/0	33/0	4	16	COMB	1580	7.1
Overall mean	*21*	*-*	*~10/1*	*~10/1*	*8*	*21*	*-*	*1718*	*4.3*

Legend. for details, see Table 1. * removed from analysis as outlier.

Table 5. Chronological summary of investigations that studied the effects of plyometric training on countermovement jump performance

Study (first author)	Age (yrs)	Fitness level	SS EXP M/F	SS CON M/F	Duration (wk)	Sessions (n)	Type of exercise	Foot contacts (n)	Δ_{tot} (%)
Brown [7]	15	A	13/0	13/0	12	34	DJT	1020	5.0
Wilson [51]	23	N-A	13/0	14/0	10	20	DJT	720	7.8
Holcomb [20]	20	N-A	10/0	9/0	8	24	DJT	1728	9.4
Holcomb [20]	20	N-A	10/0	9/0	8	24	DJT	1728	6.7
Holcomb [20]	20	N-A	10/0	9/0	8	24	CMJT	1728	6.9
Wilson [51]	22	N-A	14/0	13/0	8	16	DJT	900	12.2
Gehri [17]	20	N-A	5/6	5/5	12	24	DJT	704	10.8
Gehri [17]	20	N-A	4/3	5/5	12	24	CMJT	704	9.0
Diallo [14]	13	A	10/0	10/0	10	30	COMB	7500	20.0
Matavulj [35]	15	A	11/0	11/0	6	18	DJT	540	15.6
Matavulj [35]	15	A	11/0	11/0	6	18	DJT	540	13.8
Spurrs [43]	25	A	8/0	9/0	6	15	COMB	2064	18.2
Spurrs [43]	25	A	8/0	9/0	6	15	COMB	2064	18.2
Turner [46]	29	A	4/6	4/4	6	18	COMB	1599	4.8
Canavan [8]	20	N-A	0/10	0/10	6	18	COMB	n/a	2.9
Lehance [28]	23	N-A	10/0	10/0	6	12	DJT	640	17.8
Tricoli [45]	20	N-A	8/0	7/0	6	12	DJT	2028	4.5
Kato [24]	21	N-A	0/18	0/18	24	60	CMJT	720	5.6
Herrero [18]	21	N-A	10/0	10/0	4	16	COMB	1520	-0.3
Markovic [34]	20	N-A	30/0	33/0	10	30	COMB	1800	6.4
de Villarreal [13]	23	N-A	10/0	10/0	7	7	DJT	420	1.1
de Villarreal [13]	23	N-A	12/0	10/0	7	14	DJT	840	14.4
de Villarreal [13]	23	N-A	10/0	10/0	7	28	DJT	1680	19.3
Overall mean	*21*	*-*	*~9/2*	*~9/2*	*8*	*22*	*-*	*1509*	*10.0*

Legend: for details, see Table 1.

Table 6. Chronological summary of investigations that studied the effects of plyometric training on countermovement jump with the arm swing performance

Study (first author)	Age (yrs)	Fitness level	SS EXP M/F	SS CON M/F	Duration (wk)	Sessions (n)	Type of exercise	Foot contacts (n)	Δ_{tot} (%)
Blattner [4]	20	N-A	11/0	15/0	8	24	DJT	720	8.5
Dvir [15]	24	N-A	8/0	8/0	8	24	DJT	720	13.0
Dvir [15]	24	N-A	8/0	8/0	8	24	CMJT	720	6.9
Brown [7]	15	A	13/0	13/0	12	34	DJT	1020	6.0
Hortobagyi [21]	13	N-A	15/0	10/0	10	20	COMB	2600	6.1
Hortobagyi [21]	13	N-A	15/0	10/0	10	20	COMB	2600	12.1
Wagner [48]	17	A	20/0	20/0	6	12	COMB	1080	2.2
Wagner [48]	17	N-A	20/0	20/0	6	12	COMB	1080	2.7
Young [53]	26	N-A	5/0	9/0	6	18	DJT	468	4.3
Young [53]	26	N-A	11/0	9/0	6	18	DJT	468	1.6
Fatouros [16]	21	N-A	11/0	10/0	12	36	COMB	5480	10.3
Fatouros [16]	21	N-A	11/0	10/0	12	36	COMB	5480	10.3
Miler [36]	22	N-A	5/8	9/5	8	16	COMB	1600	-0.2
Irmischer [23]	24	N-A	0/14	0/14	9	18	COMB	2952	5.7
Lehance [28]	22	N-A	10/0	10/0	8	24	COMB	640	15.8
Stemm [44]	24	N-A	7/0	9/0	6	12	COMB	540	5.0
Stemm [44]	24	N-A	8/0	9/0	6	12	COMB	540	7.2
Overall mean	*21*	*-*	*~10/1*	*~10/1*	*8*	*21*	*-*	*1689*	*6.9*

Legend: for details, see Table 1.

Table 7. Chronological summary of investigations that studied the effects of plyometric training on drop jump performance

Study (first author)	Age (yrs)	Fitness level	SS EXP M/F	SS CON M/F	Duration (wk)	Sessions (n)	Type of exercise	Foot contacts (n)	Δ_{tot} (%)
Gehri [17]	20	N-A	5/6	5/5	12	24	DJT	704	10.1
Gehri [17]	20	N-A	4/3	5/5	12	24	CMJT	704	8.6
Young [53]	26	N-A	5/0	9/0	6	18	DJT	468	9.0
Young [53]	26	N-A	11/0	9/0	6	18	DJT	468	7.4
Chimera [9]	20	A	0/8	0/8	6	12	COMB	1950	3.7
Kyrolainen* [27]	24	N-A	13/0	10/0	15	30	COMB	7800	31.8
Lehance* [28]	22	N-A	10/0	10/0	8	24	COMB	640	25.4
de Villarreal [13]	23	N-A	10/0	10/0	7	7	DJT	420	0.3
de Villarreal [13]	23	N-A	12/0	10/0	7	14	DJT	840	8.5
de Villarreal [13]	23	N-A	10/0	10/0	7	28	DJT	1680	12.8
de Villarreal [13]	23	N-A	10/0	10/0	7	7	DJT	420	-1.4
de Villarreal [13]	23	N-A	12/0	10/0	7	14	DJT	840	5.1
de Villarreal [13]	23	N-A	10/0	10/0	7	28	DJT	1680	16.0
de Villarreal [13]	23	N-A	10/0	10/0	7	7	DJT	420	2.6
de Villarreal [13]	23	N-A	12/0	10/0	7	14	DJT	840	11.1
de Villarreal [13]	23	N-A	10/0	10/0	7	28	DJT	1680	20.2
Overall mean	23	-	~9/1	~9/1	8	19	-	1347	8.1

Legend: for details, see Table 1.

Table 8. Chronological summary of investigations that studied the effects of plyometric training on horizontal jump performance

Study (first author)	Age (yrs)	Fitness level	SS EXP M/F	SS CON M/F	Duration (wk)	Sessions (n)	Type of exercise	Foot contacts (n)	Δ_{tot} (%)
Standing long jump									
Markovic [34]	20	N-A	30/0	33/0	10	30	COMB	1800	2.4
Hortobagyi [21]	13	N-A	15/0	10/0	10	20	COMB	2600	2.9
Running long jump									
Hortobagyi [22]	16	N-A	11/0	8/0	10	30	COMB	2280	3.9
Standing five jumps									
Hortobagyi [21]	13	N-A	15/0	10/0	10	20	COMB	2600	1.4
Hortobagyi [22]	16	N-A	11/0	8/0	10	30	COMB	2280	2.7
Overall mean	*16*	*-*	*13/0*	*9/0*	*10*	*26*	*-*	*2312*	*2.7*

Legend: for details, see Table 1.

Table 9. Chronological summary of investigations that studied the effects of plyometric training on sprint performance

Study (first author)	Age (yrs)	Fitness level	SS EXP M/F	SS CON M/F	Duration (wk)	Session (n)	Type of exercise	Foot contact (n)	Δ_{tot} (%)
50 m									
Wagner [48]	17	A	20/0	20/0	6	12	COMB	1080	1.7
Wagner [48]	17	N-A	20/0	20/0	6	12	COMB	1080	1.3
40 m									
Rimmer [39]	24	A	10/0	7/0	8	15	COMB	1772	2.2
40 yd (36.6 m)									
Chimera [9]	20	A	0/8	0/8	6	12	COMB	1950	-0.3
30 m									
Hartobagyi [22]	16	N-A	11/0	8/0	10	30	COMB	2280	-0.6
Wilson [51]	23	N-A	13/0	14/0	10	20	DJT	720	1.1
Rimmer [39]	24	A	10/0	7/0	8	15	COMB	1772	1.8
Tricoli [45]	20	N-A	8/0	7/0	6	12	DJT	2028	1.4
Kotzamanidis [29]	11	N-A	15/0	15/0	10	20	COMB	1520	3.0
20 m									
Rimmer [39]	24	A	10/0	7/0	8	15	COMB	1772	1.6
Kotzamanidis [29]	11	N-A	15/0	15/0	10	20	COMB	1520	3.7
Herrero [18]	21	N-A	10/0	10/0	4	16	COMB	1520	-0.3
Markovic [34]	20	N-A	30/0	33/0	10	30	COMB	1800	0.9
de Villarreal [13]	23	N-A	10/0	10/0	7	7	DJT	420	0.8
de Villarreal [13]	23	N-A	12/0	10/0	7	14	DJT	840	0.8
de Villarreal [13]	23	N-A	10/0	10/0	7	28	DJT	1680	3.2
12 m									
Salonikidis [42]	21	A	16/0	16/0	9	27	COMB	n/a	2.1
10 m									
Rimmer [39]	24	A	10/0	7/0	8	15	COMB	1772	2.6
Lehance [28]	22	N-A	10/0	10/0	8	24	COMB	640	1.6

Study (first author)	Age (yrs)	Fitness level	SS EXP M/F	SS CON M/F	Duration (wk)	Session (n)	Type of exercise	Foot contact (n)	Δ$_{tot}$ (%)
Tricoli [45]	20	N-A	8/0	7/0	6	12	DJT	2028	2.1
Kotzamanidis [26]	11	N-A	15/0	15/0	10	20	COMB	1520	2.6
Overall mean	20	-	~12/0	~11/0	8	18	-	1486	1.6

Legend: for details, see Table 1.

Table 10. Chronological summary of investigations that studied the effects of plyometric training on agility performance

Study (first author)	Age (yrs)	Fitness level	SS EXP M/F	SS CON M/F	Duration (wk)	Session (n)	Type of exercise	Foot contact (n)	Δ$_{tot}$ (%)
20 yd shuttle run									
Markovic [34]	20	N-A	30/0	33/0	10	30	COMB	1800	2.0
4 m side steps									
Salonikidis [42]	21	A	16/0	16/0	9	27	COMB	n/a	10.2
4 m sprint with turn									
Salonikidis [42]	21	A	16/0	16/0	9	27	COMB	n/a	9.6
12 m sprint w/turn									
Salonikidis [42]	21	A	16/0	16/0	9	27	COMB	n/a	1.5
4 m agility test									
Tricoli [45]	20	N-A	8/0	7/0	6	12	COMB	2028	2.0
T-test									
Miller [37]	23	N-A	9/5	10/4	6	12	COMB	730	5.5
Illinois agility run									
Miller [37]	23	N-A	9/5	10/4	6	12	COMB	730	3.0
Overall mean	21	-	~12/2	~13/1	8	21	-	690	4.8

Legend: for details, see Table 1.

In relation to this issue, in a study conducted by the first author and collaborators [34], the PT-induced improvements in rapid movement performance (as measured by vertical jumping performance) were not accompanied by the improvements in leg extensor strength or power, which is in contrast to some [16, 35], but not all [51, 53] previous studies on PT. The authors speculate that it was possible that plyometric exercises improved jumping ability primarily by improving muscle coordination. Future studies involving electromyography (EMG) measurements should test this conjecture in the future, and provide more accurate answers on the above-mentioned question.

Summary

Summarizing the findings of PT effects on rapid movement performance, the present review encompassed 32 studies published in peer review journals and demonstrated the following:

- The effects of PT on vertical jump performance have been studied extensively; we obtained 28 published investigations that matched our inclusion criteria. PT improves vertical jump height in all four types of standard vertical jumps (i.e., SJ, CMJ, CMJA, and DJ). The observed mean effect in jump height ranged between 4.3% for SJ performance and 10.0% for CMJ performance, and these effects could be considered practically relevant. The PT effects appear to be greater in vertical jumps containing either slow (CMJ or CMJA) or fast (DJ) stretch-shortening cycle, than in concentric-only vertical jumps (SJ). From this perspective, various forms of PT can be recommended as a very effective form of physical conditioning for augmenting the vertical jump performance of healthy individuals.
- As opposed to the vertical jump performance, the effects of PT on horizontal jump performance have been investigated sparsely. Only three studies satisfied our inclusion criteria and the overall mean yielded the improvement in horizontal jump performance of 2.7%, suggesting smaller improvement gains following a PT intervention in horizontal jump performance compared to vertical jump performance. However, due to the low number of studies, we remain cautious when drawing conclusions regarding the effects of PT on horizontal jump performance. Additional well-designed studies are needed before we can draw any firm conclusions on this issue.
- In order to estimate the effects of PT on sprint performance we examined 12 studies. An overall mean of 1.6% improvement was established. Distances used for evaluating the sprint performance ranged from 10 - 50 m, and the observed effect of PT appeared to be decreasing as the sprint distance increased. The practical relevance of 1.6% overall improvement in sprint performance suggests that PT, although producing positive improvements in sprint performance, should perhaps be combined with other forms of physical conditioning in order for greater and practically more relevant improvements in sprint performance to be achieved.
- Finally, the effects of PT on agility performance were also examined in this review. Four published studies were analyzed, and the overall magnitude of improvement in

agility performance was calculated to be 4.8%. Although mechanisms behind this improvement remain to be studied, it could be speculated that this improvement could largely be contributed to the decrease in ground contact times when preparing to change direction, which is a major component of agility in tasks assessing agility performance. Suitable forms of PT, based on our results, can be recommended for improving the agility performance in healthy individuals.

CONCLUSION

In the present study we reviewed a total of 33 well-controlled studies evaluating the effects of PT on muscle function and rapid movement performance. This review showed that PT improves maximal strength of lower-limb muscles. However, we could not support the widely held belief that PT improves explosive muscle strength, with the exception of explosive strength of plantar flexor muscles, and, partly, leg extensor muscles. Interestingly, the muscle group being the most prone to improvement in both maximal strength and explosive muscle strength following a PT intervention appears to be plantar flexors. Also, the improvements in maximal and explosive muscle strength following a PT intervention are specific to the muscle group trained. Regarding muscle power, our results revealed a positive change in lower-body power as a result of PT; however, the magnitude of changes ranged from small negative changes to large positive changes. Different settings used for power assessment in the analyzed studies probably contributed to this wide range of improvements, and they prevent us from drawing any firm conclusions with regard to PT effects in muscle power improvement.

In addition to its positive effects on muscle function, PT also improves rapid movement performance, i.e., jumping, sprinting, and agility performance. Specifically, we showed that PT improves vertical jump height in all four types of standard vertical jumps (i.e., SJ, CMJ, CMJA, and DJ) and that these improvements could undoubtedly be considered practically relevant. High jumpers, volleyball, basketball and handball players are among the athletes that probably benefit the most from PT-induced improvements, since vertical jump performance directly influences their sport-specific performance. On the contrary, the effects of PT on horizontal jump performance still remain to be more thoroughly investigated. Available data indicates possible improvements in horizontal jump distance following a PT intervention; however, no firm conclusion on this issue can be drawn at this point. Sprint running performance to a smaller extent and agility performance to a greater extent also appear to improve following a PT training intervention. The mechanisms behind this improvement remain to be studied, but analyzed studies indicate that decreased ground contact times contribute to the overall improvement in sprint running and agility performance. Due to the debatable practical relevance of sprint performance improvement following a PT training intervention (i.e. 1.6% on average), perhaps other forms of physical conditioning should accompany PT in order for greater and practically more relevant improvements in sprint running performance to be achieved.

Based on the obtained results, we conclude that appropriate forms of PT may be recommended as a form of physical conditioning for augmenting muscle function and rapid movement performance in healthy individuals. Further well-designed studies are needed to address a number of open questions related to PT like 1) what are the adaptation mechanisms (i.e., neural, muscular, hormonal etc.) responsible for PT-induced changes in muscle function and rapid movement performance, 2) how different types of plyometric exercises (e.g. slow vs. fast stretch-shortening cycle jumps; horizontal vs. vertical jumps; two-leg jumps vs. one-leg jumps) influence muscle strength and power of different muscle groups, and in different types of muscular contractions, and 3) are there any age and gender effects on PT induced changes in muscle function and rapid movement performance.

REFERENCES

[1]   Aagaard, P., Simonsen, E. B., Andersen, J. L., Magnusson, P. & Dyhre-Poulsen, P. (1990) Increased rate of force development and neural drive of human skeletal muscle following resistance training. *J App Phys*, 93, 1318-26.

[2]   Abernethy, P., Wilson, G., Logan, P. (1995) Strength and power assessment. Issues, controversies and challenges. *Sports Med*, 19, 401-17.

[3]   Andersen, L. L. & Aagaard, P. (2006) Influence of maximal muscle strength and intrinsic muscle contractile properties on contractile rate of force development. *Eur J App Phys*, 96, 46-52.

[4]   Blattner, S. E. & Noble, L. (1979) Relative effects of isokinetic and plyometric training on vertical jumping performance. *Res Q*, 50, 583-8.

[5]   Bobbert, M. F. (1990) Drop jumping as a training method for jumping ability. *Sports Med*, 9, 7-22.

[6]   Bobbert, M. F, Huijing, P. A. & van Ingen Schenau, G. J. (1987) Drop jumping I. The influence of jumping technique on the biomechanics of jumping. *Med Sci Sports Exerc*, 19, 332-8.

[7]   Brown, M. E., Mayhew, J. L. & Boleach, L.W. (1986) Effect of plyometric training on vertical jump performance in high school basketball players. *J Sports Med Phys Fit*, 26, 1-4.

[8]   Canavan, P. K. & Vescovi, J.D. (2004) Evaluation of power prediction equations: peak vertical jumping power in women. *Med Sci Sports Exerc*, 36, 1589-93.

[9]   Chimera, N. J., Swanik, K. A, Swanik, C. B. & Straub, S. J. (2004) Effects of Plyometric Training on Muscle-Activation Strategies and Performance in Female Athletes. *J Athl Train*, 39, 24-31.

[10]   Cornu, C., Almeida Silveira, M. I. & Goubel, F. (1997) Influence of plyometric training on the mechanical impedance of the human ankle joint. *Eur J App Phys Occ Phys*, 76, 282-8.

[11]   Delecluse, C. (1997) Influence of strength training on sprint running performance. Current findings and implications for training. *Sports Med*, 24, 147-56.

[12]   Delecluse, C., Van Coppenolle, H., Willems, E., Van Leemputte, M., Diels, R. & Goris, M. (1995) Influence of high-resistance and high-velocity training on sprint performance. *Med Sci Sports Exerc*, 27, 1203-9.

[13]   de Villarreal, E. S., Gonzalez-Badillo, J. J. & Izquierdo, M. (2008) Low and moderate plyometric training frequency produces greater jumping and sprinting gains compared with high frequency. *J Strength Cond Res*, 22, 715-25.

[14] Diallo, O., Dore, E., Duche, P. & Van Praagh, E. (2001) Effects of plyometric training followed by a reduced training programme on physical performance in prepubescent soccer players. *J Sports Med Phys Fit*, 41, 342-8.

[15] Dvir, Z. (1985) Pre-stretch conditioning: the effect of incorporating high vs low intensity pre-stretch stimulus on vertical jump scores. Part II. *Aus J Sci Med Sport*, 17, 15-9.

[16] Fatouros, I. G., Jamurtas, A. Z., Leontsini, D., Taxildaris, K., Aggelousis, N., Kostopoulos, N., et al. (2000) Evaluation of plyometric exercise training, weight training, and their combination on vertical jumping performance and leg strength. *J Strength Cond Res*, 14, 470-6.

[17] Gehri, D. J., Ricard, M. D., Kleiner, D. M. & Kirkendall, D. T. (1998) A comparison of plyometric training techniques for improving vertical jump ability and energy production. *J Strength Cond Res*, 12, 85-9.

[18] Herrero, J. A., Izquierdo, M., Maffiuletti, N. A. & Garcia-Lopez, J. (2006) Electromyostimulation and plyometric training effects on jumping and sprint time. *Int J Sports Med*, 27, 533-9.

[19] Hewett, T. E., Stroupe, A. L., Nance, T. A. & Noyes, F. R. (1996) Plyometric training in female athletes. Decreased impact forces and increased hamstring torques. *Am J Sports Med*, 24, 765-73.

[20] Holcomb, W. R., Lander, J. E., Rutland, R. M. & Wilson, G.D. (1996) The effectiveness of a modified plyometric program on power and the vertical jump. *J Strength Cond Res*, 10, 89-92.

[21] Hortobagyi, T., Havasi, J. & Varga, Z. (1990) Comparison of 2 stretch-shorten exercise programs in 13-year old boys - nonspecific training effects. *J Hum Movt Stud*, 18, 177-88.

[22] Hortobagyi, T., Sio, A., Fodor, T. & Merkely, B. (1991) Effects of targeted skill development and plyometric conditioning on long jump performance in 16-year old boys. *J Hum Movt Stud*, 21, 1-17.

[23] Irmischer, B. S., Harris, C., Pfeiffer, R. P., DeBeliso, M. A., Adams, K. J. & Shea, K. G. (2004) Effects of a knee ligament injury prevention exercise program on impact forces in women. *J Strength Cond Res*, 18, 703-7.

[24] Kato, T., Terashima, T., Yamashita, T., Hatanaka, Y., Honda, A. & Umemura, Y. (2005) Effect of low-repetition jump training on bone mineral density in young women. *J App Phys*, 100, 839-843.

[25] Komi, P.V. (1984) Physiological and biomechanical correlates of muscle function: effects of muscle structure and stretch-shortening cycle on force and speed. *Exerc Sport Sci Rev*, 12, 81-121.

[26] Kotzamanidis, C. (2006) Effect of plyometric training on running performance and vertical jumping in prepubertal boys. *J Strength Cond Res*, 20, 441-5.

[27] Kyrolainen, H., Avela, J., McBride, J. M., Koskinen, S., Andersen, J. L., Sipila, S., et al. (2005) Effects of power training on muscle structure and neuromuscular performance. *Scand J Med Sci Sports*, 15, 58-64.

[28] Lehance, C., Croisier, J. L. & Bury, T. (2005) Optojump system efficiency in the assessment of lower limbs explosive strength. *Sci Sports*, 20, 131-5.

[29] Little, A. D. (1996) Enhancing performance: Maximal power versus combined weights and plyometrics training. *J Strength Cond Res*, 10, 173-9.

[30] Lundin, P. & Berg, W. (1991) Plyometrics: a review of plyometric training. *Nat Strength Cond Assoc J*, 13, 22-34.

[31] Markovic. G. (2007) Does plyometric training improve vertical jump height? A meta-analytical review. *Br J Sports Med*, 41, 349-55.

[32] Markovic, G. & Jaric, S. (2007) Is vertical jump height a body size-independent measure of muscle power? *J Sports Sci*, 25, 1355-63.

[33] Markovic, G. & Jaric, S. (2005) Scaling of muscle power to body size: the effect of stretch-shortening cycle. *Eur J App Phys*, 95, 11-9.

[34] Markovic, G., Jukic, I., Milanovic, D. & Metikos, D. (2007) Effects of sprint and plyometric training on muscle function and athletic performance. *J Strength Cond Res,* 21, 543-9.

[35] Matavulj, D., Kukolj, M., Ugarkovic, D., Tihanyi, J. & Jaric, S. (2001) Effects of plyometric training on jumping performance in junior basketball players. *J Sports Med Phys Fit*, 41, 159-64.

[36] Miller, M. G., Berry, D. C., Bullard, S. & Gilders, R. (2002) Comparisons of land-based and aquatic-based plyometric programs during an 8-week training period. *J Sport Rehab,* 11, 268-83.

[37] Miller, M. G., Herniman, J. J., Ricard, M. D., Cheatham, C. C. & Michael, T. J. (2006) The effects of a 6-week plyometric training program on agility. *J Sports Sci Med,* 459-65.

[38] Mero, A., Komi, P. V. & Gregor, R. J. (1992) Biomechanics of sprint running: A review. *Sports Med*, 13, 376-92.

[39] Rimmer, E. & Sleivert, G. (2000) Effects of a plyometrics intervention program on sprint performance. *J Strength Cond Res*, 14, 295-301.

[40] Roper, R. L. (1998) Incorporating agility training and backward movement into a plyometric program. *Strength Cond J*, 20, 60-3.

[41] Sale, D.G. (1992) Neural adaptation to strength training. In: Komi, P. V. (Ed.), *Strength and Power in Sport*. (pp. 249-66). London: Blackwell Scientific.

[42] Salonikidis, K. & Zafeiridis, A. (2008) The effects of plyometric, tennis-drills, and combined training on reaction, lateral and linear speed, power, and strength in novice tennis players. *J Strength Cond Res*, 22, 182-91.

[43] Spurrs, R. W., Murphy, A. J. & Watsford, M. L. (2003) The effect of plyometric training on distance running performance. *Eur J Appl Phys*, 89, 1-7.

[44] Stemm, J. D. & Jacobson, B. H. (2007) Comparison of land- and aquatic-based plyometric training on vertical jump performance. *J Strength Cond Res*, 21, 568-71.

[45] Tricoli, V., Lamas, L., Carnevale, R. & Ugrinowitsch, C. (2005) Short-term effects on lower-body functional power development: weightlifting vs. vertical jump training programs. *J Strength Cond Res*, 19, 433-7.

[46] Turner, A. M., Owings, M. & Schwane, J. A. (2003) Improvement in running economy after 6 weeks of plyometric training. *J Strength Cond Res*, 17, 60-7.

[47] Twist, P. W. & Benicky, D. (1996) Conditioning lateral movements for multi-sport athletes: Practical strength and quickness drills. *Strength Cond J*, 18, 10-9.

[48] Wagner, D. R. & Kocak, S. (1997) A multivariate approach to assessing anaerobic power following a plyometric training program. *J Strength Cond Res*, 11, 251-5.

[49] Wilk, K. E., Voight, M. L., Keirns, M. A., Gambetta, V., Andrews, J. R. & Dillman, C. J. (1993) Stretch-shortening drills for the upper extremities: theory and clinical application. *J Orthop Sports Phys Ther*, 17, 225-39.

[50] Wilson, G. J., Murphy, A. J. & Giorgi, A. (1996) Weight and plyometric training: effects on eccentric and concentric force production. *Can J App Phys*, 21, 301-15.

[51] Wilson, G. J., Newton, R. U., Murphy, A. J. & Humphries, B. J. (1993) The optimal training load for the development of dynamic athletic performance. *Med Sci Sports Exerc*, 25, 1279-86.

[52] Young, W. B., James, R. & Montgomery, I. (2002) Is muscle power related to running speed with changes of direction? *J Sports Med Phys Fit*, 42, 282-8.

[53] Young, W. B., Wilson, G. J. & Byrne, C. A. (1990) A comparison of drop jump training methods: effects on leg extensor strength qualities and jumping performance. *Int J Sports Med*, 20, 295-303.

In: Advances in Strength and Conditioning Research
Editor: Michael Duncan and Mark Lyons

ISBN: 978-1-60692-909-4
© 2009 Nova Science Publishers, Inc.

Chapter 10

STRENGTH AND CONDITIONING PROGRAMME DESIGN FOR COMBAT SPORTS

Ian Lahart[1] and Paul Robertson
University College Birmingham, UK

ABSTRACT

Effective strength and conditioning programmes are designed to optimally prepare athletes to meet the specific demands of their particular sport. Due to the unique and highly specific nature of each combat sport, strength and conditioning professionals are faced with a particularly complex challenge. This chapter presents an analysis of the three very different combat sports of amateur boxing, taekwondo, and judo. Each of these combat sports requires competitors to perform a diverse range of technical movements and skills, elicits a specific metabolic response during actual competition, and necessitates the possession of distinct physiological characteristics for performance at elite levels. Therefore, strength and conditioning programme design for each sport requires a different and multifaceted approach. Sports-specific skill-based high-intensity interval training, Olympic weightlifting exercises, circuit training, plyometrics, and complex training are strength and conditioning methods that can all be tailored to meet the specific technical and physiological demands of actual competition. The following chapter provides strength and conditioning professionals with a rationale for these training methods and sample sessions demonstrating how they can be applied to each of the three combat sports.

Keywords: Judo, Taekwondo, Boxing, Complex Training, High Intensity Training, Plyometrics

The nature of combat sport is to strike, throw or grapple with an opponent [59]. However, each combat sport is highly individualized and requires unique actions and techniques. For

---

[1] Please address correspondence and requests for reprints to Ian M. Lahart, Sports Therapy Department, University College Birmingham, Summer Row, Birmingham, England, B3 1JB or e mail i.lahart@ucb.ac.uk.

example, taekwondo involves only kicks and punches, while judo prohibits punching and kicks in favour of throws and grappling. In addition to this, individual combat sports have differing rules and regulations. For example, in freestyle wrestling only use of the arms and upper bodies are permitted, while in freestyle wrestling, athletes can also use their legs and may hold opponents above or below the waist [56]. Furthermore, combat rules have different contest formats, for example, judo consists of one continuous 5-minute bout, while taekwondo contests consist of three 2-minute rounds [49, 113]. Therefore, due to the different actions, techniques, and contest rules and formats, each combat sports represents a unique challenge to the strength and conditioning professional.

Specifically, this chapter will examine the three combat sports of amateur boxing, taekwondo, and Judo. Along with freestyle and Greco-Roman wrestling, these three combat sports represent the five Olympic combat sports. In accordance with the law of specificity, to be effective, strength and conditioning programmes for any of these three sports must stress the physiological systems specific to that particular sport. To do this we must first understand the physiological effects elicited during and after competition in the sport. Once these effects have been analysed, a strength and conditioning programme can be designed to adequately stress the physiological systems required for competition and simulate the conditions elicited during actual competition in the training environment.

With this in mind, the first part of this chapter aims to provide strength and conditioning practioners with the latest findings from the literature in regards to the specific technical and metabolic demands that these sports place on participants. In addition to this, the physiological characteristics of elite competitors will be explored to find possible determinants of successful performance in each sport. In part two of the chapter, these findings will then be applied to the design of strength and conditioning programmes for the three combat sports. Both advanced and traditional training methods, specific to each sport and supported by scientific evidence, will be investigated.

PART I. TECHNICAL AND PHYSIOLOGICAL ANALYSIS OF COMBAT SPORTS

Technical and Physiological Analysis of Amateur Boxing

Boxing is an intermittent contact sport, characterised by bouts of short duration high-intensity activity [52]. This high-intensity activity is comprised of a high punching rate and punching force, and dynamic footwork [94]. Currently, boxing in the Olympics allows only amateur participation, and consists of four 2-minute rounds, separated by 1-min rest periods, but this is due to change to three 3-min rounds in 2009. The aim of boxing is either to score more points than your opponent or stop your opponent within the contest duration. A point is scored if a punch is not blocked or guarded but lands directly with the knuckle part of the closed glove of either hand on any part of the front or sides of the head or body above the belt, but not on the arms. The outcome of a contest is either decided by the referee within its designated duration, or by 3 to 5 judges using the CSS computer scoring system if the fight goes the distance [1].

For strength and conditioning programme design purposes it is important to understand the energy pathways that predominate during sports competition. The majority of combat sports require a combination of the three energy systems. Combat sports consist of the performance of intermittent high-intensity short duration bouts of activity, which is predominantly fuelled by the anaerobic pathways of ATP and creatine phosphate (PCr) hydrolysis (phosphate system) and the degradation of muscle glycogen to lactate (lactate system) [112]. However, a significant contribution from the aerobic energy system has also been shown in high-intensity exercise lasting just 6 seconds [36]. Furthermore, this aerobic contribution has been shown to increase when high-intensity, short duration activity is repeated or sustained [14, 36, 73]. In addition to this, athlete's with a high level of aerobic fitness appear to recover faster from high-intensity activity than less aerobically fit athletes [103]. Thus, although the anaerobic energy systems predominate during boxing activities, the aerobic energy system has an important role in both the execution of and recovery from multiple high-intensity activity. The percentage contribution of the anaerobic and aerobic energy systems to boxing has been estimated as 70-80% anaerobic and 20-30% aerobic [41].

Limited research exists regarding the physiological response to boxing performance. Furthermore, the physiological impact of competition is dependent on a boxer's style and the tactics employed throughout a contest. Khanna and Manna [52] investigated the physiological response to actual boxing rounds (3 x 2 minute rounds) during competitive trials compared to graded treadmill exercise which simulated actual boxing competition (3 x 2-min bouts of exercise performed at progressively higher intensities, separated by a 1-min rest). When comparing the actual boxing rounds to graded exercise, the authors reported that the actual boxing round elicited significantly higher maximal (183-184 bpm vs. 177-180 bpm) and recovery (161-168 bpm vs. 138-146 bpm) heart rates, and blood lactate levels (7.1-9.9 mmol/L vs. 6.5-9.7 mmol/L) for all weight categories [52]. High lactic acid concentrations highlight the intense nature of boxing competition and reflect the contribution of the lactate system to meet energy demands.

Smith [93] compared post competition blood lactate values collected after different contest formats and scoring systems using data gathered between 1987 and 2004. The highest post contest blood lactate values (13.5 mmol/L) were recorded after the current format of four 2-minute rounds using computer scoring, compared to 9.5 mmol/L after three 3-minute rounds, and 8.6 mmol/L after five 2-minute rounds using computer scoring systems. The differences in lactate values between the different contest formats may be related to changes in tactical strategy and training methods [93].

In the future format (3 x 3-min rounds) there is an emphasis on the boxer to perform more frequent repeated bursts of high-intensity punching throughout the contest, thus, increasing the physiological demand on the athletes reflected by elevated lactate levels [94]. Smith [93] reported higher lactate concentrations and maximal heart rate values (>200 bpm) during actual boxing than those found in Khanna and Manna [52]. This may be explained by the shorter bout duration of the actual boxing (4 vs. 3 rounds), and the fact that Khanna and Manna [52] recorded heart rate values at the end of each round, while Smith [94] measured heart rates continuously during each round. Therefore, as Khanna and Manna [52] were unable to detect heart rates during periods of high-intensity activity during the actual rounds, the reported heart rates would be expected to be lower than in Smith [93].

Physiological Characteristics of Elite Amateur Boxers

Unfortunately, there are few studies that have investigated the physiological characteristics of amateur boxers. Furthermore, the application of this literature is limited by the changes in contest format by the AIBA, from 3 x 3 minute rounds to 5 x 2-min rounds in 1997, in 2000 to the 2008 format of 4 x 2 minutes with 1-min rest, and again to the new format of 3 x 3-min rounds with 1-min between rounds [1, 2, 93]. As seen above these modifications in contest format have changed the physiological demands of boxing and in turn the physiological characteristics of the athletes.

Guidetti and colleagues [42] investigated whether a relationship existed between certain physiological characteristics of elite amateur boxers and their ranking as decided using AIBA ranking criteria. The 8 elite Italian national middleweight (75-81 kg) boxers in this study possessed a mean VO_2max of 57.5 ml/kg/min. The mean VO_2 at which lactate threshold (LT) occurred was 46 ml/kg/min, which equated to 78.4% of the average VO_2max. The boxers mean body fat percentage was 14.5 ± 1.5 %, the mean grip strength was 58.2 ± 6.9 kg, and the mean wrist girth was 17.6 ± 0.6 cm^2. The variables found to be most related to boxing competition ranking were the individual anaerobic threshold and the handgrip strength, while moderate relationships were reported for VO_2max and wrist girth. However, wrist girth may not be a useful parameter to identify boxing talent because increases in this measure would be an expected as an adaptation to biochemical usage [42].

Recently, Khanna and Manna [52] reported mean VO_2max values of 61.7 ml/kg/min and 54.6 ml/kg/min in senior ($\geq$ 19 year of age) and junior (< 19 years of age) Indian amateur boxers, respectively. Compared to junior boxers, the senior boxers were found to possess a mesomorphic body conformation, significantly higher body fat percentage (16.4 % vs. 12.2 %), power-to-body weight ratios (6.5 W/kg BW vs. 4.9 W/kg BW), back strength (156.5 kg vs. 125.7 kg), and both left and right grip strength (left = 50.1 kg vs. 44.9 kg; right = 62.7 kg vs. 45.6 kg). In addition to this, senior boxers were able to work at higher intensities than their junior counterparts, as evidenced by the finding of significantly higher mean maximal heart rates (191 bpm vs. 186 bpm) and peak lactate levels. Due to the performance inhibiting effects that excessive blood lactate is associated with, it can be said that the higher the intensity at which an athlete can work at without an excessive accumulation of blood lactate, the longer and harder that athlete can exercise [7]. Thus, a higher LT allows a boxer to perform at a higher intensity level during subsequent rounds, delaying the detrimental affects associated with lactic acid accumulation [52].

A recent study investigated both the physiological demands of amateur boxing and the physiological profile of senior and junior England international amateur boxers [93]. A mean total skinfold of 22.3 mm and mean body fat percentage of 9.1% was reported for the senior boxers, while the junior boxers possessed higher mean total skinfold and mean body fat percentage of 23.8 mm and 10.1 %, respectively. The mean VO_2max values of senior boxers was 63.8 ml/kg/min, which was significantly higher than the 49.8 ml/kg/min reported for the junior boxers. The boxers' mean heart rate at a blood lactate of 2 mmol/L (LT) and 4 mmol/L (onset of blood lactate accumulation or OBLA) was reported as 151 bpm and 174 bpm, respectively. The lactate threshold was reached at 68% of VO_2 max, while OBLA occurred at a mean VO_2max percentage of 86%.

Along with exhibiting dynamic footwork and high punch rates, amateur boxers require the ability to punch with a high amount of force. Smith et al. [94] demonstrated using lead and rear straight punching of a boxing dynamometer (CV = 1%) that elite boxers punched with more force than both intermediate and novice boxers, and that all levels of boxers punched with greater force with their rear compared to their lead hands. The higher punch force generated by the elite boxers was said to be related to their greater experience over the intermediate and novice, and the emphasis on the production of a forceful rear punch in elite competitions that use computer scoring [94]. Whereas, the higher rear punch force (elite = 4800 N) compared to lead hand (elite = 2847 N) reported was attributed to the force generated by the legs, increased body rotation, and the greater distance over which the long-range straight rear punch is thrown [46].

In summary, actual boxing rounds elicit maximal heart rates exceeding 200 bpm and 184 bpm was measured at when measured throughout four 2-minute rounds and at the end three 2-minute rounds, respectively. Post contest lactate levels of 13.5 mmol/L and 9.9 mmol/L have been recorded after four 2-minute rounds and three 2-minute rounds, respectively. Currently, elite amateur boxers possess mean body fat percentages ranging from 9.1 % to 16.4 %, and show a mesomorphic body conformation. Mean VO_2max values of elite amateur boxers range between 57.5 ml/kg/min and 63.8 ml/kg/min, reflecting the need for boxers to perform at a high percentage of VO_2max. Previous studies have shown that elite amateur boxers possess high anaerobic capacities, such as mean LT between 68% and 78.4% of VO_2max, mean OBLA of 86% of VO_2max, and a high mean power-to-body weight ratio of 6.5 W/kg BW. In addition to this, elite amateur boxers require the ability to punch with mean forces of 4800 N with the rear hand and 2847 N with the lead hand.

Thus, the physiological demands of the amateur boxing require a well developed cardiovascular system, the ability to tolerate high levels of lactic acid, and the capacity to recover quickly between bouts of high-intensity activity. The aims of strength and conditioning for boxing should be to maintain a relatively low body fat percentage, attain a mesomorphic body conformation, improve the efficiency of the aerobic system, increase the capacity of the ATP-PC system, enhance lactate threshold and tolerance to lactic acid accumulation, improve recovery between intense bursts of activity, and increase the amount of force generated with each punch.

Technical and Physiological Analysis of Taekwondo

Taekwondo is a Korean martial art that was introduced as an Olympic sport in the 2000 Sydney Olympics. Olympic taekwondo bouts consist of three 2-min rounds (reduced from 3 x 3-min rounds in 2005), and depending on their weight category competitors may fight several times during the same day [113]. Points are scored by kicks to the torso and head or by punches to the head only, with sufficient force to displace the body segment [116]. Matches are either won by knock-out or points. Typically most points are scored from kicks, with very few points coming from punches and penalties [51].

Analysis of taekwondo competitive bouts in the 2000 Olympic Games revealed that kicking accounted for 98% of all techniques used to score, whilst offensive techniques were more commonly used to score than defensive techniques (275 vs. 204 for men, and 273 vs. 242 for women) [51]. Interestingly, non-winners scored a higher percentage of their points with offensive techniques than male winners (63% vs. 57%), while male winners scored considerably more with defensive techniques than their unsuccessful counterparts (46% vs.

38%). Similarly, another study discovered that 43% of all head blows were inflicted by an opponent's counter-attack [55]. This suggests that although an offensive technique gains a higher amount of points the ability to score with defensive techniques may differentiate between winners and non-winners.

In addition to this, Koh and Watkinson [54] investigated video analysis of 35 incidents of head blows in 48 matches in the 1999 world taekwondo championships, and reported that shorter opponents received head blows (47%) more often than taller (26%) or similar stature opponents (26%). Of these head, 66% were received in a closed sparring stance where the body is protected, which results in the head becoming the main target. No evasive manoeuvres were performed, which may be due to athletes overly concentrating on offence, poor anticipation, or greater training in kicking skills rather than blocking skills [54].

Evidence of the effectiveness and prevalence of kicking techniques can be provided by studies investigating the frequency of head blows and time-loss injury during taekwondo competition. In a previous study, roundhouse kicks followed by spinning kicks have been shown to inflict most time-loss injuries in both male and female taekwondo athletes, due to the greater velocities generated with these kicks [10, 78]. Koh and Watkinson [54] reported that head and face blows were most frequently inflicted by axe or roundhouse kicks (axe = 70%; roundhouse = 20%) involving the leading or front foot (57%). While, Beis and colleagues [10] reported that roundhouse kicks and axe kicks were responsible 50% and 33% of head blows, respectively.

Elite taekwondo athletes require the ability to kick and punch with repeatedly with great speed and force throughout a competitive contest. Chiu et al. [21] researching a new measurement system for taekwondo athletes, reported speeds of 80.2 to 90.9 km/h for roundhouse kicks and 78.9 to 85.7 km/h for back kicks. The device also measured roundhouse and back kick force values of 78.9 to 92.5 kgf and 72.1 to 85.7 kgf, respectively. Serina and Lieu [89] noted that roundhouse kicks travel at great speed (15 m/s) and have a high potential for inflicting soft-tissue injury, while back and side kicks can generate large chest compressions.

Heller and colleagues [43] analysis of two 2-min rounds of competitive taekwondo fighting revealed that typical bouts consisted of repeated 3 to 5 s of high-intensity activity alternated with periods of low-intensity. In addition to this, the authors observed heart rates of 100% of maximal heart rate and lactate concentrations of 11.4 mmol/L during competitive taekwondo. Bouhel and colleagues [17] reported that simulated taekwondo competition, consisting of a three 3-min rounds, with 1-min rest periods between each round, elicited heart rate and lactate values of 197 bpm and 10.2 mmol/L, respectively. The lactate levels in this study were only slightly higher than that found by Heller et al. [43] after two shorter rounds of 2-min duration (10.2 mmol/L vs. 9.9 mmol/L). Unfortunately, no studies to date have examined the actual physiological effects of the new three 2-min round contest format.

Physiological Characteristics of Elite Taekwondo Athletes

Due to the change in taekwondo contest format from 3-min rounds to 2-min rounds, caution is advised when interpreting data pre-2005, as it may reflect as accurately the changed physiological demands of the sport. Markovic and colleagues [65] reported that successful female taekwondo champions possessed somewhat lower body fat percentages (by 2.3%) and were slightly taller (by 5.8 cm) than less successful ones. In agreement with this, Kazemi et al. [51] although not significant found that winning taekwondo athletes tended to be younger in age, taller, and possess slightly lower BMI than their weight category average. The authors suggested that taller competitors had an advantage over opponents of lesser stature due to a longer reach, leaner body, and longer lever, which helps them cover larger distances expending less energy.

Goa [38] observed that 30 elite Chinese male Taekwondo athletes predominantly possessed an ecto-mesomorph somatotypes, well developed muscles, and low subcutaneous fat. Analysis of male and female elite taekwondo athletes from the Czech national team revealed that the athletes possessed body fat percentages 8.2% and 15.4% for male and female athletes, respectively [44]. These body fat percentages were lower than that found in Taiwanese Taekwondo athletes (male = 13.2%; female = 19.4%) [61], and in male Tunisian national team Taekwondo athletes (11.8%) [17]. Overall successful taekwondo athletes tend to possess, with lower body fat percentage, increased muscle mass and taller, leaner bodies [37, 44, 51]. Gao et al. [37] suggested that lower body fat percentages and higher lean body mass are needed to gain the highest aerobic capacity.

To enable relatively fast recovery between rounds and fights, and also during and after training sessions, it is vital taekwondo athletes possess an adequate aerobic capacity. Rapid recovery allows an athlete reduce the amount of recovery time required between the performance of high-intensity exercise, and is especially relevant in sports such as taekwondo that demands many repetitions of a sport-specific skill [65]. A study of Czech national taekwondo athletes reported VO_2max values of 54.6 ml/kg/min [44], which was lower than the value of 56.22 ml/kg/min reported in Tunisian national team elite male taekwondo athletes [17].

Due to the explosive high-intensity nature of the sport, taekwondo athletes require high anaerobic power and anaerobic capacity [44]. Markovic et al. [65] reported that successful female taekwondo athletes achieved ventilatory threshold (VT) at significantly higher speeds and lower heart rate, possessed significantly greater explosive power, anaerobic alactic power, and lateral agility than less successful competitors.

Lin and colleagues [61] investigated the anaerobic capacity of elite male Taiwanese taekwondo athletes preparing for 2004 Olympics. The Taiwanese taekwondo athletes achieved peak power (Wpeak) and mean power (Wmean) values of 8.42 W/kg and 6.56 W/kg, respectively. These Wpeak values were considerably lower than the 14.7 W/kg BW reported in Czech national Taekwondo athletes [44], elite American senior taekwondo athletes (11.8 W/kg) [76], Tunisian national team taekwondo athletes (12.1 W/kg) [17], and elite kickboxers (18.8 W/kg) [115]. The average power of the Taiwanese taekwondo athletes was also significantly lower than that of the elite American senior taekwondo athletes (9.2 W/kg) [76] and elite kickboxers (10.5 W/kg) [115].

In summary, taekwondo athletes' score most frequently from kicks, whilst adopting offensive techniques or by counter attacking. The emphasis on kicking may mean that opponents are more vulnerable to punching techniques and may not have proper defensive techniques to counter. Therefore, taekwondo athletes should work on punching techniques in addition to kicking techniques. Taekwondo is a sport which requires great kicking speed and force. Roundhouse kicks generate the highest kick speed and force, while axe, roundhouse, and spinning kicks inflict the most blows to the head and face. While, shorter athletes, a closed stance, and a lack of offensive action with an absence of blocking skills is associated with an increased risk of head and face blows. Thus, taekwondo athletes should place more emphasis on blocking kicks and perhaps adopting evasive strategies used in other sports, such as ducking in boxing.

Taekwondo competition consists of repeated bouts of 3-5 s high-intensity activity alternated with periods of low intensity. Competitive taekwondo bouts of three 3-min rounds, separated by 1-min rest intervals elicit maximal heart rates of 197 bpm and lactate concentrations of 10.2 mmol/L. Therefore, taekwondo performance mainly consists of repeated bursts of sudden, fast and powerful kicks that require a significant contribution from the phosphate and lactate systems, while the aerobic energy system aids recovery between high-intensity activity and increasingly contributes to energy expenditure as the bout continue.

Successful male taekwondo athletes tend to possess an ecto-mesomorphic somatotype, be taller than the weight category average, and possess low body fat percentages (8% to 13.2%). Taekwondo athletes have moderately high VO_2max values of 54.6 ml/kg/min to 56.22 ml/kg/min, highlighting the importance of aerobic conditioning in the recovery between rounds and fights. The importance of the phosphate system is reflected by the high Wpeak scores of 8.42 W/kg to 14.7 W/kg achieved by taekwondo athletes. In addition to this, taekwondo athletes possess high anaerobic capacity values of 6.56 W/kg to 9.2 W/kg for taekwondo athletes. Thus, Taekwondo require lean bodies with low percentages of body fat, high anaerobic power and capacity, and moderately high aerobic capacity.

Technical and Physiological Analysis of Judo

Judo is a predominantly anaerobic, intermittent combat sport [35] requiring strength [58], quickness, balance, and explosiveness [60]. In addition to the physical demands, the sport has a large technical component and as athletes wear a *gi* (jacket type garment secured with a belt) when competing it has been suggested that judo is more technical than other grappling type sports such as wrestling [4].

Judokas (judo athletes) utilise throwing techniques to force an opponent to the ground, and once on the ground, groundwork to pin an opponent or force them into submission. Similar to boxers and taekwondo athletes, *Judokas* are split into weight categories and at senior level bouts are scheduled for 5-min real-time (i.e., clock is paused when bout is paused e.g., for injury). The *judoka* accumulating the most fractional points during this period will win the bout. However, if an *ippon* (a full point) is achieved by a judoka before this period ends, the bout will cease and that player will be awarded the victory. An *ippon* can be achieved in several ways, such as by accumulating sufficient fractional points, by throwing an opponent directly onto their back, by pinning an opponent on their back for 25 s, or by forcing an opponent to submit utilising a chokehold or joint lock [49].

If scores are level at the end of the 5-min period then the first judoka to score any form of point will win the contest during a subsequent 5-min "golden score" period. If no point is scored during this period then the three judges will indicate who they believe was the most aggressive and dominant judoka throughout the bout and award them the victory. Therefore, being able to achieve *ippon* and ending the bout as quickly as possible is beneficial as *judokas* may compete several times a day with as little as 15 mins separating contests [35].

The physiological demands of judo competition can vary due to the variety of tactics and techniques available to the *judoka*. *Tachi-waza* (standing combat) predominates over *ne-waza* (groundwork combat) in simulated combat with twelve sequences of *tachi-waza* lasting on average 21 s compared to six sequences of *ne-waza* lasting on average 11 s [34], furthermore in elite judo competition *judokas* utilise *ashi-waza* (leg techniques) in preference to *te-waza* (arm techniques) possibly due to *ashi-waza* inducing less O_2 uptake than *te-waza* [34]. Furthermore, Franchini and colleagues [34] found that use of *te-waza* was positively correlated with post-bout blood lactate concentrations.

Almansba et al. [3] highlighted that judokas of different statures may adopt different approaches with lighter *judokas* (< 66kg) adopting more arm techniques such as *seoi nage* (one-arm shoulder throw) as their stature allows them to perform throws at a quicker rate and with less effort. However, Blais and colleagues [12] in their 3-dimensional analysis of the *morote seoi nage* (two-arm shoulder throw) technique identified that the main driving moments and greatest energy expenditure in this so-called arm technique come from the lower limbs and trunk through all phases of the throw. Therefore perceived demands may not necessarily match actual demands for certain techniques.

In addition to the demands of throwing actions upon the *judoka*, being thrown and avoiding conceding an *ippon* places significant stress upon the cervical region of the spine [5, 53]. The *o goshi* (hip toss) technique is executed in an average time of 0.29 s and has been found to subject the body and head to forces similar to those observed in road traffic accidents [53]. Furthermore, Kochhar and colleagues [53] observed that in elite *judokas* impact with the floor resulted in a mean posterior translation of the head of 6.2cm from a starting position of 4-5cm anterior translation, followed by mean anterior translation of 4-5cm, suggesting a significant risk of cervical injury that may be exacerbated by poor technique and inexperience. Additionally, when thrown *judokas* will often attempt to "post" on their head in order to avoid conceding an *ippon* (landing wholly on their back) further increasing the risk of cervical spine injury [5].

The high-intensity nature of judo combat is reflected by the short durations of high-intensity combat (10 to 30 s) and rest periods (10 s), in addition to the work-to-rest (W: R) ratios of 1.5 and 3: 1 reported in the literature [35, 33]. Average heart rate values of 92% of age-predicted maximum heart rate have been measured during 5-min of simulated judo combat [27], while similar heart rate values of 181 bpm (91.4% of maximum heart rate) have been reported during actual judo competition [15].

The anaerobic nature of judo combat is demonstrated by post-bout blood lactate concentrations of 10 (± 2.1) mmol/L found in male national and international Brazilian *judokas* (mass < 100kg) [35]. These findings highlight the contribution of anaerobic glycolysis to energy production, and are similar to other post-bout blood lactate concentrations found in *judokas* across weight categories and competitive levels [27, 34, 35].

However, whilst post-bout blood lactate concentrations indicate significant anaerobic contribution to energy production the high levels of aerobic power seen in judokas point to an important role played by aerobic metabolism in energy production for judo competition. Degoutte et al. [27] found significant increases above resting values in free fatty acids, triglycerides and glycerol when measured 3 mins after a simulated 5-min combat situation, thus implicating lipid metabolism despite mean post-bout plasma concentrations of lactate of 12.3 mmol/L. However, Degoutte and colleagues [27] also noted a mean carbohydrate intake of < 332g/day, well below the recommended daily amount for a non-athletic population, therefore the *judokas* glycogen stores may not have been at maximum resulting in a greater reliance on aerobic metabolism for energy production during the bouts.

Physiological Characteristics of Elite Judokas

The demands of judo combat suggest a successful *judoka* would possess specific physiological characteristics that would match these demands and that by using these characteristics *judokas* of differing levels could be distinguished. It appears that this is the case with some but not all characteristics; this could be explained by some *judokas* utilising their technical and tactical superiority to compensate for their physical deficiencies.

Anthropometric characteristics, including fat free mass, do not appear to differentiate *judokas* competing at different levels, although body fat percentage in male *judokas* regardless of level does not appear to exceed approximately 13% [33, 35]. Kubo and colleagues [58] found an average fat-free mass of 74.9 kg in a sample of *judokas* from 7 weight categories who competed at the Olympics or Asian games, which was significantly higher compared to non-competitive university judo club members. Nonetheless, fat free mass differences did not significantly differ between the higher-level *judokas* and competitive university club members suggesting that other factors may account for performances variations at higher levels.

In addition to the differences in fat free mass, Kubo et al. [58] found that the highest-level *judokas* possessed significantly greater height normalized values for elbow extensor (2.8 mm vs. 2.5 mm) and flexor (2.2 mm vs. 2.0 mm) musculature thickness compared to the non-competitive university club members. No significant differences were found with any other muscle thickness measurements taken (abdomen, forearm, knee extensor, knee flexor, plantar flexor, dorsi flexor, and subscapular). The greater elbow flexor and extensor muscle thickness characteristic of higher-level *judokas* may be due to the importance for the *judoka* to control the distance between them and their opponents, and the role that the elbow musculature plays in this [5, 58].

Whilst Kubo and colleagues [58] did not measure strength in addition to muscle thickness, Franchini et al. [33] did find a significant positive correlation between limb circumferences and measures of strength. However, neither measure differentiated between the A (starters), B and C (reserves) teams of the Brazilian national judo squad. Nevertheless, as all of these athletes could be classed as elite and undergo similar training it may be difficult to use such measures to differentiate between them. Despite not differentiating between levels, it should be noted that across the 7 weight categories tested, *judokas* achieved high 1 repetition maximum (1RM) bench press, row and squats scores of 1.24 kg/kg BW, 1.16 kg/kg BW, and 1.44 kg/kg of BW, respectively.

Although, VO_2max values exceeding 60 ml/kg/min have been measured in *judokas*, lower values of 48.3 ml/kg/min have also been found in elite competitors [34, 35]. In one study although, *judokas* with higher VO_2max values performed better in an intermittent, judo-specific throwing test, aerobic capacity was not found to be a distinguishing factor between competitive levels [35]. It must be taken into account that in these studies the sample consisted of *judokas* from a range of weight categories, and therefore, the mean scores reported may be distorted due to the variation in body mass within the sample. Franchini et al. [33] did account for this by demonstrating that in their sample as body mass increased aerobic power, as expected, decreased, and in studies consisting of athletes from a single weight category VO$_2$max values in excess of 50ml/kg/min have been obtained [27].

Franchini and co-workers [35] demonstrated that performance in high-intensity intermittent exercise (4 x upper body Wingate test, with 3 min passive recovery) significantly distinguished between levels, with the two higher-level groups achieving a greater amount of work over the 4 trials than the lower level group. Although, there were no significant differences in blood lactate at any time, Wpeak in all 4 trials, or Wmean in the first trial, it was the ability to maintain high power outputs for longer in subsequent trials that differentiated the groups. This highlights that the intermittent aspect may be the most important for judo success. Moreover, Franchini et al. [34] found positive correlations between the number of attacks initiated in combat, performance in two upper body Wingate tests separated by 3 min recovery, and performance in the intermittent specific judo test. Furthermore, the Wingate protocol and the specific judo test produced similar blood lactate values to 5-min of judo combat.

In summary, judo combat is primarily a high-intensity, intermittent anaerobic activity, as evidenced by the high average heart rates (92% of maximal heart rate) and lactate concentrations (~10 mmol/L) observed during simulated and actual judo competition. The ability to produce high levels of work repeatedly characterises high-level judo performance and distinguishes *judokas* of different competitive levels. Due to the range of VO$_2$ max values observed and the range of options available to competitors during combat in terms of technique and tactics, elite status may be achievable without high levels of aerobic capacity. However, high levels of aerobic capacity may help to maintain power output when anaerobic energy production decreases. In addition to this, due to the performance of multiple judo bouts in one day, high-levels of aerobic fitness may allow more complete recuperation between bouts.

While, strength may not differentiate between levels in elite *judokas*, high bench press, row, and squat 1RM values were achieved by elite *judokas*. *Judokas* must deal with an external resistance (i.e., their opponent) therefore a certain level of strength and power is required, although judo advocates that it is technique and the ability to utilise the mass of an opponent that can bring success. Elbow flexor and extensor musculature thickness may differentiate between levels *judokas*, perhaps due to their role in maintaining distance and controlling the opponent.

PART II COMBAT SPORTS AND STRENGTH AND CONDITIONING METHODS

Optimal sporting performance requires the use of optimal training methods. To be considered optimal, training methods must be sports-specific, that is to say they should stress the physiological systems associated with performance in a specific sport. Specific training should consist of three components, skill specificity, muscle-group specificity, and energy system specificity. To achieve specificity similarities should exist between the training conditions and those required in the field during competition. Training methods that reflect the intensity and duration of exercise bouts in competition should be incorporated into athlete's programmes.

High Intensity Interval Training (HIT)

Amateur boxing, taekwondo and judo competition involves repetitive bouts of high-intensity exercise. Successful performance in each of these combat sports is dependent on not only maintaining these bouts over the full duration of a match, but also on the ability to recover from each exercise bout [66]. To enhance the performance of and recovery from repetitive high-intensity exercise, high-intensity interval training (HIT) is recommended. HIT may be defined as repeated bouts of short-to-moderate duration exercise (5 s - 5 min) performed at intensities above VO_2max. Recovery can be either active or passive, but of a duration where sufficient recovery is not achievable. The rationale for HIT is to provide adaptation by continually stressing sports-specific physiological components above and beyond the level required during actual competition [90].

HIT is associated with a number of desirable biochemical adaptations and improvements in high-intensity exercise performance. HIT has been shown to enhance the capacity of the ATP-PC system through an increase in intramuscular ATP, phosphocreatine, and free creatine stores, and raised concentrations and activity of specific enzymes, including creatine kinase and myokinase [108]. Furthermore, HIT has been shown to elicit adaptations associated with an improved capacity of the lactate system, including increases in intracellular and extracellular lactic acid buffering capacity, enhanced enzymatic activities related to glycolysis (e.g. phosphofructokinase and lactate dehydrogenase), and raised concentrations of glycogen [62, 26, 63, 74].

In addition to this, HIT can develop the ability of combat athletes' tolerance to the accumulation of lactic acid. This tolerance may be crucial near the end of a contest, for example, Sterkowicz and Franchini [98] observed in judo that the majority of fractional points are scored in the first 2 minutes of a bout at the elite level, this lack of points may be due to fatigue, and the *judoka* who retains the ability to attack in the final minutes may hold the advantage over their opponent as they will be able to continue to accumulate points.

Moreover, HIT may provide a more time efficient method for improving endurance performance comparable to traditional endurance training [39, 57]. HIT training comprising of 4 to 7 bouts of 30 s high-intensity cycling exercise separated by 4 minute recovery, performed six times over 2 weeks, has been shown to significantly improve exercise tolerance during tasks that rely on aerobic metabolism. These HIT sessions doubled the length of time that submaximal exercise could be maintained from 26 to 51 minutes during exercise at 80% of VO_2max [18], and also improved the ability to complete a fixed amount of work (e.g. 10% reduction in time to complete a simulated 30-km cycling time trial) [40]. Findings of this nature demonstrate the effectiveness of HIT to enhance both anaerobic and aerobic capacity, and question the use of traditional non-specific training methods such as long distance running to increase combat athletes aerobic capacity.

As mentioned previously, successful combat sport athletes tend to possess lower body fat levels. In addition to this, most combat sport athletes compete at a weight classification lower than their natural body weight. To avoid the use of performance inhibiting and dehydrating weight loss methods, such as calorie restriction, saunas, and the wearing of wet-suits during exercise, in the final 3-days prior to competition, trainers must identify a time scale for safe weight reduction [94]. HIT has been shown to result in a greater reduction in sum of skinfold measures compared to continuous endurance training [96, 105]. Using interval training intensities of 120% VO_2max, Overend et al. [72] demonstrated that while HIT over 6 weeks resulted in similar increases in VO$_2$max as endurance training at 80% VO$_2$max, HIT resulted in a significant decrease in sum of skinfold values from a pre-test level of 39.6 mm to a post-test level of 36.5 mm. Therefore, HIT training provides an effective method of reducing athletes' body fat levels, and in turn controlling body weight.

Sample Sessions for Combat Athletes

The adaptations that HIT elicits are specific to the bout intensity and the work-to-rest ratio employed [43]. Brief, high-intensity ($\leq$ 10 s) bouts with longer recovery periods are proposed to induce an adaptive response in phosphocreatine metabolism, while longer higher intensity intervals (30 - 60 s) are used to produce a greater adaptive response in lactate metabolism [19, 24, 43]. Insufficient recovery periods between repeated HIT have been shown to inhibit phosphocreatine hydrolysis and anaerobic glycolysis, and result in an increased contribution from aerobic metabolism [73]. Thus, to impose adaptations upon specific energy systems the work-to-rest ratio employed must be carefully considered, whilst keeping in mind the specific demands of the sport.

A HIT session specific for boxing and taekwondo would involve repeated intervals of high-intensity sprinting or cycling matching the duration of a round (2 or 3 min), with a 1 min rest period. The aim of these sessions should be to produce concentrations of lactic acid similar to those observed post-competition (> 9.0 mmol/L) [41, 44]. While for judo, work-to-rest ratios of 1.5 and 3: 1 would accurately reflect those observed in actual competition, for example, *judokas* can perform high-intensity exercise lasting between 10 to 30 s, separated by 10 s rest periods, performed over a duration of 5-min [35]. To focus more on developing specifically the capacity of the ATP-PC system high-intensity interval durations of 5 to 10 s with work-to-rest period ratios of 1: 12 to 1: 20 are required, while for adaptations to the lactate system capacity high-intensity interval durations of 15 to 60 s with work-to-rest ratios of 1:3 to 1:5 are recommended [24].

As well as being energy system specific, optimal sports training should also be skill-specific and muscle group-specific. The importance of technique in combat sports means that time spent engaged in non-specific training modalities may be counter-productive as technique may suffer. With this in mind, skill-based HIT sessions utilising pad work, bag work, and sparring (or *randori* for judo) should be incorporated for more sport specific conditioning manipulated to reflect the work-to-rest ratios observed actual competition and effectively develop combat specific anaerobic capacity [5, 80]. For example, interval pad work, such as eight 1-minute rounds with 1-minute recovery, has been shown to be an effective method of stressing the anaerobic glycolytic energy system with lactate values frequently above 10 mmol/L [93]. Pad work is a method of training particularly effective for combat athletes because the coach dictates the training intensity.

Similarly, it has also been demonstrated that specific taekwondo racket (specific taekwondo pads) work exercises can reproduce in part the metabolic impact of competition [17]. The maximal heart rate response and blood lactate values measured during competition were significantly correlated to values measured during performance of 10 s and 3-min of repeated maximal front kicking (onto a racket held by a trainer at abdominal level).While, the 10 s bout of kicking exercise yielded maximal heart rates of 91% of maximal heart rate measured during competition, the heart rate observed in 1-min and 3-min specific exercise bouts was 92% and 100%, respectively [17].

Short duration, high-intensity sparring intervals are vital to simulate the intensity and conditions of actual competition. For this purpose, sparring bouts of 30 to 60 s for 6 to 8 sets with 1 to 3-min recovery between bouts would be effective for boxing or taekwondo. While in judo, the rest periods observed in during competition are not sufficient to allow the judoka to recover, as such rest intervals for HIT should not exceed 60 s [5, 15]. Thus for judo, *randori* intervals of 45 to 60 s with 30 s rest, repeated 5 to 6 times, would be ample to develop the judo-specific anaerobic ability of *judokas*. In addition to developing anaerobic and aerobic capacity, sparring can be used to increase the choice reaction time of athletes, i.e. sensory skills specific to an athlete's sport, described as the shortest interval needed to respond to a stimulus that is presented as an alternative to a number of other stimuli [70, 87].

However, there are some important limitations of this type of reaction time training that should be considered. For example, because training partners become familiar with one another, they can easily predict and anticipate each other's movement, and while this can be effective in training situations, in competition where the opponents are most often unknown, the reaction time will be longer [85]. Therefore, there is a need for combat sports athletes to spar with a large variety of opponents, which may involve travelling to other clubs to prevent this 'anticipation contaminated' choice reaction time training.

Skill-Based Aerobic Conditioning

Shadow boxing is a traditional boxing exercise that has been shown to elicit intensities high enough to produce cardiovascular and aerobic adaptations. Kravitz and colleagues [50] have shown that punching tempos of 108 beats/min and 120 beats/min, established with the use of a metronome, can elicit heart rates consistent with those required to elicit cardiovascular adaptations (heart rates between 85.6% and 93.1% of maximum heart rate, and 67.7 – 72.5% VO_2max). Thus, cardiovascular adaptations can be achieved by employing high tempo ($\geq$108 beats/min) shadow boxing.

In combat sports such as taekwondo, *katas* or forms-based training can be used to elicit aerobic training effects [77,118]. One study demonstrated average heart rates of 176 bpm (89% of maximum heart rate) and blood lactate concentrations as high a 5.15 mmol/L as a result of performing *wushu* (Chinese martial art) based *katas* [81]. Similarly, [25] suggested that judo *kata* (often performed with opponent) is an excellent aerobic exercise for *judokas*.

Strength and Power Training for Combat Sports

Grip strength has been indicated as predictor of boxing success [42], while, the ability to throw repeated punches of sufficient force is a key component of amateur boxing [94]. Similarly, taekwondo athletes are required to perform kicks and punches with enough force to displace their opponents. *Judokas* need to be to able to develop high forces in order to throw opponents despite their defensive resistance, and to perform a wider range of throws, so that they can incorporate more power-based throws into their technical repertoire. In addition to developing throwing specific strength, *judokas* require the development of elbow flexion/extension strength [58] and grip strength [20] in order to obtain an advantageous position, and neck strength to minimise the risk of cervical spine injury. While, isometric strength is not as important during standing fighting, it has an important role during ground fighting [33, 98].

Resistance training, through manipulation of variables such as training modality, frequency, volume, intensity, velocity and rest intervals, can elicit favourable neuromuscular adaptations [100]. Of particular benefit to the combat sport athlete is the potential to increase strength and power. However, due to combat sport athletes competing in weight categories, prudent use of resistance training is required as increases in mass can result from the use of certain protocols.

Strength gains are typically achieved with loads in excess of 80% of 1RM in order to achieve an intensity that will recruit the higher threshold fibres [47, 117]. Rest intervals must be long enough (> 2mins) to ensure that this intensity can be maintained over several sets [111]. Adaptations to training of this nature are primarily neural as the fibres do not undergo enough mechanical work to provoke sufficient protein degradation to induce muscular hypertrophy due to the lower volumes of training [117]. This may be of benefit to the combat sport athlete as greater forces can be exerted as a result of strength training without the gaining of mass, which allows the athlete to remain in their particular weight category.

Whilst increasing the amount of force a combat sport athlete can exert is important, training the athlete to be able to exert force rapidly is equally, if not more important. Working with loads greater than 80% 1RM when utilising traditional power-lifting exercises (e.g. squat, deadlift) will not improve rate of force development (RFD) as the velocity of the movement will not necessarily be sufficient to develop power [67]. Therefore, when the aim is to increase RFD using lighter loads (30-80% 1RM) for traditional power-lifting type exercises, and the use of explosive lifting techniques such as the Olympic lifts (clean and jerk, snatch) and their variations (e.g., power clean, high pull) is recommended as higher movement velocities can be achieved [8]. Similar to strength training protocols the volume for explosive lifting is low and the rest periods between sets must be of sufficient duration to ensure recovery and therefore maintenance of intensity [111]. This is of particular importance with lifts of this nature as neurally they are very demanding [117].

Improvements in throwing technique and increases in the force developed whilst throwing have been achieved utilising a validated judo specific strength-training machine. In addition, were also noted [11, 13]. In the absence of a judo-specific machine, maximal strength weight training techniques, plyometrics, and complex training methods utilising an opponent have all been shown to improve throwing speed [110] and the number of throws achieved in a judo specific throwing test [109]. Villani and Vincenzo [110] utilised a contrast throwing technique known as *butsukari* where a third *judoka* provides additional resistance to a set of throws followed by *nagekomi* (throw without the additional resistance). This method of 3 sets of 2 x 3 *butsukari* followed by a single *nagekomi* with complete recovery between sets significantly improved throwing speed compared to a group utilising *nagekomi* and lifting exercises.

Grip strength can be developed by employing supplemental resistance exercises (e.g. towel pull-ups) in addition to multi-joint, judo-specific strength training [5, 56, 101]. Elbow flexion/extension strength endurance can be developed using loads of up to 80% of 1RM with multiple sets separated by short rest intervals [117]. The need for specific neck musculature training in addition to other strength training methods has been recommended for *judokas*

[23]. Amtmann and Cotton [5] proposed 3 sets of 10 to 20 repetitions in a circuit format would be effective for developing neck musculature. All cervical spine movements (flexion, extension, lateral flexion) must undergo the same volume of training unless there is a weak movement that requires a greater volume to bring it to the same level as the other movements [114].

Combat Sports Circuit Training

The requirement of combat sport athletes to maintain force output for the duration of a bout necessitates the development of muscular endurance [71]. A method commonly used by combat sport athletes to enhance muscular endurance is circuit training. An effectively designed circuit may increase capillarization, thereby improving the potential to clear metabolic by-products which in turn can enhance the ability of the muscle to deal with metabolic acidosis during intense exercise [102]. In addition to this, circuits can be designed to safely create a metabolic state similar to that elicited during actual sports competition. This provides trainers with an effective alternative specific conditioning method that reduces the need for continuous sparring, which exposes combat sport athletes to an increased risk of injury [4].

Circuit training sessions can include resistance training exercises only, or a combination of resistance training and conditioning exercises (e.g. sprinting, skipping, shadow striking, etc.). Both dynamic bodyweight exercises, such as pull-ups/chin-ups, dips, and press-ups, and isometric bodyweight exercises, including squat holds and planks, in addition to partner assisted exercises such as lifting or carrying a partner of similar body mass, can be used in circuit training to effectively develop relative strength [71]. Upper body exercises targeting the trapezius (e.g. inverted body row) can be included in boxing circuits, as research has shown that in all boxing movements the trapezius was the most active muscle in the upper body [117]. Circuits can also include explosive resisted sprints to develop leg power and resisted punching and kicking actions to develop punching and kicking power and speed [95].

Circuit training sessions can be developed in accordance with the specific demands of the sport by matching the work-to-rest ratios of the bouts. For example, a 2-min circuit comprising of eight alternating lower and upper body exercises performed for 15 s, with no rest given between exercises, followed by a 1-min rest, repeated three times for taekwondo. For boxing, perform 8 lower and upper body exercises for 20 s with 5 s recovery between exercises, then rest for 1-min and repeat three times. A judo specific circuit could consist of a 5 min circuit consisting of 10 exercises performed for 20 s each, with 10 s given for changeovers, followed by a 10 min rest, repeated two to three times (see table below for sample exercises).

Table 1. Sample Circuit Training Sessions for Combat Sports

Sample Boxing Circuit Training Session	Sample Taekwondo Circuit Training Session	Sample Judo Circuit Training Session
1. Press-ups with feet on stability ball	1. One-legged squats	1. Pull-ups (with hold*)
2. Lunges with torso rotation holding medicine ball	2. Three-point press-up	2. Static squat
3. Sit-ups with Medicine ball throw	3. Repeated resisted kicks (10% resistance)	3. Woodchop
4. Repeated resisted sprints (10% resistance, 10 m distance)	4. Repeated unresisted kicks	4. Neck Bridge
5. Repeated unresisted sprints	5. Woodchop	5. Tractor tyre flip
6. Towel Pull-ups	6. Squat jumps on to raised platform	6. Mountain climbers
7. Dips	7. Prone dumbbell row in plank position	7. Inverted Body Press
8. Inverted Body Row	8. Side Plank	8. Rope climb
		9. Sandbag clean and shoulder
		10. 2-point plank

*isometric hold ½ way on eccentric phase for 2 s in each rep.

Plyometric Training

Both taekwondo athletes and boxers require explosive leg and trunk power in order to displace opponents and score points. While any increase in the amount of force that a *judoka* can develop in the short period of time available for a throw to be executed, provides them with a greater chance to overcome the defensive force exerted by their opponent. Due to the short duration of kick and punches, maximal power cannot be generated; therefore, it is the rate of muscular force development that increases in power are largely dependent on [91]. Plyometric training is a method of choice when aiming to enhance both lower and upper body muscular power [64]. Plyometrics seeks to improve the rate of force development and power output arising from the stretch-shortening cycle (SSC) [16]. The SSC combines mechanical and neurophysiological components, and involves a rapid eccentric muscle action to stimulate the stretch reflex and storage of elastic energy, which increases the force produced during subsequent concentric [79]. Lower body plyometric exercises are primarily based on jumping activities, such as depth jumps, standing jumps, hopping, etc., while upper body plyometric exercises typically include a variety of medicine ball throws and clap push-ups.

There are numerous studies illustrating the effectiveness of plyometric training in improving muscular power. In a meta-analytical review of studies on plyometric studies that investigated the effect of plyometrics on vertical jump height (a measure of leg power), Markovic [64] discovered that most of the previous research has shown that plyometric training is able to improve the vertical jump height in healthy individuals. Toumi et al. [104] reported improvements in jumping height in well trained handball players after combined weight training and plyometric training. Such improvements were not found in the weight-training only group. In another study, 6 weeks of training consisting of a combination of weight lifting and plyometric exercises significantly improved kicking performance, and vertical jump and sprint ability [75]. In regards to the effectiveness of upper body plyometrics, Schulte-Edelmann et al. [88] reported that after 6-weeks of plyometric training, the plyometric training group showed significant improvement in the power generated in the elbow extensor muscles compared to the control group which showed no significant changes in power output.

However, although there appears to be a large evidence base justifying the use of plyometric training for athletes, it is not recommended for inexperienced or poorly conditioned individuals, and should not be performed over prolonged periods due to the risk of injury and the rapid onset of fatigue [79]. Furthermore, due to the number of high eccentric contractions performed during plyometric training delayed onset muscle soreness (DOMS) is invariably experienced, which can impact on subsequent sessions [16]. Highlighting the effect of plyometric training on subsequent sessions, Twist et al. [106] recently demonstrated a latent impairment of balance performance following a bout of plyometric exercise, which the authors suggested has implications for both skill-based activities performed post plyometric training and for increased injury risk following high-intensity plyometric training.

Aquatic Plyometric Exercise

Aquatic plyometric training may be of particular interest to athletes and trainers as it may potentially reduce the risk of injury and the amount of post bout muscle soreness associated with plyometric training, whilst producing power gains equivalent to those seen after land-based plyometric training. Robinson et al. [82] reported that after 8 weeks of either land-based or aquatic plyometric training, participants in both groups experienced similar improvements in muscle power, torque, and velocity. However, the aquatic training group reported significantly less muscle soreness. Similarly, Stem and Jacobsen [97] demonstrated significant improvements in vertical jump performance as a result of land-based plyometric training and aquatic-based plyometric training performed in knee-deep water compared to the control group, while again no significant difference was found between the land-based and aquatic-based group. These findings suggest that aquatic training may produce similar performance improvement compared to land-based plyometric exercise, while potentially reducing injury due to a possible reduction of impact afforded by the buoyancy and resistance of the water upon landing.

However, it appears that the depth of the water has a significant effect on the performance gains possible with aquatic based plyometric exercise. Miller and colleagues [69] reported no differences in vertical jump displacement, peak force, or power values between the control group, a chest deep aquatic-based plyometric group, and a waist deep water aquatic-based plyometric training group. The advice based on current research would suggest that aquatic-based plyometric training could provide a reduced risk of injury while providing equivalent performance gains to land-based plyometric training, as long as the level of the water is knee height or below. However, further research regarding plyometric exercise effectiveness and water depth is needed, in addition to longitudinal research to confirm the potential reduced injury risk associated with aquatic plyometric training.

The following plyometric programme design recommendations have been adapted from Ebben [31]:

Plyometric Training Recommendations

- Athletes should perform only 2-3 plyometric sessions per week.
- Plyometric training should be performed in a non-fatigued state, therefore, it should not be performed after resistance training or sports conditioning sessions.
- Plyometric sets should not exceed 10 reps, and should be performed across a variety of rep ranges, such as sets of 1, 3, 5, or 10 reps, so as to develop explosiveness as well as power endurance.
- Generally, rest intervals between sets should be 5 to 10 times the duration of the set of plyometric exercises performed. For example, if a set of vertical jumps lasts 6 s, the rest interval should be 30 to 60 s duration.
- For beginners a volume of 80 to 100 foot contacts are recommended, while 100 to 120 and 120 to 140 foot contacts are recommended for intermediates and advanced level athletes, respectively.
- When possible perform in knee-deep water [82, 97]

In addition to foot contacts, the intensity of the plyometric exercise should be considered when deciding training volume. Plyometric intensity is based on the muscle activation, connective tissue and joint stress associated with various exercises. Assuming all exercises are performed maximally, a single leg exercise is more intense than its two-legged equivalent. Typically, the higher the jump the greater the ground reaction force (GRF), therefore, the greater stress caused. Jumps with added resistance (e.g. using dumbbells) are classed as moderate intensity due to the limiting effect that added resistance has on the jump height, and in turn GRF. Conversely, jumps performed while reaching the arms overhead result in higher jump heights, and therefore, greater intensity [31].

Table 2. Sample Plyometric Training Session

1. Squat Jumps	2 x 8
2. Split-squat jumps	2 x 8
3. Clap press-ups	2 x 6
4. Plyometric sit-up with Medicine ball	2 x 6
5. Box jump	2 x 5
6. 12 inch depth jump	5 x 3
Volume	81 foot contacts

Complex Training

Power can be developed with the use of heavy loads (80-90% of 1RM), plyometric exercises using body weight, and the use of explosive movements where the athlete moves 30-50% of 1RM as fast as possible [29]. Recently the use of complex training techniques has been advocated as an effective method of improving power by practioners and researchers, including most notably Verkoshanski. Complex Training involves the completion of a strength training exercise using a heavy load (1-5RM) followed after a relatively short period by the execution of a biomechanically similar plyometric exercise [32]. For example, 5 repetitions of a bench press with a 5RM load followed by 8 clap press-ups.

Advocates of complex training purport that the explosive capability of muscle is enhanced after it has just been subjected to maximal or near maximal contractions, which in turn creates optimal training conditions for subsequent plyometric exercise [29]. This effect of prior maximal or near maximal contractions appears to last up to 8-10 min, and is referred to a 'post-activation potentiation' (PAP) [30, 86, 92]. This PAP effect has been acknowledged as providing an opportunity for enhancing force and power production and exceeding performance achieve without prior loading [28]. Ebben and Watts [32] suggest that the most powerful affect of complex training may be neuromuscular, and in particular an increased motorneuron excitability and reflex potentiation, in addition to a possible increase in the motor units recruited, leading to an enhanced training state.

Complex training should only be used after functional strength is developed, basic jump training is performed, and/or after several weeks of sprint and resistance training [22, 45]. Sessions should be designed around the following recommendations of Ebben and Watts [32]:

- The volume of complex training should be low enough to guard against undue fatigue so the athlete can focus on quality.
- Sets of 2-5 of each pair with 2-8 reps of the resistance exercise and 5-15 reps of the plyometric should be performed, with 0-5 min rest between exercises and 2-10 min rest between pairs.
- 1-3 complex training sessions recommended per week with 48-96 hours recovery between sessions.

Table 3. Sample Complex Training Session

Exercises	Sets	Reps	Load	Tempo	Rest
1A. Clean and Press	3	5	5RM	Explosive	30 s sets
1B. Vertical Jump		10	-	Explosive	4 min pairs
2A. Dumbbell Chest Press	3	5	5RM	Slow	30 s sets
2B. Medicine Ball (MB) Drop		10	$\geq$10 kg	Explosive	4 min pairs
3A. Back Squat	3	5	5RM	Slow	30 s sets
3B. Depth Jump		10	-	Explosive	4 min pairs

Blais and Trilles [11] found considerable benefits for *judokas* by performing complex training methods in a 10-week training programme consisting of 2 sessions per week, with 5 sets of 10 repetitions on a judo-specific machine alternated every set with 10 repetitions of a partner throwing exercise. The utilisation of such a machine allows the maintenance, or even improvement, of technique whilst increasing the force developed at appropriate velocities whilst throwing, and minimising the amount of throws an opponent has to be subjected to if a similar protocol was to be followed using an opponent as resistance.

In addition to this, performing near maximal squats (95% 1RM) or depth jumps (plyometrics) prior to throwing also improves throwing speed as more throws can be carried out in a given period of time after using either of these techniques [109]. Both the depth jumps and maximal squats utilise lower body musculature and it is the lower limbs that provide the majority of the force when throwing [12], therefore this musculature must be targeted when developing strength and power if throwing performance is to be improved.

Table 4. Judo Specific Complex Training Pairs

Authors	Modality	Sets	Reps
Blais & Trilles [11]	Judo specific strength machine	5	10 x strength machine/10 x partner throws
Villani & Vincenzo [110]	Opponent(s) as resistance	3	(3 x *butsukari*/1 x *nagekomi*) Repeat twice = 1 set

CONCLUSION

It is clear each of the combat sports addressed in this chapter place unique metabolic demands on the competitors, and in turn requires training strategies that are specific to these demands. Effective strength and conditioning programme design for each of the combat sports is multi-faceted and must look to implement training methods that sufficiently stress the anaerobic and aerobic energy systems, while developing strength and power components in a manner specific to how they are utilised in competition. Due to the technical nature of each of the combat sports, it is recommended that combat athletes integrate specific skill-based conditioning methods, such as pad and sparring-based HIT sessions, into their training. It is advised that in combat sports where maintenance of a particular weight category is important, power and strength training that targets improvements in relative strength should be preferred to traditional high-volume bodybuilding resistance training methods. The methods recommended in this chapter include Olympic weightlifting exercises, circuit training using predominantly bodyweight exercises, plyometric training, and complex training. In closing, it is important that strength and conditioning coaches employ evidence-based practice when designing training programmes for combat athletes, and utilise training methods that are as sport-specific as possible.

REFERENCES

[1]   AIBA, International Boxing Federation. (2007) Rules for International Competitions or Tournamnets. Retrieved on 25th June 2007, available from URL: http://www.aiba.net.

[2]   AIBA, International Boxing Federation (2008) New AIBA technical and competition rules (Sept. 2008). Retrieved on 2nd September 2007, available from URL: http://www.aiba.org

[3]   Almansba, R. , Franchini, E., Sterkowicz, S., Imamura, R. T., Calmet, M. & Ahmaidi, S. (2008). A comparative study of speed expressed by the number of throws between heavier and lighter categories in judo. *Sci Sports*, 23, 186-188.

[4]   Amtmann, J. & Berry, S. (2003) Strength and conditioning for reality fighting. *Strength Cond J*, 25(2), 67-72.

[5]   Amtmann, J. & Cotton, A. (2005). Strength and conditioning for judo. *Strength Cond J*, 27, 26-31.

[6]   Artioli, G. G., Coelho, D. F., Benatti, F. B., Gailey, A. C. W., Adolpho, T. B. & Lancha Jr., A. H. (n.d.). Relationship between blood lactate and performance in a specific judo test. Retrieved on 15th August 2008, available from http://www.judobrasil.com.br/2005/rbbla.pdf.

[7]   Astrand, P-O., Rodahl, K., Dahl, H.A. and Stromme, S.B. (2003) *Textbook of Work Physiology; Physiological Bases of Exercise*. (4th Edition). Windsor, On: Human Kinetics.

[8]   Baechle, T. R., Earle, R. W. & Wathen, D. (2000) Resistance Training. In: T. R. Baechle & R. W. Earle (Eds.) *Essentials of Strength Training and Conditioning* (2nd Ed., pp.395-426). Champaign, IL: Human Kinetics.

[9]   Beekley, M. D., Abe, T., Kondo, M., Midorikawa, T. & Yamauchi, T. (2006) Comparison of normalized maximum aerobic capacity and body composition of summon wrestlers to athletes in combat and other sports. *J Sports Sci Med, CSSI*, 13-20.

[10]   Beis, K., Pieter, W. & Abatzides, G. (2007) Taekwondo techniques and competition characteristics involved in time-loss injuries. *J Sports Sci Med*, CSSI-2, 45-51.

[11]   Blais, L. & Trilles, F. (2006) The progress by judokas after strength training with a judo-specific machine. *J Sports Sci Med, CSSI*, 132-135.

[12]   Blais, L., Trilles, F. & Lacouture, P. (2007a) Three-dimensional joint dynamics and energy expenditure during the execution of a judo throwing technique (*morote seoi nage*). *J Sports Sci*, 25, 1211-1220.

[13]   Blais, L., Trilles, F. & Lacouture, P. (2007b) Validation of a specific machine to the strength training of judokas. *J Strength Cond Res*, 21, 409-412.

[14]   Bogdanis, G.C., Nevill, M.E., Lakomy, H.K.A. & Boobis, L.H. (1998) Power output and muscle metabolism during and following recovery from 10 and 20 s of maximal sprint exercise in humans. *Acta Phys Scand*, 163, 261-272.

[15]   Bonitch, J., Ramirez, J., Femia, P., Feriche, B. & Padial, P. (2005) Validating the relation between heart rate and perceived exertion in a judo competition. *Medicina Dello Sport*, 58, 23-28.

[16]   Boreham, C. (2006) The Physiology of Sprint and Power Training. In: Whyte, G. *The Physiology of Training*. (pp. 117-135). London: Elsevier.

[17] Bouhlel, E., Jouinia, A., Gmadaa, N., Nefzib, A., Ben Abdallahb, K. & Tabkac, Z. (2006) Heart rate and blood lactate responses during Taekwondo training and competition. *Sci Sports*, 21, 285–290.

[18] Burgomaster, K.A., Hughes, S.C., Heigenhauser, G.J.F., Bradwell, S.N. and Gibala, M.J. (2005) Six sessions of sprint interval training increases muscle oxidative potential and cycle endurance capacity in humans. *J App Phys*, 98, 1985–1990.

[19] Cadefau, J., Casademont, J., Grau, J.M. Fernández, J., Balaguer, A., Vernet, M., Cussó, R. & Urbano-Márquez, A. (1990) Biochemical and histochemical adaptation to sprint training in young athletes. *Acta Phys Scand*, 140, 341-351.

[20] Carvalho, M. C. G. A., Dubas, J. P., Prado, J. C., Carvalho, F. L. P., Dantas, E. H. M., Cunha, G. G., Landau, L., Drigo, A. J. & Azevedo, P. H. S. M. (2007) Judokas' hand grip strength study, according to age, weight class and championship performance. *Annals of the 5th International Judo Federation World Research Symposium.*

[21] Chiu, P.-H., Wang, H-H. & Chen, Y-C. (2007) Designing a measurement system for taekwondo training. *J Biomech*, 40(S2).

[22] Chu, D.A. (1992) *Jumping Into Plyometrics*. Champaign, IL: Human Kinetics.

[23] Conley, M. S., Stone, M. H., Nimmans, M & Dudley, G. A. (1997). Specificity of resistance training responses in neck muscle size and strength. *Eur J App Phys*, 75, 443-448.

[24] Cramer, J.T. (2008) Bioenergetics of Exercise and Training. In: Beachle, T.R. and Earle, R.W. (Eds), *Essentials of Strength Training and Conditioning*. Champaign, IL: Human Kinetics.

[25] Cree, C. D. (2007) Effects of recreational and competitive judo *kata* practice on cardiorespiratory health as evaluated by a portable gas analyzer system. A pilot study. *Annals of the 5th International Judo Federation World Research Symposium.*

[26] Dawson, B., Fitzsimons, M., Green, S., Goodman, C., Carey, M. & Cole, K. (1998) Changes in performance, muscle metabolites, enzymes and fibre types after short sprint training. *Eur J App Phys* 78, 163-169.

[27] Degoutte, F., Jouanel, P. & Filaire, E. (2003) Energy demands during a judo match and recovery. *Br J Sports Med*, 37, 245-249.

[28] Deutsch, M. and Lloyd, R. (2008) Effect of order of exercise on performance during a complex training session in rugby players. *J Sports Sci*, 26(8), 803 – 809.

[29] Docherty, D., Robbins, D. & Hodgson, M. (2004) Complex training revisited: A review of its current status as a viable training approach. *Strength Cond J*, 26(6) 52–57.

[30] Docherty, D. & Hodgson, M.J. (2007) The application of postactivation potentiation to elite sport. *Intl J Sports Phys Perf*, 2, 439-444.

[31] Ebben, W.P. (2007) Practical guidelines for plyometric intensity. *NSCA Perf Training J*, 6(5), 12-16.

[32] Ebben, W., & Watts, P. (1998) A review of combined weight training and plyometric training modes: Complex training. *Strength Cond J*, 20(5), 18–27.

[33] Franchini, E., Nunes, A. V., Moraes, J. M. & Vecchio, F. B. D. (2007) Physical fitness and anthropometrical profile of the Brazilian male judo team. *J Physiol Anthropometry*, 26, 59-67.

[34] Franchini, E., Takito, M. Y. & Bertuzzi, R. C. M. (2005) Morphological, physiological and technical variables in high-level college judoists. *Archives of Budo*, 1, 1-7.

[35]   Franchini, E., Takito, M. Y., Nakamura, F. Y., Matsushigue, K. A. & Kiss, M. A. P. D. (2003). Effects of recovery type after a judo combat on blood lactate removal and on performance in an intermittent anaerobic task. *J Sports Med Phys Fit, 43,* 424-431.

[36]   Gaitanos, G. C., Williams, C., Boobis, L. H. & Brooks, S. (1993). Human muscle metabolism during intermittent maximal exercise. *J App Phys* 75(2), 712-719.

[37]   Gao, B., Zhao, Q. & Liu, B. (1998) Measurement and evaluation on body composition and figure of taekwondo athlete. *J of Xi'an Institute of Phys Ed,* 15, 29-33.

[38]   Gao, B.H. (2001) Research on the somatotype features of Chinese elite male taekwondo athletes. *Sport Sci,* 21, 58-61.

[39]   Gibala, M.J, Little, J.P., van Essen, M., Wilkin, G.P., Burgomaster, K.A., Safdar, A., Raha, S. & Tarnopolsky, M. (2006) Short-term sprint interval versus traditional endurance training: similar initial adaptations in human skeletal muscle and exercise performance. *J App Phys,* 3, 901 – 911.

[40]   Gibala, M.J. (2007) High-intensity interval training: a time-efficient strategy for health promotion? *Cur Sports Med Rep,* 6, 211–213.

[41]   Gosh, A.K., Goswami, A. & Ahuja, A. (1995) Heart rate and blood lactate response in amateur competitive boxing. *Ind J Med,* 102, 179-183.

[42]   Guidetti, L., Musulin, A. & Baldari, C. (2002) Physiological factors in middleweight boxing performance. *J Sports Med Phys Fit,* 42, 309-314.

[43]   Harmer, A.R., McKenna, M.J., Sutton, J.R., Snow, R.J., Ruell, P.A., Booth, J., Thompson, M.W., MacKay, N.A., Stathis, C.G., Crameri, R.M., Carey, M.F. & Eager, D.M. (2000) Skeletal muscle metabolic and ionic adaptations during intense exercise following sprint training in humans. *J Phys,* 89, 1793-803.

[44]   Heller, J., Peric, T., Dlouha, R., Kohlikova, E., Melichna, J. & Vakova, H. (1998) Physiological profiles of male and female TKD black belt. *J Sports Sci,* 16, 243–9.

[45]   Hedrick, A. & J.C. Anderson (1996) The vertical jump: A review of the literature and a team case study. *Strength Cond J,* 18 (1), 7-12.

[46]   Hickey, K. (1980) *Boxing – The amateur boxing association coaching manual.* Kaye and Ward, London: England.

[47]   Hoffman, J. R., Cooper, J. Wendell, M. & Kang, J. (2004) Comparison of Olympic vs. traditional power lifting training programs in football players. *J Strength Cond Res,* 18, 129-135.

[48]   Imamura, R. T., Hreljac, A., Escamilla, R. F. & Edwards, W. B. (2006) A three-dimensional analysis of the center of mass for three different judo throwing techniques. *J Sports Sci Med, Combat Sports Special Issue,* 132-135.

[49]   International Judo Federation. (2003). *Refereeing Rules.* S.I: Author.

[50]   Karvitz, L., Greene, L., Burkett, Z. & Wongsathikun, J. (2003) Cardiovascular response to punching tempo. *J Strength Cond Res,* 17, 104-108.

[51]   Kazemi, M., Waalen, J., Morgan, C. & White, A.R. (2006) A profile of Olympic taekwondo competitors. *J Sports Sci Med,* CSSI, 114-121

[52]   Khanna, G.L. & Manna, I. (2006) Study of physiological profile of Indian boxers. *J Sports Sci Med,* 5, 90-98.

[53]   Kochhar, T., Back, D. L., Mann, B. & Skinner, J. (2005) Risk of cervical injury in mixed martial arts. *Br J Sports Med,* 39, 444-447.

[54] Koh, J.O. & Watkinson, E.J. (2002) Video analysis of blows to the head and face at the 1999 World Taekwondo Championships. *J Sports Med Phys Fit*, 42, 348–353.

[55] Koh, J.O., Watkinson, E.J. & Yoon Y-J (2004) Video analysis of head blows leading to concussion in competition Taekwondo. *Brain Injury*, 18 (12), 1287–1296.

[56] Kraemer, W. J., Vescovi, J. D. & Dixon, P. (2004) The physiological basis of wrestling: implications for conditioning programmes. *Strength Cond J*, 26, 10-15.

[57] Krustrup, P., Hellsten, Y. & Bangsbo, J. (2004) Intense intervals training enhances human skeletal muscle oxygen uptake in the initial phase of dynamic exercise at high but not at low intensities. *J Phys*, 559 (1), 335-345.

[58] Kubo, J., Cchishaki, T., Nakamura, N., Muramatsu, T., Yamamoto, Y., Ito, M., Saitou, H. & Kukidome, T. (2006) Differences in fat-free mass and muscle thickness at various sites according to performance level among judo athletes. *J Strength Cond Res*, 20, 654-657.

[59] Lane, A. (2006) Introduction to the special issue on combat sport. *J Sports Sci Med*, CSSI, i-iii.

[60] Lidor, R., Melnik, Y., Bilkevitz, A. & Falk, B. (2006) The ten-station judo ability test: a test of physical and skill components. *Strength Cond J*, 28, 18-20.

[61] Lin, W.-L., Yen, K.-T., Doris, C.-Y. Lua, Y.-H. & Huanga, C.-K. (2006) Anaerobic capacity of elite Taiwanese Taekwondo athletes. *Chang Sci Sports,* 21, 291–293.

[62] Linossier, M.T., Dormois, D., Perier, C., Frey, J., Geyssant, A. & Denis, C. (1997) Enzyme adaptations of human skeletal muscle during bicycle short-sprint training and detraining. *Acta Phys Scand*, 161, 439-445.

[63] MacDougall, J.D., Hicks, A.L., MacDonald, J.R., McKelvie, R.S., Green, H.J. & Smith, K.M. (1998) Muscle performance and enzymatic adaptations to sprint interval training. *J App Phys*, 84, 2138-2142.

[64] Markovic, G. (2007) Does plyometric training improve vertical jump height? A meta-analytical review. *Br J Sports Med*, 41, 349–355.

[65] Markovic, G., Misigoj-Durakovic, M. & Trninic, S. (2005) Fitness profile of elite Croatian Taekwondo athletes. *Collegium Antropologicum*, 29, 93-9.

[66] Maughan, R.J. and Gleeson, M. (2004) *The Biochemical Basis of Sports Performance*. Oxford University Press: Oxford.

[67] McBride, J. M., Triplett-McBride, T., Davie, A. & Newton, R. U. (1999) A comparison of strength and power characteristics between power lifters, Olympic lifters and sprinters. *J Strength Cond Res, 13,* 58-66.

[68] McGuigan, M. R., Winchester, J. B. & Erickson, T. (2006) The importance of isometric strength in college wrestlers. *J Sports Sci Med, Combat Sports Special Issue,* 108-113.

[69] Miller, M.G., Cheatam, C.C., Porter, A.R., Richard, M.D., Hennigar, D. & Berry, D.C. (2007) Chest- and waist-deep aquatic plyometric training and average force, power, and vertical-jump performance. *Int J Aquatic Res Ed*, 1, 145-155.

[70] Morris, P.M.V. & Trimble, A. (1989) *Advanced Karate Manual*. Stanley Paul: London.

[71] Murlasits, Z. (2004) Special considerations for designing wrestling-specific resistance training programs. *Strength Cond J*, 26 (3), 46-50.

[72] Overend, T.J., Paterson, D.H. & Cunningham, D.A. (1992) The effect of interval training and continuous training on the aerobic parameters. *Can J Sports Sci*, 17, 129-134.

[73] Parolin, M.L, Chesley, A., Matsos, M.P., Spriet, L.L., Jones, N.L. & Heigenhauser, G.J. (1999) Regulation of skeletal muscle glycogen phosphorylase and PDH during maximal intermittent exercise. *Am J Phys Endocrin Metab,* 277, 890–900.

[74] Parra, J. Cadefau, J.A ., Rodas, G., Amigo, N. & Cusso, R. (2000) The distribution of rest periods affects performance and adaptations of energy metabolism induced by high-intensity training in human muscle, *Acta Phys Scand,* 169, 157-165.

[75] Perez-Gomez, J., Olmedillas, H., Delgado-Guerra, S., Royo, I., Vicente-Rodriguez, G., Ortiz, R., Chavarren, J. & Calbet, J. (2008) Effects of weight lifting training combined with plyometric exercises on physical fitness, body composition, and knee extension velocity during kicking in football. *App Phys Nut Metab*, 33 (3), 501-510.

[76] Pieter, W. (1991) Performance characteristics of elite Taekwondo athletes. *Kor J Sports Sci*, 3, 94–117.

[77] Pieter, W., Taaffe, D. & Heijmans, J. (1990) Heart rate response to taekwondo forms and technique combinations. *J Sports Med Phys Fit,* 30, 97–102.

[78] Pieter, W., Van Ryssegem, G., Lufting, R. & Heijmans, J. (1995) Injury situation and injury mechanism at the 1993 European Taekwondo Cup. *J Hum Movt Stud,* 28, 1-24.

[79] Potach, D.H. & Chu, D.A. (2000) Plyometric Training. In: Beachle, T.R. & Earle, R.W. (Eds). *Essentials of Strength Training and Conditioning.* Champaign, IL: Human Kinetics.

[80] Ratamess, N. A. (1998) Weight training for jiu jitsu. *Strength Cond J,* 20, 8-15.

[81] Ribeiro, J.L., Ogoday, B. de Castro,S. D., Rosa, C.S., Baptista, R.R. & Oliveira, A.R. (2006) Heart rate and blood lactate responses to *changquan* and *daoshu* forms of modern *wushu*. *J Sports Sci Med,* CSSI, 1-4.

[82] Robinson, L.E., Devor, S.T., Merrick, M.A. & Buckworth, J. (2004) The effects of land vs. aquatic plyometrics on power, torque, velocity, and muscle soreness in women. *J Strength Cond Res,* 18, 84–91.

[83] Ronnestad, B. R., Egeland, W., Kvamme, N. H., Refsnes, P. E., Kadi, F. & Raastad, T. (2007) Dissimilar effects of one and three-set strength training on strength and muscle mass gains in upper and lower body in untrained subjects. *J Strength Cond Res*, 21, 157-163.

[84] Roosen, A., Compton, G. & Szabo, A. (1999) A device to measure choice reaction time in karate. *Sports Engineering*, 2, 49-54.

[85] Roosen. A, & Pain. M.T.G. (2006) Impact timing and stretch in relation to foot velocity in a taekwondo kicking combination, *J Biomech,* 39, S562.

[86] Sale, D. G. (2002) Postactivation potentiation: Role in human performance. *Exer Sports Sci Rev*, 30, 138–143.

[87] Schmidt, R.A. (1990) *Motor Learning & Performance: From Principles to Practice.* Champaign, IL Human Kinetics,.

[88] Schulte-Edelmann, J.A., Davies, G.J., Kernozek, T.W. & Gerberding, E. (2005) The effect of plyometric training of the posterior shoulder and elbow. *J Strength Cond Res.* 19(1), 129-134.

[89] Serina, E.R., & Lieu, D.K. (1991) Thoracic injury potential of basic competition Taekwondo kicks. *J Biomech*, 24, 951-60.

[90] Shave, R. and Franco, A. (2006) The Physiology of Endurance Training. In: Whyte, G. (Ed) *The Physiology of Training* (pp. 61-85). London: Elsevier.

[91] Siff, M.C. (2000) Supertraining (5th ed), Denver, CO: Super-training Institute.

[92] Smilios, I., Pilianidis, T., Sotiropoulos, K., Antonakis, M. & Tokmakidis, S.P. (2005) Short-term effects of selected exercise and load in contrast training on vertical jump performance. *J Strength Cond Res,* 19 (1), 135-139.

[93] Smith, M.S. (2006) Physiological profile of senior and junior England international Amateur boxers. *J Sports Sci Med* CSSI, 74-89.

[94] Smith, M.S., Dyson, R.J., Hale, T. & Janaway, L. (2000) Development of a boxing dynamometer and its punch force discrimination efficacy. *J Sports Sci,* 18, 445-450.

[95] Solovey, B.A. (1983) Exercises with weights as a means of improving hitting speed in young boxers. *Sov Sports Rev,* 18, 100-102.

[96] Stepto, N.K., Hawley, J.A., Dennis, S.C. & Hopkins, W.G. (1999) Effects of different interval-training programs on cycling time-trial performance. *Med Sci Sports Exerc,* 31 (5), 736-741.

[97] Stemm, J.D. & Jacobson, B.H. (2007) Comparison of land- and aquatic-based plyometric training on vertical jump performance. *J Strength Cond Res,* 21 (2), 568-71.

[98] Sterkowicz, S. & Franchini, E. (2000) Techniques used by judoists during the world and Olympic tournaments 1995-1999. *Hum Mov,* 2, 24-33.

[99] Sterkowicz, S., Zuchowicz, A. & Kubica, R. (n.d.) Levels of anaerobic and aerobic capacity indices and results for the special fitness test in judo competition. Retrieved on 14th August 2008 from http://www.judoinfo.com/research.doc.

[100] Stone, M.H. Collins, D., Plisk, S., Haff, G. & Stone, M.E. (2000) Training principles: Evaluation of modes and methods of resistance training. *Strength Cond J,* 22 (3), 65-76.

[101] Szymanski, D. J., Szymanski, J. M., Molloy, J. M. & Pascoe, D. D. (2004) Effect of 12 weeks of wrist and forearm training on high school baseball players. *J Strength Cond Res,* 18, 432-440.

[102] Tan, B. (1999) Manipulating resistance training programme variables to optimize maximum strength in men: a review. *J Strength Cond Res,* 13, 289-304.

[103] Tomlin, D.L. & Wenger, H.A (2001) The Relationship Between Aerobic Fitness and Recovery from High Intensity Intermittent Exercise. *Sports Med,* 31 (1), 1-11.

[104] Toumi, H., Best, T.M., Martin, A. & Poumarat, G. (2004) Muscle plasticity after weight and combined (weight + jump) training. *Med Sci Sports Exerc,* 36, 1580–8.

[105] Tremblay, A., Simoneau, J.A. & Bouchard, C. (1994) Impact of exercise intensity on body fatness and skeletal muscle metabolism. *Metabolism,* 43 (7), 814-8.

[106] Twist C., Gleeson, N. & Eston, R. (2008) The effects of plyometric exercise on unilateral balance performance. *J Sports Sci,* 26 (10), 1073–1080.

[107] Valentino, B., Esposito, L. C., & Fabozzo, A. (1990) Electromyographic activity of a muscular group in movements specific to boxing. *J Sports Med Phys Fit* 30, 160-162.

[108] van Someren, K. (2006) The Physiology of Anaerobic Endurance Training. In: Whyte, G. (Ed.) *The Physiology of training* (pp. 85-117). London: Elsevier.

[109] Vecchio, F. B. D., Miarka, B. & Franchini, E. (2007) Effects of different muscle actions on special judo fitness test performance. *Annals of the 5th International Judo Federation World Research Symposium.*

[110] Villani, R. & Vincenzo, V. D. (2002) Increase the speed of judo throwing techniques using a specific contrast method. *Proceedings of the 7th Annual Congress of the European College of Sports Science.*

[111] Willardson, J. M. (2006) A brief review: factors affecting the length of the rest interval between resistance exercise sets. *J Strength Cond Res,* 20, 978-984.

[112] Withers, R.T., Sherman, W.M. & Clark, D.G. (1991) Muscle metabolism during 30, 60, and 90 s of maximal cycling on an air-braked ergometer. *Eur J App Phys*, 63, 354-362.

[113] World Taekwondo Federation (2004) Available from: URL: www.wtf.org

[114] Ylinen, J. J., Julin, M., Rezasoltani, A., Virtapohja, H., Kautiainen, M., Karila, T. & Malkia, E. (2003) Effect of training in Greco-Roman wrestling on neck strength at the elite level. *J Strength Cond Res*, 17, 755-759.

[115] Zabukovec, R. and Tiidus, P.M. (1995) Physiological and anthropometric profile of elite kickboxers. *J Strength Cond Res*, 9, 240–2.

[116] Zar, A., Gilani, A., Ebrahim, K.H, and Gorbani, M.H. (2008) A survey of the physical fitness of the male taekwondo athletes of the Iranian national team. *Phys Ed Sport,* 6 (1) 21 – 29.

[117] Zatsiorsky, V. M. & Kraemer, W. J. (2006) *Science and Practice of Strength Training.* Champaign, IL: Human Kinetics.

[118] Zehr, E.P. & Sale, D.G. (1993) Oxygen uptake, heart rate and blood lactate responses to the Chito Ryu Seisan kata in skilled karate practitioners. *Intl J Sports Med,* 14, 269-274.

In: Advances in Strength and Conditioning Research
Editor: Michael Duncan and Mark Lyons

ISBN: 978-1-60692-909-4
© 2009 Nova Science Publishers, Inc.

Chapter 11

THE DEVELOPMENT OF MENTAL TOUGHNESS IN SPORT

Tony D. Myers[1] and Jamie B. Barker[2]*
1Newman University College, UK
2Staffordshire University, UK

ABSTRACT

The purpose of the current chapter was to review the literature on mental toughness with a focus on developing mental toughness in athletes using psychological skills. Research into mental toughness and its development is in its infancy and as a result there have been conceptual, measurement and methodological inconsistencies. The chapter presented definitions of mental toughness on a conceptual level, provided an overview of current models of mental toughness and associated measures. It explored the development of mental toughness attributes using psychological skills training, focusing particularly on the consensual attributes self-confidence and self-efficacy, motivation and commitment and coping with adversity. Empirical evidence on the efficacy of a number of psychological skills in developing these attributes was examined. Psychological skills discussed included self-talk, imagery, goal setting, and hypnosis. A speculative model of the relationship between mental toughness and psychological skills training was presented based on the literature reviewed. Conclusions drawn included the refinement of measurement tools in order to provide direction for future research and the need to establish efficacious mental skills in developing mental toughness. In particular a recommendation was made to explore the efficacy of hypnosis. It was suggested hypnosis may be used to integrate a range of other mental skills in the developmental of mental toughness.

Keywords: Mental toughness, Psychological skills, Hypnosis, Self-efficacy, Motivation, Applied sport psychology, Mental skills training, Elite athletes

---

* Please address correspondence and requests for reprints to Tony D. Myers, Department of Physical Education and Sport Studies, Newman University College, Genners Lane, Birmingham, B32 3NT or email tony.myers@staff.newman.ac.uk.

For many years physical conditioning and technical expertise have been widely accepted as being essential for success in elite sporting competition by athletes and coaches alike. However, the importance of psychological characteristics and skills has been less widely accepted until more recently. One psychological attribute that has been frequently associated with sporting success by athletes, coaches and sport psychologists is mental-toughness [72]. The term originally popularised by Loehr [80, 81] who considered at least 50% of superior athletic performance was attributable to mental factors, has been in currency since that time. Mental toughness has become a frequently used layman's term for individual tolerance to stress and performance maximisation [34, 56]. For example, mental toughness is often the all-encompassing term many coaches, spectators, and commentators use to describe the superior mental characteristics of successful elite athletes. Indeed, separating "great" from "good" athletes may be due to mental toughness when physical, technical, and tactical skills are equal [61]. Typically, good athletes are those who make it to the elite level but do not achieve with the same consistency and magnitude that great athletes with mental toughness do. It could therefore be argued that whilst unprecedented physical ability is needed to make it to an elite level, mental toughness may be the major distinction between "good" and "great" athletes.

Mental toughness is a relatively new and growing area of sport psychology, but has received increasing recent interest from various parts of the world that include the United States [59], United Kingdom [13, 40, 72, 73, 112), and Australia [63, 87]. This research has predominantly focussed on understanding the construct of mental toughness by interviewing athletes deemed to be or have been "mental tough" and elite coaches who have worked alongside "mentally tough" athletes. Data have therefore indicated a number of characteristics ascribed to mental toughness. These include self-belief, concentration and focus, motivation, thriving on competition, resilience, handling pressure, positive attitude, quality preparation, goal-setting, determination and perseverance, and commitment.

In this chapter, we begin by providing a discussion on defining mental toughness. We then outline the various models and frameworks used to extend understanding mental toughness in sport. Measures of mental toughness and the emanating issues are then explored. Recommendations are posited for developing mental toughness and suggestions are made regarding pertinent psychological skills. A model for using psychological skills to enhance mental toughness is then presented. The chapter ends with a summary and recommendations for future research.

DEFINING MENTAL TOUGHNESS

Although frequently identified as being essential to consistent high level performance, operationalization of mental toughness has been hampered by a lack of clear conceptualisation, with definitions being informed by anecdotal evidence, speculation and introspection of athletes, coaches and psychologists [34]. Lacking in scientifically driven conceptualisation numerous definitions have been produced ranging from an ability to handle pressure, stress, and adversity [34, 56] to the possession of superior mental skills [13]. However, the construct has more recently been investigated with more scientific rigour and the resulting definitions have received a level of acceptance amongst researchers in the area [e.g., 13, 73, 112].

Jones, Hanton, and Connaughton's [72] definition of mental toughness emerged from interview and focus group techniques. Echoing some elements of previous mental toughness definitions, the authors suggested mental toughness represents the ability of a person to cope with the demands of training and competition, increased determination, focus, confidence, and maintaining control under pressure. Their research found 12 attributes associated with mentally tough performers: self-belief, desire and motivation, performance and lifestyle distractions, pressure and anxiety associated with competition, and physical and emotional pain. Clough, Earle, and Sewell [18] also provided a scientifically derived definition informed by constructs from mainstream psychology. They suggested that mentally tough people have "a high sense of self-belief and an unshakable faith that they control their own destiny, these individuals can remain relatively unaffected by competition and adversity" (p. 38). Their findings suggested mental toughness is closely related to resilience, physiological toughness but principally hardiness. Crust and Clough [26] also found mental toughness was related to physical toughness by finding evidence of a relationship with pain tolerance.

In a two-part study that attempted to confirm Jones, Hanton, and Connaughton's [72] definition with soccer players, Thelwell, Weston, and Greenlees, [112] used a combination of semi-structured interviews with professional players followed by confirmation of the attributes identified with a wider population using a likert- scale. Their investigation found a general consensus with Jones, Hanton, and Connaughton's [72] definition of mental toughness in a specific soccer population. Further support for Jones et al.'s [72] came in a more recent study by Jones, Hanton, and Connaughton [73] investigating superelite athletes. The superelite athletes (Olympic or world champions) appeared to have a more detailed perception of the concept than elite athletes identifying 30 attributes that they deemed essential to being mentally tough clustered under four separate dimensions (attitude/mindset, training, competition, post-competition). In this study participants also stated that 'natural' mental-toughness was developed throughout their careers but interestingly pointed to the possibility that mental toughness may fluctuate over time therefore indicating mental toughness to be transient in nature. Although generally there is support for this view of mental-toughness, some researchers have passed criticism. For example, Middleton, Marsh, Martin, Richards, and Perry [87] and Crust [25] argued that Jones et al.'s [72] definition merely describes what mental toughness allows an athlete to do, rather than actually defining the concept or composite nature of mental toughness itself. Middleton et al. [87] offered their own definition suggesting mental toughness is an "unshakeable perseverance and conviction towards some goal despite pressure or adversity "(p.6). These differences appear to suggest that although the construct of mental toughness has developed considerably on a conceptual level 'it is still research in progress'. Indeed, although somewhat impressive in providing an insight into the composite nature of mental toughness, previous research has only focussed on describing the key characteristics of mental toughness. Research has therefore failed to identify when these characteristics are required, what they enable a mentally athlete to do, and what overt behaviours mentally tough athletes exhibit [63].

MODELS/FRAMEWORKS OF MENTAL TOUGHNESS

Despite a level of conceptual ambiguity, mental toughness has been investigated across a range of sports including cricket [13] soccer [112], golf [34], rugby [55], flying kilometre skiing [41], wushu athletes [78] Australian rules football [63], adventurers/explorers [40], ice hockey [28] and sports coaches [110]. The findings suggest that although aspects of mental toughness may vary in emphasis from sport to sport, there is enough commonality for a general framework to be considered irrespective of sport. Therefore, Clough *et al.* [18], suggested a preliminary model of mental toughness they refer to as the four Cs model. This consisted of four components: control, commitment, challenge and confidence. They proposed, control is related to an individual's appraisal of a situation and includes aspects of controlling emotions, challenge to the perception of potentially stressful situations as positive opportunities, commitment to 'stickability' or an ability to complete what has been started despite difficulties, and finally, confidence to self-belief on a personal level and in ones abilities [18]. Although, the model appears to have some ecological validity, the authors acknowledge this model was constructed largely from a study on physiological stress combined with hardiness research and anecdotal evidence [18]. There has been no significant attempt by the authors to quantitatively validate the model, focusing instead on definition and measurement issues pertaining to mental toughness. Middleton et al. [87] also proposed a model that separated mental-toughness into 'orientation' and 'strategy'. 'Orientation' composed of self-belief, task familiarity, motivation and goal commitment, while 'strategy' is composed of perseverance, task specific attraction and emotional management. While the model represents a valiant effort at using both quantitative and quantitative approaches with strong theoretical links, the approach taken had some limitations. The use of a cross sectional research design did not allow for an exploration of how mental toughness may fluctuate over time and failed to triangulate athletes' perspectives with that of coaches and other observers. In addition, Middleton [88] highlighted a failure to deal with issues of temporal proximity to an event that was associated with a requirement for an athlete to be mentally tough. To address these limitations, Middleton [88] proposed multi-method assessment with temporal proximity to the actual experience of mental toughness is needed to address these issues.

Bull, Shambrook, James, and Brooks, [13] identified the critical role of a cricketer's environment influencing 'Tough Character', 'Tough Attitudes', and 'Tough Thinking'. Consequently, they developed a mental toughness pyramid or framework to understand the development of mental toughness in elite English cricketers and how to disseminate mental toughness education into cricket coaching and playing populations in England. The pyramid represents key elements involved in developing mental toughness as derived from interview data collected on 12 English cricketers identified as being the mentally toughest during the previous 20 years. Thus 'Environmental influence' underpins the whole framework, and is therefore the most important area upon which to focus resources. The environment is suggested to set the base upon which 'Tough Character' is developed. This aspect is considered to be fairly stable and generalisable across different situations and is a precursor to the manifestation of 'Tough Attitudes'. Finally, 'Tough Thinking' forms the top of the pyramid and represents the key psychological properties of being "mentally tough". The framework includes being able to account for individuality within the development of mental toughness and concurs with views on developing broader psychological skills and characteristics in elite athletes [59]. In sum, this framework not only supports previous research in detailing the key attributes of mental toughness [e.g., 72], but also provides practitioners with guidance on how to develop mentally tough athletes. A limitation of the framework is that it is not explicitly linked to theory.

More recently, Jones et al. [73] investigated mental toughness in individuals who had achieved ultimate sporting success to address the issues of defining mental toughness, identifying essential attributes, and developing a framework of mental toughness. Eight Olympic or world champions, three coaches, and four sport psychologists took part in the study. Using qualitative methods (including focus groups and individual interviews), data supported Jones et al. [72] definition of mental toughness and revealed 30 essential attributes to being mentally tough. The clustering of these attributes into 4 separate dimensions (attitude/mindset, training, competition, post-competition) was the basis for a framework of mental toughness. Specifically, the model proposed i) belief and focus to be key components of the attitude/mindset dimension, ii) using long-term goals as a source of motivation, controlling the environment, and pushing oneself to the limit as components of the training dimension, iii) belief, staying focussed, regulating arousal, handling pressure, awareness and control of thoughts and feelings, controlling the environment as key components of the competition dimension of mental toughness, and iv) handling failure and handling success under the post-competition dimension of mental toughness. Although the model has received support, Crust [24] highlighted concerns with the research using small numbers in the initial focus group stage of the research. However, overall this framework represents a precise dissection of the mental toughness construct. In doing so, sport psychologists, coaches, and performers have a better understanding of what is required to achieve a state of mental toughness in each dimension. Consequently, mental skills training could be implemented to enhance strengths in the appropriate dimensions. Although this is a positive suggestion, a reliable and valid measure of mental toughness is needed so that effective mental skills can be determined.

Collectively this research provides a description of what mental toughness and a conceptual insight into how mental toughness may be developed. However, recent research has criticised this work as being a-theoretical and therefore lacking conceptual clarity [63]. Therefore the use of theoretical frameworks in which an individual's views, experiences, meanings and perceptions can be detailed and understood are posited to allow for a greater examination of mental toughness. Gucciardi, Gordon, and Dimmock. [63] thus adopted Personal construct psychology [PCP; 76] framework in an attempt to reveal a holistic understanding of mental toughness in the specific context of Australian Football. PCP [76] places emphasis on the meanings an individual sees in the events of his or her life and this distinguishes the troubled from the untroubled, as well as these meanings directly influencing an individual's behaviour. Indeed, by adopting PCP Gucciardi et al. [63] deemed it is possible to understand how constructs (e.g., mental toughness) are organised and to what situations they apply. Accordingly, using a PCP-based interview protocol with 11 elite football coaches' three independent categories (characteristics, situations, behaviours) were derived along with 11 key characteristics and these were integrated into a mental toughness model of Australian Football, which emphasises the importance of the categories and characteristics. Overall, several of the characteristics revealed as keys to mental toughness were consistent with previous research. These included self-belief, motivation, tough attitude, concentration and focus, and handling pressure. Importantly, several characteristics including personal values, emotional intelligence, sport intelligence, and physical toughness were unique to understanding and defining mental toughness in Australian Football and highlighted that whilst there appear to be several global mental toughness characteristics there also appear to be certain characteristics that are specific to particular sports. For example, adventure/explorer sports consistently involve more life threatening situations than sports such as tennis, golf, and badminton. Therefore, one can see how the characteristics of safety, survival, and no fear would be considered key components of mental toughness in adventurer/explorers but not athletes. Indeed, the identification and understanding of unique and sport-specific characteristics will have important implications for defining, measuring and developing toughness in sport [63]. Overall, this study uses innovative methods and provides a holistic understanding of mental toughness specific to Australian Football. Particularly, the study revealed mental toughness characteristics might be sport-specific along with supporting previous postulations surrounding mental toughness.

Despite a move towards greater scientific exploration and conceptualisation there still remains a need for even greater scientific rigour in establishing a model of mental toughness. Given the range of contributing factors to mental toughness, it is unlikely that a single measurement method can capture the true nature of mental toughness and so a greater use of multi-method assessment is recommended.

MEASURING MENTAL TOUGHNESS

Although in a conceptual sense mental toughness is still in its infancy, measures of mental toughness have been produced and used in research. Loehr's [81] Psychological Performance Inventory (PPI; 1986) currently remains the most widely used mental toughness instrument [88]. The PPI is a 42-item inventory that measures what Loehr considered the seven most important psychological factors that reflect mental toughness: self-confidence, negative energy, attention control, visual and imagery control, motivation, positive energy, and attitude control. It includes items describing athletes' specific psychological behaviours and self-evaluations. The seven subscale scores are obtained, with scores ranging from six (low) to 30 (high) and a total score ranging from 42 to 210. While the instrument continues to be used in practice it has been criticised for a lack of appropriate psychometric properties [88]. Middleton et al. [88] found factors of the PPI to have good face validity and could be considered conceptually compelling. However, after examining the PPI factor structure using Confirmatory Factor Analysis (CFA) they found a priori model resulted in a poor fit to the data and an improper solution. Indeed, the associated correlation matrix for the instrument revealed numerous factor correlations approaching or exceeding unit value. The author suggested that from a within-network perspective, support for the PPI instrument was problematic.

In response to the inadequate psychometric properties they found with the PPI, Middleton [88] produced a measure of mental toughness based on his own conceptualisation (i.e., the Mental Toughness Inventory, MTI). The MTI instrument was piloted with 479 (200 females; 279 males) young elite athletes (12 to 19 years of age) who were competing in several major team and individual sports. The 67-item Inventory measures 12 separate components of mental-toughness (self-efficacy, potential, mental self-concept, task familiarity, task value, personal bests, goal commitment, perseverance, task specific attention, positivity, stress minimisation, positive comparisons) along with a global mental-toughness score [87]. The authors found that the MTI provided a reliable and valid measure of their model of mental toughness, suggesting it to be strong on both conceptual between-network and within-network grounds. Within-network validation suggested that internal properties of the MTI (e.g., internal reliability, factor structure, uniqueness, and cross loadings) were sound. Similarly, the MTI was found to have between-network validity with the scales of MTI relating with a range of established constructs that were differentially stronger or weaker as predicted (i.e., based on content analyses and theory). For example, the author found that the MTI factor "Task Focus" related more strongly with *Flow Trait Scale* (FLOW) factor "Concentration" than with other, less theoretically related factors such as *Review of Personal Effectiveness and Locus of Control Questionnaire* (ROPELOC), "External Locus of Control" and "Social Effectiveness". This said, the authors did acknowledge that validation was based on responses from a single point in time and this should be addressed in future work.

Another measure was produced by Clough et al. [18] who developed the Mental Toughness Questionnaire 48 (MTQ48) to assess their proposed characteristics of mental toughness. The MTQ48 assesses global mental toughness and four subcomponents that relate to their four C's model: challenge, commitment, confidence, and control. The items on the MTQ48 rated on a 5-point Likert-type scale anchored at 1 = strongly disagree to 5 = strongly agree. Adequate reliability, face, construct, and criterion validity has been reported for the MTQ48 [18, 88]. It has been reported as being able to differentiate between elite, regional and recreational athletes but not discriminate across gender [18]. The measure has recently been used to examine mental toughness in 677 athletes where it gained some support for its psychometric properties [91]. Along with the MT48, the original authors developed a MT18 (18-item questionnaire) to offer a shorter user-friendly instrument providing a quick global mental-toughness score for coaches and sportspersons in practical settings. The authors report a correlation of $r=0.87$ between the two instruments (MT48 and MT18) indicating a strong relationship [18]. Although the authors attempted to demonstrate construct validity of the measure by describing how it relates to other constructs (i.e., optimism, self-image, life satisfaction, self-efficacy and stability), they did this by relating the constructs to the overall mental toughness score achieved, rather than the individual MT48 scales. This has been highlighted as a significant flaw in the validity of the measure [88]. This, along with methodological shortfalls, means that validity of the MT48 remains undetermined and further investigation into its validity required before it becomes a more widely accepted measure.

There has been a suggestion that while there seem to be several key components of mental toughness that are common to most sports, there is the possibility that some components of mental toughness may be specific to particular sports [63]. Recognising this possibility, Gucciardi et al. [63] recently produced the Australian Football Mental Toughness Inventory (AFMTI), a sport specific measure of mental toughness for Australian rules football. The 24-item inventory measures four components of mental toughness in Australian football: thrive through challenge, sport awareness, tough attitude, and desire success. The study provided preliminary support for the factor structure, internal reliability, and construct validity of the AFMTI. However, it was acknowledged that these must be verified through further psychometric examinations before the AFMTI can be considered a useful tool for measuring mental toughness in Australian football.

Recently, the English Cricket Board (ECB) has developed the Mental Toughness Profiler [MTP; 12] as a mechanism with which to help cricketers, coaches and support staff develop performance. The MTP includes four dimensions of mental toughness in cricket (i.e., 'Fight', 'Inner Drive', 'Critical Moment Control', 'Resilience') as identified in winning minds research conducted by Bull et al. [13]. The MTP is completed based upon discussions about cricketers held between a sport psychologist and coach. Ratings are given on each the four mental toughness dimensions. The results are used to provide player feedback, developmental training interventions or for selection to national squads. Currently, validation work including the collection of normative values is being undertaken on the MTP.

The current drive to produce valid and reliable measures is welcomed and should play a role in advancing understanding of mental toughness by enabling more quantitative research to be undertaken. However, more work needs to be conducted on an agreed conceptualisation of the construct both across sports and in specific individual sports, before a globally accepted measure can be adopted by the research community. On a cautionary note, a level of scepticism should be maintained regarding whether mental toughness measures should be used as a means for selecting athletes for national squads (e.g., the MTP). Indeed, a similar debate has raged within the sport psychology literature regarding personality inventories.

DEVELOPING MENTAL TOUGHNESS

Defining, describing and measuring mental toughness is of limited value to the coach or athlete without the possibility of offering practical strategies to improve the attributes associated with it. Despite the importance placed on the construct by coaches, athletes and other stake holders, only 9% of coaches suggested that they were successful in developing or improving mental toughness in the performers [61]. Despite this disappointing level of success in the intentional development of mentally tough individuals, it does appear possible to develop the attribute [73]. Mental toughness has been reported as being both a naturally occurring and developed phenomenon [112]. It has been likened to body composition where an individual is predisposed to a certain size or shape, however this can be altered by lifestyle changes [34]. For example, research evidence suggested components of mental toughness are both socialised and directly coached. The role coaches and parents play in facilitating a number of desirable psychological attributes associated with mental toughness has been identified in studies on gifted and talented school children [27, 40, 50] and athletes [10, 20, 21]. Earle et al. [34], suggested that if athletes don't develop mental toughness as a result of formative experiences, psychological skills training (including goal-setting, imagery, anxiety control and relaxation) offer the possibility of improving mental-toughness. Currently, no research has evaluated the efficacy of such mental skills in facilitating mental toughness in athletes [34].

Connaughton et al., [19] examined different stages of athletes' careers, outlining the temporal development and maintenance of mental-toughness, namely early years, middle years, later years and maintenance years. There was a consensus from the elite athletes interviewed that sport psychology support should commence from a young age and not when athletes' achieve elite status. The interviews suggested that in the early years of an athlete's career the appropriate motivational climate is important in fostering mental toughness. The suggestion being that this climate is created by coaches and other stakeholders, including family members and other athletes, and should aim to provide a supportive, enjoyable environment that encourages skill development but also expose athletes to competitive stressors and failure in sport [19]. In addition, the athlete's interviewed by Connaughton and colleagues [19] revealed early in their careers they developed an unshakable self-belief i) in their ability to achieve competition goals and ii) in their unique qualities and abilities, and iii) an insatiable desire to succeed years. These attributes were nurtured and strengthened in the middle years of their sporting careers. In this middle career period, those interviewed also revealed they experienced a number of formative experiences associated with training and competition that helped develop the attributes of mental toughness. These included experiencing performance setbacks, enduring physical and emotional pain, experiencing anxiety, the pressure of competition, and having to cope with a number of uncontrollable events. The perception being that these experiences allowed the athletes' to develop in a number of ways. First, increased their determination for success. Second, allowed them to endure increasing amounts of physical and emotional pain while still maintaining technique and effort under distress. Third, accepted the inevitability of competition anxiety and coping with it. Fourth thrived on the pressure of competition. Finally, regained psychological control following unexpected and uncontrollable events. In the later years of their career they felt they developed their ability to switch their sport focus on and off as required, an ability to remain fully focused on the task at hand in the face of competition-specific distractions, to not be adversely affected by others' performances- good or bad and remaining fully focused in the face of personal life distractions.

What is clear from Connaughton and colleagues [19] study is that although these career and life challenges forged mental toughness in the elite athlete's interviewed, similar challenges could well have produced very different outcomes and may well have done so in less successful athletes. For example, psychological skills offer the possibility of assisting athletes develop appropriate positive responses to competition and training challenges that could help thus help to forge their mental toughness. Although the current evidence for developing mental-toughness using psychological skills training is largely anecdotal, there is evidence of psychological interventions improving a number of the associated attributes: self-confidence and self-belief, coping with adversity, and motivation and commitment.

Self-Confidence and Self-Efficacy

Self-confidence or self-efficacy is a key component in a number of definitions of mental toughness [e.g., 18, 72, 87]. The terms self-confidence and self-efficacy have been used synonymously with aspects of each have been theorised using constructs such as self-efficacy, self-concept, and self-image [70]. The term confidence tends to be used in an applied sport psychology setting and self-efficacy in a significant body of theory and research originating in mainstream psychology. Self-efficacy has been defined as a specific form of self-confidence that includes both an affirmation of capability along with the strength of belief [4]. Butler [14] proposed a model of self-belief that shows a relationship between efficacy and self-belief. The model suggested an individual athlete's estimate of their efficacy determines how they will approach a task and that this is driven by that athlete's self-belief. Butler [14] illustrated this by suggesting that if an athlete's estimate of efficacy is validated by a goodness of fit (either positive or negative) a sense of mastery strengthens their self-belief. Butler [14] further suggested if the estimate of efficacy is invalidated, it leads an athlete to respond with what he terms as hostility or guilt responses. The hostility response enables an athlete to preserve self-belief by skewing attributions; the guilt response requires an athlete to readjust their belief accordingly in the light of performance information.

Self-efficacy theory has been used as a theoretical framework for exploring the impact efficacy in both sports and general psychology related research [4]. Self-efficacy beliefs are considered to be one of the most influential psychological constructs mediating achievement in sport [42, 43, 44, 46, 89]. Finding strategies and techniques that effectively enhance or maintain these beliefs is an important part of much applied psychology research [cf. 124]. The efficacy of Bandura's model in the sport domain has been well documented [e.g., 44, 46, 106] with perceived self-efficacy being illustrated as being a strong and consistent predictor of individual athletic performance [e.g., 39, 45, 46, 89, 114].

Because the correlation between confidence and performance success is well documented and consistent [e.g., 44], sport psychologists have become intrigued with developing psychological techniques to enhance self-confidence and self-efficacy. There is empirical evidence that suggests self-efficacy can be enhanced by using techniques to influence the various sources of self-efficacy information as identified in Bandura's [4] model. Generally, research supports the use of hypnosis, imagery, modelling, self-talk, and feedback in developing athletes' self-efficacy.

Hypnosis

Hypnosis has been suggested to influence self-efficacy by facilitating behaviours and cognitions that will impact upon all of the antecedent sources of self-efficacy information as presented in Bandura's self-efficacy theory [4, 69]. First, with regards performance accomplishments, the use of hypnosis could help a performer to recall and imagine future mastery experiences and therefore facilitate self-efficacy regarding future sport performance. Second, hypnosis could be used to provide information on vicarious experiences. Moreover, an athlete could be presented with suggestions that relate to the successful performance or confident behaviours of a team-mate. Third, hypnosis could be used as an internal verbal persuasive technique, whereby suggestions could be given to give a performer encouragement, support and hence build self-efficacy about a particular task. Finally, hypnosis could impact the physiological and emotional state (e.g., reduce arousal and increase relaxation) as well as improve the imaginal experience (i.e., the quality of the athletes imagery ability) of the performer prior to and during performance. This could be achieved via the use of suggestions to control and alter perceptions, emotions, and behaviour. According to a neo-dissociation theory of hypnosis, responses to suggestions focussing on mastery experiences, vicarious experiences, internal verbal persuasion, emotional and physiological arousal control and the imaginal experience of the individual will cause the subconscious part of an athlete's central control structure to attenuate to the given suggestion without the conscious part of the central control structures' knowledge [109]. In turn, by communicating with the subconscious part of the mind, long-term behaviours and cognitions can be impacted upon without the conscious part interfering. In addition to suggestions facilitating dissociation, it is also posited, hypnosis will bring about changes in behaviour due to positive expectations, beliefs, attitudes held by participants, and the interpersonal nature of hypnosis [109, 117, 118].

Based upon theory, research has demonstrated hypnotic interventions containing ego-strengthening suggestions to enhance self-efficacy in an elite judoka [5], a leg-spin cricket bowler [6] and a professional soccer player [7]. In addition, using group methods significant increases between pre and post intervention self-efficacy beliefs and soccer volley performance was found in a sample of 30 experienced collegiate soccer players following a hypnosis intervention. Importantly, self-efficacy beliefs and soccer volley performance were also maintained 4-weeks post-intervention [8].

Imagery

Self-efficacy represents an important cognition related to imagery use [86]. Beliefs about personal efficacy influence the types of imaginal futures that individuals construct [4]. Individuals with high self-efficacy should maintain images of successful performance. There is increasing evidence that imagery can have a positive impact on self-efficacy, although the type of imagery used is important [86]. Using Paivio's original taxonomy of imagery function as a basis, Hall, Mack, Paivio, and Hausenblas [65] identified five functions of imagery in the development of the Sport Imagery Questionnaire (SIQ), and these were incorporated by Martin et al.[86] into their conceptual model of imagery use in sport settings. Martin et al. [86] proposed that motivational general-mastery imagery (MG-M), which refers to effective coping and mastery of challenging situations (e.g., a cricket bowler would imagine feeling able to cope with bowling in a pressure situation) may be used to increase self-efficacy and this is supported by recent research [e.g., 15, 74]. The use of motivational-specific (MS) imagery (e.g., imagining setting and attaining training and performance specific goals) is also suggested to facilitate an athlete's intrinsic motivation towards training and performance [85] which in turn may impact self-efficacy beliefs [4]. Motivational general-arousal imagery (MG-A) focuses on the emotional responses associated with sport performance, such as, feeling excited prior to an important competition [85]. MG-A imagery has been associated with changes in athletes' emotional responses [e.g., 74, 116] and generating a desired emotional state for competition, which could have a positive impact on self-efficacy levels [107, 113].

Research also indicates that those athletes who were more self-confident prior to competition also reported a greater use of MG-M imagery than less self-confident athletes [90, 116]. For example, pre-competition MG-M imagery accounted for significant variance in both self-efficacy and performance for collegiate golfers. Self-efficacy was also found to be predictive of golf performance and MG-M imagery use mediated the relationship between self-efficacy and performance [9].

Modelling

Observing competent models successfully perform actions conveys information to observers about the sequence of actions one should use to succeed [107]. Furthermore, the belief that one knows what to do to perform a task raises self-efficacy and thus can also motivate observers to perform the task (4, 104]. Research illustrates that models can have profound effects on self-efficacy, motivation and achievement towards a given task [104, 98, 123]. By observing similar others succeed, observers' self-efficacy may be raised which may motivate them to try the task, as they believe that if others can succeed (e.g., peers, team mates) so can they [4, 105].

The highest degree of model-observer similarity is attained through self- modelling [32]. Hence, one is videoed while performing a task and subsequently views the tape (e.g., a cricketer watching a video of their bowling action from a variety of angles). The use of modelling as an effective technique to develop self-efficacy is well documented [32, 107]. Participants who view similar models perform a task better and judged self-efficacy higher than participants who observe dissimilar models [51, 58]. However, research exploring the effectiveness of self-modelling on self-efficacy within the physical domain appears to be inconclusive [97]. For example, Dowrick and Dove [33] noted that self-modelling contributed to increases in self-efficacy and swimming performance and decreased anxiety within spina-bifida children. In contrast, Winfrey and Weekes [122] found no differences in self-efficacy and performance between self-modelling and control groups. Similarly, Ram and McCullagh [97] using a single-subject design with five volleyball players found that self-modelling did not contribute towards increases in self-efficacy and performance.

Self-Talk

Research relating to the contribution of positive self-talk on efficacy expectations is inconclusive [e.g., 46]. For example, Wilkes and Summers [121] found positive self-talk to enhance performance but not efficacy related cognitions. In contrast, using a multi-modal intervention consisting of goal-setting, imagery and self-talk on swimmers debilitated by anxiety [66]. Data indicated the cognitive restructuring techniques altered the athletes' perceptions of their anxiety response, increased levels of self-confidence, and improved swimming performance.

Feedback

Feedback has been advocated to affect self-efficacy, motivation and performance [106]. Performance feedback that highlights individuals are performing well or making progress should raise self-efficacy motivation and performance [106]. This outcome is likely to occur for individuals who cannot reliably determine progress on their own (e.g., gymnasts or swimmers). Furthermore, goal progress feedback provides information about progress towards a goal. The outcome of such feedback is an increase in self-efficacy, motivation, and performance as it highlights a level of competence, encourages persistence and the setting of new goals [108].

Research has examined the impact of feedback on self-efficacy, performance and task choice and the mediating effects of self-efficacy in the feedback-performance and task choice relationships [39]. Through the use of manipulated feedback and estimates of self-efficacy relative to an athletic task (i.e., hurdling) it was concluded that performance feedback was significantly related to self-efficacy, performance and task choice. In addition, data also highlighted that self-efficacy is a cognitive variable that mediates the relationship between feedback and task choice (e.g., if one receives positive feedback from a team mate about the execution of a particular task then one is more likely to attempt it again in a similar situation).

Other Techniques

In addition to the direct use of psychological skills, there are a number of strategies that impact positively on an individual's efficacy or confidence. As predicted by self-efficacy theory, previous performance appears to be the most pertinent source of information athletes use to inform their perceptions of self-efficacy or sport confidence [4, 39, 108]. This suggests that it is important that athletes are able to experience success in order to enhance confidence. An appropriate motivational climate is useful in facilitating this, where success is framed in an achievable way and is not just outcome focused. Framing success and attempting to manage attributions may be important in fostering self-confidence. The attributions an athlete makes about their performance can directly impact on confidence [84]. Attributing success to stable causes and failure to external factors may lead athletes to believe that future outcomes will be similar and so see any additional exertion of effort as rather futile. On the other hand, attributing failure to poor strategies or technique and success to personally controllable causes would seem helpful in enhancing confidence [52]. A novel way of allowing athletes to focus on success is self-modelling [119]. Dowrick [31] proposed the use of edited video to present only successful performances of a particular athlete. A variation of self-modelling, feed-forward [119] also offers the possibility enhancing confidence by offering athlete's an insight into possible future successes. In this intervention, a video is produced presenting constructed successful performances of a behaviour or skill not yet accomplished by that particular athlete [119].

Along with using information of success in past performances, athletes have also been found to use additional sources of information to evaluate their potential future performances. In a study of world-class athletes, Hays et al. [68] found that along with performance accomplishments, appropriate preparation, and coaching are also important in enhancing confidence. Taylor [111] suggested that preparation was pivotal in developing confidence. This preparation can involve physical preparation, technical preparation, tactical preparation and psychological preparation [120] and suggests the psychological benefits of appropriate physical conditioning, good technical coaching along with psychological skills training. Additional sources of confidence identified by Hays et al. [68] included innate factors, social support, experience, competitive advantage, self-awareness and trust. The research team found that athletes could distinguish between where their confidence was derived from and what they were confident about without any difficulty. The team also indentified some gender differences, male athletes suggested superiority to opposition and tactical awareness were pertinent sources of confidence but females did not consider these sources important. Given that reductions in an athlete's confidence are directly related to the sources of confidence from which they derive, it has been suggested that the most successful interventions for enhancing confidence may involve identifying a particular athlete's pertinent sources and types of confidence and attempting to ensure that these are intact during competition preparation phases [68]. Other studies have also found social support an important source of confidence in the form of encouragement and feedback from other athletes, coaches, family members and friends [61]. Encouraging athletes to derive confidence from a multitude of sources, and develop an understanding of how and why they perform successfully, might enable them to develop a more robust sport confidence. [68].

In summary, a range of psychological techniques can be used to increase athletes' self-efficacy. Through enhancing self-efficacy beliefs, athletes will also experience changes in their level of effort and persistence, along with the setting of challenging goals; characteristics which have been reported as key to mental toughness in sport [e.g., 63, 87].

Coping with Adversity

The importance of coping with adversity has been identified as a key factor in mental-toughness (e.g., 13,72, 73, 112). Coping has been defined as the "constantly changing cognitive and behavioural efforts to manage specific external and/or internal demands that are appraised as taxing or exceeding the resources of the person" [79; p. 141]. In competitive sport, athletes use both approach and avoidance coping styles; the former involving an athlete dealing with a stressor by engaging with it, and later involving dismissing it as unimportant [2]. Although each style has advantages and disadvantages depending on the context [99], Nicholls et al. [91] found mentally tough athletes use more approach coping strategies and less avoidance strategies. Avoidance-focused coping strategies include avoidance and isolation [62] creating a private world [48], detachment, denial, and wishful thinking [82]; ignoring or blocking things out [71] (and suppression of competing activities, wishful thinking, behavioural disengagement, denial, and self-blame [23]. Examples of successful approach strategies identified include constructive evaluation, positive images, distraction control, keeping sight of the whole picture, positive thinking [94, 95].

Poczwardowski and Conroy [96] highlighted four theoretical components in what they described as an integrated coping response: avoidance coping, problem-focused coping, emotion-focused coping, and appraisal-focused coping. Avoidance coping involves both behavioural and cognitive efforts by an individual to disengage from a challenging situation [2, 38, 77]. Problem-focused coping where an individual uses problem-oriented strategies directed to both the environment and the self [79]. Emotion-focused coping involves an individual managing their emotional responses to stress using behavioural strategies and cognitive reappraisals of demands [57]. Finally, Appraisal-focused coping refers to an individual appraising or reappraising stressful situations using [22] positive appraisal of particular competition stressors has been found useful in coping [64]. For example, it is better for athletes to interpret a potentially stressful situation as a challenge and an opportunity to perform well, than to interpret it as being pressured.

The ABC formula provides a practical model of coping that highlights a strategy for dealing with failure or setbacks by using positive reappraisal. The model was based on the work of rational emotional therapists, Ellis and Harper [37]. The model suggests a failure or set back generates self-talk which can be either positive or negative. Positive self-talk tends to be specific, external and temporary. However, if self-talk is negative it is loaded with permanent, pervasive and personal. Whichever type of explanations or attributions are used explain to failure they lead to a particular affect; positive or negative. Positive self-talk leads to positive emotions and underlying hopefulness that leads to determination, self-confidence, motivation and persistence. Conversely, negative self-talk leads to negative emotion such as hopelessness, inadequacy, powerlessness, and low motivation. If the emotions generated are negative, the model offers the possibility of a defence to the negative transforming the negative evaluations and associated self-talk with more positive, specific, temporary and external self-talk that offer counter-arguments to the negative self-talk thereby replacing the negative feelings with more positive and productive ones. Each of the stages are represented by a letter: 'A' stands for a failure or setback, 'B' represents the self-talk generated by 'A', this self-talk leads to particular feelings represented by 'C' and the possibility of a defence to negative emotions that leads to positive affect 'D' [56].

Gould, Finch, and Jackson [60] identified a number of psychological skills used in successful coping including self-talk, reflection on positive past performances, pre-performance routines and relaxation techniques. Self-talk has been associated with coping with physical pain [54, 53]. Although the support for self-talk appears relatively broad, support the use of relaxation techniques such as biofeedback and mediation has been equivocal. For example, there has been criticism of techniques that use relaxation type interventions for developing physiological toughness. Dienstbier [30] suggested that relaxation techniques that provide short-term relief may possibly be removing the very situations that lead to toughening. Anshel and Sutarso [2] argued that, rather than instruct athletes to use coping strategies for individual stressful events, by grouping sources of stress into categories, athletes should be able to create a set of rules based on previous experience from which to determine the best coping strategy.

Hypnosis could also be used to help athletes' develop their coping skills. First, hypnosis and self-hypnosis (including relaxation procedures) could be used to facilitate feelings of relaxation prior to competition. Second, presenting athletes' with hypnotic suggestions that resonate to feelings, thoughts, and behaviours of successfully undertaking and coping with challenging sporting situations could facilitate their coping resources. Currently, no research evidence exists in the sport psychology literature supporting this postulation.

In summary, psychological skills such as self-talk and appropriately attributing success and failure, offer the possibility of developing approach style coping strategies that tend to used by mentally tough athletes. Although currently speculative and supported purely by anecdotal evidence, hypnosis may also be useful in this. Certainly we would encourage researchers to explore this further.

Motivation and Commitment

Motivation and commitment have been seen as important attributes in mentally tough athletes [72, 53]. From a theoretical perspective a number of motivational theories and models adopted from general psychology have been used within a sporting context including competence motivation theory [67], cognitive evaluation theory [29], expectancy-value theory [35], and achievement goal theory [1, 36, 93]. In an attempt at a sport specific model Scanlan and Simons [92] presented a conceptual model of motivation that they called the sport commitment model. Focusing on commitment in youth sport, this model breaks down commitment in sport to five key factors. These factors include level of enjoyment, involvement alternative, personal investment, social constraints and involvement opportunities; all of which are suggested to exhibit an effect on an individual's commitment to a specific sporting activity. In researching the model, Scanlan and Simons [101] reported that enjoyment and involvement opportunities emerged as the most salient determinants of sport commitment. They also found that enjoyment permeated the discussion of several other constructs. Despite the preliminary support for the model's propositions, Scanlan, Carpenter, Schmidt, Simons, and Keeler [102] argued that the model is developmental. They pointed to issues that merit additional consideration. Certainly in subsequent investigations, social constraints have been found to be either unrelated or negatively correlated with commitment [16, 17].

Athletes have reported that an appropriate motivational climate is important in nurturing mental toughness. [19]. Ryan and Deci [100] recommended training and competitive environments that support basic human needs of competence, autonomy and relatedness. Environments where mutual respect is fostered, individual differences excepted, autonomy in decision making encouraged, performance is facilitated by positive modelling, process goals are focussed on rather than an outcome goals, and performance improvements are informed by using positive and constructive feedback. Ideally, such a climate is created by coaches, other athletes as well as friends and family members [19]. Parents influence their children's initial participation motivation in sport by either providing a role model, social support and social influence [119]. Walker, Foster, Daubert and Nathan, D [119] suggest that some young athletes may need extra support in optimizing their motivation particularly those who do not appear to be benefitting from parental/guardian support or where that support might be too critical. Motivational climate should extend beyond individual factors and be fostered even outside of the training and competitive environment. Athletes have indicated the importance of social factors in their achievement motivation [103]. This type of climate can be operationalised by coaches incorporating social motives into team practices and competitions, including team contribution alongside individual accomplishments when evaluating performance and rewarding behaviour, and providing opportunities outside of the sport setting that promote affiliation and belonging [103].

A range of interventions are proposed to both maintain and enhance motivation. Observing inspirational performances, listening to motivational stories involving successful athletes along with vicarious experience of other athletes during training and competition have been recommended to maintain or reignite diminishing motivation and commitment [119]. Hypnosis could also be used to help athletes' develop their motivation. For example, presenting athletes' with hypnotic suggestions containing motivational stories and instructions could help to develop motivational thoughts and images; therefore positively affecting thoughts, feelings, and behaviours about up and coming training and performance. Currently, no research evidence exists in the sport psychology literature supporting this postulation.

USING PSYCHOLOGICAL SKILLS TRAINING TO ENHANCE MENTAL TOUGHNESS

In this chapter we have outlined a number of strategies that could be used to enhance mental toughness. In this section of the chapter we present a tentative model of the relationship between mental toughness and psychological skills training, in an attempt to highlight how the psychological skills training discussed may support the development of mental-toughness (see figure 1). It should be noted that this model is speculative and based on current evidence on mental toughness and current understanding of the efficacy of a range of psychological techniques in enhancing certain attributes identified as being associated with mentally tough individuals. This model is presented to help inform practitioners and focus their efforts to create an environment that may facilitate athletes' developing mentally tough attributes.

Commonalities in describing mental toughness attributes across research teams and authors revolve around several areas but generally make reference to self-belief or confidence, motivation or commitment and coping. It is these areas of consensus that this model uses as a focus for the psychological interventions detailed. The model highlights the need for an appropriate motivational climate being established from the outset of an athlete's career to provide support for all experiences and challenges particularly during formative years and periods of fluctuating mental toughness (e.g., dealing with set-backs and making senior debut). This climate is reinforced by coaches, parents, friends and family members as well as other athletes, something seen as important by elite athletes in their own development [21]. Sport psychologists should be encouraged to work, when and where possible, with coaches and parents of athletes, as well as the athletes themselves. It is a combination of the attitudes and feedback from these key stakeholders along with an individual athlete's personal views, which cultivates the motivational climate an athlete operates in. This climate should provide support on a number of different levels (e.g., social, technical and emotional) and be process and developmentally focused to support athletes' as they face the sporting and life challenges that athletes have suggested is necessary to develop mentally tough attitudes [e.g., 73, 19]. In such a climate feedback and goals are intrinsically linked. For example, the climate created has the potential to impact on the extrinsic and intrinsic feedback received by athletes and influence self-efficacy, motivation and future performance [107].

A climate focusing on process and developmental goals, that facilitate the development of task orientation, which is enforced by all stakeholders means athletes can frame a difficult opponent or high pressure situation as a challenge that provides an opportunity to facilitate development rather than a barrier to success that needs to be overcome [47]. This type of motivational climate offers the possibility of encouraging athletes to try out new techniques and seek out tough opposition, in the knowledge it will be a positive and successful developmental experience whatever the competition outcome. Appropriate goals have also been found to be important in developing and maintain the necessary motivation and commitment required to develop into mentally tough athletes [72]. Such a climate has been positively associated with adapted sources of confidence, social sources, and the belief that motivation and effort is the cause of success and satisfaction [127, 115]. However, it should be noted that the environment created should not discount the potential importance of ego involvement in developing mentally tough performers [25]. Certainly an environment where athletes are facilitated in developing both high ego and high task involvement provides may provide an opportunity for athletes to develop the intrinsic motivation and the competitiveness necessary to be mentally tough competitors.

In addition to making suggestions on how the general motivational climate may be shaped, the model points to a range of psychological techniques that can support an athlete in facing sport and life challenges, developing appropriate coping strategies to turn these into positive opportunities for developing mentally tough attributes. As discussed in detail earlier in the chapter, the appropriate use of self-talk, imagery and hypnosis (hetero and auto) offer sports psychologists and athletes the tools to enhance the key attributes highlighted in the model with the athlete (i.e., motivation/commitment and confidence) and can help cultivate appropriate coping strategies and skills. While basic psychological skills would be useful being taught to athletes alongside sports skills, an integrated approach using a combination of techniques could be used to help athletes cope with particular challenges as they arise throughout their career. These may involve sport or life challenges, both of which offer the opportunity for developing mental toughness. This contention suggests that role of a practitioner needs not only provide support and training to a range of individuals important to an athlete's career (i.e., coach, parents and other athletes), but also that they may need to support an athlete outside of their immediate sporting environment. Should such an approach be adopted it could mean that education for sport psychologists in the future may need to include more breadth and include general mainstream psychological input including pertinent aspects of clinical psychology.

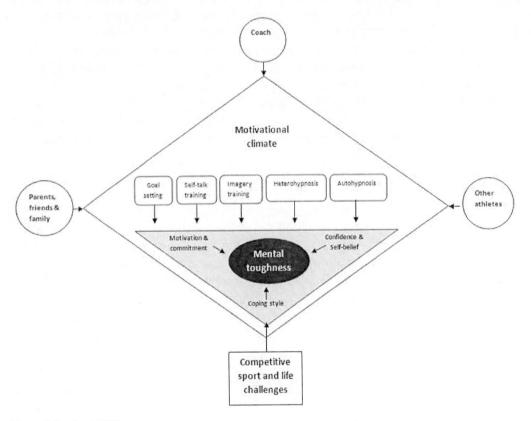

Myers & Barker, 2008.

Figure 1. A model of the relationship between mental toughness and psychological skills training.

CHAPTER SUMMARY AND RECOMMENDATIONS FOR FUTURE RESEARCH

In this chapter we began by exploring definitions of mental toughness on a conceptual level, went on to provide an overview of models and associated measures, moving on to discuss the development of mental toughness attributes and propose a model for their cohesive implementation. Clearly recent research has increased our understanding of the construct of mental toughness in sport. That said, although there appears to be a level of agreement on a definition and to an extent on a conceptual framework, this is still work in progress and there is a need for an agreed definition. Further research may wish to consider what mental toughness is not (i.e., the mislabelling of positive psychological characteristics as mental toughness) and therefore reduce some of the conceptual confusion existing in the area [73].

It is clear that the current models of mental toughness need exploring with even greater rigour and across a wider range of populations before we can be confident in our full understanding of the concept. The instruments available to measure mental toughness are of varying quality. Certainly along with conceptual clarity, the psychometric properties of the measures need to be clearly established. While our understanding of how athletes' feel their own mental toughness has been developed has been significantly enhanced by recent studies, there is still a considerable journey to embark upon in terms of developing mental toughness. There are a number of areas we still need to explore. For example, we need to determine what might cause fluctuations in mental toughness during an athlete's career. Longitudinal research approaches, cross-sectional studies, along with a combination of quasi-experimental designs (e g., single-subject, switched replication) should be used to compliment case studies in evaluating intervention efficacy..

Future mental toughness research should consider developing a valid and reliable measure of mental toughness to enable researchers and practitioners to assess perceived levels of mental toughness. Once developed, such a measure would enable comparisons of groups of individuals, thus highlighting areas that require further investigation [73]. Interventions can then be implemented and evaluated with mentally weak performers. Indeed, research needs to identify appropriate and efficacious mental skills because currently evidence is scant in this area. One technique, which may be useful, is hypnosis. Hypnosis could assist in the development of athletes' mental toughness in a number of ways. First, hypnosis and self-hypnosis (including relaxation procedures) could be used to facilitate feelings of relaxation prior to competition. Second, hypnotic suggestions containing self-talk and imagery information on the attributes of mental toughness (e.g., perseverance, handling pressure, maintaining effort) may facilitate positive changes in an athletes' feelings, thoughts, and behaviours. Therefore enabling to cope better and display enhanced mental toughness when they are in mentally challenging sporting situations (e.g., as penalty shoot-out in soccer or Olympic final). Third, the development and use of self-hypnosis will also allow athletes to self-regulate during stressful performance. Currently, no research evidence exists in the sport psychology literature supporting this postulation.

In summary, understanding, measuring and facilitating mental toughness has obvious benefits for those involved in elite sport. The recent research has certainly increased an understanding of mental toughness per se. Despite this increase in knowledge sport psychologists should be cautious about measuring mental toughness and how scores from current measures are used. Indeed, it is possible sports coaches and managers may seek to select players based upon scores from measures that lack appropriate psychometric rigour.

REFERENCES

[1]   Ames, C. (1992). Classrooms: Goals, structures, and student motivation. *J of Ed Psych, 84*, 261 271.

[2]   Anshel, M. H &. Sutarso, T. (2007). Relationships between sources of acute stress and athletes' coping style in competitive sport as a function of gender. *Psych of Sport Exer, 8*, 1–24.

[3]   Anshel, M. H. (1996). Examining coping style in sport. *J of Soc Psych, 53*, 337–348.

[4]   Bandura, A. (1997). *Self-efficacy: The exercise of control*. New York: Freeman

[5]   Barker, J. B., & Jones, M. V. (2005). Using hypnosis to increase self-efficacy: A case study in elite judo. *Sport Exer Psych Rev, 1*, 36-42.

[6]   Barker, J. B., & Jones, M. V. (2006). Using hypnosis, technique refinement and self-modeling to enhance self-efficacy: A case study in cricket. *The Sport Psychologist, 20*, 94-110.

[7]   Barker, J. B., & Jones, M. V. (2008). The effects of hypnosis on self-efficacy, affect, and sport performance: A case study from professional English soccer. *J of Clin Sport Psych, 2*, 127-147.

[8]   Barker, J. B., Jones, M. V., & Greenlees, I. (in prep). The effects of hypnosis on collegiate soccer players self-efficacy and soccer wall-volley performance.

[9]   Beauchamp, M. R., Bray, S. R., & Albinson, J. G. (2002). Pre-competition imagery, self-efficacy and performance in collegiate athletes. *J of Sports Sci, 20*, 697-705

[10]   Bloom, B. S. (1985) *Developing talent in young people*. New York, NY: Ballantine.

[11]   Bull, S. J., Albinson, J. G., & Shambrook, C. J. (1996). T*he mental game plan: Getting psyched for sport*. Eastboune, UK: Sports Dynamics.

[12]   Bull, S., James, W., & Brooks, J. (2008). The Mental Toughness Profiler (MTP) for cricket. *On the Up*: *English Cricket Board (ECB) Coach Edu*, August, 34-36.

[13]   Bull, S., Shambrook, C., James, W., & Brooks, J. (2005). Towards an understanding of mental toughness in elite English cricketers. *J of Applied Sport Psych, 17*, 209-227.

[14]   Butler, R.J. (1996). *Sports Psychology in Action*. Oxford: Butterworth-Heinemann

[15]   Callow, N., Hardy, L., & Hall, C. (2001). The effects of a motivational general-mastery imagery intervention on the sport confidence of high-level badminton players. *Res Quart Exer Sport, 72*, 389-400.

[16]   Carpenter, P. J., & Coleman, R. (1998). A longitudinal study of elite youth cricketers' commitment. *Int J of Sport Psych, 29*, 195–210.

[17]   Carpenter, P. J., & Scanlan, T. K. (1998). Changes over time in determinants of the sport commitment model. *Pediatric Exer Science, 10*, 356–365.

[18]   Clough, P., Earle, K., & Sewell, D. (2002). Mental toughness: The concept and its measurement. In I. Cockerill (Ed.), *Solutions in sport Psychology* (pp. 32–46).). London: Thompson.

[19]   Conaughton, D., Wadey, R., Hanton, S., & Jones, G. (2008). The development and maintenance of mental toughness: perceptions of elite performers. *J of Sport Sci, 26*, 83-95.

[20]   Cote, J. (1999). The influence of the family in the development of talent in sports. *The Sports Psychologist, 13*, 395-417.

[21]   Cote, J., Baker, J., & Abernethy, B. (2003). From play to practice: A developmental framework for the acquisition of expertise in team sports. In J. Starkes & K.A.Ericsson (Eds.), *Expert performance in sports: Advances in Research on Sport Expertise* (pp. 89-110). Champaign, IL: Human Kinetics.

[22] Cox, T., & Ferguson, E. (1991). Individual differences, stress and coping. In C. L. Cooper & R. Payne (Eds.), *Personality and stress: Individual differences in the stress process* (pp. 7–30). Chichester, UK: Wiley.

[23] Crocker, P. R. E., & Isaak, K. (1997). Coping during competitions and training sessions: Are youth swimmers consistent? *Int J of Sport Psych, 28,* 355–369.

[24] Crust, L. (2007). Mental toughness in sport: A Rev. *Int J of Sport Exer Psych,* 5(3), 270–290.

[25] Crust, L. (2008). A Review and conceptual re-examination of mental toughness: Implications for future research. *Personality Ind Diffs* 45 576–583

[26] Crust, L., & Clough, P. J. (2005). Relationship between mental toughness and physical endurance. *Percept & Motor Skills,* 100, 192–194.

[27] Csikszentmihalyi, M., Rathunde, K., & Whalen, S. (1993). *Talented Teenagers: The roots of success & failure.* Cambridge, UK: Cambridge University Press.

[28] Davis, H., & Zaichkowsky, L. (1998). Explanatory style among elite ice hockey athletes. *Percept and Motor Skills,* 87, 1075–1080

[29] Deci, E.L., & Ryan, R.M. (1985). *Intrinsic motivation and self determination in human behaviour.* New York: Plenum Press.

[30] Dienstbier, R. A. (1991) Behavioral correlates of sympathoadrenal reactivity: The toughness model. *Med Sci Sports Exer, 23,*846-852.

[31] Dowrick, P. W. (1991) *Practical guide to using video in the behavioural Sciences.* New York: Wiley.

[32] Dowrick, P. W. (1999). A Rev of self-modelling and related interventions. *App Prevent Psych, 8,* 23-39.

[33] Dowrick, P. W., & Dove, C. (1980). The use of self-modelling to improve the swimming performance of spina-bifida children. *J of App Behav Anal, 13,* 51-56.

[34] Earle, K., Earle, F., & Clough, P. (2008). Mental toughness and its application for golfers. *Sport Exer Psych Rev, 4,* 22-27.

[35] Eccles (Parsons), J. S., Adler, T.E., Futterman, R., Goff, S. B., Kaczala, C. M., Meece, J. L., & Midgley, C. (1983). Expectancies, values, and academic behaviours. In J. T Spence (Ed.), *Achievement and achievement motivation* (pp. 75-146). San Francisco: Freeman.

[36] Elliott, E. S., & Dweck, C. S. (1988). Goals: An approach to motivation and achievement. *J of Person Soc Psych,* 54, 5-12.

[37] Ellis, A. and Harper, R.A. (1975). *A new guide to rational living.* Hollywood: Wilshire Book Company.

[38] Endler, N. S., & Parker, J. D. A. (1990). Multidimensional assessment of coping: A critical evaluation. *J of Person Soc Psych,* 58, 844–854.

[39] Escarti, A., & Guzman, J. F. (1999). Effects of feedback on self-efficacy, performance and choice in an athletic task. *J of App Sport Psych, 11,* 83-96.

[40] Fawcett, T. (2006). An investigation into the perceptions of mental toughness of adventurers/explorers, elite athletes, and elite coaches. Unpublished doctoral dissertation, University of Newcastle at Northumbria, UK.

[41] Fawcett, T. (2008). The Psych of competing in the flying kilometre-unexplored cognitions and emotions. poster presentation BASES annual conference Brunel University

[42] Feltz, D. L. (1988). Self-confidence and sports performance. In K. B. Pandolf (Ed.), *Exercise and Sport Sciences Reviews* (pp. 423-456). New York: Macmillan.

[43] Feltz, D. L. (1994). Self-confidence and performance. In D. Druckman & R. A. Bjork (Eds.), *Learning, remembering, believing: Enhancing human performance* (pp. 173-206). Washington, DC: National Academy Press.

[44] Feltz, D. L., & Lirgg, C. D. (2001). Self-efficacy beliefs of athletes, teams and coaches. In R. N. Singer, H. A. Hausenblas, & C. M. Janelle (Eds.), *Handbook of Sport Psychology* (2nd ed; pp. 340-361). New York: Wiley.

[45] Feltz, D. L., Chow, G., & Hepler, T. J. (2006). Path analysis of self-efficacy and performance: Revisited. *J of Sport Exer Psych, 28,* S66.

[46] Feltz, D. L., Short, S. E., & Sullivan, P. J. (2008). *Self-efficacy in sport*. Champaign, IL: Human Kinetics.

[47] Fraleigh, W.P. (1984). *Right actions in sport: Ethics for contestants.* Champaign, IL: Human Kinetics.

[48] Fredrickson, J., & Rooney, J. F. (1988). The free-lance musician as a type of non-person: An extension of the concept of non-personhood. *Soci Quart, 29,* 221–239,

[49] Gagne, F. (1996) *A thoughtful look at talent development*. Montreal: University of Quebec Press.

[50] Gagne, F. (2003) Transforming Gifts into Talents: The DMGT as a Developmental Theory. In N. Colangelo & G. A. Davis *Handbook of Gifted Education* (pp. 130-140). Boston: Pearson Education).

[51] George, T. R., Feltz, D. L., & Chase, M. A. (1992). Effects of model similarity and model talk on self-efficacy and muscular endurance: A second look. *J of Sport Exer Psych, 14,* 237-248.

[52] Gernigon, C., & Delloye, J. B. (2003). Self-efficacy, causal attribution, and track athletic performance following unexpected success or failure among elite sprinters. *The Sport Psychologist, 17,* 55-76.

[53] Girodo, M., & Roehl, J. (1980). Cognitive preparation and coping self-talk: Anxiety management during the stress of flying. *J of Consult Clin Psych*, 46, 978-989.

[54] Girodo, M., & Wood, D. (1979). Talking yourself out of pain: The importance of believing that you can. *Cog Therapy Res, 3,* 23-33.

[55] Golby, J., & Sheard, M. (2004). Mental toughness and hardiness at different levels of rugby league. *Personality Ind Diff, 37,* 933–942.

[56] Goldberg, A.S. (1998). *Sports slump busting: 10 steps to mental toughness and peak performance.* Champaign, IL: Human Kinetics.

[57] Gould, D. Hodge, K. Peterson, K., & Giannini, J. (1989). An exploratory examination of strategies used by elite coaches to enhance self-efficacy in athletes. *J of Sport Exer Psych, 11,* 128-140.

[58] Gould, D., & Weiss, M. R. (1981). Effect of model similarity and model self-talk on self-efficacy in muscular endurance. *J of Sport Psych, 3,* 17-29.

[59] Gould, D., Dieffenbach, K. & Moffett, A. (2002). Psychological Characteristics and their Development in Olympic Champions. *J of Applied Sport Psych, 14,* 172–204.

[60] Gould, D., Finch, L. M., & Jackson, S. A. (1993). Coping strategies used by national champion figure skaters. *Res Quart Exer and Sport, 64,* 453–468.

[61] Gould, D., Hodge, K., Peterson, K., & Petlichkoff, L. (1987). Psychological foundations of coaching: Similarities and differences among intercollegiate wrestling coaches. *The Sport Psychologist, 1,* 293-308.

[62] Gould, D., Udry, E., Bridges, D., & Beck, L. (1997). Coping with season ending injuries. *The Sport Psychologist, 11,* 379–399,

[63] Gucciardi, D. F., Gordon, S., & Dimmock, J. A. (2008). Towards and understanding of mental toughness in Australian football. *J of App Sport Psych, 20,* 261-281.

[64] Hale, B. D., & Whitehouse, A. (1998). The effects of imagery-manipulated appraisal on intensity and direction of competitive anxiety. *The Sport Psychologist, 12,* 40-51.

[65] Hall, C. R., Mack, D., Paivio, A., & Hausenblas, H. A. (1998). Imagery use by athletes: Development of the Sport Imagery Questionnaire. *Inter J Sport Psych, 29,* 73-89.

[66] Hanton, S., & Jones, G. (1999). The effects of a multimodal intervention program on performers: II. Training the butterflies to fly in formation. *The Sport Psychologist, 13,* 22-41.

[67] Harter, S. (1978). Effectance motivation reconsidered: Towards a developmental model. *Human dev, 21,* 34-64.

[68] Hays, K ., Maynard, I., Thomas, O., & Bawden, M. (2007). Sources and Types of Confidence Identified by World Class Sport Performers. *J of App Sport Psych, 19,* 434-456.

[69] Hilgard, E. R. (1986). *Divided consciousness: Multiple controls in human thought and action* (expanded edition). New York: Wiley.

[70] Horsley, C. (1995). Confidence and sporting performance. In Morris, T. & Summers, J., *Sport Psychology: Theory applications and issues* (pp. 311-337).. Brisbane Wiley

[71] Jackson, S. A., Mayocchi, L., & Dover, J. (1998). Life after winning gold: II. Coping with change as an Olympic gold medallist. *The Sport Psychologist, 12,* 137–155.

[72] Jones, G., Hanton, S., & Connaughton, D. (2002). What is this thing called mental toughness? An investigation of elite sport performers. *J of App Sport Psych, 14,* 205-218.

[73] Jones, G., Hanton, S., & Connaughton, D. (2007). A framework of mental toughness in the world's best performers. *The Sport Psychologist, 21,* 243–264.

[74] Jones, M. V., Mace, R. D., Bray, S. R., MacRae, A., & Stockbridge, C. (2002). The impact of motivational imagery on the emotional state and self-efficacy levels of novice climbers. *J of Sport Behav, 25,* 57-73.

[75] Kane, T. D., Marks, M. A., Zaccaro, S. J., & Blair, V. (1996). Self-efficacy, personal goals and wrestlers' self-regulation. *J of Sport & Exer Psych, 18,* 36-48.

[76] Kelly, G. A. (1991). The Psych of personal constructs: A theory of personality (Vol 1). London Routledge (Original work published 1955).

[77] Krohne, H. W. (1993). Vigilance and cognitive avoidance as concepts in coping Res. In H. W. Krohne (Ed.), *Attention and avoidance: Strategies in coping with aversiveness* (pp. 19–50). Seattle, WA: Hogrefe & Huber.

[78] Kuan G., & Roy J. (2007). Goal profiles, mental toughness and its influence on performance outcomes among Wushu athletes. *J of Sports Sci Med 6,* 28-33.

[79] Lazarus, R., & Folkman, S. (1984). *Stress, appraisal, and coping.* New York: Springer.

[80] Loehr. J. E. (1982). *Athletic excellence: Mental toughness training for sports.* New York: Forum.

[81] Loehr. J. E. (1986). *Mental toughness training for sports: Achieving athletic excellence*. Lexington, MA: Stephen Greene press.

[82] Madden, C. C., Kirkby, R. J., & McDonald, D. (1989). Coping styles of competitive middle distance runners. *Int J of Sport Psych, 20*, 287–296,

[83] Magyar, T. M., & Feltz, D. L. (2003). The influence of dispositional and situational tendencies on adolescent girls' sport confidence sources, *Psych of Sport Exer, 4 2*, 175-190

[84] Manzo, L. G., Mondin, G. W., & Clark, B. (2005). Confidence. In Taylor J. & Wilson G. *Applying Sport Psychology: four perspectives*. Champaign, IL: Human Kinetics

[85] Martin, K. A., & Hall, C. R. (1995). Using mental imagery to enhance intrinsic motivation. *J of Sport Exer Psych, 17*, 54-69.

[86] Martin, K. A., Mortiz, S. E., & Hall, C. R. (1999). Imagery use in sport: A literature Rev and applied model. *The Sport Psychologist, 13*, 245-268.

[87] Middleton, S. C., Marsh, H. M., Martin, A.J ., Richards, G. E., & Perry, C. (2004). Discovering mental toughness: A qualitative study of mental toughness in elite athletes. *Self Research Centre Biannual Conference, Berlin.*

[88] Middleton, S.C.(2007). Mental toughness: conceptualisation and measurement. Doctoral dissertation University of Western Sydney. http://handle.uws.Ed.au:8081/1959.7/18959.

[89] Moritz, S. E., Feltz, D. L., Fahrbach, K. R., & Mack, D. E. (2000). The relation of self-efficacy measures to sport performance: A meta-analytic Rev. *Res Quarterly for Exer Sport, 71*, 280-294.

[90] Moritz, S. E., Hall, C. R., Martin, K. A., & Vadocz, E. (1996). What are confident athletes imaging? An examination of image content. *The Sport Psychologist, 10*, 171-179.

[91] Nicholls A. R., Polman R. C. J., ,Levy, A. R. & Backhouse S. H. (2008) Mental toughness, optimism, pessimism, and coping among athletes *Person Ind Diff*, 1182–1192,

[92] Nicholls, J. G. (1989). *The competitive ethos and democratic Education*. Cambridge, MA: Harvard University Press.

[93] Nicholls, J.G. (1984). Achievement motivation: Conceptions of ability, subjective experience, task choice, and performance. *Psych Rev*, 91, 328 346

[94] Orlick, T. (1986). *Psyching for sport: Mental training for athletes*. Champaign, IL: Human Kinetics.

[95] Orlick, T. (1992). The Psych of personal excellence. *Cont Thought on Perform Enhance, 1*, 109–122.

[96] Poczwardowski J A. & Conroy D. E.(2002) Coping Responses to Failure and Success Among Elite Athletes and Performing Artists, *J of App Sport Psych, 14*,313–329.

[97] Ram, N., & McCullagh, P. (2003). Self-modelling: Influence on psychological responses and physical performance. *The Sport Psychologist*, 17, 220-241.

[98] Relich, J. D., Debus, R. L., & Walker, R. (1986). The mediating role of attribution and self-efficacy variables for treatment effects on achievement outcomes. *Cont Edu Psych, 11*, 195-216.

[99] Roth, S., & Cohen, L. J. (1986). Approach, avoidance, and coping with stress. *Am Psychologist, 41*, 813–819.

[100] Ryan, R. M., & Deci, E. L. (2000). Self-determination theory and the facilitation of intrinsic motivation, social development, and well-being. *Am Psychologist, 55,* 68-78

[101] Scanlan, T, K. & Simons, J. P. (1992). The construct of sport enjoyment. In Roberts G.C. (Ed.), *Motivation in sport and Exercise* (pp. 199~215). Champaign, IL: Human Kinetics.

[102] Scanlan, T. K., Carpenter, P. J., Schmidt, G. W., Simons, J. P., & Keeler, B. (1993). An Introduction to the Sport Commitment Model. *J of Sport Exer Psych, 15,* 1-15.

[103] Schilling, T. A. and Hayashi, C. T. (2001)'Achievement Motivation among High School Basketball and Cross- Country Athletes: A Personal Investment Perspective', *J of App Sport Psych, 13,,*103-128.

[104] Schunk, D. H. (1981). Modelling and attributional effects on children's achievement: A self- efficacy analysis. *J of Ed Psych, 73,* 93-105.

[105] Schunk, D. H. (1987). Peer models and children's behavioural change. *Rev of Ed Res, 57,* 149-174.

[106] Schunk, D. H. (1995). Self-efficacy, Education and instruction. In J. E. Maddux (Ed.), *Self-efficacy, adaptation and adjustment: Theory, Res and application* (pp. 281-303). New York: Plennum.

[107] Schunk, D. H. (1995). Self-efficacy, motivation, and performance. *J of App Sport Psych, 7,* 112-137.

[108] Schunk, D. H., & Rice, J. M. (1991). Learning goals and progress feedback during reading comprehension instruction. *J of Read Beh, 23,* 351-363.

[109] Spanos, N. P. (1991). A socio-cognitive approach to hypnosis. In S. J. Lynn & J. W. Rhue (Eds.), *Theories of hypnosis: Current models and perspectives* (pp. 324- 361). New York: Guildford Press.

[110] Stannard, P., Thelwell, R. C.,& Weston, N. J. V. 2008). Examining mental toughness within sports coaches presentation BASES annual conference Brunel University.

[111] Taylor, J. (2001).*Prime Sport: Triumph of the athlete mind*. New York :iUniverse.

[112] Thelwell, R., Weston, N., & Greenlees, I. (2005). Defining and understanding mental toughness in soccer. *J of App Sport Psych*, 17, 326-332.

[113] Treasure, D. S., Monson, J., & Lox, C. L. (1996). Relationship between self-efficacy, wrestling performance and affect prior to competition. *The Sport Psychologist, 10,* 73-83.

[114] Treasure, D. S., Monson, J., & Lox, C. L. (1996). Relationship between self-efficacy, wrestling performance and affect prior to competition. *The Sport Psychologist, 10,* 73-83.

[115] Treasure, D.C., & Roberts, G.C. (2001). Students' perceptions of the motivational climate, achievement beliefs, and satisfaction in physical Education. *Res Quart for Exer Sport,* 72(2), 165.

[116] Vadocz, E., Hall, C. R., & Moritz, S. E. (1997). The relationship between competitive anxiety and imagery use. *J of App Sport Psych, 9,* 241-253.

[117] Wagstaff, G. F. (1981). *Hypnosis, compliance, and beliefs*. Brighton; Harvester Press,

[118] Wagstaff, G. F. (1991). Compliance, belief and semantics in hypnosis: A non-state socio-cognitive perspective. In S. J. Lynn & J. W. Rhue (Eds.), *Theories of hypnosis: Current models and perspectives* (pp. 362-396). New York: Guildford Press.

[119] Walker, B., Foster, S., Daubert, S. & Nathan, D. (2005). Motivation. In Taylor J. & Wilson G. *Applying sport Psych: four perspectives*. Champaign, IL: Human Kinetics

[120] Weiss, M. R., Wiese, D. M., & Klint, K. A. (1989). Head over heels with success: the relationship between self-efficacy and performance in competitive youth gymnastics. *J of Sport Exer Psych, 11*, 444-451.

[121] Wilkes, R. L., & Summers, J. J. (1984). Cogntitions, mediating variables, and strength performance. *J of Sport Psych, 6,* 351-359.

[122] Winfrey, M. L. & Weekes, D. L. (1993). Effects of self-modelling on self-efficacy and balance beam performance. *Percept and Motor Skills, 77,* 907-913.

[123] Zimmerman, B. J. & Ringle, J. (1981). Effects of model persistence and statements of confidence on children's self-efficacy and problem solving. *J of Ed Psych, 73,* 485-493.

[124] Zinsser, N., Bunker, L. & Williams, J. M. (2006). Cognitive techniques for building confidence and enhancing performance. In J. M. Williams (Ed.), *Applied Sport Psychology: Personal growth to peak performance* (5th ed., pp. 349-363). New York: McGraw-Hill.

In: Advances in Strength and Conditioning Research   ISBN: 978-1-60692-909-4
Editor: Michael Duncan and Mark Lyons   © 2009 Nova Science Publishers, Inc.

Chapter 12

ENHANCING PERFORMANCE IN ICE-HOCKEY

Michael R. Bracko[1]
[1]Institute for Hockey Research, Canada

ABSTRACT

For the strength and conditioning professional and hockey coach, designing training programs to improve performance in ice hockey can be hard because of the multiple physiological demands on the body. In addition, there is limited recent research on the best training programs for enhancing hockey and skating skills. However, because of the nature of hockey it is believed that all the components of fitness are important. These components of fitness include muscle strength, power, and endurance, and cardiovascular endurance and anaerobic capacity. The research on training for hockey and skating suggests that upper and lower body muscle strength, power, and endurance are important for skating acceleration and upper body power is important for stick velocity when shooting. It is unclear what off-ice training, if any, can improve skating agility which resembles game-performance skating the most. Research on skating can be confusing if a coach relies on resent research done with subjects skating on treadmills. There appear to be biomechanical differences when skating on a treadmill compared to skating on ice. The most obvious difference is that treadmills can require a player to skate uphill, whereas every hockey rink in the world has an ice surface that is completely flat. Conversely, there is a good line of research from studies done on ice that can clearly show a coach what characteristics are important for fast, high-performance skating. If coaches review skating research and understand the skating characteristics that are important for fast skating and high-performance skating, they will have a lot of information to develop drills to improve skating. Future research could focus on studies to assess the training protocols that best improve all hockey and skating skills.

Keywords: Ice Hockey, Skating, Hockey Training, Performance Enhancement, Skating Biomechanics

---

[1] Please address correspondence and requests for reprints to Michael R. Bracko, Institute for Hockey Research, 73 Wimbledon Cr. S.W., Calgary, Alberta, Canada, T3C 3J2 or e mail bracko@hockeyinstitute.org

The physical demands of ice hockey are complex. Howie Green, Ph.D., University of Waterloo, Canada [11] gives a unique and intriguing description of hockey physiology when he says "Hockey is uniquely stressful in ways scientists don't really understand. The heat and humidity of the protective gear, the high level of co-ordination required, the repeated demands made on the muscles with little rest and the 'astounding' requirement that it's played while balancing on skate blades are all factors in fatigue."

Dr. Green's comments about scientists not understanding the demands of hockey is somewhat corroborated by the lack of research studies that investigate specific off-ice training programs that have an effect on skating performance or hockey skills [1, 2, 8, 10, 12, 13, 14, 15]. Of the eight studies that were found through reviews of literature that had specific training protocols, three [8, 10, 11] could be considered "recent." As such, there is little objective evidence to support the choice of training programs for hockey players. Most coaches, physiologists, and strength and conditioning coaches must rely on the few training studies, but more so the studies on the physiological of hockey and studies that investigate the off-ice fitness variable that predict skating performance. This is despite the fact the prediction studies to not show a cause and effect interpretation of the fitness variables that calculate superior performance on skating tests.

Interestingly, there are few recent data-based research studies [6, 16, 17, 22, 24] on the most important skill in ice hockey which is skating [9]. However, if one understands the complexity and cost of conducting research on skating performance [16, 26] it becomes clear why so few studies have been conducted. Much of the current skating research is performed with players skating on skating treadmills which do not replicate the on-ice performance or biomechanics of game-performance skating. The research on skating has its limitations because it has investigated primarily forward skating, which leaves the understanding and enhancement of all the other skating characteristics [6] to interpretation.

The purpose of this chapter is to review the research on ice hockey training, skating research, and the off-ice fitness variables that predict skating performance. In addition, conclusions will be made based on the research as to the best way to develop strength and conditioning programs for hockey players.

TRAINING STUDIES IN ICE-HOCKEY

Brocherie et al., [8] investigated the effects of electromyostimulation (EMS) on seventeen division II hockey players from the French Ice Hockey League. There was an EMS group and a control group. The electrostimulated group (ES) had a total of nine EMS sessions over three weeks in addition to their regular hockey training. The vastus medialis and vastus lateralis muscles of each subject were stimulated for twelve minutes per session. During each session 30 EMS contractions to at least 60% of maximum voluntary were completed.

The subjects were pre and posttested on the following variables: maximal voluntary torque of the right knee extensor, vertical jump (squat jump, countermovement jump, drop jump, and fifteen consecutive countermovement jumps), and 10-m and 30-m on-ice skating sprints. The results showed that before training started there were no significant differences on any testing variable between the ES and control group. After testing, the results show that eccentric and concentric isokinetic torque increased significantly for the ES group whereas the control group had no improvements. Vertical jump performance on squat jump, countermovement jump, and the drop jump decreased significantly from pretest scores. No differences were found in the control group. On the fifteen consecutive countermovement jumps the ES group improved power but there was no gain in height jumped. Of the most importance as it relates to hockey and skating performance, the ES group significantly decreased (improved) 10-m sprint time but there was no difference in the 30-m sprint time. The control group stayed the same from pre to posttest.

The results of this study are intriguing as it relates to hockey training. Considering that the players improved their 10-m skating sprint time with EMS, and the restricted time that many hockey teams have available for off-ice training, EMS may have its merits as a form of off-ice training to improve skating acceleration. However, because the EMS subjects improved only their muscle contraction torque but decreased their vertical jump performance on squat jump, countermovement jump, and the drop jump, the use of EMS as an off-ice training tool might be questioned. Perhaps more importantly, EMS training may have its merits as a rehabilitation tool for injured hockey players in an attempt to improve and maintain muscle torque and 10-m skating acceleration. Hockey teams would have to think "outside of the box" in terms of traditional strength and conditioning for EMS to be used as a training tool.

Fergenbaum and Marino [10] investigated the effects of upper body plyometrics, medicine ball throws, and weighted hockey stick slap shots with no puck on upper body isometric strength, stick velocity, and puck velocity using the slap shot. The subjects were twenty-one male Canadian university hockey players (mean age = 23 yrs). The subjects were assigned to a control group or a plyometric group. The control group continued their regular hockey training with no specific plyometric training, whereas the plyometric group performed a warm-up then four exercises: 1) wheelbarrow hops, 2) abdominal shockers 3) two-handed underhand side throw of a four kilogram medicine ball, and 4) slap shots with no puck using a .45 kilogram weighted hockey stick. Sets and repetitions ranged from one set of eight repetitions to three sets of ten repetitions.

In pre-testing the subjects were not different in strength and puck velocity. Posttesting showed there were no differences in chest and shoulder strength and no interaction between groups. Bicep and tricep strength significantly improved in both groups but there was no interaction. Puck velocity increased in both groups from pre to posttesting, but there were no significant difference between groups. Stick velocity significantly improved by 13% in the plyometric group. There was a strong positive correlation (r=0.977; p=0.004) between changes in off-ice stick velocity and changes in on-ice puck velocity. However, the 13% increase in stick velocity did not produce a 13% increase in puck velocity. This could be related to poor skill in performing a slap shot.

The authors conclude that plyometric training, medicine ball throws, and weighted hockey stick slap shots with no puck can improve the coordination between upper and lower body limbs in six training sessions. Moreover, performing off-ice training with a weighted hockey stick for ten weeks showed that it can improve puck velocity when shooting on the ice. However, these results do suggest that in order to improve hockey skills, the training has to be very specific to the actual movement that is used on the ice.

Bracko and Fellingham [2] investigated the effect of an eight week jump training program on the skating performance of 29 male hockey players (mean age; 12.5 yrs, playing experience; 6.93 yrs). There were two groups: 1) jump training (JT) and 2) control (C), however, in order to maintain participation in the study by the control group, the researchers assigned upper body exercises (push-ups and curl-ups) to the control group. As such, the control group was not a control group in true sense of a group that had no treatment. On the contrary, the control group was actually an "upper body group." All subjects were one to three weeks into their postseason but were all taking skating lessons one to three times per week.

The JT group used a progressive overload for the jump training exercises. The jump training exercise program adhered to the guidelines of the National Strength and Conditioning Association for "Explosive Exercises and Training," and "Plyometric Exercises," and "Youth Resistance Training," [23]. The jump training group was supervised by an investigator once per week, and performed their training on their own twice per week. The jump training group started their program during weeks one and two with three sessions per week, two sets of ten foot strikes, and used skipping, vertical jump, and a split squat jump. During weeks three and four, the jump training increased to three sets of 15 foot strikes using the same exercises and three days per week. In weeks five and six, the jump training group stayed at three sets, fifteen foot strikes, but increased the intensity of the jump and added a one-footed jump training exercise. In weeks seven and eight, the jump training group maintained three sets of fifteen foot strikes, but were told to jump as high and hard as they could and had one and two footed vertical and horizontal jumps.

The "control" or upper body group started their program in weeks one and two with two sets of ten repetitions of either regular or modified push-ups and half abdominal curl-ups. During weeks three and four the upper body group increased the sets to three and performed ten to fifteen repetitions. Weeks five and six maintained the same sets but increased the repetitions to fifteen to 25. In weeks seven and eight the subjects were instructed to perform three sets of maximum push-ups and curl-ups.

Subjects had their skating performance evaluated with the following tests: Acceleration: 6.10-m, Speed: 47.85-m, Full Speed: 15.2-m, and Agility Cornering S Turn. Off-ice tests included: counter movement vertical jump height, vertical jump anaerobic power, vertical jump peak and average mechanical power, standing long jump, and maximum curl-ups and push-ups per minute.

The JT group significantly improved skating acceleration, vertical jump height, vertical jump peak mechanical power, and vertical jump average mechanical power. The upper body group significantly improved skating acceleration and push-ups per minute. In this study, skating speed, agility and full speed were not enhanced by any form of off-ice training.

The authors conclude that total body training should be used for improvement of skating acceleration in youth hockey players. Moreover, a possible combination of jump training with counter movements of arms and specific upper body exercises appeared to be important factors for improving acceleration in youth hockey players. Improvements in skating speed (over longer distances) may be associated with higher intensity exercise, longer periods of training, and/or strength training for the legs.

Improvements in skating speed over 47.85-m and 15.2-m in youth hockey players may also be a function of neuromuscular coordination. Young hockey players who have 6.93 years playing experience may not have the coordination of arm and leg movement in order to maintain speed over a longer distance compared to a short acceleration skate.

There may be merit to the upper body group improving acceleration due to the improved strength/endurance of the glenohumeral adductors and abductors. Bracko, Fellingham &

Lyons [4] found that proper glenohumeral joint movement was an important aspect of acceleration in high school hockey players.

The players' not improving their agility skating makes sense since the vertical jump and upper body group performed no lateral movements, except for one jump training exercise. In addition, it is questionable if their would be transfer from dry land exercises to developing the ability to perform gliding and crossover turns and accelerating out of a turn. Performance on the agility test is of particular importance because it may be the closest skating test to game-performance skating [5] with acceleration, turning in both directions, acceleration from a dynamic position, and maintaining balance while skating as fast as possible.

Finally, it is interesting that despite the fact that the players were taking skating lessons one to three times per week, this practice apparently did not improve their skating speed and agility. As such, it may take longer than eight weeks for young hockey players to improve their skating ability.

Conclusion

Based on the limited number of studies that investigate an actual training effect on skating of hockey skill performance, it is hard to make specific conclusions about the proper forms of training. However, it one was to surmise information from these studies and put it into practical application it would appear that improving muscle strength, weather by electromyostimulation or weight training, it would have a positive effect on skating acceleration. Improving upper body power with plyometrics can have a somewhat positive effect on the velocity of hockey player's stick during a slap shot. And if plyometrics can have an positive effect on the slap shot, it might be reasonable to assume plyometrics will improve stick velocity of other types of shots. But as the authors of this study [10] indicated, skill factors are important in the enhancement of shooting skills. Although strength and conditioning professionals are taught that improving muscle strength, power and endurance, it appears that off-ice training has some limitations when it comes to improving a complex motor skill such as skating. And, of interest, and excitement, for strength and conditioning professionals, it was shown by Bracko and Fellingham [2] that both lower body and upper body plyometric training can have a positive effect on skating acceleration.

Although the studies reviewed focused on muscle strength, power, and endurance, there are still many other components of fitness that are important to understand as it relates to improving performance in ice hockey. Some of the components of fitness that are important to investigate include: cardiovascular endurance, anaerobic capacity, and weight training protocols.

SKATING RESEARCH

In the most recent research study on skating biomechanics, Upjohn et al., [26] had ten high and low caliber hockey players (mean age = 37 yrs) skate on a skating treadmill to describe lower limb kinematics of forward skating. Four digital video camcorders were used to film the subjects. The investigators had the subjects skate on the treadmill with a two degree incline which, according to the investigators, simulated on-ice skating conditions. Skating on an incline of two degrees does not simulate on-ice skating conditions [16] because every hockey rink ice surface in the world is flat, with no incline. The results of this study as they relate to practical application to game-performance skating, skating on ice, or improving skating performance can be questioned.

The investigators measured many skating characteristics of the forward stride such as, stride length, stride width, hip flexion when the skate blade landed on the treadmill (weight acceptance), knee extension and plantar flexion during push-off phase of the stride, and knee and ankle ranges of motion. There were some findings that were similar to previous studies which have been the hallmark of skating biomechanics research done by Marino [18, 19], Marino and Weese [21], Marino [20], and Page [25]. Some of consistent findings that corroborate previous research include: high caliber players had significantly greater stride width than low caliber players and a deeper knee flexion throughout the skating phases with rapid extension during push-off. However, there are some contradictions that do not translate to practice for improved skating such as: high caliber players had significantly greater stride length. Greater stride length could be caused by skating uphill. When skating uphill on a skating treadmill a hockey player has to alter his or her skating stride to push-off with more hip extension and less hip abduction. Moreover, Marino [20] found that as speed increased stride rate increased and there was no change in stride length. High caliber players had significantly greater hip flexion when the skate blade landed on the treadmill after a push-off (weight acceptance). However, this may just be a function of the fact that when skating uphill the hip has to be in a greater degree of flexion when the recovery skate lands on the treadmill. There is research to indicate that fast skaters have significantly more hip flexion then slower skaters [25].

Interestingly, the investigators indicated that both groups had a neutral hip position at weight acceptance with full external rotation of the hip at the end of the push-off phase. This final hip rotation position is completely the opposite of what other studies have found with little hip external rotation in the final stages of the push-off phase [7, 27]. Again, this external rotation of the hip may be caused by skating uphill. When skating uphill a player has to produce more hip extension (pushing backward). With hip extension there is hip external rotation so as to stay up on the treadmill to prevent from falling off.

Practical applications from this study are hard to make because the subjects were skating uphill. Moreover, the investigators reported that the high caliber hockey players in this study had a lower stance which means that increased strength of the knee and hip extensors may help a hockey player to maintain a deep knee bend and hip flexion. They based this conclusion on the significantly different vertical jump height and long jump distance. However, in one table they report no significant differences in vertical and long jump, but in the conclusions report that the high caliber players were faster than the low caliber players because they were able to jump higher and longer. Based on the conflicting results of this study, it could be surmised that skating uphill on a treadmill is not a practical idea for improving skating performance.

In another skating study done on a skating treadmill Lockwood and Frost [17] investigated the changes in skating kinematics during a six week skating treadmill habituation process. This study had the treadmill at a zero degree grade. Seven male hockey players (mean age = 10.58 yrs, skating experience = 5.71 yrs) who have no previous skating treadmill experience performed four, one minute skating bouts at progressively increased treadmill speeds each week for the six weeks of the study. The kinematic criteria for habituation included: decrease in stride rate, increase in stride length, increase in trunk angle, and increase in vertical movement of the center of mass.

The results of the study indicate that over the six weeks of skating treadmill training, the subjects were assessed as having successfully habituated to the treadmill because they significantly decreased stride rate and significantly increased stride length. Interestingly, previous research has indicated that a decrease in stride rate and an increase in stride length are characteristics of slower skaters [20]. Nobes et al., [14] found that stride rate was significantly lower while skating on a treadmill compared to skating on ice. But they also found that stride rate increased significantly as velocity increased when skating on ice.

The investigators also report that although trunk angle was not significantly different, the subjects skated more upright toward the end of the study. If the subjects were skating faster, they would skate with more trunk flexion (less upright) as has been previously found in fast skaters [6, 22, 25].

These findings are important because it helps the strength and conditioning professional to understand how skating on a treadmill affects skating kinematics compared to when a player skates on ice. It can also lead a coach and strength and conditioning professional to question the skating treadmill as an effective training tool because there are inconsistent findings in the present study with other research, as well as observation of fast skaters. The investigators conclude their discussion by indicating that skating treadmills allow for ice hockey players to train all year. However, hockey rinks with ice are available all year as well. Moreover, skating on a treadmill focuses on forward skating only, which is one of 27 important characteristics of high performance skating [6]. Skating on ice in a more practical teaching setting and has the ability to improve all skating characteristics.

Lafontaine [16] investigated the kinematics of the right knee and ankle over three strides on ice. Seven adult male hockey players were tested. Data were collected by pushing a cart carrying the camera equipment along the ice at the same speed as the subject skated. The kinematics that were analyzed included: knee flexion, tibial abduction, tibial external rotation, ankle dorsiflexion, ankle abduction, and ankle eversion.

The results of the study indicate that four of the seven subjects increased knee flexion during the first 70% of the push-off followed by extension in the last 30% of the stride. All skaters maintained slight knee flexion (20 – 30 degrees) until toe-off. Knee flexion range of motion increased with each stride. No clear tendency was analyzed for tibial abduction. In the initial push-offs tibial external rotation gradually increased until reaching a maximal value of 59%. In the second and third push-offs it reached a peak of 79% at skate contact with the ice. Ankle dorsiflexion gradually increased when each skate landed on the ice after recovery. A slight increase from twelve degrees to sixteen degrees was analyzed during the second push-off. The angle remained constant for the third push-off. Ankle abduction was small during all push-offs. Ankle eversion was the prime indicator of differences in ankle motion between push-offs.

The authors conclude that knee flexion was the angle most affected by increased skating velocity. Translating the results into direct practical application the author suggests that hockey players would benefit from training programs involving large ranges of motion. The author suggests exercises such as multiple-stride plyometric style training where players produce deeper knee flexion. Acceleration is an important component of high-performance skating and should be a key focus of off-ice training. As such, players would benefit from explosive motions of short duration and large ranges of motion.

Nobes et al., [24] compared oxygen uptake, heart rate, and skating economy on subjects while they skating on ice and on a skating treadmill. Fifteen male university hockey players (mean age = 21.0 yrs) skated for four minutes at submaximal speeds of 18, 20, and 22 km·h$^-$1, with five minutes of passive recovery between skating tests. A VO$_2$max test was completed on the treadmill and on ice.

The results indicate that VO$_2$ and heart rate were significantly higher at each speed on the treadmill compared to on the ice. However, there was no difference in VO$_2$max between on-ice (54.7 ml·kg$^-$1·min$^-$1) and treadmill (53.4 ml·kg$^-$1·min$^-$1). Adding to the questionable use of treadmills for skating improvement was the fact that in this study there were no differences in stride rate as skating speed increased on the treadmill. Conversely, as have been found in previous research [23], stride rate increased significantly as speed on the ice increased. Moreover, on-ice stride rates were significantly lower than when skating on a treadmill.

The practical applications that can be derived from this study are that skating on a treadmill may be good as a conditioning tool, but is questionable for improvement of skating performance.

The final skating study that will be reviewed was conducted by Bracko, et al., [6] who analyzed NHL forwards to investigate the time and frequency of 27 skating characteristics during a game (Tables 1 and 2). Fifteen timed skating characteristics and 12 frequency characteristics were analyzed. For the timed skating characteristics, the total time spent performing each characteristic during a shift was measured. For the frequency characteristics, the total number of occurrences during a shift was counted. The results of the study indicate that NHL forwards spend the highest percentage of ice time, 39%, gliding on two feet, suggesting that this position is an important characteristic in hockey. It is important for hockey players to maintain balance on two feet while gliding straight, turning, and engaging in body contact. Each of the other skating characteristics are derived from a two-foot balance position, and eventually go back to a two-foot glide position. Body contact is initiated from a two-foot balance position. The typical balance position, while gliding and stationary, is for a player to have his skates positioned slightly wider than shoulder width apart, ankles dorsiflexed, knees flexed, trunk flexed, and the hockey stick close to, but not always on, the ice. The ability to maintain balance while placing the center of gravity outside the base of support appears to be important for game-performance skating, and would be for young hockey players trying to develop motor programs for efficient skating.

Even though high-intensity skating was utilized for a low percentage of total on-ice time, it is also considered an important characteristic as it relates to the nature of ice hockey. Using quick bursts of speed to maintain position or possession of the puck, to maintain speed, or to initiate body contact, is how hockey players gain advantage over opposing players.

Table 1. Timed Skating Characteristics of NHL Forwards

Skating Characteristic	% Of Total Time on ice
Two-foot glide	39.0
Cruise slide	16.2
Medium intensity skating	10.0
Struggle for puck or position	9.8
Low-intensity skating	7.8
Backward skating	4.9
High-intensity skating	4.6
Two-foot stationary	3.0
Two-foot glide with puck	1.4
Medium-intensity skating with puck	0.8
Cruise stride with puck	0.6
Struggle with puck	0.6
Low-intensity skating with puck	0.5
High-intensity skating with puck	0.4
Two-foot stationary with puck	0.4

Table 2. Frequency Skating Characteristics of NHL Forwards

Skating Characteristic	% of Total Occurences
Left cross-over turn	20.2
Gliding left-turn	17.8
Right cross-over turn	17.7
Gliding right-turn	16.4
Stop and start	10.4
Forward to backward pivot	7.6
Backward to forward pivot	6.3
Gliding left turn with puck	1.0
Right cross-over turn with puck	1.0
Left cross-over turn with puck	1.0
Gliding right turn with puck	0.4
Stop and start with puck	0.2

The practical application of this research is to understand all the skating characteristics used during a hockey game. Therefore, it is important for coaches to have their players practice all skating characteristics in order to improve their game-performance skating. This type of training can only be accomplished when skating on an ice rink compared to skating on a treadmill. From a strength and conditioning perspective, it could be surmised that since a lot of time is spent gliding on two skates in a somewhat low knee range of motion position, it would be prudent to train the knee and hip extensors for strength and endurance. Likewise, although a small percentage of time was spent skating at a high intensity, it is important for hockey players to develop muscle power to accommodate the repeated bouts of quick skating.

Conclusion

Based on the skating research that was reviewed in this chapter, it appears that the strength and conditioning professional and the hockey coach might be confused by the conflicting findings of the research. It can be confusing to understand skating when studies are conducted on skating treadmills and the results are presented in a manner that are recommended as similar to skating on ice or game-performance skating. In fact, skating on a treadmill appears to change the biomechanics of skating compared to studies that have been done on ice.

Moreover, the research is still lacking studies that measure cause and effect of training programs. As such, it is hard to understand what skills and drills are important for improving skating performance of players of all ages and abilities levels. However, there does seem to be rather consistent line of research that indicates same characteristics that are important for fast skating. As such, it recommended having a good understanding of the characteristics of game-performance skating, and the characteristics of fast skaters in order to do develop skills and drills to improve skating.

REFERENCES

[1]   Alexander, J.F., Drake, C.J., Reichenbach, P.J., & Haddow, J.B. (1964). Effect of strength development on speed of shooting of varsity ice hockey players. *Res. Q.* 35, 101 – 106.

[2]   Bracko, M.R. & Fellingham, G.W. (1997). Effect of jump training on skating performance of ice hockey players. *J Strength Cond Res,* 11, Abstact, 278.

[3]   Bracko, M.R. Fellingham, G.W., & Lyons. D., (1996), Glenohumeral kinematics: a comparison of three techniques during an ice hockey acceleration test. *Med. Sci Sports Exerc.* 28, Abstract, 455.

[4]   Bracko, M. R. & George, J. D. (2001) Prediction of ice skating performance with off-ice testing in women's ice hockey players. *J Strength Cond Res*, 15, 116 - 122.

[5]   Bracko, M.R., Hall. L.T., Cryer, W., Fisher, G., & Fellingham, G.W. (1998), Skating characteristics of professional ice hockey forwards. *Sports Med, Rehab, and Training*, 8, 251 - 263.

[6]   Bracko, M.R. & Moeller, J.L., Ice hockey., In: J.L. Moeller & S.R. Rifat, Eds. Winter Sports Medicine: McGraw-Hill, New York. 2004, 233 – 294.

[7]   Brocherie, F., Babault, N., Cometti, G., Maffiuletti, N., & Chatard, J. (2005). Electrostimulation training effects on the physical performance of ice hockey players. *Med. Sci Sports Exerc.* 37, 455 – 460.

[8]   Brown, J. (2001) *Sports Talent: How to Identify and Develop Outstanding Athletes*. Champaign, IL: Human Kinetics.

[9]   Fergenbaum, M.A. & Marino, G.W. (2004) The effects of an upper-body Plyometrics program on male university hockey players. In: D.J. Pearsall and A.B. Ashare, Eds. Safety in Ice Hockey: Fourth Volume, ASTM International, West Conshohocken, PA., U.S.A. 2004; 209 - 223.

[10]   Green, H.J. Personal communication, October 2008.

[11] Greer, N., Serfass, R., Picconatto, W., & Blatherwick, J. (1992). The effects of a hockey-specific training program on performance of bantam players. *Can. J. Spt. Sci.,* 17, 65 – 69.

[12] Hermiston, R.T. (1976) Resistance machine for power skating of hockey players. *J. Sports Med Phys Fitness,* 16, 233 – 236.

[13] Hollering, B.L. & Simpson, D. (1977). The effect of three types of training programs upon skating speed of college ice hockey players. *J. Sports Med Phys Fitness,* 17, 335 – 340.

[14] Hutchinson, W.W., Maas, G.M., & Murdoch, A.J. (1979). Effect of dry land training on aerobic capacity of college hockey players. *J. Sports Med Phys Fitness,* 19, 271 – 276.

[15] Lafontaine, D. (2007) Three-dimensional kinematics of the knee and ankle joints for three consecutive push-offs during ice hockey skating starts. *Sports Biomechanics,* 6, 391 - 406.

[16] Lockwood, K.L. & Frost, G. (2007). Habituation of 10-year-old hockey players to treadmill skating. *Sports Biomechanics,* 6, 145 – 154.

[17] Marino, G.W., (1984), Analysis of selected factors associated in the ice skating strides of adolescents., *CAHPER J.,* January-February, 4 – 8.

[18] Marino, G.W., (1983), Selected mechanical factors associated with acceleration in ice skating. *Res. Q.,* 54, 234 – 238.

[19] Marino, G.W., (1977), Kinematics of ice skating at different velocities. *Res. Q.,* 48, 93 – 97.

[20] Marino G.W. & Weese R.G., A kinematic analysis of the ice skating stride; In: Terauds J, Gros HJ, eds. *Science in skiing, skating, and hockey.* Proceedings of the International Symposium of Biomechanics in Sports. Del Mar, CA: Academic Publishers, 1979, 65-74.

[21] McPherson, M.N., Wrigley, A., & Montelpare, W.J. The biomechanical characteristics of development-age hockey players: determining the effects of body size on the assessment of skating technique. In: D.J. Pearsall and A.B. Ashare, Eds. Safety in Ice Hockey: Fourth Volume, ASTM International, West Conshohocken, PA., U.S.A. 2004; 272 – 287.

[22] National Strength and Conditioning Association, 2008. Available from www.nsca-lift.org.

[23] Nobes, K.J., Montgomery, D.J., Pearsall, R.A., Turcotte, R.A., Lafebvre, R., &Whittom, F. (2003) A comparison of skating economy on-ice and on the skating treadmill. *Can J App Phys* . 28, 1 – 11.

[24] Page P. (1975), Biomechanics of forward skating in ice hockey. Unpublished master's thesis, Dalhousie University.

[25] Upjohn, T., Turcotte, R., Pearsall, D.J., & Loh, J. (2008). Three-dimensional kinematics of the lower limbs during forward ice hockey skating. *Sports Biomechanics,* 7, 206 – 221.

[26] Van Ingen Schenau, G.L., de Groot, G., & de Boer., (1985), The control of speed in elite female speed skaters. *J. Biomechs.,* 18, 91 – 96.

INDEX

H

I

J

K

L

M

U

V

W

Y

Z